Human Rights, Labor Rights, and International Trade

Human Rights, Labor Rights, and International Trade

edited by
Lance A. Compa and
Stephen F. Diamond

PENN

University of Pennsylvania Press

Philadelphia

Copyright © 1996 University of Pennsylvania Press
All rights reserved
Printed in the United States of America on acid-free paper

First paperback edition 2003

Published by
University of Pennsylvania Press
Philadelphia, Pennsylvania 19104-4011

Library of Congress Cataloging-in-Publication Data

Human rights, labor rights, and international trade / edited by Lance A. Compa and
    Stephen F. Diamond.
        p.   cm. — (Pennsylvania studies in human rights)
    Includes bibliographical references and index.
    ISBN 0-8122-3340-9 (cloth : alk. paper). — ISBN 0-8122-1871-X (pbk. : alk. paper)
    1. Labor laws and legislation, International—Economic aspects. 2. Human
rights—Economic aspects. 3. Commercial policy. I. Compa, Lance A. II. Diamond,
Stephen F. III. Series.
K1705.4.H86   1996 2003
    341.7'63—dc20
                                                                                96-1825
                                                                                 CIP

Contents

Acknowledgments

The editors thank Professor Drew Days III and George Andreopoulos, Director and Associate Director respectively of the Schell Center for International Human Rights at Yale Law School, for initiating and supporting the symposium on human rights, labor rights, and international trade held at Yale Law School in March 1992, and their successors, Professors Harold Koh and Ronald Slye, for continuing to support the publishing of this volume.

We also thank student editors Sydney Patel, Victoria Clawson, and Sherry Moore from Yale Law School, Jon Bailey from the Yale School of Management, Misha Cornes and Curt Lambrecht from the Yale Graduate School Master's program in International Relations, and Nicole Duda of the University of Connecticut School of Law.

We finally thank our colleagues Joan Paquette-Sass, Jill Tobey, and Renee DeMatteo of the Yale Law School staff, and Mary Mattie and Karen Donegan of the Yale School of Management staff, for their assistance in preparing the papers for publication.

Introduction

Lance A. Compa and Stephen F. Diamond

Worker rights in the global economy arise at the intersections of trade law, human rights law, labor law, and related public policy concerns. The Orville H. Schell Center for International Human Rights at Yale Law School sponsored a symposium in March 1992 titled "Human Rights and Labor Rights: A New Look at Workers in the Global Economy" to illuminate these intersections and chart paths for further inquiry. This volume is based on papers presented at the symposium, supplemented by new materials to account for developments since then.

Linking international commerce to human rights and labor rights concerns has become a critical issue in trade bargaining and trade policy debates. Bringing the Uruguay Round of negotiations for a new General Agreement on Tariffs and Trade (GATT) to a close in 1994, ministers of the 123 GATT member countries approved a declaration that worker rights must be on the agenda of the new World Trade Organization (WTO) set up to enforce GATT rules.

Leaders of several developing countries have criticized a worker rights-trade linkage as a protectionist ploy to close markets to their exports. They also charged advocates of a trade-linked "social clause" with a form of "cultural imperialism" seeking to impose "Western" notions of human rights and labor rights, and Western models of labor-management relations, on non-Western societies, governments, and enterprises.

The Clinton administration was torn for months by a policy struggle over China's most-favored-nation (MFN) trade status after the President demanded human rights and labor rights reforms as a condition for maintaining MFN. Pressed by U.S. multinational companies seeking billions of dollars in Chinese business, the President dropped his demands in May 1994 despite Chinese government intransigence on human rights. Similar corporate pressure has staved off U.S. sanctions for human rights and labor rights violations in Indonesia, Malaysia, and other authoritarian countries with large-scale U.S. investments. At the same time, hoping to appear responsive to human rights concerns, several corporations and U.S. government officials announced plans for a "code of conduct" for businesses operating in countries with authoritarian regimes.

Some human rights and labor rights advocates in Mexico, the United States, and Canada, along with their environmental counterparts, challenged the terms of the North American Free Trade Agreement for failing to address sufficiently their concerns. In response, the Clinton administration obtained supplemental agreements covering labor rights and environmental protection, creating new arenas for advocacy in those areas. NAFTA was approved and took effect January 1, 1994.

In July 1994 the U.S. Congress approved a labor rights clause in a bill authorizing funding for the Inter-American Development Bank, the World Bank, and the International Monetary Fund. The amendment obligates U.S. representatives to multilateral lending institutions to ensure respect for international labor rights as a condition of approval for countries seeking development loans. The first instance of labor rights linkage to international lending programs, this amendment adds to an array of U.S. worker rights clauses in statutes governing the Generalized System of Preferences, the Overseas Private Investment Corporation, Section 301 of the Trade Act, the Caribbean Basin Initiative, and Agency for International Development trade promotion programs.

In Europe, an ambitious Social Charter and the related Social Chapter of the Maastricht Treaty on economic and political union have run headlong into a stubborn recession. Faced with budget deficits, many governments have begun scaling back social protections. Pressured by global competition, many European companies have eliminated jobs and shifted operations abroad, including to the now relatively low-cost United States. At the same time, social obligations under the Europe-wide legal system are shown still to be effective: a European Court of Justice decision in June 1994 found the United Kingdom—the most reluctant "unionist" in Europe—to have violated a European Union directive on worker consultation, raising the prospect of substantial damage payments to affected workers.

These and other examples indicate the frequency with which human rights and labor rights issues are arising in the international trade arena. A distinction somewhat comfortably maintained by "trade hands" who managed the post–World War II international economy—that trade is strictly a commercial function with no immediate connection to social concerns—has evaporated under the pressure of political and social forces generated by the globalization of the economy. Shifting patterns of investment and disinvestment have brought large-scale job losses in many countries, and cultural upheaval in countries where new jobs are created.

Developments in the international labor rights field raise a series of critical questions for trade policy analysts and advocates. To what extent should worker and trade union rights be treated as economic claims to be regulated by national governments and subordinated to the demands of the marketplace in a rapidly liberlizing world economy? In contrast, to what extent can worker and trade union activities be viewed and treated as irreducible human rights, protected by international norms, superior to market discipline and economic regulation?

Can one distinguish among worker and trade union rights, identifying some as fundamental human rights, while exposing other "rights" as, upon closer examination, assertions of privileges or claims for benefits? Can the status of fundamental rights be adjusted to a country's level of development? Can varying national labor laws and policies be harmonized through internationally recognized standards, or should national policies be permitted to deviate from international standards for purposes of economic development or in light of cultural differences?

Can the United States or other developed industrial nations take unilateral measures to enforce worker rights in developing countries seeking access to their markets? Or do such unilateral actions breach principles of sovereignty in international relations, or evince hypocrisy when, in many cases, the United States itself fails to enforce workers' rights or to ratify international labor rights covenants?

Human rights advocates, labor and international law analysts, and trade specialists have been slow in coming to grips with these issues. Worker concerns in the global context have usually been treated as a narrow, even technical matter for the International Labor Organization (ILO), a United Nations body that sets, but has no power to enforce, international labor standards. Trade law specialists rarely discuss whether worker rights conflict with market dictates. When they mention the subject, it is usually by a passing reference to the ILO. For their part, human rights and international law commentators frequently point to the ILO as the sole forum for consideration of worker and trade union rights, and turn greater attention to egregious violations of civil and political rights.

Labor law scholars are more at home with issues of union organizing, trade union independence, internal union democracy, collective bargaining, the right to strike, and so on, but in the United States, at least, they still concentrate on domestic law. Labor relations under the National Labor Relations Act, and union governance under the

Landrum-Griffin Act, remain the mainstay of labor law offerings. New scholarship explores employment law in the non-union context, such as changes in the employment-at-will doctrine, discrimination law, employee benefits, and individual rights in the workplace. These studies, too, focus on the domestic context. While occasional courses on comparative labor law are offered, we are just beginning to explore the prospect of a new, more unified international labor law that permits assertions of rights and demands for remedies by workers and unions in the global economy.

Working people themselves are forcing international labor rights onto the agenda of government trade policy administrators, multinational corporate executives, and trade union leaders. An upsurge of strikes and organizing shook Korea in the late 1980s as worker sought a greater share of the export "miracle" so admired by economists and so dependent, to that point, on suppression of worker rights. In Brazil, political organizing by trade unionists nearly launched labor leader Luis Ignacio da Silva into the presidency of that huge nation in 1989, and sustained another energetic, although unsuccessful, campaign in the 1994 election.

In South Africa, the trade union movement served as a training ground in democratic organization, leadership, and discipline as the country moved toward majority rule. Now the same traits give pause to foreign investors wary of militant South African unions. In Nigeria, a nationwide strike movement led by the key oil workers union challenged military control of the government. In many developing countries, and in economically reforming Eastern European countries, labor movements have mounted strong campaigns against austerity and privatization programs imposed by their governments, often at the insistence of the World Bank or International Monetary Fund.

Whether they like it or not, when they make policy or investment choices, those who command the heights of the new global economy must take into account the interests, passions, and rights of workers and trade unionists on the ground below. Legal analysts and practitioners, too, must move international labor rights, which for most has been a marginal concern, to the center of their work.

The papers collected here articulate a concern for labor rights and labor law in the global context. Coming from a variety of backgrounds, including academic, labor, and management experience, the authors, most (but fortunately not all) of whom are lawyers, examine developments in the field of international labor rights and their implications for scholars, policymakers, and activists. Each chapter makes a distinct contribution to the discussion. Together, they review changes in the world economy that require a new analysis of international worker rights; they grapple with conflicting views of labor rights as fundamental human rights; they relate worker rights to trade policy and development strategies; and they contrast the adequacy of national labor law and policy against the demands of an internationally competitive economy.

Part I introduces the central notion of labor rights as human rights, and examines the extent to which labor rights *are*, and must be treated as, basic human rights and alternatively the extent to which labor rights diverge from basic human rights in a way that requires separate analysis and treatment. The premier labor historian in the United States, David Montgomery of Yale University, sets the stage for the modern global context in an introductory essay describing past examples of concern for international labor rights. He reminds us that the issue is really timeless. As long as nations have traded, states and employers have usually resisted moves to erect enforceable labor standards. At the same time, Montgomery points out, some countries have promoted the principle of labor rights across national boundaries, and working people themselves have created many forms of international labor solidarity.

Montgomery stresses the centrality of freedom of association as the bedrock right on which all else rests. He insists, though, that the right cannot remain abstract, but must take shape in concrete social standards. Montgomery evokes international solidarity traditions in the U.S. labor movement, and points to the worldwide movement for the eight-hour working day as an example of working people using their right of association to promote social justice.

With wide experience in international labor and human rights affairs, including several years at the International Labor Organization and service on the Board of Directors of Asia Watch and the International Labor Rights Fund, Virginia Leary of the SUNY Buffalo Law School presents a penetrating analysis of ILO standards and procedures as they relate to the human rights of workers. Leary first examines the failure of human rights organizations and trade union groups to forge a close relationship and joint action projects. Rather than despairing, however, she outlines the potential for such an alliance.

Leary offers a frank assessment of the strengths and flaws of the ILO as the *locus* of labor rights treatment in the global economy. She suggests ways to improve the use of ILO mechanisms. At the same time, she creates the context needed for consideration of forums outside the ILO where worker rights claims can be made. A detailed discussion of the right of association, with particular emphasis on the right to strike, informs her treatment of basic international norms affecting workers and trade unions. Leary counsels caution in laying claim to expanded international labor rights, suggesting that worker rights would be better served now by concentrating on freedom of association and the abolition of forced labor as consensus labor rights.

Philip Alston of the Australian National University's Centre for International Human Rights argues that recent "labor rights amendments" in U.S. trade laws might conflict with general principles of international human rights law on several grounds. For example, while these statutes refer to "internationally recognized worker rights," they neither define the rights in any way that could set a standard for compliance nor adopt ILO standards. Moreover, they omit one of the most basic internationally recognized worker rights: non-discrimination in employment because of race or sex.

The U.S. labor rights amendments also run afoul of international law precepts because they seek to apply sanctions against countries for purported violations of standards they have not agreed to, or standards that have not risen to the level of customary international law to which all countries are bound. Even worse, they demonstrate a certain hypocrisy on the part of U.S. policymakers, given that the United States itself has failed to ratify most of the ILO's basic human rights conventions, and has thus far failed to ratify the United Nations' International Covenant on Economic, Social and Cultural Rights, which contains the most detailed statement of labor rights in a UN charter.

In effect, says Alston, U.S. "aggressive unilateralism" on labor standards risks retarding the protection of worker rights by failing first to gain an international consensus for such conditions to trade. Instead, Alston suggests a greater U.S. commitment to the ILO and its mechanisms, and adoption of a multilateral approach. To the extent the U.S. maintains a unilateral labor rights conditionality policy, he concludes, it should be reformed to enhance consistency in application and regard for due process concerns.

Part II focuses more directly on labor rights and trade. Labor economist Stephen Herzenberg opens this section with a discussion of the movement of international standards from the margin of economists' concerns to a central consideration in fashioning trade policy. Herzenberg speaks from both research and policy stands: while at the U.S. Labor Department's Bureau of International Labor Affairs, he was a member of the U.S. negotiating team for the NAFTA labor supplemental agreement.

Herzenberg makes an important distinction between a "list" of fair labor norms, perhaps useful for the sake of denouncing violations, and a strategy for genuinely improving labor rights and labor conditions around the world. He suggests that the choice between an "upward harmonization" of worker rights and labor standards, on one hand, and a "downward spiral" because of cost-cutting pressures without labor rights protections, on the other hand, is still to be made. Herzenberg defends labor rights amendments in U.S. trade statutes, but cautions that such initiatives must be linked to a broader movement by workers, trade unions, and their allies to promote worker rights in the global economy.

A Martin Luther King-Cesar Chavez-Rosa Parks Visiting Professor in the African Studies and Women's Studies programs at Wayne State University, Cecilia Green is intimately familiar with the apparel and electronics assembly industries of the Caribbean region. The explosive growth of "export processing zones" and other labor-intensive work-sites in developing countries is an important feature of the new global economy. No study of worker rights in trade would be possible without an analysis of this phenomenon. Green provides both a well-grounded political and sociological consideration of these export zones and a passionate critique of the policies of multinational corporations that set up shop in the Caribbean islands.

R. Michael Gadbaw and Michael T. Medwig bring to this volume the equally important perspective of one of the world's largest multi-national firms, the General Electric Company. Gadbaw is vice president and senior counsel for international trade; Medwig is his associate counsel. An experienced Treasury Department trade negotiator and attorney in private practice before joining G.E., Gadbaw and his colleague discuss the competing pressures on multinational enterprises from national governments, international trade regulators, workers, and unions. They suggest that economic development is the surest way to create conditions for advanced labor rights and labor standards, and caution that too-aggressive policing of labor rights will slow investment and growth, to the detriment of working people in both developing and developed countries.

International trade attorney Daniel Ehrenberg provides a review of international mechanisms for dealing with labor rights and labor standards, especially as they relate to child labor and forced labor. In addition to such analysis, he develops an innovative proposal for collaboration between the ILO and the new World Trade Organization (WTO) on a concrete means of enforcing labor rights and standards through trade sanctions, while remaining sensitive to development and sovereignty concerns.

Attorney and law teacher Lance Compa and management consultant Tashia Hinchliffe Darricarrère offer an account of "codes of conduct" on worker rights fashioned as a private alternative to state action. They review the various origins of such codes: some developed by governmental coordinating bodies like the Organization for Economic Cooperation and Development; others proposed by independent groups or individuals for companies to adhere to voluntarily, like the Sullivan Principles for business in South Africa or the MacBride Principles for business in Northern Ireland. Finally, these contributors examine in greater detail codes of conduct created and enforced by individual corporations, particularly the Levi Strauss & Company "terms of engagement" for business partners and the Reebok Corporation's "human rights production standards."

Political scientist, lawyer, and former union representative Stephen F. Diamond takes one of the first critical looks at the recently negotiated labor side agreement to NAFTA, the North American Agreement on Labor Cooperation (NAALC). In an innovative effort to bridge the intellectual divide between traditional international law concerns with dualism, monism and the sources of legitimacy, on the one hand, and emerging transnational economic realities, on the other, he suggests that the NAALC can be an international institution of a new and useful type. He argues that response to the deepset crisis of both employment and trade union membership must recognize the potential in such institutions. At the same time, he points out the inherent structural flaws of the NAALC and outlines the uphill battle facing those who recognize the importance of a strong labor movement to a democratic society.

Part III moves to specific examples of worker rights litigation in U.S. courts. A "first generation" of worker rights cases has emerged in recent years, the result of both statutory developments and the novel application of traditional causes of action. Judges are typically slow to warm to such attempts to break new legal ground. But these efforts begin to educate the judiciary to the realities of the new global economy and the potential for legal remedies in well-grounded cases.

Terry Collingsworth, General Counsel to the International Labor Rights Fund, discusses the Fund's case against the Bush administration for its politically selective enforcement of the labor rights amendment to the Generalized System of Preferences (GSP). While *Labor Rights Fund v. Bush* ultimately failed to go forward to trial, its consideration by the federal courts yielded differing, sometimes conflicting analyses of administrative law, standing and justiciability doctrines, jurisdictional issues, and the relative powers of the three branches of government in matters of trade and foreign relations. Collingsworth reviews the arguments and decisions of the case and suggests methods of addressing the courts' concerns in both new legislation and refined litigation strategies.

As Legal Director at the Center for Constitutional Rights in New York, Frank Deale litigated the pathbreaking case of *Labor Union of Pico Korea v. Pico Products, Inc.* This was the first case ever brought in a U.S. court by a foreign trade union against a U.S. multinational corporation alleging violation of worker rights. As should be expected in a case involving novel claims by foreign plaintiffs, the court was cautious in making new law. While the ultimate ruling on appeal of this case went against the plaintiffs, it contains critical lessons for future labor rights initiatives in U.S. courts.

As important as the legal lessons, argues Deale, now a Professor of Law at the Queens College of Law of the City University of New York, are the "cross-cultural" lessons learned by U.S. attorneys representing foreign clients. Since similar cases will surely take shape in future disputes, a solid preparation for the "human side" of international labor rights litigation will be a necessary adjunct to legal expertise.

Emily Yozell, a human rights attorney based in San José, Costa Rica, analyzes the important case of *Castro Alfaro et al. v. Dow Chemical Co.* Here the claimants were Costa Rican farmworkers rendered sterile by the use of DBCP, a pesticide banned in the United States, without notice or warning as to the potential harmful effects of the product. In a landmark procedural ruling, the Texas Supreme Court rebuffed Dow's defense of *forum non conveniens*, by which the company sought to have the case sent to Costa Rica as the more convenient site for adjudication.

Financial recovery in Costa Rica was limited to less than $1,500 per worker. By winning the right to sue in a U.S. court, the farmworker plaintiffs ultimately settled the case for approximately ten times that amount on the eve of trial. While summarizing analyses of the *forum* issue, Yozell also discusses cultural issues faced by U.S. attorneys representing working-class foreign clients, and by those clients faced with the mysteries of the United States judicial system.

From the rarefied atmosphere of human rights instruments and international trade law to the harsh reality of Korean factories and Central American plantations, the papers in this volume provide the first comprehensive view of the variety of forums now available for pressing worker rights claims in the global economy, and the theories and arguments surrounding such claims. In years to come, the place of workers and trade unions in a globally competitive economy will continue to be shaped by employers, regulated by government policymakers, and debated by scholars. Inevitably, workers and unions will fight back against restraints on fundamental rights. As this process advances, the papers collected here will serve to inform the protagonists and, it is hoped, persuade decision makers in government and industry of the importance of protecting human rights and labor rights as the new global economy unfolds.

Part I
Labor Rights
and Human Rights

Chapter 1
Labor Rights and Human Rights
A Historical Perspective

David Montgomery

This volume considers the role of international action and of national and international law in defining and enforcing the human rights of working people in today's world. New features of the global economy, which have emerged during the past twenty-five years, have undermined working conditions, economic standards, and collective rights that workers in the industrialized portions of the globe had come to enjoy over the course of this century. These new features have also placed the question of workers' rights and patterns of economic and social change in developing countries at the top of history's agenda of new business. At the same time, they have opened some noteworthy possibilities for international action to improve the conditions and liberties of working people. The purpose of this volume is to discuss the potential contributions of national and international law, effective forms of social action, and perhaps most relevant of all, the ways in which improved laws can encourage social action on behalf of human rights in the present worldwide version of what R. H. Tawney called "the acquisitive society."

The nation-state provided industrializing societies with the coercive authority that not only established the framework for commercial activity but also defined and enforced whatever social and economic rights of working people were recognized under the law. Over the course of the twentieth century the rights of citizenship in highly industrialized countries came to include entitlements to specified minimal standards of social welfare, and protection for forms of collective action, which were granted to wage earners and their families in exchange for loyalty to the nation-state. Elsewhere in the world struggles for national independence shaped both the destinies of workers' movements and the social programs of emerging nations. By the 1960s, in Latin America, and in much of Asia and Africa, import-substitution policies had become linked to the promotion of more or less official trade union organizations.

Those formulas for linking economic and social development were decisively abandoned in most parts of the world after the early 1970s. What had been intended as a social shelter became instead a source of special privilege, inept management, massive national debts, public corruption, and chronic stagflation, unleashing attacks from both the left and the right against the roles nation-states had come to play. Chile experienced both alternatives to its own earlier policies in ruthlessly quick succession. First, the Popular Unity government subjected the economy to direction by governmental agencies and workers' organizations in hopes of supplying the material needs of its working people, and then a military dictatorship rapidly reversed social regulation of market activity and threw open the national economy to imports and investments from abroad.

The decisive moment in reordering the world economy, however, came with the global debt crisis of the 1980s. While many African nations simply sank under the weight of debt payments that far exceeded their incomes from trade, South American countries settled with their creditors and with the World Bank by dismantling their public sectors, import barriers, and restrictions on foreign investors. Mexico's reversal of its historic opposition to the General Agreement on Tariffs and Trade (GATT) and the trade agreement between the United States and Canada paved the way for the North American Free Trade Agreement. NAFTA, and the recently completed Uruguay Round of GATT negotiations, have profoundly altered the relative roles of national and international governing bodies in reshaping the recognized rights of working people.

The decade closed with the dramatic collapse of the Soviet Union. Although the states that emerged from its wreckage and those of Eastern Europe introduced capitalist economic relations into the region only to a very limited degree, and often in grotesque forms, the ideological significance of the transformation was profound. On the one hand, the claims of men and women to speak, act, and associate on their own behalf without governmental restraint were vindicated in ways that visibly affected the thinking of working people in many other parts of the world. On the other hand, the living example of a different way of arranging economic life from that found in North America and Western Europe not only disappeared but was thoroughly discredited. Democracy and free market economies came to be almost universally (if mistakenly) discussed as if they were interchangeable and inseparable. The discussion of human rights and labor rights in this volume has inevitably been framed by these events.

Today, although some states, most notably the United States of America, wield prodigious influence over the economic and social development of other countries, the very capacity of all nation-states to regulate their own internal economic life has been decisively limited. Multinational corporations, able to move operations and processes around the world to the environments they find most attractive, exert a powerful force homogenizing economic, social, and environmental standards globally.

Countries that play host to branch plants of the multinationals confront an unresolved question of utmost importance. Will those enterprises forge effective developmental linkages to the regional economy, or will they become "footloose" operations, exploiting local labor and befouling the local environment while creating goods for sale in wealthier lands and remaining always prepared to move on to some other and still cheaper source of labor? The answer to that question may turn out to be quite different in Scotland than in Indonesia.

We must also consider the demonstrated power of multilateral lending agencies like the World Bank and the International Monetary Fund to impose austerity budgets, privatization, and the elimination of social controls on foreign investment. What investors see as "obstacles" often are policies intended by governments to encourage domestic industries to produce for home consumption. In countries like Argentina, Mexico, and Brazil, nationalistic measures that are now held in disdain had previously provided important shelters for some sectors of the working class, those who worked in state-operated industries under more privileged circumstances than most of their neighbors encountered. The primary purpose of the North American Free Trade Agreement is to lock future governments of Mexico and Canada into the free market policies that have been in vogue since the late 1970s. Moreover, the Clinton administration has made it clear that if other countries in the Americas wish to share in the trade benefits of that agreement, they must first demonstrate their good intentions over the course of several years by undertaking domestic policies similar to those Mexico has adopted during the last eight years.

Perhaps most important among issues raised in this volume, we face an urgent responsibility to consider the social impact of negotiations for multilateral trade agreements. In recent years such negotiations have turned from such obvious questions as tariffs and import quotas to the privatization of public assets and services, and to environmental and social legislation. Such legislation has increasingly been depicted as an obstacle to the free movement of goods, investment, intellectual property, and profits, as have efforts to link social issues to trade.

The connection between social issues and trade, however, can also be framed in a more positive way. We can ask whether "social charters," which safeguard workers' rights and the environment, can or should be negotiated into trade agreements. An important contrast between NAFTA and the European Union comes immediately to mind. NAFTA requires the participating governments to pursue their goals almost exclusively through market mechanisms. It created small offices to hear complaints about labor rights and environmental problems, but those offices can do no more than oversee enforcement of the existing laws of the three participating countries. NAFTA contains no plan to move, even in the long term, toward "upward harmonization" of labor rights and environmental standards.

In sharp contrast, the Maastricht Treaty contains a Social Chapter prescribing worker rights in all participating countries (except the United Kingdom, which refused to accept the chapter). It suggests that strong national labor movements can influence the shape of international trade agreements. The total absence of a social chapter in NAFTA bears witness to the humbling of the labor movement in the United States that preceded the drafting of the treaty.

Nevertheless, there has been another aspect of the recent historic changes that can provide the basis for a much more positive reshaping of international agreements: the profound surge of popular demands in many parts of the world for human rights, in the sense of basic freedom to speak, to associate, and to be spared the arbitrary authority of police. For working people the freedom to associate is the most important right of all. A consideration of U.S. experience may help clarify our thinking about that right.

Here in the United States freedom of association has long provided an essential link between the exercise of human rights and conditions of employment. Nineteenth-century workers justified their collective action, before the courts and before public opinion, as constitutionally sanctioned freedom of speech and association. The courts tended in the opposite direction: extracting from the common law doctrines of master and servant a legal sanction for claims of the employers to impose rules of conduct on those whom they hired, on pain of fine or dismissal.

When twentieth-century legislation prescribed important, but carefully bounded, protection for workers' collective action, it couched that protection in a discourse that categorically distinguished between human rights and industrial relations. The outcome was neatly summarized by the lawyer (and former Yale historian) Staughton Lynd: "In the private sector, when you punch in you leave your constitutional rights in the glove compartment of your car."[1] Face to face with the employer, the U.S. worker has only such rights as collective bargaining contracts and specific legislation stipulate.

There is also, however, a judicial legacy of broader scope, which links human rights to workplace activity and conditions directly, in a way that is more relevant to the international issues we are confronting in this volume. There is the legacy, however limited in time and impact, of such decisions as *Thornhill v. Alabama* and *Haig v. Congress of Industrial Organizations (C.I.O.).*[2] The Supreme Court in those decisions of the late 1930s and early 1940s refused to separate industrial rights from freedom of speech and association. *Thornhill* opened the way for public agitation of labor issues in Alabama timber camps, where the state had declared picketing by members of the American Federation of Labor illegal. *Haig* had the same effect in closed towns like Jersey City, where anyone who handed out literature favoring the CIO had been subject to arrest by the municipal authorities for disturbing the peace and littering the streets, and to deportation across the Hudson river to New York.

These decisions of a half-century ago are directly related to the question posed in this volume about the different levels of human rights recognized by government and the relationships among them. Although it approved the International Covenant on Civil and Political Rights, the government of the United States has thus far refused to recognize the socioeconomic rights specified in the International Covenant on Economic, Social and Cultural Rights as "true human rights." The United States has ratified only one of the core human rights conventions of the International Labor Organization (ILO), that on the abolition of forced labor. Moreover, the annual survey of trade union rights released by the International Confederation of Free Trade Unions cited the United States among the 87 countries that had violated fundamental trade union rights as formulated by the ILO. Consequently, any attempt to use the U.S. government as an exemplar, let alone an agency to advance human and labor rights in the international economy, will require broadening this government's definition of human rights far beyond that prescribed by the doctrines of the free market economy.

Moreover, although human and social rights were first defined within the arena of the nation-state, the developments of the past twenty years underscore the importance of specifying and enforcing rights today through social actions and charters, covenants, and conventions that operate in an international arena. Contributions here from people who are not from the United States are especially welcome, because the experience of the U.S. labor movement with internationalism is a rather limited one. U.S. experience offers something of value for our discussion, but also leaves us in need of instruction.

At its very best, the U.S. labor movement welcomed into its fold every man or woman from any place in the world who came to the United States. Most of the time it fell far short of doing even that. The sense of urgent need for working relations with unions in neighboring countries has been much less a part of the U.S. experience than it has been for Germans or Swedes, for example. Those societies developed strong national trade union and political movements in economies that were thoroughly immersed in international trade. Collaboration with their neighbors was for them a question of more immediate and pressing importance than it was to Americans. We need to learn from people who have had such experience.

To be sure, there is some largely forgotten legacy of mutual assistance across international boundaries in North America. When the Mine, Mill and Smelter Workers unionized the smelting and refinery workers of El Paso, Texas, between 1939 and 1943, organizers assigned to help them by the Confederación de Trabajadores de México (CTM) played a decisive role in recruiting local Mexican citizens and Mexican-Americans for the CIO union. Activists from the CTM also visited Mexican nationals across the river in Juarez to counteract El Paso's county sheriff, who disrupted meetings in his jurisdiction and deported CIO members. The House Un-American Activities Committee investigated this trade union cooperation, which the sheriff described in his testimony as "designed to instill in Mexican aliens living in the United States the principles of the Mexican Communist form of government."[3] During the decisive copper strike of 1946 the CTM in Juarez pledged not to allow strikebreakers to cross the border, and the U.S. and Mexican unions sent hundreds of members to each other's demonstrations.

Such mutual assistance in organizing provides important precedents for our time. In fact, in 1992 the United Electrical, Radio and Machine Workers of America (UE) established a "strategic organizing alliance" with an independent Mexican labor federation, the Authentic Labor Front, to jointly organize branch plants of U.S. companies in the Mexican *maquiladora* factory zones along the U.S.-Mexican border.

More commonly today, however, the most urgent need is simply for the protection of individual trade unionists who are prosecuted, or threatened with disappearance, in Guatemala, in South Korea, or even in Los Angeles, where exiled Salvadoran union activists have been pursued by agents of the Salvadoran military. In 1992 alone, according to the records of the International Confederation of Free Trade Unions, 260 people were killed around the world for trade union activity, and some 2,500 were imprisoned. Although we have valuable traditions for coping with persecution at home—like the coal miners' practice of accompanying an arrested miner en masse to the police station—we are only beginning to learn how to keep alive and safe workers who have been incarcerated in other countries. Perhaps no single form of activity is more essential in the struggle for freedom of association. Several U.S. unions participate in "rapid response" appeals to foreign governments to safeguard arrested trade unionists. Often such defense takes the form of calling for the enforcement of existing laws, laws that on paper, at least, usually proclaim more rights for working people than U.S. labor laws.

There is one question pertinent to today's discussions on which Americans have had useful experience: the protection of immigrant workers. It is not only capital that is moving rapidly around the globe today, but also masses of workers. The question of how rights can be secured for, say, Haitians migrating to the United States, Turks in Germany, Algerians in France, Eritreans in Italy, or Guatemalans in Mexico poses a challenge to labor movements, to national governments, and to international agencies. Early in this century foreign consuls sometimes assisted persecuted immigrant workers in the United States. In 1907, for example, when there was a strike of miners at Copper Cliff, Michigan, Finnish miners jailed by U.S. authorities were successfully defended in court by eight attorneys hired by the Russian consul in Chicago.

The fact that the Czar's government was reeling under the impact of revolution may have had more than a little to do with its unusual concern for his subjects abroad, but its action was not unique. The consul of the Austro-Hungarian Empire came to the aid of striking Slovaks and Ruthenians who were arrested at steel mills in McKees Rocks, Pennsylvania in 1909. He appealed on the immigrants' behalf to U.S. statutes prohibiting peonage. Italian consuls in the early years of the twentieth century sometimes joined in the battle against the *padrone* system. In cities like Boston and New York they actively assisted Italian subjects to free themselves from debt bondage and extortion on their jobs in North America. During the same period Japan protested formally and vigorously against the racial segregation of children of its emigrants by the schools of California.

All such activity, of course, conflicts with claims to sovereignty by the state in which immigrants are being abused. Vigorous objection is raised to what is labeled the imposition of alien standards by foreign agents. Nevertheless, intervention by consulates is a practice worth remembering in the context of our discussion here. So, too, is the long tradition of international covenants combatting the slave trade, and later regulating the conditions under which contract laborers were shipped across the Pacific. There is precedent aplenty for intervention from without in defense of the human rights of immigrant workers.

Finally, since much of the discussion in this volume will involve the value and limits of international agreements in promoting economic and social standards, it may be useful to reflect briefly on one historic precedent: the international effort to make eight hours the standard working day. As Gary Cross noted in his history of the protracted struggle for the eight-hour day in Europe,[4] regardless whether the hours of labor had tended to be twelve or thirteen as in France, indefinite as in Bulgaria or Russia, or eight and one-half as in England, the eight-hour standard was established everywhere at the same time: the end of World War I. He concluded that, while Woodrow Wilson sought world parliamentary democracy in vain, and Lenin failed to achieve his goal of world revolution, "the eight-hour day swept across Europe as governments and employers conceded this major reform to exhausted and sometimes militant people."[5] Indeed, the new global standard was written into the Treaty of Paris, where it was described as the social norm on which any just society would be based. No less a figure than Georges Clemenceau proposed that there be an international covenant to establish the eight-hour day for all countries.

The treaty never materialized. It was the first major undertaking of the International Labor Organization, and it faced great difficulties from the outset. The host country of the ILO's founding convention, the United States, refused to join the Organization. Two of the most important industrial countries of the world, Germany and Russia, were excluded from the deliberations. Japan insisted that it was just beginning its industrial development and needed an exemption. And England said it arranged hours of labor by trade agreements between employers and unions, and would tolerate no legislation on the question. Bulgaria signed, Czechoslovakia signed, Switzerland signed, and many other countries signed, but the international agreement had little effect. Afterwards, normal working hours drifted upward again, in Europe as well as in the United States, usually under the rubric of overtime.

One of the major questions for us to consider here, therefore, is the systematic abstention of the United States from agreements on international labor standards. We need to consider how domestic life in the United States, as well as human rights elsewhere, might benefit from adherence to some of the ILO conventions. The problem we face in establishing global standards is not imposing those of the United States on the rest of the world, but rather using international agreements to improve the socioeconomic standards of both the United States and the countries in which multinational corporations based here are investing.

In short, our problem is to consider ways in which human rights, including both freedom of association for working people and social standards, might be expanded by the internationalization of markets and investments, rather than being undercut in what has been called a "race to the bottom" by countries and companies constantly seeking a competitive edge in international trade. We need to consider also what such provisions mean for the developing world, and what they mean for those portions of the world, particularly in Africa, that hold no interest for any major power since the collapse of the Cold War.

Shaping such international standards will require new legislation by national bodies, refined instruments from international bodies, and social struggles waged by popular organizations around the world. The goal is the establishment of high standards of human rights and social welfare to which multinational corporations and all other forms of international activity must conform.

Notes

1. Staughton Lynd, *Labor Law for the Rank and Filer* (rev. ed.; San Pedro, CA: Singlejack Books, 1982), 10.

2. 310 U.S. 88 (1940); 307 U.S. 496 (1939).

3. See Mario T. Garcia, *Mexican-Americans: Leadership, Ideology and Identity, 1930–1960* (New Haven and London: Yale University Press, 1989), 183.

4. Gary Cross, *A Quest for Time: The Reduction of Work in Britain and France, 1840–1940* (Berkeley: University of California Press, 1989).

5. Ibid., 129.

Chapter 2
The Paradox of Workers' Rights as Human Rights

Virginia A. Leary

Workers' Rights and Human Rights: Parallel Tracks

Workers' rights are human rights, yet the international human rights movement devotes little attention to the rights of workers. At the same time, trade unions and labor leaders rarely enlist the support of human rights groups for the defense of workers' rights. A regrettable paradox: the human rights movement and the labor movement run on tracks that are sometimes parallel and rarely meet.

Nevertheless, the catalogue of international human rights includes numerous rights relating to work: The Universal Declaration of Human Rights, the International Covenant on Economic, Social and Cultural Rights (ICESCR), the International Covenant on Civil and Political Rights (ICCPR), and especially the conventions adopted by the International Labor Organization (ILO), which enshrine the right of association (the right to form and join trade unions), the right to free choice of employment, the right to equal remuneration for work of equal value, and the right to just and favorable conditions of work and which prohibit forced labor and discrimination in employment.

The status of workers' rights in a country is a bellwether for the status of human rights in general. The first sign of a deteriorating situation is often the violation of freedom of association, the most fundamental of workers' rights. Repressive regimes inevitably attempt to suppress or control trade unions; thus, labor leaders are among the most frequent victims of repression. Conversely, the development of free trade unions signals the dissolution of authoritarian regimes, as the example of Poland's Solidarity movement demonstrates.

Acts of repressive regimes aimed at controlling or destroying trade unions are well documented in recent history. In the first week of the Pinochet regime in Chile, following the overthrow of President Salvador Allende in September 1973, widespread killings and arrests of trade union leaders occurred and the legal personality of the main trade union organization was canceled.[1] Similarly, the maintenance of apartheid in South Africa required the subjection and harassment of trade unions and labor leaders. Although South Africa maintained its membership in the United Nations during the period of apartheid, it withdrew from the International Labor Organization in 1966 following persistent criticism of its treatment of unions and labor leaders. As recently as 1991, it was reported that "Police and vigilante activities continued to hamper the normal functioning of the union. Union offices were raided by the police and there were instances of their being bombed. A number of prominent union leaders . . . were arrested."[2]

The protection of the right of association has been a major concern of human rights monitors involved in the peace process in El Salvador. The International Confederation of Free Trade Unions reported in 1992 that, despite the signing of peace accords between the government and Farabundo Martí National Liberation Front (FMLN), "sadly the human and trade union rights situation has not improved. . . . The trade union movement is still one of the prime targets of government and employer repression."[3]

There are indications that the government of the People's Republic of China is more fearful of workers' demands for the right to organize free labor unions than the students' clamor for democracy. Asia Watch has reported that

ordinary workers have borne the brunt of the Chinese government's crackdown on pro-democracy activists. At least 45 workers are known to have been executed in connection with the anti-government demonstrations in April, May and June 1989. No student or intellectual has been sentenced to death for his or her participation. Workers appear to have received longer sentences; a greater percentage of them have been tried; fewer have been released or had their sentences remitted. Many more have disappeared into the Chinese labor camp system. Lacking the access to the international network enjoyed by many Chinese students and scholars, workers have received very little public attention.[4]

The suppression of the rights of workers to organize are evident in many other countries. Given this close association between workers' rights and the general human rights situation, it is surprising that human rights non-governmental organizations (NGOs) have evinced slight concern for workers' rights per se (such as the right to organize trade unions or the right to a safe and healthy worker environment), while recording arbitrary killings, torture, and detention of labor leaders. This is likely due to the tendency of most human rights organizations to focus on civil and political rights and to neglect economic, social, and cultural rights, such as the right to housing, the right to food, and workers' rights. The right of association, however—including the right to form and join trade unions—is considered both a civil right and an economic right; provisions for freedom of association are included both in the ICCPR and the ICESCR.[5]

Non-governmental organizations send few missions to investigate violations of economic and social rights and few studies or reports are issued on such rights. Recently, however, the New York–based Lawyers' Committee for Human Rights has published several studies on workers' rights and international trade.[6]

A notable and surprising exception to the failure to regard workers' rights as human rights are the U.S. State Department's annual *Country Reports on Human Rights Practices*, which include analyses of workers' rights in each country report. However, the State Department has not reported on other economic and social rights since 1981, because such rights were considered "aspirations" or "goals" rather than rights by the Reagan/Bush administrations.[7] "Internationally recognized worker rights," for the purpose of inclusion in the State Department reports, are those defined in Section 502(a) of the Trade Act of 1974[8]: namely, (1) the right of association; (2) the right to organize and bargain collectively; (3) a prohibition on the use of forced or compulsory labor; (4) a minimum age for the employment of children; and (5) acceptable conditions of work with respect to minimum wages, hours of work, and occupational safety and health.[9]

The main international forum for the defense of labor rights has been the International Labor Organization. Human rights organizations, while extremely active at the annual meetings of the United Nations Human Rights Commission in Geneva, rarely attend the ILO annual conference, also in Geneva, where states are subject to more effective monitoring than by the Human Rights Commission.[10]

At a recent meeting of the UN Human Rights Commission, sixty-three non-governmental human rights organizations made oral interventions under the agenda item concerning the violation of human rights and fundamental freedoms.[11] In contrast, Amnesty International (AI) appears to be the only major human rights NGO that regularly attends the ILO Conference and the only human rights NGO that has developed a strategy for working with the ILO.[12] AI has emphasized the close relationship between workers' rights and civil and political rights and has pointed out that it shares common concerns with much of the ILO's work, particularly freedom of association, freedom from forced labor, and indigenous peoples' rights.[13]

The failure of most NGOs to develop strategies to work with the ILO is regrettable given the greater effectiveness of the ILO system in comparison with the work of the UN Human Rights Commission and the common human rights issues raised in the two forums.[14] The preference for action at the Human Rights Commission may be due to the more formal structure of the ILO, which does not facilitate the participation of non-occupational NGOs and, perhaps, even to the very effectiveness of the ILO system, which seems less in need of NGO pressure. Trade union representatives, who participate fully in all ILO activities, provide the much needed pressure on governments to promote worker rights.

While U.S. human rights organizations have actively pressed the U.S. Congress to ratify the Genocide Convention, the Convention against Torture, and the ICCPR, they have not demonstrated equal concern for the ratification of the ILO human rights conventions dealing with the rights of workers.[15]

Human rights scholars—other than ILO officials or former officials—also give little attention to workers' rights.[16] Lance Compa has pointed out that a perusal of human rights literature reveals few references to "labor," "workers," "trade unions," or "unions," although the ILO is frequently mentioned.[17] The better known international law casebooks include sections on human rights with rare references to labor rights, although they usually include a passing reference to ILO conventions and the admired ILO system of supervision of treaties. Texts and casebooks more narrowly focused on human rights, more surprisingly, also give little space to the subject of labor rights.[18]

Workers' rights should be of interest to human rights scholars and activists since they are among the most well-defined rights and are subject to a better enforcement procedure than most rights. Workers' rights have been elaborated and clarified by ILO conventions and by ILO organs that supervise the application of these conventions. Indeed, the international human rights movement may be said to have begun with the founding of the ILO in 1919 and the adoption soon thereafter of the first international labor conventions. Scholars would find ample material for study in the ILO's extensive experience in developing and promoting labor rights.

The failure to address workers' rights as human rights is also attributable, in part, to labor advocates. Labor advocates and trade unions tend to rely on their own organizations for promoting and protecting worker rights and to ignore the additional support that could be provided by well-known human rights organizations. Representatives of the two movements have little contact with each other. A happy exception to the failure to work together is the Washington-based International Labor Rights Fund, a non-profit organization founded in 1986 to promote respect for worker rights. This organization includes members of human rights groups on its Board and reaches out beyond the traditional trade union constituency.

What accounts for these parallel tracks—the human rights movement and the labor movement rarely working together? The reasons appear to be multiple. It has already been mentioned that human rights organizations tend to ignore economic and social rights in general—perhaps because of the controversy (largely in the United States) over whether they are "rights" or merely "claims" and perhaps because of the greater complexity involved in protecting such rights.

Human rights organizations have been mainly concerned with countries in which there are serious violations of human rights and where there is a large informal, non-unionized sector. The right to physical security, the right to life, and the right not to be tortured have been seen as more urgent than the right to organize trade unions or the right to non-discrimination in employment. But, as mentioned earlier, repressive regimes choose their victims with care—and the victims of arbitrary execution, torture, and detention without trial are frequently those who are active in trade unions or other workers' associations. It is not only the leaders of trade unions who are subject to such threats to their security, but also rubber tappers in Brazil, sugar workers in the Philippines, and plantation workers and hired farm laborers in many countries who attempt to organize in defense of their rights. It is because of the defense of their rights as workers that some of the more vulnerable populations in many countries are most in danger.

In addition to the reasons discussed above for the failure of the two movements to work together, there may also be a difference in the "cultural context" of human rights activists and trade union activists. Here "cultural context" does not refer to academic learning or interests in cultural activities, but rather to the general milieu and interests of the two groups. In most industrialized countries trade unionists are deeply involved in local economic issues—organizing at the shop level or working on issues of importance within a particular enterprise or industry. They are pragmatic and concerned about specific economic interests. The national organizations may attempt to elicit an interest in their union counterparts elsewhere, but the average unionist is not deeply concerned about the development of workers' rights abroad, except to the extent that his or her own livelihood may be threatened by imported goods. Union members are often regarded as protectionist, objecting to the importation of goods, whether or not such trade may be assisting the economic situation of workers from the importing country. The argument often made by union leaders—and it is certainly a valid argument—is that goods produced under unfair labor standards should not be allowed to compete with goods made in the home country under better standards.

The subject of workers' rights and trade is a major focus of other papers in this volume and will not be further discussed here, other than to illustrate the differences in attitude between union members and human rights advocates. Human rights activists are, by and large, internationally oriented. Their concern is with human rights problems elsewhere, usually in Asia, Africa, and South and Central America. The pragmatic, local, and protectionist concerns of the average U.S. union member or local organizer are unlikely to be those of the human rights activist.

While ordinary union members and local branches of the union may be focused on their immediate economic interests, national and international federations of unions and trade secretariats have always evidenced a more general international concern with labor rights. For many years this concern was influenced largely by the Cold War. The international trade union movement, like so many other movements, was ideologically divided into the "free" and the "Communist" camps. The concern for human rights, as espoused by the national and international federations, appeared to be largely a political weapon in the Cold War rather than a true humanitarian concern. In the United States, the international activities of the major unions seemed to be mere extensions of U.S. foreign policy. As a result, non-governmental human rights organizations were hesitant to ally themselves with the activities of U.S. labor organizations abroad; political neutrality was felt to be essential by human rights organizations. Amnesty International took particular care not to be allied with either side in the Cold War, but rather emphasized violations of human rights wherever they occurred.

Finally, the failure of the human rights movement and the trade union movement to work together may be largely a U.S. phenomenon. It appears to be less accentuated in Canada and in many European countries. In developing countries, movements for workers' rights are considered human rights issues and the dichotomy is scarcely evident.

What Are Internationally Recognized Workers' Rights?

Current interest in workers' rights has been stimulated by the perceived link between competitive advantages in trade and low labor standards. Long hours of work, low wages, child labor, and poor working conditions are said to be a type of "social dumping" or "unfair subsidy" permitting developing countries or newly industrializing countries to market goods at a low price on the international market. Responses to these allegations of social dumping include U.S. legislation linking various trade benefits and "internationally recognized worker rights" and efforts within GATT to link trade and workers' rights.[19]

In the previous section, workers' rights were discussed as a concept without defining them or distinguishing which of the rights are fundamental or "minimum" international labor standards. The invocation of "internationally recognized worker rights," or "minimum international labor standards" (a phrase that is also used in the context of international trade), however, requires clarification.

Conventions adopted by the ILO provide the best reference for defining "internationally recognized worker rights"; however, the ILO has adopted 177 conventions establishing labor standards on a multitude of issues ranging from the most general (freedom of association) to very specific ones relating to working conditions in particular industries (road transport, seafaring, glass making, etc.). In addition it has adopted hundreds of recommendations, codes, and guidelines that lay down labor standards. It is clearly inappropriate to consider all of these standards as "minimum international labor standards." The ILO itself has established a priority among these standards by listing conventions on a number of subjects as "basic human rights" conventions and emphasizing the importance of ratifying and implementing the following "basic human rights" conventions; those on freedom of association and collective bargaining, on forced labor, equal remuneration, and on discrimination in employment.[20] These are the most widely ratified of ILO conventions and are those to which the ILO devotes most of its attention. The United States has ratified only one of these conventions: Convention No. 105 on the Abolition of Forced Labor. The rights included in these "basic human rights" conventions might logically be considered to form the corpus of "minimum international labor standards" or "internationally recognized worker rights."

Workers' rights are also delineated in the Universal Declaration of Human Rights the ICCPR and the ICESCR. These instruments refer to the following rights: the right to work; the right to just and favorable conditions of work, including fair wages and safe and healthy working conditions; the right to protection against unemployment; the right to equal pay for equal work; the right to form trade unions; the right to rest and leisure and reasonable limitation of working hours; and the right not to be subjected to forced labor. Recently, the UN General Assembly adopted the Convention on the Rights of Migrant Workers, which reiterates many of the fundamental human rights of workers while elaborating on the rights of migrants.[21] Conventions on safe working conditions, employment protection, and limits on working hours are not included among the ILO human rights conventions.

Freedom of Association

Freedom of association—the right of workers to form and join trade unions for the protection of their interests—is a fundamental, internationally recognized right of workers. It is mentioned in the 1919 ILO Constitution, reaffirmed in the 1944 ILO Declaration of Philadelphia, and codified by the adoption of ILO Conventions No. 87 on Freedom of Association and Protection of the Right to Organize Convention, 1948 and No. 98 on the Right to Organize and to Bargain Collectively, 1949. It is included in the provisions of the Universal Declaration of Human Rights and the two main human rights covenants.

Most importantly, membership in the ILO implies a commitment to freedom of association, regardless of whether the relevant ILO conventions on freedom of association have been ratified. This commitment is explicit in the ILO Constitution and the Declaration of Philadelphia. It has subsequently been reiterated in the annual conferences and in the bodies of the ILO, namely the Governing Body Committee on Freedom of Association, in the Commissions of Inquiry, and in the Committee on the Application of Conventions and Recommendations. Similarly this right has received recognition by member states who have not ratified the relevant ILO conventions (including the United States), but who, nevertheless, routinely respond to allegations of violations of the right to freedom of association that have been brought before the ILO Governing Body Committee on Freedom of Association.[22]

In 1974, following the overthrow of the Allende regime in Chile, the ILO established a Fact-Finding and Conciliation Commission to investigate allegations of violations of trade union rights in that country. The Conclusions of the Commission clearly stated that ILO member states are bound to protect the right to freedom of association even if they have not ratified relevant conventions:

Chile has not ratified the Freedom of Association and Protection of the Right to Organize Convention, 1948 (No. 87), which, accordingly, has no binding effect for this country. However, by its membership of the International Labour Organisation, Chile is bound to respect a certain number of general rules which have been established for the common good of the peoples of the twentieth century. Among these principles, freedom of association has become a customary rule above the Conventions.[23]

Current discussions between the Governing Body Committee on Freedom of Association and the People's Republic China (PRC) also evince the PRC's acceptance of an obligation to respect the rights of workers to organize, although there is disagreement over the application of the norm in China. China has not ratified the two main ILO conventions on freedom of association and the right to organize. However following the massacre in Tiananmen Square in 1989 and complaints filed by the International Confederation of Free Trade Unions (ICFTU), the ILO Governing Body on Freedom of Association examined the question of violations of freedom of association by China. The ICFTU complaint alleged that by killing, imprisoning, and harassing workers attempting to establish an independent trade union (the Workers' Autonomous Federation, WAF), China was violating its obligation to the principle of freedom of association. The Committee on Freedom of Association undertook examination of the case in accordance with its usual terms of reference.[24] Exchanges between the government and the ILO are ongoing, and China has demonstrated its willingness to cooperate with the ILO by providing information concerning imprisoned workers.[25]

In these exchanges the PRC has not contested its commitment to the principle of freedom of association. Rather, it has insisted that its actions are in conformity with the principle:

China, one of the founder Members of the ILO, remains faithful to its commitments towards the ILO. . . . The Chinese Government has at all times upheld the principle of freedom of association and protects organizations and associations established pursuant to the law as well as their activities in keeping with the Constitution and the legislation.[26]

The PRC contends that its actions against the workers had nothing to do with freedom of association, but rather that the punishment imposed on workers resulted from their criminal acts and not their acts in pursuance of the right to organize. In its 281st Report in 1992, the Committee urged the government of China to put an end to the detention of workers in custody, to refrain from taking measures of administrative detention and forced labor against workers who had engaged in trade union activities, and to take the necessary steps to ensure that the right of workers to establish organizations of their own choosing and the right of such organizations to function freely be recognized in the legislation and guaranteed in practice.[27]

Why was it necessary to adopt conventions on freedom of association and urge states to ratify them if States were already committed to that norm by virtue of membership in the ILO? There are two possible explanations. First, the two main ILO conventions on freedom of association were adopted in 1948 and 1949, while the obligation of freedom of association by virtue of ILO membership was raised in the context of specific cases only at a later date. Second, the ratification of a convention obligates the state to regularly furnish information concerning the application of the convention to an ILO monitoring body (the Committee of Experts on the Application of Conventions and Recommendations) and to take into consideration the comments of that body as well as the comments of the comparable committee of the Annual Conference. Thus, accepting the norm of freedom of association through ratification of the conventions provides a more regular system of supervision of the norm than the occasional complaints brought before the Governing Body on Freedom of Association, although these complaints, as explained previously, have the advantage of calling attention to countries that have not ratified the conventions.

The question of the obligation of freedom of association for states that are not members of the ILO remains to be examined. Is it a norm of customary international law thereby binding on all states? In pointing out the limitations of U.S. legislation relating to worker rights and trade, Philip Alston questions the binding force in international law of the concept of "freedom of association" for states that have not ratified the relevant ILO conventions nor the ICESCR.[28] Norms are binding in international law either through international agreement or as customary international law; Alston suggests that none of the rights referred to in U.S. legislation as "internationally recognized worker rights" (including freedom of association) have attained the status of customary international law. He also points out that some of the states against which U.S. legislation on worker rights has been invoked have not accepted these norms through adherence to international agreements, such as the relevant ILO conventions or the ICESCR.

Alston does not refer to the commitment to freedom of association entailed by membership in the International Labor Organization—a commitment by international agreement. Whether "freedom of association" is a rule of customary international law is irrelevant for the member states of the ILO. ILO member states include the great majority of the states in the world, including the United States and those against whom allegations of violation of worker rights have been raised in the United States.

A strong argument can also be made for the status of freedom of association and protection of the right to organize as customary international law for non-members of the ILO. Alston cites the Restatement (Third) of the Foreign Relations Law of the United States as supporting the view that none of the worker rights referred to in U.S. legislation (including freedom of association) have become customary international law "especially from an official US perspective".[29] The Restatement lists only the following as comprising the customary international law of human rights: genocide; slavery or slave trade; the murder or causing the disappearance of individuals; torture or other cruel, inhuman, or degrading treatment or punishment; prolonged arbitrary detention; systematic racial discrimination; and a consistent pattern of gross violations of internationally recognized human rights.[30]

In evaluating the relevance of the omission of freedom of association from the list in the Restatement, the following comments should be kept in mind.

(1) It is explicitly pointed out in the Restatement that the list is not exclusive of other rights: "The list is not necessarily complete, and is not closed: human rights not listed in this section may have achieved the status of customary law, and some rights might achieve that status in the future."[31]

(2) The criteria used by the authors of the Restatement to determine whether a particular human rights norm has become customary international law would equally support the contention that freedom of association has become customary international law. Those criteria include widespread adherence to international instruments containing the norm (ILO Constitution, International Covenants on Civil and Political Rights and on Economic, Social and Cultural Rights, etc.), declarations by international bodies (ILO commissions and committees), the incorporation of human rights provisions in national constitutions and laws, and international organization activities and actions.[32] Freedom of association might more clearly satisfy these criteria than some of the norms listed in the Restatement.

(3) The authors of the Restatement include as customary law "only those human rights whose status as customary law is generally accepted (as of 1987) and whose scope and content are generally agreed."[33] Since the great majority of states are committed to freedom of association by international agreement—membership in the ILO—it is not surprising that freedom of association for the protection of worker rights has seldom been discussed as a norm of customary international law (and hence is absent from usual lists of human rights customary norms). The general scope and content of freedom of association has been elaborated over a considerable period by ILO bodies.

(4) While authoritative by virtue of its authorship, the Restatement remains a statement of U.S. conclusions concerning international law and is not itself proof of the existence of a particular norm of international law. Its listing of customary international law human rights norms is not conclusive either as to inclusions or omissions. Alston accords attention to the Restatement, particularly, because he wishes to emphasize the inconsistency between two U.S. approaches: that of U.S. trade legislation and that of the Restatement.[34]

The basic elements of the norm of freedom of association are contained in ILO Convention No. 87, Freedom of Association and Protection of the Right to Organize, and in Convention No. 98, The Right to Organize and to Bargain Collectively:

Workers and employers without distinction whatsoever, shall have the right to establish and, subject only to the rules of the organisation concerned, to join organizations of their own choosing without previous authorisation. (Article 2 of Convention No. 87)

Workers shall enjoy adequate protection against acts of anti-union discrimination in respect of their employment. (Article 1 of Convention No. 98)

Machinery appropriate to national conditions shall be established, where necessary, for the purpose of ensuring respect for the right to organize. (Article 3 of Convention No. 98)

Further provisions of Convention No. 87 provide that organizations have the right to draw up their constitutions and rules and to elect their representatives in full freedom, that the should not be dissolved or suspended by administrative authority, and that they should have the right to establish federations and affiliate with international organizations. Convention No. 87 also provides that each state may determine the extent to which freedom of association applies to the police and armed forces. Convention No. 98 specifies certain acts that are considered anti-union discrimination.

The scope of the right, as a commitment of ILO membership, has been interpreted by ILO bodies as substantially the same as the commitments under Conventions No. 87 and 98. As with all legal rules, the problem comes in applying the general rule to the specific facts. It is evident from the ILO's own criticisms of the legislation and practice of member states that freedom of association is frequently violated by ILO members. Such violations do not negate the legal validity of the rule but do challenge the ability of the organization to ensure conformity with its fundamental principles. Essentially the same problem of enforcing widely accepted human rights norms exists for all UN and other international organizations enunciating human rights standards. The efforts of the ILO to promote and protect ILO standards are discussed in the next section.

Disagreements between member states and the ILO regarding freedom of association relate less to the legal validity of the norm than to whether certain specific actions of a state contravene the norm. Many of the cases brought before the ILO Governing Body Committee on Freedom of Association relate to killings, arrests, and harassment of trade union activists or persons attempting to organize workers. While persecution of worker representatives is a clear violation of freedom of association, there are other issues relating to freedom of association that appear less clear-cut; for example, does freedom of association necessarily imply the right to strike and does it exclude union security clauses?

The Right to Strike

Neither of the two major ILO conventions on freedom of association expressly refer to the right to strike. However, ILO supervisory bodies have held that the right to strike is one of the essential means available to workers and their organizations for promoting and protecting their economic and social interests.[35] This right, however, has been qualified and limited by the ILO. Strikes must be peaceful, they may be made subject to certain preconditions, and the right to strike may be denied to public servants and workers engaged in "essential services." Article 8 of the ICESCR on freedom of association provides that states that are parties to the Covenant should undertake to ensure the right to strike, provided that it is exercised in conformity with the laws of the particular country. In contrast there is no comparable provision in the ICCPR. Article 22 of the ICCPR relating to freedom of association does not refer to the right to strike. The Human Rights Committee monitoring the ICCPR ruled in the Alberta case that the norm "freedom of association" in the ICCPR does not imply the right to strike. However, the opinion of the committee is unpersuasive and its credibility is lessened by the forceful individual dissenting opinion in the case signed by five of the most respected members of the Committee, including Rosalyn Higgins, Professor of International Law at the London School of Economics, and Torkel Opsahl, Professor of Constitutional Law at the University of Oslo.[36]

The divergence among the freedom of association obligations of ILO Convention No. 87, the ICESCR provisions, and the obligations of the ICCPR has been noted by the United States government.[37] Ratification of the ICCPR was not thought to bind the United States to ensure the right to strike. It should be noted, however, that no reservation, declaration, or understanding was made concerning this issue at the moment of ratification, presumably because the United States would not wish to state officially that it did not accord workers the right to strike. However, the administration evinced concern regarding the conformity of U.S. legislation with international norms regarding the right to strike in ILO conventions and in the ICESCR.

Despite the administration's view concerning the ICCPR, the United States is, nevertheless, committed to freedom of association, and to the ILO's interpretation that this freedom implies the right to strike, by virtue of its membership in the ILO. The U.S. government has not directly denied this commitment. It has, however, denied in a case before an ILO body that the permission that U.S. law accords to employers to replace striking workers does not infringe on the right to strike.

In 1990, the AFL-CIO brought a complaint against the United States before the ILO Governing Body on Freedom of Association relating to the so-called "Mackay doctrine," which permits employers to hire permanent replacement workers for strikers in certain types of strikes.[38] The United States maintained that its laws guaranteed the right of association and the right to strike and that the "Mackay doctrine" did not violate the right to strike. The Committee held, however, that the

right to strike is one of the essential means through which workers and their organizations may promote and defend their economic and social rights. The Committee considers that this basic right is not really guaranteed when a worker who exercises it legally runs the risk of seeing his or her job taken up permanently by another worker, just as legally. The Committee considers that, if a strike is otherwise legal, the use of labour drawn from outside the undertaking to replace strikers for an indeterminate period entails a risk of derogation from the right to strike which may affect the free exercise of trade union rights.[39]

The difference between the United States and the ILO on the right to strike, thus, does not relate to whether freedom of association implies the right to strike, but rather whether a specific U.S. legal doctrine infringes upon that right.

Efforts to amend the "Mackay doctrine" by legislation have been pushed by labor groups in the United States. Although it was passed by the House of Representatives and enjoyed majority support in the Senate, the "striker replacement" bill failed passage in July 1994 when the U.S. Senate failed to muster sixty votes to end debate to force a final vote. Regrettably, little attention was paid to the views of the ILO on the question by U.S. legislators.

The Right Not to Join an Association

ILO conventions assert the right to form and join labor unions; however, there is no correlative right recognized by the ILO not to join an association. The ILO Conference that adopted Convention No. 87 on the Right to Freedom of Association refused to include in it a provision stipulating the right not to join an organization, leaving to each member state the decision regarding union security clauses. Nevertheless, the ILO Committee of Experts has specified that union security clauses imposed by law, as contrasted with those agreed upon between unions and employers, are incompatible with the freedom of association conventions.[40] The European Court of Human Rights has interpreted the provision on freedom of association in the European Convention on Human Rights to impose limitations on union security or closed shop arrangements,[41] and the Universal Declaration of Human Rights contains a provision stating that "No one may be compelled to join an association" — a provision that is, however, missing in the ICCPR and the ICESCR.

Freedom of association is the most fundamental of all the rights of workers and is so recognized in U.S. legislation and other instances of the linkage of trade and workers' rights. Should other standards such as the prohibition of child labor, the regulation of hours of work, and safety and health standards also be considered "minimum international labor standards" or fundamental "worker rights" under U.S. legislation and other efforts that link worker rights and trade? One of the most comprehensive efforts to define the specific content of "minimum international labor standards" was undertaken in the Netherlands in 1984.

The Dutch Study on Labor Standards and Trade

In 1984, the Netherlands grappled with the problem of defining the minimum content of internationally recognized labor standards in connection with the possible linking of trade and worker rights. The Dutch Minister of Development Cooperation requested the Netherlands National Advisory Council for Development Cooperation to give its views regarding the advisability of incorporating "a provision concerning minimum labour standards into international agreements" on economic cooperation and trade policy. The resulting report is a thoughtful and thorough discussion of the linkage of trade and international standards. It is particularly useful in the effort to determine what rights may constitute "minimum international labor standards."[42]

The report defines minimum labor standards, in an absolute sense, as those that "*all* countries ought to introduce and observe under *all* circumstances." It points out that there are minimum standards "in a relative sense which develop more or less in line with economic growth."[43] The report should be compulsory reading for all of those who are concerned about worker rights and labor standards.

The Advisory Council had recourse to ILO standards to define the content of "minimum internationally recognized labor standards," concluding that the standards in eight ILO conventions constituted a minimum package of international labor standards that might be incorporated in international agreements: the two major conventions on freedom of association, two conventions on forced labor, and conventions on discrimination in employment, equal remuneration, employment policy, and minimum age for employment. In reaching that conclusion the Council applied three criteria: a social criterion, a political and legal criterion, and an economic criterion. The social criterion limited the choice to conventions related to basic human needs and human rights. The second criterion, the political and legal criterion, related to the degree of international acceptance of the standard. The Council checked whether the relevant convention was ratified by a geographically and economically diverse group of states. The final, economic, criterion was applied to ensure that the convention would not impose economic hardship or impair economic development. Applying these criteria, the Council arrived at the decision that the eight conventions previously mentioned constituted the minimum package of international labor standards.

The Council also recommended that this minimum package of labor standards provisions should be included in international agreements only if certain conditions are met: first, the agreement itself must first contribute to the attainment of conditions needed to facilitate observance of the minimum international labor standards; second, the agreement must provide a satisfactory procedure for settling disputes by an independent body; and third, the enforcement of minimum international labor standards must be based on reciprocity; that is, it must not be used by countries that have not themselves accepted the standards.

The careful examination of the issue of worker rights and trade in the Dutch report may be contrasted with the approach used in U.S. legislation. As Alston has pointed out, U.S. legislation has not sufficiently linked the concepts of worker rights in U.S. legislation with ILO standards and has failed to use the criterion of reciprocity in its criticisms of the labor standards of other countries.[44] The determination of "minimum international labor standards" or "fundamental workers' rights" by the Dutch Advisory Group is a serious and comprehensive effort to define these concepts in the context of international trade. Their inclusion of the standards of minimum age for employment and employment policy may be controversial, but their examination of the issues involved in the linkage of worker rights and trade is persuasive.

Apparently there has not been any practical follow-up, within the Netherlands, on the conclusions reached by the Dutch report, although there was a suggestion of renewed interest in the subject by the Minister of Development Cooperation in March 1993.[45] In view of current U.S. interest in the subject, the Report may eventually have a practical import not limited to the Netherlands. This 1984 Report deserves resuscitation.

A Minimal Approach to Defining Internationally Recognized Workers' Rights

The issue of whether economic cooperation agreements and international trade should be linked with fundamental workers' rights is discussed in other chapters. However, defining the concepts of "worker rights" and "minimum international labor standards" arises in every consideration of that issue. A minimal approach should be taken to the meaning of these concepts in the context of international trade and economic agreements—without negating the importance of the full panoply of workers' rights. In this context, the concept of workers' rights may most appropriately and productively be limited to freedom of association and the prohibition of forced labor.

Why only these rights? They are both clearly "basic human rights" (probably customary international law and, in any event, included in major human rights instruments that have been widely ratified) and not simply technical labor standards. As other basic human rights, they should not be denied for reasons of economic development or lack of resources. There is less international agreement about the normative value and interpretation of equal remuneration, minimum wages, working hours, child labor, and safe working conditions than concerning freedom of association and the prohibition of forced labor. The use of the lowest common denominator in this context may be the wisest course; the common arguments used against the linking of trade and workers' rights have less force if the concept of workers' rights is limited to freedom of association and the prohibition of forced labor.

Freedom of association has been discussed extensively above. Without discussing the prohibition of forced labor extensively here, it is sufficient to point out that it is included in the Universal Declaration of Human Rights, the ICCPR, the ICESCR, and two ILO conventions (one of which has been ratified by the United States) and has been extensively interpreted by ILO organs. The same arguments that support the allegation that freedom of association may now be a rule of customary international law apply equally to the prohibition of forced labor. Other worker rights referred to in the Dutch study and in U.S. legislation are extremely important, but the adherence to these additional norms by countries that have not ratified the relevant ILO conventions is problematic and economic development arguments against their implementation appear more persuasive. Since the U.S. is committed to freedom of association, by virtue of ILO membership, and has ratified an ILO convention on the prohibition of forced labor, the United States is on solid ground in using only these two norms as the fundamental elements of worker rights; it would not then be imposing standards on other countries that it has not itself adopted.[46]

At the same time, trade unions and human rights groups should continue to press for improvement in other international labor standards, both at the UN and the ILO and in countries reaching a more advanced stage of industrial development. However, the definition of worker rights in national legislation linking trade and worker rights (hence unilateral determinations) is likely to be less controversial if limited as suggested.

Implementing Workers' Rights: Contributions and Limitations of the International Labor Organization

When created by the Treaty of Versailles following World War I, the ILO did not use the term "human rights" either in its constitution or in early documents; the phrase "social justice" described its aims. Since World War II, however, when the ILO became a specialized agency of the United Nations and human rights became a focus of international attention, the ILO has emphasized the relationship of labor rights to concepts of human rights and social justice.[47] In contrast with other UN specialized agencies, it has consistently collaborated with UN human rights activities, submitting detailed and useful information concerning the implementation of workers' rights in specific countries to the monitoring committees set up under the two international covenants, particularly the Committee on Economic, Social and Cultural Rights (ECOSOC). ILO reports and studies have emphasized the close interrelation between civil and political rights and trade union rights.[48]

A unique organization within the UN system, the ILO antedates the founding of the United Nations and, unlike other UN agencies, provides for full participation of non-governmental representatives of employer and workers' organizations in all its activities. Non-governmental organizations do not participate on an equal footing with governments in any other UN agency. NGOs with consultative status in ECOSOC may speak at many UN meetings and may present reports and comments for consideration by governments, but they remain secondary members participating by permission and not by right.

In retrospect, it appears surprising that the Treaty of Versailles, focusing on issues of peace after World War I, included Part XIII, which established the ILO. It is rare today to hear references to the link between peace and workers' rights. Yet the link between democracy and peace is often invoked—and freedom of association is an essential element of democracy. Samuel Gompers of the AFL and other labor leaders of the victorious powers emphasized the contribution of workers to the war effort and urged the drafting of a labor magna charta contemporaneously with the post–World War I peace negotiations. The link between issues of peace and the rights of the working class was underscored by the Bolshevik Revolution of 1917; the establishment of the ILO in 1919 was the Western response to the demands of the working class. The famous AFL premise, "labor is not a commodity or an article of commerce," was adopted as a basic principle of the newly established organization.[49]

Although Samuel Gompers was Chairman of the committee that created the ILO at the Versailles peace negotiations, and despite the fact that the first annual Conference of the ILO was held in Washington, D.C., the United States did not join the Organization until 1934, and never joined the League of Nations, also created by the Treaty of Versailles. The relations of the United States with the ILO have been ambivalent. The United States left the ILO in 1977 over allegations that it was "Soviet dominated" and that it employed a double standard in its human rights activities.[50] Since its return in 1980, the United States has had a more temperate and positive role within the organization, but, to date, it has ratified only 12 of the 177 ILO conventions, including only one of the basic human rights conventions (The Convention on the Abolition of Forced Labor).

The ILO has maintained a more holistic approach to human rights than the United Nations by referring more generally to "human rights" rather than categorizing them as "civil and political rights" or "economic, social and cultural rights." Its broader philosophical approach to human rights is contained in a succinct phrase in the ILO Declaration of Philadelphia,[51] a restatement of its original aims adopted in 1945:

All human beings, irrespective of race, creed or sex have the right to pursue both their material well-being and their spiritual development in conditions of freedom and dignity, of economic security and equal opportunity.

Are ILO conventions effective instruments in promoting and protecting worker rights? Many critics argue that the ILO lacks enforcement powers and that some state members of the ILO give little attention to its efforts to protect labor rights. In evaluating these assertions it is necessary to consider realistically the current context of international political relations, particularly with regard to the protection of human rights.

Neither the ILO nor any other international body, with the exception of the UN Security Council, has enforcement powers in the sense that one may speak of enforcement in a national legal system. Even in the case of the egregious violations of human rights occurring in former

Yugoslavia and in Somalia, for example, it has been difficult to initiate effective military action, despite the Chapter VII enforcement powers of the Security Council contained in the United Nations Charter. The political climate and fears of inroads on state sovereignty consistently block enforcement measures in the overwhelming majority of cases.

The ILO Constitution does not authorize the use of armed force or economic sanctions against countries violating labor rights. To that extent, it lacks "enforcement" powers. Like all international human rights bodies, it must ultimately rely on voluntary acceptance of its strictures. What realistically then can be done—and has been done—to promote and protect human rights and labor rights?

The first and essential task in protecting and promoting human rights is to define rights and to obtain an international acceptance of these definitions. In this regard, the ILO has been preeminent. Through the adoption of conventions and recommendations and, especially, through the interpretation of rights by ILO monitoring bodies in particular cases, the ILO has made an outstanding contribution to the definition of worker rights. It has, to borrow a phrase from the Universal Declaration of Human Rights, established a "common standard of achievement" relating to worker rights.

But the ILO has also developed a complex monitoring system aimed at protecting labor rights. The ILO system of monitoring the application of its conventions has been extensively discussed and praised in numerous books and articles, and the description of that system will not be repeated here.[52] It includes a reporting system, a comprehensive analysis of state reports by ILO officials and by the ILO Committee of Experts, open questioning of state representatives at the annual ILO conference, commissions of inquiry, personal country visits by ILO officials, and, finally, the "mobilization of shame" through publication of failure to implement conventions.

The ILO must necessarily, as with all international human rights bodies at the present stage of international life, rely primarily on publishing its findings. In the on-going exchanges between the government of China and the ILO, for example, the ILO Committee on Freedom of Association has clearly, but diplomatically, pointed out to the government the serious nature of the violations of freedom of association and urged the government to take immediate measures to put an end to the detention of workers still in custody and to ensure the right of workers to establish organizations of their own choosing.[53] What more can be done by the ILO to contribute to freedom of association in China and elsewhere?

In a review of ILO procedures for protecting freedom of association in 1979, trade union organizations urged the ILO to cut off technical as-

sistance and close regional ILO offices in states that are egregious violators of labor rights.[54] Their suggestions were not supported by the other
members of the ILO constituency, governments, or employer organizations. Is it more productive to maintain contact with states violating
standards or to terminate relationships? China, for example, has been
willing to engage in a continuing discussion with the ILO on the question of freedom of association. The answer to this question is not self-
evident and depends on the specific situation. South Africa terminated
its membership in the ILO during the period of relentless criticism of
apartheid within the organization but continued as a member of the
United Nations.

It should be noted that U.S. efforts to enforce human rights through
trade legislation or conditions attached to most-favored-nation status
run up against the same obstacles as those encountered by the ILO.
They have also not been noticeably effective in fundamentally changing
the system of human rights in various countries. Much more could be
done both nationally and internationally to promote and protect human
rights, but security interests, desire to continue trade, and many other
factors block progress.

Is the ILO system effective enough? Clearly not. No international system for protecting human rights is yet good enough. Nevertheless, the
ILO system has been consistently praised as one of the best systems, and
it has had results. Walter Galenson, an American academic, in one of the
most thorough studies by a non-ILO official, has documented the adoption of improved labor laws in a number of countries following the countries' ratifications of ILO conventions.[55] Countries that have been the
subject of ILO criticism have tended to turn to the organization for assistance, or have accepted closer contact with the ILO when the regimes
change. South Africa, which left the ILO after criticism of its apartheid
policy, agreed in 1992 to the constitution of an ILO Fact-Finding and
Conciliation Commission on Freedom of Association in South Africa,
in response to a complaint originating from the Congress of South African Trade Unions.[56] South Africa has since rejoined the ILO.

The Broader Context: Workers' Rights, Human Rights, and Democracy

The concept of workers' rights has been given too narrow a focus.
We have excluded workers' rights in practice from the broader realm
of human rights and we have narrowed the concept of human rights
to exclude social rights, including workers' rights. The significance
of workers' rights in the development of democratic institutions has
largely been ignored in current discussions of that important subject,

yet democracy necessarily implies the right of association, including the right to form and join trade unions. We have consigned issues of worker rights to a specialized UN agency, but we have forgotten the context in which the ILO and international labor standards were originally created: the link between workers' rights and peace. What was perceived as important in the tumultuous period of the Bolshevik revolution should be reemphasized today: the importance of social justice to a stable and peaceful world, and social justice implies rights for the great majority of the world's population—the workers. Today, we use the terminology of "human rights" rather than "social justice," but human rights cannot exist without social justice. The rights of workers must be seen as essential to issues of social justice, human rights, and democracy and must be promoted as such.

Notes

1. See *The Trade Union Situation in Chile: Report of the Fact-Finding and Conciliation Commission on Freedom of Association* (Geneva: ILO, 1975).

2. *Special Report of the Director-General on the Application of the Declaration Concerning Action Against Apartheid in South Africa* (Geneva: ILO, 1991).

3. *Peace Agreements and Violations of Human and Trade Union Rights in El Salvador* (Brussels: International Confederation of Free Trade Unions, Oct. 1992).

4. "Chinese Workers Receive Harsh Sentences," *News from Asia Watch* 3, 9 (March 13, 1991).

5. Article 8, International Covenant on Economic, Social and Cultural Rights; Article 22 of the International Covenant on Civil and Political Rights.

6. See Lawyers Committee for Human Rights. "A Report on Legal Mechanisms to Protect Worker Rights" (mimeo, 1991) and "Worker Rights Under the U.S. Trade Laws" (1989).

7. See Dobriansky, *U.S. Human Rights Policy: An Overview*,Current Policy No. 1091 (Washington, DC: U.S. Department of State, Bureau of Public Affairs, 1988), 2–3.

8. Pub. L. No. 93-618, 88 Stat. 2066 (1975), codified at 19 U.S.C.A. sec. 2462(b) (1)–(6) (1980).

9. U.S. Department of State, *Country Reports on Human Rights Practices for 1989*, Report Submitted to the Senate Committee on Foreign Relations and the House Committee on Foreign Affairs, 101st Cong., 2nd sess. 1 (1990).

10. See below concerning the ILO for information on its monitoring of labor rights. For a comparison of UN and ILO human rights systems, see Virginia A. Leary, "Learning from the Experience of the ILO," in *The United Nations and Human Rights*, ed. Philip Alston (Oxford: Clarendon Press, 1992).

11. The great number of NGO interventions at recent meetings of the UN Human Rights Commission is increasingly regarded as excessive and may be counterproductive, leading to restrictions on NGO rights to intervene. The sixty-three interventions mentioned in the text relate to only one agenda item among many others on which NGOs also spoke.

12. This difference in participation in UN and in ILO activities is not entirely due to neglect by the NGOs. The UN system for a variety of reasons is more

open to participation by non-governmental human rights organizations with consultative status with ECOSOC than is the ILO system. At the United Nations, registration to attend human rights meetings is relatively simple, a full-time UN official is responsible for relations with NGOs, NGOs are given the opportunity to make oral as well as written interventions, and seating is arranged for them in meetings. The ILO is the only international organization to provide for full participation in its activities of some non-governmental organizations—specifically, employers' and workers' organizations—but non-occupational NGOs, such as human rights organizations, find it more complicated to participate in ILO activities. Little assistance or encouragement is given to them by the ILO.

13. "The 77th International Labour Conference: Amnesty International's Concerns Relevant to the Effective Implementation of International Labour Organization Conventions." *Amnesty International* IOR 42/01/90 (April 1990).

14. See note 10.

15. A notable exception was the testimony in 1991 of the Washington representative of Human Rights Watch urging ratification of ILO Convention No. 105 on Abolition of Forced Labor during hearings on that convention.

16. Publications on workers' rights by ILO officials or former officials include numerous writings by C. Wilfred Jenks, former Director-General and Legal Advisor of the ILO; Ernest Landy, *The Effectiveness of International Supervision: Thirty Years of ILO Experience* Dobbs Ferry, NY: Oceana Publications (1991); Virginia A. Leary, *The Application of International Labour Conventions in National Law* (The Hague, Netherlands, Kluwer 1982) and "Learning from the Experience of the ILO"; Stephen I. Schlossberg, "United States Participation in the ILO: Redefining the Role," *Comparative Labor Law Journal* 11 (1989); and Nicolas Valticos, *International Labour Law* (The Hague, Netherlands, 1979).

17. Lance Compa, "International Labor Standards and Instruments of Recourse for Working Women," *Yale Journal of International Law* 17 (1991): 152, n. 5.

18. See, for example, Richard Pierre Claude and Burns H. Weston, eds., *Human Rights in the World Community: Issues and Action* (Philadelphia: University of Pennsylvania Press, 1989), in which there are only a few brief references to the ILO, including a two-paragraph summary of its work, and no discussion of workers' rights in general or of freedom of association for workers. See also Frank Newman and David Weissbrodt, *International Human Rights* (Boston: Little Brown, 1990), in which there are a number of references to "worker rights" and to the ILO, but no substantial development of either subject.

19. See, for example, Sec. 502(b) (7) of the Trade Act of 1974, Pub. L. No. 93-618, 88 Stat. 2066 (1975), codified at 19 U.S.C.A. sec. 2462(b) (1)–(6) (1980), relating to the Generalized System of Preferences.

20. ILO Conventions and recommendations are published in ILO, *International Labour Conventions and Recommendations, 1919–1981*. Conventions adopted subsequent to 1981 are available in individual format from the ILO, Geneva. The ILO also publishes a *Classified Guide to International Labour Standards* in which it lists the following conventions as "basic human rights conventions": Freedom of Association and Protection of the Right to Organize Convention, 1948 (No. 87); Right to Organize and Collective Bargaining Convention, 1949 (No. 98); Workers' Representatives Convention, 1971 (No. 135); Rural Workers' Organizations Convention, 1975 (No. 141); Labour Relations (Public Service) Convention, 1978 (No. 151); Right of Association (Agriculture) Convention, 1921 (No. 11); Right of Association (Non-Metropolitan Territories) Convention, 1947 (No. 84); Forced Labour Convention, 1930 (No. 29); Abolition of Forced Labour

Convention, 1957 (No. 105); Discrimination (Employment and Occupation) Convention, 1958 (No. 111), Equal Remuneration Convention, 1951 (No. 100).

21. International Convention on the Protection of the Rights of All Migrant Workers and Members of Their Families, adopted by the United Nations General Assembly, 45th Session, Dec. 18, 1990 (A/RES/45/158).

22. For information concerning a case brought against the United States by the AFL-CIO before the ILO Governing Body Committee on Freedom of Association see Section II (a) concerning the right to strike. The Governing Body Committee on Freedom of Association is composed of nine members of the ILO Governing Body appointed by the Governing Body as a whole and representing governments, workers, and employers. It has become the major ILO organ for examining allegations of freedom of association. Its responsibility is to determine whether cases are worthy of examination by the Governing Body. As of May 1993, it had presented findings and recommendations to the Governing Body for decision in almost 1,600 cases of allegations of violations of freedom of association.

23. Fact-Finding and Conciliation Commission on Chile, International Labour Organisation, Geneva, 1975, para. 466.

24. Information concerning the procedure of the Committee on Freedom of Association is contained in Outline of the Existing Procedure for the Examination of Complaints Alleging Violations of Trade Union Rights, GB/LS/May 1982.

25. See the following reports of the ILO Committee on Freedom of Association Relating to the Complaint Against the Government of China Presented by the International Confederation of Free Trade Unions (ICFTU), Case No. 1500: 270th Report, *ILO Official Bulletin* 73 ser. B, no. 1 (1990): paras. 287–334 (plus Annex); 275th Report, *ILO Official Bulletin* 73 ser. B, no. 3 (1990): paras. 323–363 (plus Annex); 279th Report, *ILO Official Bulletin* 74 ser. B, no. 3 (1991): paras. 586–641 (plus Annex); 281st Report, *ILO Official Bulletin* 75 ser. B, no. 1 (1992): paras. 68–83.

26. "Report of the Committee on Freedom of Association" (275th and 276th Reports), *ILO Official Bulletin* 73 ser. B, no. 3 (1990): paras. 340, 344.

27. "281st Report of Committee on Freedom of Association," *ILO Official Bulletin* 75 ser. B, no. 1 (1992): para. 83.

28. Philip Alston, "Labor Rights Provisions in U.S. Trade Law: 'Aggressive Unilateralism'?" *Human Rights Quarterly* 15, 13 (1993).

29. Ibid., 14.

30. 2 Restatement (Third) of the Foreign Relations Law of the United States, sec. 702.

31. Ibid., Sec. 702(a).

32. Ibid., Sec. 701, Reporters' Notes No. 2.

33. Ibid., Sec. 702(a).

34. Alston, "Labor Rights Provisions," 14: "Thus, if most of the enumerated worker rights could not, *especially from an official U.S. perspective,* be considered to form part of customary law" (emphasis added).

35. See *Reports of the Committee on Freedom of Association, 1–14* 2nd Report, Case No. 28, para. 68; 4th Report, Case No. 5, para. 27; 13th Report, Case No. 181, para. 94 (Geneva: ILO). See also Hodges-Aeberhard and Odero De Dios, "Principles of the Committee of Association concerning Strikes," *International Labour Review* 126 (1987): 544–45; *Freedom of Association: Digest of Decisions of the Freedom of Association Committee of the Governing Body of the ILO* (3rd ed.; Geneva: ILO, 1985).

36. "Decision of the Human Rights Committee under the Optional Protocol to the International Covenant on Civil and Political Rights," 28th session, concerning Communication No. R.26/118, submitted by John Booth, Paul Duteau, Lorraine Snyders, Tom Minhinnett, David Potter, and Donald Sloan; State Party concerned Canada; CCPR/C/D/R.26/118, July 29, 1986, individual opinion by Rosalyn Higgins, Rajsoomer Lallah, Andreas Mavrommatis, Torkel Opsahl, Amos Wako.

37. U.S. Senate Committee on Foreign Relations, *Report on the International Covenant on Civil and Political Rights*, Jan. 30, 1992, reproduced from U.S. Senate Executive Report 102–23 (102d Cong., 2nd sess.), app. B, *International Legal Materials (I.L.M.)* (1992): 31, 645, 661.

38. Case No. 543, "Complaint Against the Government of the United States Presented by the American Federation of Labor and Congress of Industrial Organizations," 278th Report of the Governing Body Committee on Freedom of Association, 1991, paras. 60–93.

39. Ibid., para. 92.

40. Principles and Procedures of the ILO Relating to Freedom of Association.

41. Case of Young, James, and Webster, Judgment, European Court of Human Rights, Aug. 1981, ser. A, No. 44.

42. National Advisory Council for Development Cooperation, *Recommendation on Minimum International Labour Standards* (The Hague: Ministry of Foreign Affairs, Nov. 1984), Plein 23. The working group that prepared the report consisted of the following members of the National Council: L. J. Emmerij, chair, K. Fibbe, H. Hofstede, M. J. 't Hooft-Welvaars, E. Postel-Coster, P. J. I. M. de Waart, and Y. B. de Wit.

43. Ibid., 17.

44. Alston, "Labor Rights Provisions," 32.

45. Telephone discussion with Paul de Waart, March 19, 1993.

46. In 1989, the *Worker Rights News*, a newsletter of the International Labor Rights Fund, reported that "the State Department has instructed embassies that while ILO standards concerning working conditions permit flexibility in implementation based on a country's level of economic development, the flexibility applies only to standards concerning working conditions. In applying the flexibility variable, the State Department has told embassies that, 'The U.S. position is that there should be no flexibility in according such basic worker rights as freedom of association, the right to organize and bargain collectively and the prohibition of forced labor'" (*Worker Rights News* 1, 2 [Feb. 1989]: 1). As has been pointed out earlier, the United States may contest certain ILO interpretations, but it has not contended its commitment to freedom of association. But see Edward Potter, *Freedom of Association, the Right to Organize and Collective Bargaining: The Impact on U.S. Law and Practice of ILO Conventions No. 87 and No. 98* (Washington, DC: Labor Policy Association, 1984), pointing out discrepancies between the ILO Conventions and U.S. law.

47. See C. Wilfred Jenks, "Human Rights, Social Justice and Peace: The Broader Significance of the ILO Experience" in Eide and Schou, eds., *International Protection of Human Rights* (Washington, DC: Labor Policy Association, 1968); *Human Rights—Common Responsibility: Report of the Director-General* (Geneva: International Labour Conference, 75th Session, 1988).

48. In 1970, the International Labor Conference adopted a resolution stating that "the absence of civil liberties removes all meaning from the concept of trade union rights" (ILO, Record of Proceedings, ILC, 54th Session, 1970, 733).

See also ILO, "Freedom of Association and Collective Bargaining, General Survey," ILC, 69th Session, 1983, para. 49–75.

49. For the history of the founding of the ILO, see Shotwell, *The History of the International Labor Organization*, vols. 1–2 (New York: Columbia University Press, 1934).

50. See Bruce L. Rockwood, "Human Rights and Wrongs: The United States and the I.L.O.—A Modern Morality Play" *Case Western Reserve Journal of International Law* (1978): 358.

51. Declaration Concerning the Aims and Purposes of the International Labour Organisation (commonly referred to as the "Declaration of Philadelphia"), Oct. 9, 1946, 62 Stat. 3485, 15 U.N.T.S. 35.

52. "Its [ILOs] history is often regarded as a success story of the international protection of human rights. In recognition of its achievements, the ILO was awarded the Nobel Peace Prize in 1969." (Vincent-Daviss, "Human Rights Law: A Research Guide to the Literature, Part II," *New York Journal of International Law and Policy* [1982]: 213).

53. "281st Report of the Committee on Freedom of Association", *ILO Official Bulletin* ser. B, no. 1 (1992): para. 83. The willingness of the ILO to forthrightly criticize human rights in China may be contrasted with the actions of the Human Rights Commission of the United Nations at its 1993 session, where efforts to pass a resolution criticizing human rights in China generally did not succeed.

54. 193rd Report of the Committee on Freedom of Association, GB.209/6/9, 209th Session, Geneva, Feb. 27–March 2, 1979, para. 33.

55. Walter Galenson, *The International Labor Organization: An American View* Madison: University of Wisconsin Press, 1981).

56. See *Report of the Fact-Finding and Conciliation Commission on Freedom of Association concerning the Republic of South Africa* (GB. 253/15/7, 253rd sess.: Geneva: ILO Governing Body, May–June 1992).

Chapter 3
Human Rights and Labor Rights
A European Perspective

Denis MacShane

During much of the 1980s labor lawyers who met me in Britain often paused to look me hard in the face. "Not *the* MacShane, as in *MacShane v. Express Newspapers*" they would say. The case was simple. The National Union of Journalists (NUJ) of which I was then president had ordered journalists in the British Press Association, the British news agency, not to supply copy to provincial newspapers whose journalists were on a wage strike. Using news agency copy, the editors and strikebreakers could produce papers, thus rendering the strike ineffective. Without the copy their task became much more difficult. The NUJ's call for solidarity to the Press Association journalists, while obvious enough to a trade unionist, raised questions of secondary action, third-party involvement, and the contractual obligations of the agency—itself part-owned by the provincial press—as well as technical questions of interference with telex landlines.

The newspapers sought an injunction. I quickly appeared in front of Lord Denning, Master of the Rolls, which is English law-speak for the Chief Appeal Judge. Denning was one of Britain's most anti-union and anti-labor jurists, even by the standards of the English legal system. (In his retirement he also let loose his racist views, but that is another story.) During the 1970s he had taken every opportunity to interfere judicially in favor of employers and capital. In the NUJ case, he naturally found for the newspaper owners. The case was considered important enough to be taken to the House of Lords, Britain's Supreme Court. There the Law Lords (Supreme Court Justices) found Denning was wrong and the law, as it stood at the time, had permitted what my union had ordered.

But it was all too late to affect the conflict. As I write, I have on my desk an ILO ruling published in March 1992 on a case involving

Hitachi in Malaysia. The ILO upheld the trade union position and condemned the Malaysian government. The dispute took place in 1989. The workers who had organized the trade union had been dismissed and no longer work for Hitachi. The Japanese multinational continues its arrogant course. The Malaysian government will file the ILO finding with all the others that condemn its violation of ILO Conventions and go on denying workers the right to organize.[1] As with PATCO in 1981, judges act like lightning to do down workers and unions but imitate the snail when it comes to supporting them.

In my case, Lord Denning was acting only months ahead of a change in the law. The incoming Conservative government in 1979 legislated to make illegal the kind of solidarity action my union had ordered. It changed the law governing trade unions in many other areas as well, contributing significantly to the weakening of the British trade unions, which now have one-third fewer members than in 1980 (though employment, social, and other changes have also contributed to this process, of course). The Conservative government in Britain has been condemned for its violations of international and European Community laws and norms.[2] At the same time, some of its legally imposed changes governing trade union practice, such as the membership election of union leaders or secret strike-ballots, have been welcomed by unions. Indeed such changes have strengthened the moral authority of the unions, and would likely not change with the election of a pro-union Labour government.

In short, normative universality in the application of workers' rights is difficult to achieve. What in 1980 was defended as an age-old British right to choose union leaders without secret ballot elections or to call strikes by virtue of executive decision has been superseded a decade later by new norms. These were externally imposed, politically driven, and designed to weaken unions. However, they actually reinforced the internal democratic procedures of British unions and gave a new validity to militant leaders because they were now sanctioned by the full membership's participation in the decision-making procedures.

Democracy, Labor Rights, and the Rule of Law

As a trade union official I agree with the emphasis that the writer Basil Davidson puts on the rule of law. Writing about the goals of the wartime resistance movement in Europe, Davidson wrote:

The absolute demands of the liberation fight [was] that democracy should prevail and be seen to prevail. . . . [The] resistance did in fact achieve by 1945 one of the greatest democratizing insurrections of European history. And this achievement stood foursquare within the tradition which linked, and which still links, anti-authoritarian and anti-colonial ideas and aspirations with the belief that freedom, the rule of law, is a supreme good in itself.[3]

The "rule of law" (not, please, rule by lawyers) is thus a goal in itself, essential to the trade unionist, who is a fish only able to swim in the waters of plural democracy with its separation of powers and its independent judiciary. In turn, the use of law and legal interventions by workers and their representatives has been valuable in promoting democracy and allowing some space for social organization. Felipe González, Spain's Socialist premier, began his professional and political life defending workers arrested in Franco's Spain. The KOR (The Polish acronym for Workers' Self-Defense Committee) set up in Poland in 1976 was based on campaigning for the full respect of Polish laws, especially as they affected workers. In South Africa, brilliant tactical use of the law by union jurists in the 1970s and 1980s strengthened the South African labor movement. In Korea, labor activists have welcomed Korea's entry into the ILO as since that organization provides a set of international legal benchmarks by which anti-union behavior in Korea can be condemned.

I write as a labor activist, not a lawyer, but naturally the constant search of the trade unionist is for what the Fabian historian-theoreticians of the British labor movement, Beatrice and Sydney Webb, called the "Common Rule."

In the absence of any Common Rule, the conditions of employment are left to 'free competition', this always means in practice, that they are arrived at by individual bargaining between contracting parties of very unequal economic strength. Such a settlement it is asserted invariably tends, for the mass of the workers, towards the worst possible conditions of labor—ultimately, indeed, to the barest subsistence level—whilst even the exceptional few do not permanently gain as much as they otherwise could. We find accordingly that the Device of the Common Rule is a universal feature of Trade Unionism, and that the assumption on which it is based is held from one end of the Trade Union world to the other.[4]

What officials of the Congress of Industrial Organizations and union-friendly lawyers in the 1940s called "industrial jurisprudence"[5] remains a goal for labor. In recent years, as labor has woken up to the internationalization of production, finance, and trade, and regulations governing all three, this search for common rules or industrial jurisprudence has taken on increasingly transfrontier features.

Global Economy, International Labor

Three recent developments have underlined this process. First, the extraordinary impact of new trade union movements in countries as diverse as Poland, Brazil, South Africa, and Korea have shown the continuing vitality of the idea of trade unionism while it was coming under relentless attack for various reasons in northern industrial countries. It is fashionable—and statistically justifiable—to note labor's relative decline worldwide, but in Western Europe there are still 47 million trade unionists grouped in the European Trade Union Confederation. Countries such as Spain, Greece, and Portugal, which twenty years ago did not have democratic labor movements, now do. The end of the Cold War has produced near unity among the unions in Italy (though not yet in France[6]) and in other countries where socialist-communist rivalries had prevented internal, let alone transnational, labor unity.

Second, the regionalization of the world economy (Europe, Americas, Japan/Asia) has encouraged manageable transnational union contacts. This is most evident in the European context, although NAFTA, the North American Free Trade Agreement, has provoked more contacts and dialogue between the United States and Mexican labor movements (unions and groupings of activists) than ever existed previously.

Third, the rise of international social movement issues such as human rights, the environment, and feminism have given rise to a growing commitment to global solidarity. In the past, international relations were perceived as simply intrastate relations and the search for world government or world law or world regulations was an upscaling of the rule of the nation-state to the entire globe. The new "social" internationalism is changing the way labor activists see things everywhere in the world, though not always smoothly. This process is in conflict with a rising tide of nationalism in many areas of the world, and there is no way of telling which will prevail in any single context. However, what is happening is that workers and unions everywhere are far more conscious of transfrontier developments that affect their economic existence and political priorities than was previously the case.

In this context, the precise interface between human rights and labor rights is difficult to describe, let alone prescribe. Describing what it meant for France to be liberated from Nazi rule, General de Gaulle wrote:

On peut, du jour au lendemain, parler tout haut, rencontrer qui l'on veut, aller et venir à son gre! (From one day to the next, you could say what you liked, meet whom you wished, come and go as you pleased!)[7]

De Gaulle was neither a lawyer nor a trade unionist, nor was he especially known as a lover or defender of human rights, but his one-sentence summary has a simple attraction with wider validity than the specific historical conjuncture about which he was writing. The three freedoms—or rights—of speech, assembly, and travel (not, let it be noted, property, a "human" right that has drifted into the spectrum in recent years) were denied the people of communist Eastern Europe and Russia until recently and are still denied to millions in China and in many third world countries.

Human Rights and Labor Rights

Free speech, free assembly, and free contact or travel are human rights with great relevance to workers. If applied to the workplace, for example, the abilities to say what you like, meet with whom you wish, or establish contact with other workers remain central rights. Their denial constitutes the difference between a society with labor freedoms and one without. The citizen does not lose her human rights upon entering the workplace.

A few years ago I was drafting the agenda for a seminar for workers in Asia. I set aside one period to discuss human rights but was politely corrected by a senior Japanese colleague who said that what unions discussed were trade union rights, not human rights. Frankly, I did not then, and I do not now, see the difference. Clearly there is no point proclaiming the end of human or labor rights without willing the means. Free speech without a free press is meaningless; granting the right to travel but withholding passports is a contradiction. Similarly, to extol labor rights but deny basic ILO Conventions is sheer hypocrisy and a denial of human rights.

Can a line be drawn between human rights and labor rights? Is there a moment when the instrumentalization or application of labor rights ceases to be universal and becomes a matter of political power, negotiation, and resolution by compromise, law, or force?

The question has exercised professors and theoreticians for many years. It will continue to do so. Without entering the merits of relativism, essentialism, or determinism (three "isms" I wish could become "wasms"), I believe it is difficult to avoid the need to respond to new movements, new pressures, and new realities created in economic and social relations that constantly alter what was once taken as a given.

In Europe, the European Court recently ruled that bans on night work for women are against regulations permitting equality of opportunity for women.[8] European governments have had to redraft laws and to denounce—to use the formal legal term—the ILO Convention (one of the earliest ever adopted) that forbids such night work. The ruling is hailed as a victory for equal rights by many feminists but is also welcomed by manufacturers, who can now use female labor during the night. In newly industrializing countries in Asia, a complete adherence to ILO Conventions banning such night work for women would be a progressive move strengthening the rights of women workers. In Europe, it is seen as denial of a woman's right to have access to the same jobs—and pay—as men.

I mention this case because I think it is necessary to avoid the trap of thinking that it is easy to draw up a list of universal rights that are good for now and for all time. For a trade unionist, the argument is one of pragmatic possibility and advance. He or she does not care much about doctrinal dissertations on the exact nature of international law. The ILO for him is a bit like the International Olympics Committee; we need the Committee to draw up rules, but what counts are the teams and the relative strength of the players.

The world is awash with international regulations such as the ILO's 177 Conventions, or the OECD (Organization for Economic Cooperation and Development) guidelines on multinationals, or the European Union charter, or the Sullivan guidelines for multinationals in South Africa, or the never quite elaborated guidelines from the United Nations on transnational corporations.

Defining World Labor Standards

For more than a century, governments have expressed a generalized desire to declare—but not to enforce—world labor standards. The International Labor Organization was set up in 1919 to define such standards. Kaiser Wilhelm called the first international labor standards conference in Berlin in 1890. Like the Republican presidents who ruled the United States in 1980–1992, the Kaiser was an advocate of a new world order. Please note, I am careful to avoid any suggestion of moral equivalence. Wilhelmine Germany was much more progressive in promoting workplace standards and national health and social security schemes than the Bush or Reagan administrations. One of the biggest challenges facing President Clinton and his Labor Secretary, Robert Reich, is to extend democracy into the workplace both domestically and internationally. With Soviet communism dead, the new global contest is between democratic capitalism and confucianism capitalism, as practiced in tyrannical China, and in other human rights-suppressing ways in many Asian industrial export-centered economies.

The Atlantic Charter signed between the United States and Britain in August 1941 said that the two countries desired "improved labour standards, economic advancement and social security"[9] for the postwar world. The 1948 UN Covenant on Economic, Social and Cultural Rights contains extensive provisions on the right to form trade unions, child labor, forced labor, discrimination, and fair wages and safe working conditions.

But all these instruments that purport to declare international labor rights, and in particular, the ILO group of conventions, cut little ice with employers or unions. Indeed, they are not known to many workers precisely because they are just that—fine resolutions, helpful benchmarks, and useful sources for moral condemnation. They remain a negation of law because they have no means of enforcement.

I have drafted too many complaints to the ILO myself to undervalue the usefulness of having some court to hear labor complaints, nor do I dismiss the cumulative effect on a country's civil servants or leaders of coming under ILO criticism. The arguments of ASEAN (Association of South East Asian Nations) labor ministers for a derogation from ILO standards[10] is an example of how the ILO does stand for something. Anything that is criticized with such passion by anti-labor spokespersons must be useful. The United States' refusal to ratify ILO Conventions certainly undermines both the ILO and the strength of U.S. condemnations of the repression of labor rights in other countries. Korea, for example, is citing the United States as an example to follow in being an ILO member but not ratifying ILO conventions.[11]

On the other hand, it carries the formal argument too far in the other direction to suggest that only the creation of a system of effective ILO judgments and enforcement is worth working toward and all other interventions linking the upholding of human or labor rights are simply ex parte interventions, special pleading, double-standard operations, disguised protectionism, or "aggressive unilateralism," as Philip Alston calls it.

From a worm's eye view, that of the worker trying to persuade his government to permit the right to form a union, or to join an international labor federation, or to stop a multinational from flouting elementary workplace safety precautions, there is simply a resounding cheer when the threat of removing Generalized System of Preferences (GSP) privileges, or Overseas Private Investment Corporation (OPIC) cover is made. We do not hear workers or their genuine representatives—not those like the head of the government-sponsored Singaporean trade union federation, who is a cabinet minister—saying they are glad to endure low wages, unsafe conditions, child labor, the exploitation of women and minorities, and the absence of an effective voice in the workplace so that their countries can attract multinational corporations and become internationally competitive, nor do they reject trade unions as a form of Western imperialism.

To be sure, the Bush administration imposed sanctions in the name of human rights against Cuba, but none against China. Over Reagan's veto, Congress imposed restrictions on trade with South Africa to pressure the apartheid administration over its treatment of blacks. But Congress did nothing similar to pressure the rulers of Israel over repression of human and labor rights of Palestinians living under the Israeli administration.

A double standard? Yes, but pro-democracy activists in Cuba and anti-apartheid campaigners in South Africa were delighted with the position the United States took in their particular cases and would have been disappointed to be told to wait until the United States had agreed upon a universal position with a common application everywhere in the world. In the meantime, the precedents created were of political value for those campaigning for the same standards to be applied to China or Israel.

For trade unions in general, the use of the law to solve workplace problems or to achieve social justice has always been only one weapon in the armory and often a double-edged one. What the Wagner Act or the National Labor Relations Board (NLRB) gives can also be taken away, like solidarity strikes, also called "secondary boycotts"—the action that brought me to the bench of Judge Denning. Lawyers generally work for money and unions usually have less money than corporations. Far more important has been collective action, solidarity, and the old labor movement trinity of "Agitation, Organization, Education."

The Webbs' Common Rule is never in steady state. It comes under continual pressure from new demands as new technologies or new categories of workers alter previous givens. Europe is now an interesting case study of how the internationalization of capital and production is forcing changes in labor regulation across frontiers.

European Transfrontier Labor Organization

The end of the Cold War and Europe's division since 1947 opens the possibility for reuniting the European working class, or rather uniting it, since at no period in its history has ever been united.

The creation of a capitalist single European market in the western European Community has brought into play an opposite—though far from equal—reaction. That is the call for a Social Charter of Workers' Rights, which in the view of more and more labor movement organizers needs to be extended to workers in Eastern Europe to prevent its becoming our *maquiladora*.

A U.S. audience should first be acquainted with a taxonomy of the "social charter" phenomenon in Europe. There are actually several such "charters" of varying weight and effectiveness:

(1) the social provisions of the 1950 European Convention for the Protection of Human Rights and Fundamental Freedoms, and a series of protocols that followed, which have given rise to many cases involving labor rights and labor standards brought before the European Court of Human Rights;

(2) the social provisions of the 1957 Treaty that created what was then called the EEC, now applicable to the 15-member states of the European Union (EU);

(3) the 1961 European Social Charter adopted by the Council of Europe, applicable to all the countries of Europe;

(4) the 1987 Protocol to the 1961 European Social Charter, which added to the formulation of social rights affecting workplace equality between men and women, rights to information and consultation in the workplace, and worker participation in setting working conditions;

(5) the 1989 Social Charter approved in the formation of the European Free Trade Area (EFTA), which includes the members of the EU plus other Scandinavian states and the historically neutral states, along with Eastern European countries that have gradually been joining the EFTA;

(6) the 1989 EC Social Charter, distinct from the 1989 EFTA Charter and the 1961 European Social Charter, yet drawing on them as foundations for elaborating the EC Charter; it is this 1989 EC Charter, for example, that created the right of free movement by workers who are citizens of the European Union (EU) states;

(7) an "Action Programme" initiated under the 1989 EC Charter, which has produced some fifty proposals for community legislation, about twenty of which have been adopted under existing EU procedures (most in non-controversial areas such as safety and health);

(8) the 1992 Maastricht Social "Chapter," as it is actually called—the social provisions of the Maastricht Treaty that move the EC toward a greater degree of political and financial union (reflected in the Community's new name, the European Union)—which the United Kingdom vetoed as an integral feature of the Treaty.[12] The U.K. rejection forced the other (then-eleven) EU members to adopt the Maastricht Social Chapter as a free-standing charter among themselves, hoping that an eventual change of government or change of policy in Britain would bring the United Kingdom on board and restore the Social Chapter to the Treaty as a whole.

The EC Social Charter, the Action Programme, and the Maastricht Social Chapter are made even more complicated by EU structures and procedures that require that some issues be decided by unanimous vote and others by a weighted majority vote, that some issues can be brought to the European Commission and appealed to the European Court of Justice and some cannot, and other intricacies.

In whatever manifestation, the European Union's Social Charter of Workers' Rights has been long on generous intention and short on concrete delivery. Still, its underlying philosophy, which accepts the right of workers to construct a socially acceptable political economy, was enough to provoke a visceral hostility from the British government, the most anti-labor government Europe has seen since World War II.

In contrast to Britain's hard free-market approach is what might be called Christian consensual corporatist capitalism, which is especially evident in Germany, with its concept of social partnership. This vision is now predominant in Western Europe and has been enshrined by the Maastricht Treaty. It will only be reinforced by the addition of the Nordic countries and Austria, with their strong labor movement traditions. Despite Britain's opting out of the clauses of the treaty that offer greater rights to workers, it is likely that British workers will enjoy some of its protection, either through a front door opened by a new Labour government that accepts the Social Chapter or through the side door of participation with their continental comrades working for U.K.-based "European companies"—those with at least 1,000 employees in two or more EU countries. Most major U.K. enterprises meet this definition, and thus must consult with unions that represent their employees on many aspects of the Social Chapter.

For workers and their unions at least the European Social Charter offers a serious chance for building transfrontier links with workers in other countries. Volkswagen, Europe's biggest car manufacturer, for example, signed in February 1992 an agreement with unions from Germany, Spain, and Belgium recognizing a pan-European Works Council for VW workers. As VW also bought a controlling stake in Skoda, the Czech automaker, the unions will seek to include Czech worker representatives from Skoda on the Volkswagen Euro Works Council.

The central importance of the Social Charter is the extent to which an intergovernmental treaty now includes a range of regulations and directives concerning labor rights. For the first time in history, supranational law will determine the nature of labor rights in more than one country. From a British labor point of view there is much in the Social Charter that represents an advance on labor rights after thirteen years of being battered by anti-union Conservative governments.

Works Councils

One central development that will creep into British workplace organization (and that is of great interest to the United States and Canada,
with their emphasis on adversarial collective bargaining at the expense
of legally enshrined rights for workers) is the arrival of works councils
as a result of British membership of the European Community and the
effect of the Social Charter. Britain and Ireland are now the only EC
members without legislation that permits workers some direct representation vis-à-vis employers.

In Britain, a worker only has rights face to face with the employer if
he or she is a union member. As in the United States, massive struggles
have taken place over union recognition in Britain in recent years. The
de-recognition of civil servants working for intelligence communications
operations and Rupert Murdoch's move to non-union newspaper production in East London in 1985 are the most notorious cases, but every
union reports a significant political assault on union recognition by employers.

This problem does not arise in Germany or Italy or the Netherlands,
where workers, not unions, have legal recognition rights. The working
class on the continent of Europe is part of a dual power system, seeking
rights in the workplace as a workforce and concurrently seeking to build
up effective unions. Unions in Germany, Italy, and the Nordic countries
have been more able than British unions to resist the anti-labor aggres-
sion of contemporary capitalism.

The signing of the Maastricht Treaty permitted majority voting on laying down new transfrontier workplace rights for European workers and
for creating pan-European works councils. Beforehand, such proposals
required unanimity, thus giving one recalcitrant government—in recent
years invariably Conservative Britain—the opportunity to block any new
proposals for social legislation.

Labor rights are an important though far from key issue in the
whole process of forging greater European unity. The referendums held
in France and Denmark in 1992, as well as many opinion polls, show
great uncertainty about the idea of giving up national sovereignty to
a European entity whose accountability, democratic transparency, and
economic direction were far from certain.

But with the construction of both the single European market, enshrined by treaty in 1986, whose open borders came into force in 1993,
and the greater political, economic, and social union implicit in the
Maastricht Treaty, transfrontier regulation of workers' rights has passed
from declaration to enforceable reality. This development is not due
simply to trade union pressure. Many employers in North Europe were

concerned that their competitiveness, based as it was on labor and social costs significantly higher than those in southern Europe, could be undermined to the point of destruction if there were not commonality at least on basic minimum standards and workers' rights that were applied across the European labor market playing field.

The exact impact of Maastricht and European integration on labor rights remains to be evaluated. While productionist European capitalism, represented by the industrial manufacturing firms, is willing to enter into a dialogue with labor nationally, and is even willing to have limited consultation between European employers and labor federations, it is reluctant to concede transfrontier bargaining rights.[13] European unions have organized about 150 prototype European Works Councils but only twenty have won recognition from employers. U.S. and Japanese firms are particularly hostile to European Works Councils. Meanwhile, European employers outside the manufacturing sector, represented especially in England by giant trading companies, banks, and financial service firms, remain extremely hostile to any link-up between their employees on a transfrontier basis.

The full legal implications of the Treaty remain to be tested in the European Court but the shift in the direction of supranational regulation of labor rights is unmistakable.

International Labor-Management Dialogue

Just prior to Maastricht, in November 1991, a highly significant transfrontier labor relations agreement was signed between UNICE, the European employers federation, and the European Trade Union Confederation (ETUC). The agreement, cleared with the EU, allowed the two parties representing European employers and unions to intervene in the Community's proposals concerning industrial relations and to have a joint role in drawing them up.

In addition, the EU would allow UNICE and ETUC to substitute a collectively bargained agreement between these so-called social partners for an EU directive. The advantage of this agreement from the employers' point of view is that it replaces some of the legal direction with an employer-union agreement. But even under this generous interpretation, the UNICE-ETUC agreement represents the thin edge of a corporatist wedge at the European level plus the acceptance by the European employers federation and the EU of the right of European unions collectively to lay down joint agreements with the employers federation covering workplace rights.

Antoine Riboud, president and chief executive officer of BSN, a French-based food multinational, has agreed to the creation of a European works council and sees transnational union links as a means of regenerating trade unions in France, where the proportion of union membership has fallen below 10 percent of the private sector workforce (though collective bargaining covers many non-union members, as well as dues-payers). Declares Riboud:

BSN has 22 biscuit factories in the European Community. These no longer operate as national entities. They are linked in a network, each producing a European biscuit. It is the outcome of this network that produces the financial resources so that there can be distribution between profit, pay, jobs and working time. But this distribution is not automatic. It is best negotiated in a social dialogue. And since the growth is European, since the profit is European, the negotiations have to be European. I would add that this new field of negotiation will permit the rebirth of trade unionism.[14]

There is now a marked difference between European continental partnership trade unionism and the Anglo-Saxon adversarial traditions prevalent in Britain, Ireland, and North America. Instead of seeking a victory by knocking out the enemy, Europeans prefer sumo labor relations in which the workforce permanently grapples with the employer but victory is celebrated in no-loss-of-face rituals instead of in a desire to see the opponents' blood and brains splattered on the floor. Instead of pretending to be industrial behemoths, unions have to learn judo tactics, using effective points of leverage to outwit the employer. The struggle goes on (it never ends), but the tactics are different. Major European unions such as IG Metall or Italy's CGIL are class-conscious, militant worker organizations but prefer to win without fighting by propaganda and mobilization rather than charging into industrial valleys of death. I would note that several U.S. unions have begun experimenting with "corporate campaigns," "in-plant strategies," and other alternatives to the do-or-die strike.

The unions of the European Union are actively setting up Euro Works Councils. It is important to keep in mind that these are organically distinct organizations. Works Councils are organizations of employees granted statutory rights to consult with employers separately from trade unions. Trade unions, for their part, engage in industry-wide bargaining and broad-based political action. In some countries—Germany, for example—the Works Councils are de facto controlled by the trade unions because union officials are elected by workers as their Works Council representatives. In other countries—France in particular—the Works Council is often entirely divorced from the union. Indeed, some Works Council candidates are elected on an anti-trade union platform.

The formation of these works councils in Europe-wide context is raising new problems that force labor unions to consider what kind of organizations they seek to be and how they should relate to workers in other countries. For some there are fears that Works Councils quickly get dominated by employers and become docile, company-controlled bodies that replace shop steward organization in the workplace.

Much depends on whether they follow the German *Betriebsrat* model, which is a worker-only Works Council with rights to have representatives on the board of big companies, or the French *comité d'enterprise* format, which is a joint worker-management council open to employer manipulation. Also the role of unions is vital. Where they are sectarian and politically divided, and have low membership, as in France, the works councils can drift off into independent existence. Where they are organized on a one-workplace, one-union system and under social democratic (in Britain, read Labour) hegemony as in Germany or Austria, they reinforce the class consciousness of works council delegates by constant education and mobilization.

In Britain, the drift toward mega-unions through mergers and single-union representation in companies opens the way for a German works council system. For British workers, in particular, it could be a win-win situation. The 60 percent of the country's workforce that is not unionized, currently denied any collective workplace rights, would start to think, organize, and act collectively and would undoubtedly turn to unions for guidance, advice, and help. This, in turn, might bring unions into workplaces from which they are excluded.

Thus in three areas—consultation, regulation, and organization—the impact of European developments on international workers' rights is extremely important. Insisting on a social dimension governed by supra-national regulation with full legal impact clearly has implications for the rest of the world, notably in the area covered by the North American Free Trade pact. The key element has to be law that grants workers rights to combine. It is necessary, if problematic, to note that EC Social Charter provisions emphasize *workers'* rights, not specifically *union* rights, even if the worker-union link is taken as a given. To privilege unions as institutions, rather than their members as individuals, is difficult in many countries in Europe, where intraunion rivalries and hatreds often render common agreement on which union is representative (or even a genuine union) very difficult.

Furthermore, to extend rights to unions qua unions makes them the focus for opposition. To extend rights to workers as individuals, including the key right of combination across frontiers, is more difficult to oppose. The difference between the unions and the collective of workers may appear—and often is—semantic. But in the debate over what the rights of workers are, justifying collective rights expressed as formal support of a union is difficult to sustain whereas emphasizing the human rights of the individual as a worker permits a more powerful case to be made.

This approach does have serious implications for some traditional forms of unionization. The closed or membership shop has been explicitly repudiated by the labor movement in Britain as part of its embrace of the Social Charter. No obligatory union membership exists for any worker in the Nordic countries or Germany, yet powerful mass-membership unions exist there.

Obviously, there are dangers in arguing for worker rights as if these can exist independent of democratic trade unions to negotiate and enforce them. The ILO recognizes in its case law that the concept of freedom of association (ILO Convention No. 87) or the right to collective bargaining (ILO Convention No. 98) is meaningless without effective trade unions. But freedom of association also permits the creation of a multiplicity of unions. Sometimes these are set up with government or employer backing, such as the Solidarismo movement in Latin America or the Malaysian Labour Organization in Malaysia. Yet the alternative, which is to confer exclusive union rights on one organization, as in China, where the law recognizes only the All-China Confederation of Trade Unions, or Korea, where up to 1993 it recognized only the Federation of Korean Trade Unions was legally recognized, and where independent union organizing in both countries was treated as a crime, is also unacceptable. So often the search for some universally applicable and enforceable code for trade union rights stumbles not only on relativities but also on the complex country-specific, industry-specific, history-specific nature of trade union organization in different parts of the world.

Codes of Conduct

In addition to transnational European directives conferring rights on workers on an international basis there are other examples of collectively bargained agreements. One is the fourteen-point code of labor rights for German companies operating in South Africa that was developed in the late 1980s. This was drawn up jointly by German and South African metalworkers unions, and then the German union pressed leading German companies such as Daimler-Benz and Volkswagen to sign. These formalized agreements broke new ground as they stipulated in great detail how a multinational should behave overseas on the basis of demands from its workers. In effect, the companies agreed to grant the same rights of trade union freedom and organization in the workplace in South Africa as they had to live with in Germany, even though German labor freedoms were far in excess of custom, practice, and law in apartheid South Africa. It was an important break with the conventional platitude of multinationals that they cannot go beyond what local law and conditions (however repressive both may be) permit in their treatment of workers in subsidiaries.

Similarly, in the United States, the Amalgamated Clothing and Textile Workers Union pressured Sears Roebuck and Co. to agree that the company would monitor its overseas suppliers to make sure they were not buying goods or material made by forced labor in China where an estimated 10 million people are in labor camps. Levi Strauss also issued similar guidelines following press exposure that their jeans were being produced by workers denied basic freedoms.[15]

Sensitivity over human rights in China or under apartheid have pushed companies to accept interference in their labor relations policies overseas, and these examples show the possibility of relating worker rights to trade or investment considerations.

All these efforts reflect the growing sense that the global economy requires global regulation—whether by law or by contractual agreement. It also shows the complications of applying human rights in the labor field internationally since very quickly one hits the question of sanctions, which almost inevitably mean some kind of trade-related measure. Even banning landing rights for planes is a form of a trade-related sanction.

GATT and a Social Clause of Workers Rights

The long history of seeking to have GATT (General Agreement of Tariffs and Trade) look at worker rights in its member countries as a condition for trading privileges such as "most-favoured nation" status and access to the U.S. market illustrates both the search for a mechanism of global regulation in this field and the obstacles that exist. Attempts to persuade GATT to introduce a so-called "social clause" go back to the organization's founding in the 1940s. Indeed, the reason why GATT is still technically a provisional agreement and not a treaty lies in the rejection by the U.S. Congress of proposals after 1945 to set up an International Trade Organization that would have included in its tasks the responsibility for social and economic advance for humankind. Since then there have been various attempts to obtain a social clause but they have always fallen at two hurdles. The first is the classical economics argument that such "externalities" as labor rights or environmental issues should not be linked to trade questions. The second, more serious, is the objection that such linkage represents interference in national sovereignty, the right of government to organize its internal affairs as it wishes.

We need to be blunt here. Human rights in the workplace as laid down even in the minimal standards of the ILO, if applied, would considerably reduce arbitrary government. In 1987, the United States proposed setting up a GATT working party on the "possible relationship between international trade and respect for international labor standards."[16] The U.S. proposition met with opposition. Between 1987 and 1990 the United States reduced its demand to examination of the links between trade and three international labor standards—freedom of association, freedom to organize and bargain collectively, and freedom from forced or compulsory labor. But even this concession was insufficient. At the GATT council that considered the issue in November 1990, the third world countries lined up to denounce the proposal. The nations that were opposed—Mexico, the Philippines, Korea, Thailand, Tanzania, Chile, Bolivia, Nigeria, Egypt, Morocco, and Cuba—regularly headed the list of human rights violators worldwide.[17]

It may well have been that the United States, the European Community, and the Nordic countries, all of which supported setting up a GATT working party on the trade-labor rights link (the issue for decision) were happy to find shelter behind the opposition of the third world, but the question of GATT and the linkage of human and labor rights to trade will continue to resurface as the world economy continues its relentless globalization and the need for international regulations in a wide range of economic relationships that cross frontiers continues to manifest itself. As with the European Union, it will not be possible to abolish national frontiers to the flow of capital without creating transfrontier rules to regulate this process.

International Law

Although international law is very weak, it did make a major entry during the Gulf War in two areas to a sufficient degree to have an impact on public opinion, including that of trade unionists. First, the United States and United Nations sought to justify armed intervention against Saddam Hussein in quasi-judicial terms. Second, and more importantly, there was agreement to support international intervention into two areas that are the prerogatives of nation-states—the setting up a safe haven for the Kurds and the investigation inside Iraq and other countries of those companies and/or governments that had been responsible for selling arms, particularly nuclear arms, to Iraq.

But law has to come from somewhere; it cannot be simply be, as in Arthur Miller's maxim, "an expression of what is right, should happen." Law needs law-givers with a democratic base to sanction the laws being enacted. The 1930s and 1940s were the heyday of passing laws, whether Stalin's Soviet constitution, Eleanor Roosevelt's Human Rights as they were taken up by the United Nations, or, indeed, some of the ILO's most legalistic conventions, the ones most commonly flouted on organizing and collective bargaining. Like Shakespeare's Hotspur calling up spirits from the vasty deep, the law-makers of the mid-twentieth century felt they were laying down a law, but neither Stalin, nor the United Nations, nor the ILO had a democratic base, in the sense of having an electorate willing to abide by the laws as part of a social contract of government.

The other essential aspect that makes law is its enforceability, and in the field of much of what we call international law it is clear that there exists no judicial system accepted in the way we accept judge's rulings as part of the idea of living under the rule of law. In the case of the mining of the Nicaraguan ports, the United States flouted the World Court. Where the World Court has been used, it has been as an arbitration service willingly used by two conflicting parties rather than a court of law with plaintiff, accused, defense, and prosecution. Where international law has been appealed to, as in the case of Iraq, it has been treated as a set of political decisions by the executive—in this case the United Nations—where, by chance, there was a temporary majority of yay-sayers, and not as a judicial application and enforcement of international law.

Nevertheless, important precedents have been set by the Iraq case. As Mohammed Bedjaoui, a member of the Court of International Justice at the Hague, which is technically the United Nation's principal judicial organ, has said: "To seek to invoke international law, whether in good faith or not, means that for a time one has to adhere to it." How long that process lasts depends on "the vigilance of everyone in the world."[18]

Enforcing Transfrontier Rules or Laws

Enforceability of course is the major stumbling block for all systems of international law and until laws can be enforced it may be questioned whether even referring to them as law is appropriate. The one example of international law that does sort of work are the so-called laws of war. What is surprising about the Geneva conventions is not how often they are broken but rather how widely they are observed. Yet clearly laws to govern relations in the economic, ecological, financial, property, trade, copyright, pollution, and other spheres have to be either fully or partly internationalized.

This process has left the realm of possibility and theory in Europe where the fifteen nation-states in the European Union have transferred significant powers to regulate in the above areas to a supranational authority. As much as possible is regulated by agreement among the ministers of the fifteen states but there exists both a higher executive authority in the form of a European Commission, a kind of cabinet government for the entire European Union, and a European court, which can and has issued rulings that have had superior legal force over national law and have forced individual countries, notably Britain in recent years, to change national rules and laws in various fields.

The enforceability lies in the acceptance of a concept of greater good, that is, that each member nation-state in Europe will draw more benefit from being part of a larger whole than it would derive from resting outside and ploughing an individual furrow. This development, however, marks the beginning of the end of national sovereignty in the continent that gave birth to the nation-state and to the political philosophy that justified or lauded its existence. There is an embryonic European Parliament that is gradually increasing its powers though of course it faces resistance not just from nation-state governments but from national legislatures as well. Interestingly it has been Germany, a country with perhaps the greatest historical need to subsume national(ist) political drive in a wider setting that has most forcefully argued for increased powers for the European Parliament. As yet we have no Locke or Rousseau or Kant to explain what is now taking shape in Europe, but it is a powerful force that Americans should examine as they seek to understand how the United States might better fit in with other countries around the world.

Conclusion

What international trade needs is international law, just as domestic trading practices are governed by endless legal controls and interventions. But to concede a world trade court means abiding by legal traditions of transparency, democratic consent, and equality for rich and poor alike. There is a growing interest in Europe in extending the idea of law to international relations beyond the new arrangements and institutions of the European Union. In France, an organization called L'Association Européen Droit contre Raison d'Etat (European Association of Law Against the Reason of the State) has been set up to promote the idea that citizens can sue states for damages caused by their permitting international crimes, such as the selling of arms to Iraq, that threaten the upholding of international law. A low-level court has already received one such action launched by the Association, which is seeking, as its chair, Olivier Russbach, argues, to move such questions from the realm of political morality into that of the law.[19]

In a related move, Robert Badinter, president of France's Constitutional Court and a former Justice Minister in the Mitterrand administration, has suggested setting up a European Conciliation and Arbitration Court. His argument is as follows:

For the first time, there are no more irreconcilable ideological, political, or religious conflicts in Europe. For the first time, all the countries of Europe claim to follow the same principles — human rights, democracy, a market economy based on social or neo-liberal values according to the state.[20]

Europe, adds Badinter, is nonetheless faced with immense problems:

minorities, linguistic, religious or cultural rights, environmental problems, access to energy, the free movement of peoples, migration flows and economic problems arising from the collapse of Comecon. All these differences have to be resolved in order to avoid them irreconcilable hostilities.

The venue for resolving these differences should be a European Conciliation Court, not as a replacement for interstate diplomatic relations but to complement them. Badinter calls for the progressive juridicialization of relations between European states.

In the field of international labor rights both conciliation and arbitration mechanisms and juridical enforcement are rudimentary in Europe and missing elsewhere in the world. Setting them up will require a step-by-step process. To set too high a target, to demand universalism because anything less is particularist, to reject the good because it is not the best, will continue to leave too many of the world's workers and the world's weak without protection. In the search for human rights in the workplace, enforceability and commonality, anywhere and anyhow, remain the key, and the area for this search now embraces transfrontier mechanisms, rules, and worker connections.

The applicability of law itself will come under challenge as enforcement beyond the nation is not developed. In the field of labor rights many factors come into play. The comparative advantage between nations is one. Yet just as national law developed to provide common minimum social rights to all citizens of a nation while dictating neither their economic behavior nor imposing particular wages and benefits, so the challenge of international regulation of labor or social questions will be to enforce common rights for workers based on definitions laid down by the ILO that have stood the test of time. This is also the mechanism for rebutting the argument of many third world countries that labor rights–trade linkages are simply a new form of industrialized country protection against the challenge of more cheaply made products from overseas.

These labor rights must be universal and must be enforceable, but their application will be a matter of local agreement. It may well be that unions will agree with employers on particular arrangements covering wages when they seek to strengthen the overall productive capacity of the economy and not to maximize the income of workers in the most profitable companies or industries. It may be, as for example in Sweden, that unions will seek to limit individual wage increases in exchange for wider social provisions such as health insurance and public expenditure on education, housing, and welfare. Nothing will replace the relationship between those who possess capital and those who offer their minds or bodies for hire. In many countries, unions face a challenge that requires a revolutionary alteration in their thinking, tactics, and relationship with employees and companies.

All these developments should call for a process of negotiation, compromise, and—yes—temporary victory or defeats for one side or another. There is no stable state in the social sphere. However, there should be given rights that no longer can be spurned or ignored on account of the right of nation-states to suppress rights that belong to all humankind at work in the name of economic development or any other excuse that comes to hand.

The rule of law internationally cannot be limited to relations between companies. It must protect the rights of humans or the idea of law will cease to command respect. Arriving at a rule of law for social relations globally requires exploring every path. Transfrontier union-employer dialogue, international worker organization, and enforceable transfrontier regulation are the next major goals for the labor movement as it contemplates the twenty-first century and the question of its continuing existence.

Notes

1. See *Malaysia and the ILO: Two Decades of Violating ILO Conventions* (Geneva: International Metalworkers Federation, 1992) and ILO Freedom of Association Reports, 1990–1992.

2. Rulings by the EC and the European Court of Justice obliged the British government to amend labor law to benefit workers in the following acts: Transfer of Undertakings (Protection of Employment) Regulations of 1981, the Equal Pay (Amendment) Regulations of 1983, the Sex Discrimination Act of 1986, and parts of the Employment Act in 1989. See Anthony Ferner and Richard Hyman, eds., *Industrial Relations in the New Europe* (Oxford; Blackwell, 1992), 15. The ILO repeatedly found Britain guilty of violating its Freedom of Association conventions after the then prime minister, Margaret Thatcher, withdrew the right to belong to a trade union from the Government Communications Agency, which, as a branch of the intelligence services, eavesdropped on telecommunications between foreign powers and portable telephone conversations between adulterous members of Britain's royal family.

3. Basil Davidson, *Special Operations Europe: Scenes from the Anti-Nazi War* (London: Grafton, 1987), 303–4.

4. Sydney and Beatrice Webb, *Industrial Democracy* (London: Longman, 1897), 560.

5. See Nelson Lichtenstein, "Great Expectations: The Promise of Collective Bargaining and its Demise, 1935–1965" in *Industrial Democracy, Past and Present*, ed. Howell Harris and Nelson Lichtenstein, (New York: Cambridge University Press, 1991).

6. See Denis MacShane, "France: The Missing Link in European Labor," *New Politics* 3, no. 2 (Winter 1991).

7. Charles de Gaulle, *Mémoires de guerre: Le Salut 1944–1946* (Paris: Plon, 1959), 3.

8. See *European Industrial Relations Review* 11 (1991).

9. For the full text of the Atlantic Charter, see Hugh Thomas, *Armed Truce: The Beginning of the Cold War, 1945–46* (London: Hamish Hamilton, 1986), 556–557.

10. For example, Malaysia's Human Resources Minister at the ASEAN labor ministers' conference, December 1992, quoted in the *Star* newspaper (Malaysia), Dec. 8, 1992. The former prime minister of Singapore, Lee Kuan Yew, has repeatedly told the United States that it should drop concerns about labor rights in Asia. On the eve of President Clinton's inauguration, he said Clinton "should not muddy the situation by bringing in the politics of democracy and human rights and pressing it too hard because that would upset the economic growth that's on the way in East Asia" (*International Herald Tribune*, Jan. 21, 1993). The opposite view is that the denial of human rights, especially linked to information, and labor rights, especially those of collective bargaining, is preventing the creation of a broad-based middle-class community able to purchase what it makes and make informed decisions about expenditure, consumption, and investment because what might be called Jeffersonian rights are not available. See Denis MacShane, Is the Working Class Waking Up in Asia, *Pacific Review* 1 (1992).

11. See the complaint and attendant documentation to the ILO by the Korean Trades Union Congress submitted in March 1992.

12. The Maastricht Social Chapter covers the following issues:

1) freedom of movement
2) employment and remuneration
3) living and working conditions
4) social protection
5) freedom of association and collective bargaining
6) vocational training
7) non-discrimination based on gender
8) information, consultation and participation
9) workplace health and safety
10) children and adolescents in employment
11) protection of the elderly
12) protection of the disabled

13. These themes are more fully discussed in Denis MacShane, "The European Social Charter After Maastricht" in *European Labour Forum*, and Denis MacShane, *The New Politics of Global Labor*, forthcoming.

14. *Le Nouveau Quotidien* (Lausanne), May 16, 1992.

15. Workers and democratic trade unionists have faced torture and imprisonment in China since the pro-democracy movement and the workers autonomous federations were crushed in 1989. See Amnesty International report, "Torture in China," Dec. 1992.

16. GATT document L/6243, Oct. 28, 1987.

17. Minutes of GATT Council, Nov. 1, 1990, C/M/245.

18. *Nouvel Observateur*, Feb. 27, 1992.

19. Ibid.

20. Ibid.

Chapter 4
Labor Rights Provisions in U.S. Trade Law
"Aggressive Unilateralism"?

Philip Alston

Legislatively mandated measures designed to protect the labor rights of workers in foreign countries constitute an increasingly important dimension of United States human rights policy. Perhaps because those measures have been enacted under the rubric of U.S. trade law, rather than in the context of human rights legislation, they have attracted rather limited critical (as opposed to essentially descriptive) attention from international lawyers in the human rights field.[1] But this relative neglect is unjustified. As international trade becomes even more important in a post-Cold War world with its many additional would-be market economies, and as protectionist pressures increase in the United States and other developed market economies, the more attractive punitive or retaliatory trade measures become. This is especially true if they can be justified not solely by reference to economic considerations but also on human rights grounds. While measures in response to "market dumping" are a form of economic self-defense, measures to combat "social dumping" can be defended in largely altruistic or humanitarian terms.[2]

It is submitted, however, that the policy assumptions embodied in current U.S. "international worker rights" legislation (a phrase that, at least to a non-American, is surely ungrammatical), as well as the manner in which that legislation is being implemented, are highly questionable from an international law perspective. Specifically, there are several matters that warrant careful examination by proponents of an international rule of law in relation to both trade and human rights matters. These include: the use of the rhetoric but not the substance of "international standards"; the application to other countries of standards that have not been accepted by those countries and that are not generally considered to be part of customary international law; the invocation of international instruments that the United States itself has not ratified; and the neglect of existing and potential international mechanisms for achieving comparable objectives. In brief, the current approach to worker rights would appear to be incompatible with some of the key principles on which the emerging international human rights regime is, or should be, premised. U.S. trade law since the mid-1980s has been characterized by some commentators as an exercise in "aggressive unilateralism."[3] There are strong grounds for applying a similar label to the worker rights provisions of the relevant legislation.

This chapter suggests the need for a much closer, and considerably more critical, examination of that legislation and of the related implementing machinery than has been undertaken to date. It concludes by suggesting some reforms that could make existing approaches more compatible with the efforts to develop an effective international labor rights regime.

An Overview of the Principal Worker Rights Programs

For the purposes of the present analysis four programs are of particular relevance. The first consists of the preferential trade access under the Generalized System of Preferences (GSP).[4] Under the 1974 Trade Act the GSP's privileged trading partner status could not be accorded to any country that, inter alia, was communist, was uncooperative in international drug control efforts, or was terrorist-abetting.[5] Under the Generalized System of Preferences Renewal Act of 1984 (the "Renewal Act") various other grounds for exclusion from the program were added.[6] One of the most important additions prohibits the President from designating as a GSP beneficiary any country that "has not taken or is not taking steps to afford internationally recognized worker rights" to its own workers.[7]

The second program is the Caribbean Basin Initiative,[8] which provides for duty-free entry of specified products from any of the 27 countries that are eligible for beneficiary status. In determining whether to grant duty-free treatment to the country concerned, the President must take into account the extent to which workers enjoy "reasonable work place conditions and enjoy the right to organize and bargain collectively."[9]

The third program, the Overseas Private Investment Corporation (OPIC),[10] seeks to insure U.S. investment in foreign countries against losses due to political turmoil or nationalization. OPIC is not permitted to participate in a project unless the government of the country concerned is "taking steps to adopt and implement laws that extend internationally recognized worker rights" to its workers.[11]

Under the fourth program, created pursuant to the Omnibus Trade and Competitiveness Act of 1988,[12] the systematic denial of internationally recognized worker rights constitutes an unreasonable trade practice.[13] A country engaging in such practices may be subjected to a wide variety of sanctions imposed by the executive branch without the right of appeal, including the cancelation or suspension of a country's most-favored-nation trading status as a whole or the revocation of such status for particular products. It is not necessary that the target of the sanctions be in the same sector that is responsible for the violations that gave rise to the sanctions.[14]

While all these programs are cause for concern from an international human rights perspective, an especially troubling dimension relates to the potential for existing concerns to be exacerbated in the years ahead. This could happen in two ways. The first would be for the Congress to continue adopting such programs, some of which might be even less satisfactory than the present model. The second would be for other countries to begin to adopt comparable legislative approaches in the context of their trade policies. The fear that other countries will eventually retaliate in this fashion has been mooted by a number of trade experts[15] and was one of the reasons that Reagan administration cited when it opposed the worker rights provisions in a revised trade bill.[16]

Comparing Worker Rights Programs with Assumptions Underlying the International Human Rights Regime

The various trade policy issues raised by these programs are important and far-reaching, but they are not the focus of this analysis.[17] Rather, the objective here is to examine the compatibility of the principles reflected in the worker rights programs with some of the major assumptions on which the international human rights regime is constructed. Among those assumptions are the following: (1) that international endeavors to promote respect for human rights should be based upon internationally agreed-upon standards; (2) international human rights standards should be applied only to the extent that the target state is bound by way of treaty or customary law provisions, especially in a punitive context; (3) normative consistency should be sought as far as possible between the standards being applied by one government and those of other governments and the relevant international standards; and (4) mechanisms for sanctioning violations of human rights should be based upon reasonably clear criteria, should follow fair and consistent procedures, and should avoid double standards as far as possible.

Internationally Agreed-Upon Standards

The Brandt Commission Report of 1980, which surveyed the entire gamut of north-south relations, supported the general principle of linking respect for labor standards to enhanced trading opportunities. Its recommendation was not unqualified, however. It was based explicitly on the premise that "Fair labor standards should be internationally agreed in order to prevent unfair competition and to facilitate trade liberalization."[18] In 1974, when the United States Congress first sought to link the two issues, it acknowledged the desirability of doing so within a multilateral framework.[19] Congress has continued to propose multilateral action, most notably in the context of the Uruguay Trade Round in 1986.[20] However, these initiatives have garnered little support from other states, most of which have seen the proposals as being essentially protectionist in motivation.[21]

Nevertheless, the very use of the qualifier "internationally recognized" to describe the relevant "worker rights" would seem to imply clear recognition that it is desirable to avoid applying subjectively determined norms to the countries that might be affected by the U.S. legislation. This impression is further reinforced by the list of relevant rights, which, according to the Renewal Act,[22] include:

(i)   the right of association;
(ii) the right to organize and bargain effectively;
(iii) a prohibition on the use of any form of forced or compulsory labor;
(iv) a minimum age for the employment of children; and
(v)   acceptable conditions of work with respect to minimum wages, hours of work, and occupational safety and health.

The specific rights in question are not defined at all for the purposes of the Caribbean Basin Initiative,[23] while the OPIC legislation[24] refers to the definition contained in the Renewal Act. The Omnibus Trade and Competitiveness Act[25] also uses a definition that, for all intents and purposes, is identical to that contained in the Renewal Act.

From the perspective of international human rights law the list of worker rights is a very familiar one. The terminology is essentially that developed by the International Labor Organization (ILO), which has evolved a detailed set of "international labor standards" or "labor rights" that could readily be used for the purpose of giving substance to the Renewal Act's rather cryptic formulations.[26] But the U.S. legislation carefully eschews any reference to the ILO standards per se. Rather the legislation "mirrors"[27] the issues dealt with in the principal ILO human rights conventions without specifically endorsing the actual formulations used therein. As one commentator has noted defensively, "The standards reflect the legitimate concerns embraced by the most fundamental ILO Covenants".[28]

The problem is that the reflection provided in the legislative mirror is a distorted one. In the first place, the list of standards is artificially restricted in that it does not cover all the issues internationally recognized as being necessary to ensure the basic human rights of workers.[29] A notable omission, for example, is the issue of non-discrimination in employment on the basis of "race, colour, sex, religion, political opinion, national extraction or social origin."[30]

In the second place, the form in which the standards are stated amounts to a carte blanche to the relevant U.S. government agencies, enabling them to choose which standards they will apply in any given situation. Most academic commentators, a substantial majority of whom are in favor of the worker rights initiatives,[31] have simply glossed over, or "fudged," the subjectivity of the U.S. standards and the fact that they bear no necessary or even authentic relationship to ILO standards. Thus, for example, a non-governmental group formed specifically for the purpose of promoting the application of the worker rights legislation offers the following justification for the standards used:

The labor rights and standards enumerated in the legislation are the ones that most governments claim on paper to support; most of the violators have ratified ILO conventions to this effect. Hence, this is not a case of imposing U.S. regulations; they are internationally recognized standards to which most countries are bound by international law.[32]

As noted below,[33] the problem is that many of the "violators" have not in fact ratified the ILO standards and that, in any event, the U.S. legislation does not contain detailed standards. It simply misappropriates some of the terminology developed by the ILO, without involving any commitment whatsoever to make use of the specific standards that have been drawn up and very carefully negotiated within the ILO framework.

Another commentator, Steve Charnowitz, recognizes that "what constitutes 'unfair' working conditions presents a thorny problem of definition."[34] However, having invoked the detailed history of ILO standards in support of the concept of "worker rights," he then seeks to distance the U.S. program from that background:

One could define unfair conditions to be any which do not meet the standards of the ILO. But such a definition has the undesirable consequence of putting just about every nation in the doghouse on at least one of the ILO's 161 Conventions.[35]

Charnowitz makes no reference to the easy way out of this dilemma, which is to link any such program to that group of rights that the ILO itself has designated as constituting "basic human rights."[36] Instead, he simply rejects the possibility of establishing "one set of standards that would be acceptable" to all nations.[37] This proposition contradicts the argument used by other proponents who defend the programs on the grounds that the standards already enjoy very widespread international support.

Charnowitz's rejection of the feasibility of universal standards does not prevent him from concluding that "it may be possible for the democratic nations to agree to a definition of fairness" based on two principles: that "the labor market should operate under voluntary choice, not coercion" and that "there should be a floor for work place conditions below which no nation can go".[38] However, this purported solution does little more than reveal the weaknesses of virtually any set of standards not based on those adopted by the ILO. It is apparent that the proposed definition of "fairness" remains essentially subjective and devoid of precise content. The consequences of such subjectivity are best illustrated by reference to the cases of child labor and freedom of association.

Child Labor

One of the requirements of U.S. legislation is the existence of legislation requiring "a minimum age for the employment of children."[39] During the congressional debates on the legislation it was suggested that,[40] in this case, the sponsors had in mind ILO Convention No. 5, which was adopted in 1919.[41] Convention No. 5 was rendered effectively obsolete by a revision adopted in 1937,[42] which in turn was revised in 1973.[43] The standards specified in the latest Convention (No. 138) are complex and quite detailed. They provide for the possibility of different minimum ages in different occupations and under different circumstances, and they require the adoption of a wide range of other measures that are aimed at eliminating exploitative child labor.[44]

The only official U.S. government statement concerning the appropriate standards to be applied under the worker rights legislation appears to reflect the approach contained in Convention No. 138 rather than that contained in Convention No. 5, as had been proposed by the legislation's principal sponsor. This statement is printed in an appendix to the annual State Department Country Practices report. According to these "additional guidelines" for "reporting on worker rights":

Minimum age for employment of children concerns the effective abolition of child labor by raising the minimum age for employment to a level consistent with the fullest physical and mental development of young people. In addition, young people should not be employed in hazardous conditions or at night.[45]

But even this clarification fails to mirror adequately the variety and precision of the provisions contained in Convention No. 138. It thus remains entirely unclear which standards are applicable. Moreover, these "additional guidelines" are provided only for the purposes of reporting by State Department officials. They do not appear to have been accorded any standing in the determinations made by the U.S. trade representatives, despite the fact that those reports are supposed to be taken into account.[46]

Under these circumstances, it is hardly surprising that one of the staunchest advocates of the U.S. legislation, the International Labor Rights Fund, seems largely ignorant of the complexity of the actual ILO standards. They characterize the minimum age issue as one involving "absolute rights."[47] In its view, "Either a country has child labor or it doesn't."[48] Yet the ILO itself has acknowledged that the problem is, in effect, a relative one. Many countries, including the United States,[49] have experienced significant and continuing problems in their endeavors to eliminate child labor. Legislative measures are far from adequate for dealing with the issue and may well be entirely ineffective if they are not supplemented by a range of other measures.[50] An ILO study of the situation in India has even suggested that a straight-out prohibition of child labor may not always be the best strategy in the short term:

The possibilities for the application of the full force of legislation in the unorganized sectors where child labor is concentrated and child exploitation most pronounced are also severely limited. Even if it were possible, it may not necessarily be in the best interest of the families concerned and, to be sure, of the nation at large.[51]

Freedom of Association

While many other examples could be provided, one more will suffice to make the point. In responding to a complaint that worker rights were violated in El Salvador in 1989–1990, the relevant interagency committee characterized death squad attacks on labor leaders as violations of human rights rather than as violations of worker rights.[52] According to interviews with the officials involved:

The Administration's position . . . is that the definition of internationally recognized worker rights is very clear, and does not speak of basic political freedoms.[53]

While such a distinction might seem plausible to a general observer, the ILO's Committee on Freedom of Association has made it very clear that such acts do indeed directly contravene the right to freedom of association. In summing up its own jurisprudence it has noted that

A climate of violence such as that surrounding the murder or disappearance of trade union leaders constitutes a serious obstacle to the exercise of trade union rights; such acts require severe measures to be taken by the authorities.[54]

The result is that the relevant United States government agency is adopting an interpretation of the scope of the right to freedom of association that is considerably narrower than that which has long been accepted internationally. Confusion as to the scope of labor rights in general, and of the specific right concerned in particular, would seem a very likely result of such discrepancies.

Such problems, which stem from the extraordinary vagueness of U.S. worker rights legislation, are only two examples of the range of complexities in the case of each of the formulations used in the legislation. It is no surprise that a comprehensive analysis of the standards actually applied by the relevant U.S. government agencies to date concluded that the process of formulation is characterized by a total lack of normative clarity. According to the study, "It is virtually impossible to identify or predict with any certainty the standards the [Trade Policy Staff Committee] will use in future worker rights determinations."[55] For present purposes, it may be added that whatever the standards may be, they are highly unlikely to be the "internationally recognized" ones that they purport to be.

Application of Standards Only to States Bound Thereby

International human rights obligations, including those dealing with labor rights issues, are applicable to a given state either through the undertaking of specific treaty obligations or by virtue of customary international law.[56] If the norm in question has attained the latter status "not only the treaty non-parties, but also the parties [can] have recourse to international law remedies not provided for in the treaties."[57] While some commentators have suggested that all the rights recognized in the Universal Declaration of Human Rights have attained the status of customary law,[58] the more widely accepted view is that reflected in the Restatement (Third) of the Foreign Relations Law of the United States. In that view, only a limited number of civil and political rights are part of customary law.[59] According to the *Restatement*, none of the five categories of worker rights listed in the U.S. legislation have attained such status.

The other possibility is that some international labor standards might have become part of general international law in the form of "general principles of law recognized by civilized nations."[60] In Meron's view this could be the case with respect to any of the relevant rights that "have been recognized by the internal laws of most states (e.g. as a result of ratifications of ILO's international labour conventions)."[61] However, in the case of those ILO conventions cited by the principal sponsor of the U.S. worker rights legislation as being the basis for the list enumerated in the latter,[62] this approach could only be even potentially productive with respect to the conventions dealing with forced labor and freedom of association. For the remainder, the relevant convention on hours of work had been ratified by only 49 states as of January 1, 1991, the relevant minimum age convention had 69 ratifications, and the convention on minimum wages had only 34 ratifications.[63] It is thus extremely difficult to sustain the proposition that, despite their relatively low level of ratification, the principles contained in these conventions have acquired the status of general principles of law.

In addition, many of the governments under U.S. scrutiny have failed to ratify or accede to the appropriate ILO conventions. For example, if we take five of the most commonly cited ILO human rights conventions (Nos. 11, 98, 105, 111, and 138) we find that, as at January 1, 1991, Thailand had ratified only one (No. 105), Indonesia had ratified only one (No. 98), Myanmar (Burma) had ratified only one (No. 11), and Chile had ratified only two (Nos. 11 and 111). South Korea, which was not then a member of the ILO, had ratified none of the conventions. Moreover, if the relevant treaty obligations were taken as providing the justification for U.S. action, then the actual standards contained in those treaties would have to be applied. As we have seen, this is far from being the case.

It is difficult to escape the conclusion that the United States is, in reality, imposing its own, conveniently flexible and even elastic, standards upon other states. The effect is that states are being required to meet standards that are not formally binding upon them by virtue either of treaty undertakings or of customary international law. It is unlikely that the United States would look kindly upon such an approach if it were targeted in a similar fashion.

The major harm flowing from the U.S. Congress's failure to use internationally agreed-upon standards may be to the human rights movement. As Meron has correctly noted, the attempt to hold non-parties accountable to human rights treaty norms "generates tension between the important human rights values advocated . . . and the sovereignty of non-parties. The credibility of international human rights therefore requires that attempts to extend their universality utilize irreproachable legal methods." [64]

Consistency with Existing International Norms

The future effectiveness of efforts to promote respect for human rights within the framework of interstate relations depends to a very large extent upon the ability of the international community to agree not only upon the appropriate normative standards but also upon efforts to interpret those standards with as great a degree of precision and consistency as possible. In the area of worker rights, furtherance of these objectives requires a major effort to achieve a normative approach that is generally consistent with that pursued by the ILO. Since the ILO is the preeminent international organization in the field whose standards have often been relied upon by the United States in the past,[65] any approach that is predicated upon circumventing that body or on undermining its effectiveness should be strenuously avoided.

Although a House of Representatives Foreign Affairs Committee Report accompanying the 1985 OPIC amendments suggested that one indication that a government was serious about worker rights was membership in the ILO,[66] the procedures implementing the worker rights legislation appear to ignore, in an almost studied fashion, the various ways in which ILO norms could be taken into account. While the interagency subcommittee that administers the GSP program is said to take account of the "findings of the . . . ILO,"[67] there is no evidence to indicate that any of the relevant agencies have, in practice, made any significant reference to the jurisprudence emanating from the ILO.

The problems that may result from the neglect, or circumvention, of existing international doctrine is illustrated by the case of freedom of association. The State Department's "guidelines" for "reporting on worker rights" indicate that the right to association has been defined by the ILO to include various specific subrights, including for example "the right of workers and employers to establish and join organizations of their own choosing without previous authorization."[69] In interpreting this right the ILO has had to consider a very wide range of obstacles and deterrents that prevent or inhibit the right, in order to determine which are compatible with the terms of the relevant ILO conventions.[70] By failing to take account of this jurisprudence, there is a very great likelihood that the U.S. agencies will create a different and probably inconsistent set of standards for evaluating a country's compliance.

The Need for Fair and Consistent Procedures

Another concern in the use of "internationally recognized" human rights standards as a basis on which potentially punitive measures might be taken is to ensure that the relevant procedures are fair and consistent and that double standards are avoided as far as possible. Such concerns have long featured prominently in the criticisms by U.S. officials and academics of the UN's human rights programs. David Forsythe, for example, has said that the United Nations must exhibit "a balanced commitment to human rights" if it is to warrant full U.S. government support.[71] Similarly, a former senior administration official warned that a double standard on human rights "undermines the United Nations' moral authority—and some would say its legitimacy."[72] The concerns underlying these comments are entirely justified.[73] They apply equally well to a national body that purports to be applying international standards.

The worker rights procedures do respect some of the fairness requirements that can reasonably be expected under the circumstances. These include, for example, an opportunity for a country under scrutiny to make detailed submissions on its own behalf, in order to rebut allegations, and to participate in public hearings. The major procedural problem, however, stems from the unpredictability of the outcome in any given case and the virtually overwhelming element of discretion that is vested in the President. It has been noted, for example, that "the executive branch has complete and ultimate authority and can inject strategic and political considerations into review decisions".[74] This point was further emphasized by the U.S. District Court for the District of Columbia, which, in dismissing a complaint under the GSP legislation on the grounds that it was not justiciable, observed:

Given [the] apparent total lack of standards, coupled with the discretion preserved by the terms of the GSP statute itself and implicit in the President's special and separate authority in the areas of foreign policy, there is obviously no statutory direction which provides any basis for the Court to act.[75]

Such unfettered discretion vested is far from ideal in a situation in which one state's human rights practices are being judged by another.

One of the key problems are the open-ended requirements that the legislation imposes upon other states. To take the example of the GSP legislation, the President shall not designate a country as a beneficiary "if such country has not taken or is not taking steps to afford its workers internationally recognized worker rights."[76] Under the OPIC legislation the language is similar, although expressed in the affirmative.[77]

Under these terms, the relevant U.S. government agencies have been prepared to accept undertakings of a very vague and general nature as evidence that appropriate steps are being taken. In some cases, when the measures subsequently failed to effect improvements, no follow-up action has been taken.[78] Even when the standard used is somewhat stronger, as in section 301, the government concerned must have taken, or be taking, "actions that demonstrate a significant and tangible overall advancement" in protecting worker rights.[79] The emphasis in practice has been on the word "overall," thus permitting a wide range of factors to be taken into account.

As a result, virtually all available analyses of the actual approach to implementation have concluded that political factors are generally the overriding consideration in determining the outcome of cases. One review of Reagan administration decisions to terminate GSP and OPIC status for Nicaragua, Romania, Ethiopia, Chile, and Paraguay concluded that human rights factors had been of only minor importance in the decisions taken.[80] Instead, "strategic, or national security considerations" were determinant.[81] This view is strengthened by the fact that, at the same time as these states were penalized, the President found that worker rights practices were satisfactory in El Salvador, Guatemala, Haiti, Singapore, Suriname, and Gambia.[82] Malaysia has been left untouched by labor rights sanctions, and Indonesia, despite labor practices as egregious as any, was placed on a probationary status in the most recent round of GSP decisions.[83]

A further problem with the procedures is the lack of human rights expertise available to the decision-making bodies. The office of the United States Trade Representative, which is the key agency in this area, is primarily concerned with promoting U.S. trade opportunities. It does not consider itself a human rights agency,[84] and most observers would probably not think it is in a good position from which to act objectively in worker rights matters. Even where inputs are sought from a range of different agencies, as is the case with the GSP subcommittee, there is apparently no representative with human rights expertise.[85]

This situation stands in marked contrast to the various procedural safeguards that exist in relation to proceedings in the ILO context. While far from perfect, the relevant safeguards at least seek to promote fairness, impartiality, objectivity, and transparency in the process of assessing a government's compliance with international standards. The importance of these safeguards were eloquently underscored in an address by the U.S. Secretary of Labor, Elizabeth Dole, to the International Labor Conference in June 1989:

The ILO must continue to promote and protect human rights and the rights of workers in every corner of the globe. The strength of the ILO, however, lies not just in the legal obligations undertaken by its Members. More fundamentally, its strength derives from its moral force among governments, workers and employers. But, this moral force in turn depends upon the ILO's strict adherence to its founding principles, and to its continued impartial role in supervising the application of its international standards. Respect for such due process is fundamental, because it is nothing more than—or less than—a respect for law. Without such respect, the ILO will lose its integrity and purpose.[86]

The same sentiments could appropriately be adapted as a basis upon which to impugn the procedures followed in implementing the U.S. worker rights legislation.

Assessing Criticisms of the Worker Rights Legislation

How Have Human Rights Groups Reacted?

Various U.S.-based non-governmental human rights groups have voiced their support for the worker rights initiatives.[87] Criticisms have been limited to proposed procedural improvements rather than any major re-thinking of the present approach. Yet in view of the problems that have been identified in the analysis above, the question that arises is why criticism of the programs has been so limited and so muted? One explanation is that low priority is often attached to the need to ground advocacy and sanctions approaches in international standards. Another is that, outside of the U.S. labor movement, there is very limited knowledge, or even awareness, of the ILO's international labor standards in any technical sense. Thus the occasional invocation of that agency's name by the proponents of the U.S. legislation seems to have been sufficient to allay any fears of inconsistency between the two sets of standards. Similarly, the organization's structure and procedures are sufficiently unknown in the United States to deter any serious proposals to make more effective use of the opportunities that might exist. A third, and related, explanation is that most of the groups have evaluated the worker rights legislation only in terms of its objectives rather than in terms of the means by which those objectives are to be sought.[88]

Trade and Human Rights Issues Should Be Kept Separate

It has often been argued that human rights issues ought to be kept entirely separate from trade and international development policy. However, the international community has already become significantly more sophisticated than such positions would lead one to expect. Many forms of linkage are now recognized to be not only appropriate but inevitable. The World Bank, the International Monetary Fund, and the

United Nations Development Program (UNDP) have all adopted measures of one kind or another that recognize that human rights performance ought to be a factor in their decision-making.[89]

This type of linkage is nothing new. While this is not the place to embark upon a detailed historical analysis of the position of economic factors in early human rights initiatives, it is appropriate to recall that early nineteenth-century efforts to outlaw international slavery, as well as much of the concern to protect the rights of aliens (especially when they were representing U.S. business in South America) were strongly supported by economic considerations. Similarly, there is an even more direct analogy to be drawn between the current U.S. worker rights initiatives and the concerns that initially gave rise to the creation of the International Labor Organization. The preamble to the ILO's Constitution of 1919 explicitly proclaimed that "the failure of any nation to adopt humane conditions of labour is an obstacle in the way of other nations which desire to improve conditions in their own country."[90]

The Legislation Is Not Really Motivated by Human Rights Concerns

The suggestion that the worker rights legislation is motivated by protectionist concerns with little or no genuine concern for human rights has often been made. Proponents of the legislation have generally been enthusiastic in rejecting it. In 1984, for example, a report by the House Ways and Means Committee stated that

The denial of internationally recognized worker rights in developing countries tend [sic] to perpetuate poverty, to limit the benefits of economic development and growht, to narrow privileged elites, and to sow the seeds of social instability and political rebellion.[91]

Most subsequent analyses of the various programs have followed a similar line. Charnowitz has suggested two objectives. The first is to respond to "a growing public concern about U.S. abatement of foreign human rights violations," and the second is to support the "goal of promoting private sector development and democratization."[92] Similarly, Harlan Mandel has argued that "the immediate U.S. goal to be attained . . . is humanitarian: to improve the working conditions and rights of foreign labor."[93]

Human rights legislation is rarely motivated by purely altruistic concerns.[94] Thus, even if it were possible to demonstrate convincingly that the worker rights programs have been driven by varied motives, some of which are undeniably protectionist, this fact would not of itself discredit them. Nevertheless, if it were to be shown that there is little or no congruence between U.S. human rights policies on the one hand and its worker rights policies on the other, it would seem reasonable to question the authenticity of the purported human rights motivation.

One such incongruity arises insofar as successive U.S. administrations have consistently argued, and Congress has tended to agree, that sanctions should only be used as a last resort in response to human rights violations. The Clinton administration shifted to this view with respect to most-favored-nation status for China after campaigning on the opposite grounds.[95] Yet, in marked contrast, the worker rights legislation opts for the imposition of sanctions, albeit on a discretionary basis, as the principal form of response to perceived violations of worker rights. That approach would seem to be designed less to achieve the cessation of human rights abuses than to bring offending states to the negotiating table so as to improve the relative trade position of the United States vis-à-vis those states.

The Worker Rights Approach Is Unlikely to Achieve Human Rights Goals

There is little doubt that the worker rights legislation will, over a period of time, contribute to the adoption of reforms in a number of states that are significantly dependent on access to the U.S. market, and in those states in which legislative or administrative changes can be achieved at relatively little real cost. In such cases states can almost certainly be persuaded to comply with some of the "suggestions" emerging from the worker rights review process. In addition, the legislation provides yet another means by which pressure can be applied against governments which are *non grata* with the United States, either for ideological or for human rights reasons (or, more likely, both). However, the question remains; do the ends justify the means?

While acknowledging that the worker rights provisions are likely to have a positive impact on labor rights in certain situations, that impact must be weighed against the negative consequences of the legislation. Moreover, it must be asked whether alternative approaches might be available that would be reasonably effective at a lower negative cost.

The U.S. Should Not Apply Standards to Other States That It Has Failed to Ratify Itself

The argument that the United States should not apply standards to other states that it has failed to ratify itself was a favorite refrain of countries that were the targets of U.S. human rights criticism or sanctions in the 1970s and 1980s, and was advanced with particular gusto by the then socialist countries of Eastern Europe. Before considering its merits in the present context it is appropriate to examine the U.S. ratification record in respect to the ILO Conventions that are cited as the basis for the worker rights programs.

As of January 1, 1995, the ILO had adopted a total of 175 conventions, not all of which deal directly with human rights per se. The United States has ratified only one of the seven core human rights conventions. Convention No. 105 on the Abolition of Forced Labour, which was ratified in September 1991.

The AFL-CIO and various human rights groups have frequently called upon the United States to ratify the ILO's basic human rights conventions and have warned of the greatly diminished credibility of the United States as a human rights defender in the absence of such ratification.[96] But the longstanding position of the U.S. government is that "although an improved record of ratification [is] an important objective towards which to strive," the important fact is that "in practice United States law [meets] or [exceeds], in almost every case, that which [is] set out in international labor conventions."[97] Consistent with this approach, the leading worker rights advocacy group has suggested that the U.S. failure to ratify is of little relevance:

The U.S. Congress has long been reluctant to ratify international accords that will constrain U.S. laws. For example, the Congress has never ratified the major GATT rules. It has nonetheless generally complied with GATT rules as though they were binding. Concerning worker rights, the important point is that the United States has adopted and enforced domestic laws that guarantee each of the five basic rights and standards enumerated in the legislation.[98]

In fact, it is the reluctance of the United States to subject itself to internationally binding "constraints" that lies at the very root of the problem. Any state can assert that its own laws conform to international standards, but such assertions are unconvincing when there is no element of international accountability and no regular independent reviews of the laws undertaken. This issue is underscored by the position of the Washington-based Labor Policy Association, the principal U.S. employer group concerned with international labor affairs. It argues that the provisions of some of the basic ILO human rights conventions are actually in direct conflict with U.S. law and that their ratification would require a number of major amendments to that law.[99]

The U.S. record in agreeing to be formally bound by the same standards that it purports to be applying to other states is thus rather poor, both in absolute and comparative terms.[100] When the United States is speaking out, or taking action, in response to violations of those human rights that are the subject of *erga omnes* obligations, the discrepancy between its poor record of human rights treaty ratification and its proselytizing stance is of no great import apart from the few propaganda opportunities thereby afforded to its ideological adversaries. However, in relation to worker rights, which are not yet the subject of such obligations, it is apparent that the United States would be acting on much stronger and certainly more persuasive grounds if it were itself a party to the relevant international conventions, and if these standards were the ones being applied. In contrast, what emerges is a major discrepancy between the United States' refusal to submit itself to multilateral accountability (through the ILO) and its preparedness to subject others to a form of accountability in which the United States acts as the sole legislator, judge, jury, and enforcement authority. In the final analysis, protestations to the effect that the United States already conforms fully to the relevant standards will ring hollow until the United States is prepared to take the only steps that can effectively give substance to the claim: ratification of the relevant ILO standards.

Conclusion

As noted at the outset, the great majority of commentators who have analyzed the U.S. worker rights programs have been favorably disposed towards them. They have suggested the need for procedural reforms but have not concluded that the programs in their existing forms are unacceptable. The conclusion of the present analysis, however, is far less sanguine. It seems clear, on the basis of experience to date, that the legislation is aimed almost exclusively at improving the U.S. trading position. This goal is not in itself inappropriate, but it does not follow that international lawyers should be supportive of it without weighing very carefully any adverse consequences it might have in human rights terms.

From the perspective of international human rights law, the programs are not only seriously flawed in the specific ways described above but also have the potential, over the longer term, to undermine significantly both the standards and the procedures that together make up the labor rights regime that the international community has devoted most of the twentieth century to establishing and developing. The key question that remains to be answered is whether it might be possible to redesign the U.S. worker rights programs in such a way as to make them compatible with, and even complementary to, that regime. The advantages of such an approach are obvious. As Oscar Schachter noted in 1978 in relation to human rights-inspired sanctions:

"When such judgments are made by the United States unilaterally, they are likely to be perceived by others as political and self-interested. To avoid this negative perception, one would have to have impartial international procedures founded on adequate inquiry and international criteria of some specificity." [101]

While a system that depends significantly upon multilateral standards and procedures makes good sense in theory, it must be asked whether it is feasible in practice. Although such approaches have been outlined before by different commentators, including myself,[102] it has to be acknowledged that, in this and other fields, multilateralism has always tended to attract considerably more than its fair share of idealistic but naive and largely impractical proposals. There is good reason to think, however, that a multilateral effort to promote fair labor standards in the context of international trade should not be lightly dismissed.

Perhaps one of the strongest indications of the proposal's feasibility in both practical and institutional terms is the fact that more than one ILO director-general has drawn attention to the opportunities that already exist for an investigation of unfair labor practices, and has also suggested that ad hoc conciliation procedures might be initiated in this context. Such a proposal was first put forward in 1973[103] and was reiterated with a significant degree of specificity in 1988.[104] On the latter occasion the director-general even indicated his preparedness to draft a composite set of labor standards that might be used specifically for this purpose.[105] Yet the United States has taken no action to activate such procedures, or to propose entirely new mechanisms within the ILO framework that could resolve specific disputes over worker rights issues when they arise in a bilateral (or multilateral) trade context.

Although the United States has made such an effort in the Uruguay Round negotiations, its trading partners have apparently all assumed that its proposals were a form of very thinly concealed protectionism.[106] However, there are strong reasons for doubting whether GATT is the most appropriate forum in which to pursue such an initiative. GATT has no existing role or expertise in relation to labor standards, it has no readily adaptable institutional arrangements for this purpose, and it has none of the ILO's experience in fact-finding, conciliation, the exertion of pressure, or the provision of technical cooperation in the field of labor policy. Thus the prospects of successfully developing a multilateral worker rights program would appear far greater in the ILO. A cynic might suggest that this explains why no initiative has been taken by the United States in that forum.

Finally, it must be emphasized that even if the United States is unable to obtain satisfaction in this matter from the ILO, there remain a number of measures that Congress could take to make its worker rights programs both more convincing and more acceptable in the eyes of its trading partners, as well as to reduce greatly the potential harm that they might cause to the international labor rights regime. These measures include: (1) ratifying some, if not all, of the ILO's basic human rights conventions; (2) encouraging U.S. trading partners to ratify the same conventions, combined with technical assistance, if requested, to facilitate such measures; (3) using the standards contained in these ILO conventions as the basis for the worker rights programs; (4) using consistently ILO-generated information in assessing the situation of workers in a given state; (5) opening up opportunities for any interested parties to participate in the hearings dealing with alleged violations; (6) preparing a clear and detailed report listing the unacceptable practices pursued or tolerated by the government under scrutiny; (7) removing the excessively indulgent flexibility arrangements for developing countries that currently apply; and (8) reducing the President's discretion by requiring reasons to be given for decisions and by providing an opportunity to appeal against those decisions.

Acknowledgments. An earlier version of this chapter appeared under the same title in *Human Rights Quarterly* 15 (1993). Reprinted by permission of *Human Rights Quarterly*.

Notes

1. On the linkage between labor standards and international trade see generally Lawyers Committee for Human Rights, "A Report on Legal Mechanisms to Protect Worker Rights" (mimeo, 1991) (hereinafter "Lawyers Committee (1991)"); Lawyers Committee for Human Rights, "Worker Rights Under the U.S. Trade Laws" (1989) (hereinafter "Lawyers Committee (1989)"); Harlan Mandel, "In Pursuit of the Missing Link: International Worker Rights and International Trade?" 27 *Columbia Journal of Transnational Law* 27 (1989): 443; International Labor Rights Education and Research Fund, "Trade's Hidden Costs: Worker Rights in a Changing World Economy" (mimeo, 1988) (hereinafter "Trade's Hidden Costs"); Steve Charnowitz, "The Influence of International Labour Standards on the World Trading Regime: A Historical Overview," *International Labor Review* 126 (1987): 565; Ian C. Ballon, "The Implications of Making the Denial of Internationally Recognized Worker Rights Actionable under Section 301 of the Trade Act of 1974," *Virginia Journal of International Law* 28 (1987): 73; Steve Charnowitz, "Fair Labor Standards and International Trade," *Journal of World Trade Law* 20 (1986): 61; G. Hansson, *Social Clauses and International Trade* (1983) London: Croom Helm; Philip Alston, "Commodity Agreements: As Though People Don't Matter," *Journal of World Trade Law* 15 (1981): 455; and Gus Edgren, "Fair Labour Standards and Trade Liberalization," *International Labor Review* 118 (1979): 523.

2. For example, Owen Bieber, former president of the United Auto Workers, in congressional testimony in support of worker rights legislation, stated that:

There are many countries around the world that have built an advantage in international trade by preventing workers from exercising the right to organize and bargain with employers, by failing to adopt minimum standards for conditions of work, or by allowing forced or child labor. The US should officially repudiate any trading advantage obtained in this way and retaliate against the exports of such countries.

Mastering the World Economy: Hearings before the Senate Committee on Finance, 100th Cong., 1st sess., 59–60 (1987).

"Market dumping" is generally used to refer to the practice of selling goods in international trade at a lower price than the cost of production and marketing, with a view to destroying competition in the target country or artificially stimulating a market that, when subsequently consolidated, is expected to support a higher price that exceeds actual production and marketing costs. "Social dumping," on the other hand, usually refers to the practice of relying upon low "social" costs (whether in the form of low wages, poor working conditions, or neglect of basic environmental, safety, or health standards) to produce goods that can then be sold in another market at a price that is well below the cost of production in that market, primarily because producers in that market would not be permitted to tolerate such low social standards.

3. *Aggressive Unilateralism: America's 301 Trade Policy and the World Trading System,* ed. Bhagwati and Patrick (Ann Arbor: University of Michigan Press 1990).

4. See Ballon, "Worker Rights Actionable under Section 301," 78–82; Lawyers Committee (1991), 2–19.

5. See Trade Act of 1974. sec. 502, Pub. L. 93-618, 88 Stat. 2066 (1975), codified at 19 U.S.C.A. sec. 2462 (b) (1)–(6) (1980).

6. Enacted as Title V of the Trade and Tariff Act of 1984. Pub. L. 98-573, sec. 502, 98 Stat. 3020, codified at 19 U.S.C.A. 2462 (West Supp. 1988).

7. Ibid., sec. 502 (b) (7).

8. See generally Ballon, "Worker Rights Actionable Under Section 301," 75–78, and Lawyers Committee (1991), 19–22.

9. Caribbean Basin Economic Recovery Act, 19 U.S.C. sec. 2702 (c) (8) (Supp. IV 1986). In the view of one commentator, "Because of its general wording and discretionary language, the potential impact of the CBI provision does not appear great" (Mandel, "In Pursuit of the Missing Link," 446, n. 16). In my opinion, it is precisely because of its flexibility and open-endedness that the provision is troubling.

10. See Ballon, "Worker Rights Actionable Under Section 301," 82–84, and Lawyers Committee (1991), 22–26.

11. Overseas Private Investment Corporation Amendment Act of 1985, Pub. L. 99-204, 99 Stat. 1670 (1985), codified at 22 U.S.C.A. sec. 2191 a (a) (1) (West Supp. 1988).

12. See generally Ballon, "Worker Rights Actionable Under Section 301," 88–127, and Lawyers Committee (1991), 26–31.

13. Trade Act of 1974, as amended by the Omnibus Trade and Competitiveness Act of 1988, Pub. L. 100-418, 102 Stat. 1107 (1988), sec. 1301, codified at 19 U.S.C.A. sec. 2411 (a).

14. Ibid., sec. 301 (b) (2), and sec. 301 (c) (1) (A) and (B).

15. Helen Milner, "The Political Economy of U.S. Trade Policy: A Study of the Super 301 Provision," 180 and Section 301," 214, both in *Aggressive Unilateralism,* ed. Baghwati and Patrick.

16. *Presidential Authority to Respond to Unfair Trade Practices: Hearings on Title II of S.1860 and S.1862 before the Senate Comm. on Finance,* 99th Cong., 2d sess., 39 at 52 (1986) (testimony of C. Yeutter, U.S. trade representative).

17. One careful analysis has concluded that the 1988 Trade Act provisions concerning worker rights could well be in violation of United States obligations as a signatory to the General Agreement on Tariffs and Trade (opened for signature Oct. 30, 1947, 61 Stat. pts. 5–6, T.I.A.S. No. 1700, 55 U.N.T.S. 194; the current version of the Agreement is reprinted in General Agreement on Tariffs and Trade, Basic Instruments and Selected Documents, Supps. I–XXXIII (1987). The most-favored-nation (MFN) clause (ibid., art. 18) prohibits discriminatory trade and tariff practices. It has been suggested that:

> Without an internationally recognized basis on which to impose trade sanctions, any United States action under Section 301 to address the denial of worker rights by a fellow signatory would appear to constitute a substantive violation of GATT's MFN clause, or at least a procedural evasion of GATT's dispute resolution mechanism. Such an action by the United States could invite retaliatory trade action by the other signatory and its allies.

Lawyers Committee (1989), 66. For a careful and persuasive analysis of the circumstances under which it might be appropriate for the relevant GATT rules to be ignored or broken see Robert Hudec, "Thinking About the New Section 301: Beyond Good and Evil," in *Aggressive Unilateralism,* ed. Baghwati and Patrick, 113.

18. Independent Commission on International Development Issues. *North-South: A Programme for Survival* (London: Pan Books, 1980), 182–183.

19. Trade Act of 1974, sec. 121 (a) (4).

20. General Agreement on Tariffs and Trade, Preparatory Commission, Doc. (86) W/43, June 25, 1986.

21. See Charnowitz, "Fair Labor Standards and International Trade."

22. Trade Act of 1974, sec. 502 (a) (4), 19 U.S.C. sec. 2462 (a) (4).

23. See note 9 above.

24. Overseas Private Investment Corporation Amendment Act of 1985, Pub. L. 99-204, 99 Stat. 1670 (1985), codified at 22 U.S.C.A. sec. 2191 a (a) (1) (West Supp. 1988).

25. Trade Act of 1974, as amended by the Omnibus Trade and Competitiveness Act of 1988, Pub. L. 100-418, 102 Stat. 1107 (1988), sec. 1301, codified at 19 U.S.C.A. sec. 2411 (a).

26. See Nicolas Valticos, *Le Droit international du travail* (Paris: Dalloz, 1983).

27. "Internationally recognized worker rights, such as those included in the GSP and OPIC legislation, mirror those spelled out in bedrock International Labor Organization (ILO) Conventions" "Trade's Hidden Costs," 6.

28. Mandel, "In Pursuit of the Missing Link," 460.

29. See text accompanying notes 102–105.

30. Article 1 (a), ILO Convention (No. 111) Concerning Discrimination in Respect of Employment and Occupation, adopted June 25, 1958, entered into force June 15, 1960: reprinted in *United Nations, Human Rights: A Compilation of International Instruments,* p. 84 (Geneva: UN Centre for Human Rights, 1988).

31. For a negative view see Ballon, "Worker Rights Actionable Under Section 301."

32. "Trade's Hidden Costs," 8.

33. See text accompanying notes 62–63 below.

34. Charnowitz, "Fair Labor Standards and International Trade," 68.

35. Ibid.

36. See text accompanying note 103 below.

37. Charnowitz, "Fair Labor Standards and International Trade," 69 (the justification offered is that "the nations of the world not share a common set of values").

38. Ibid.

39. E.g., 19 U.S.C. sec. 2462 (a) (4).

40. Rep. Don Pease (Ohio) indicated that the formulations contained in the legislation that he was co-sponsoring were based on the following ILO Conventions: Hours of Work (Industry) Convention of 1919 (No. 1): Minimum Age (Industry) Convention of 1919 (No. 5); Right of Association (Agriculture) Convention) of 1921 (No. 11); Right to Organize and Collective Bargaining Convention of 1949 (No. 98); Abolition of Forced Labour Convention of 1956 (No. 105); and Minimum Wage-Fixing Convention of 1970 (No. 131). See 133 *Congressional Record* H1499 (daily ed., March 19, 1987).

41. The convention is reprinted in International Labor Organization, *International Labour Conventions and Recommendations, 1919–1981* (Geneva: ILO, 1982), 22.

42. Minimum Age (Industry) Convention (Revised) of 1937 (No. 59), reprinted in *International Labour Conventions and Recommendations, 1919–1981*, 720.

43. Minimum Age Convention of 1973 (No. 138), reprinted in *International Labour Conventions and Recommendations, 1919–1981*, 730.

44. See H. T. Dao, "ILO Standards for the Protection of Children." *Nordic Journal of International Law* 58 (1989): 54.

45. Department of State, *State Department Country Reports on Human Rights Practices for 1990*, Report Submitted to the Senate Committee on Foreign Relations and the House Committee on Foreign Affairs, 102d Cong., 1st sess. (1991), app. B, 1694 (hereafter *County Reports on Human Rights 1990*).

46. The GSP Subcommittee of the Trade Policy Staff Committee, which is chaired by a representative of the Office of the United States Trade Representative, is supposed to consider the State Department's annual country reports in its deliberations. See generally Lawyers Committee (1991), 6.

47. "Trade's Hidden Costs," 7.

48. Ibid.

49. General Accounting Office, *The Fair Labor Standards Act: Enforcement of Child Labor Provisions in Massachusetts*, doc. GAO/HRD-88-54, April 1988.

50. One study concluded that the legislative approach will only yield significant results where determined efforts are made to secure its implementation, where the bureaucracy charged with responsibility for such implementation is technically and financially equipped to do so, where there exists a degree of difficulty in concealing the existence of the problem, and where there is relatively little to be gained from employing children rather than adults (Rodgers and Standing, "The Economic Roles of Children: Issues for Analysis," *Child Work, Poverty and Underdevelopment*, [1981] (39).

51. International Labor Office, *Towards an Action Program on Child Labour: Report to the Government of India of an ILO Technical Mission* (Geneva: ILO, 1984), 29.

52. GSP Subcommittee, *1990 GSP Annual Reviews: Worker Rights Summary, El Salvador*, April 1991, 2, cited in Lawyers Committee (1991), 17, n. 65.

53. Ibid., 17–18.

54. International Labor Office, *Freedom of Association: Digest of Decisions and*

Principles of the Freedom of Association Committee of the Governing Body of the ILO, 3rd ed.; Geneva: ILO, 20. ILO, 1985).

55. Lawyers Committee (1989), 33.

56. See Meron, *Human Rights and Humanitarian Norms as Customary Law* (Oxford: Clarendon Press, 1989).

57. Oscar Schachter, "International Law in Theory and Practice" *Recueil des Cours* 178 (1982-V): 334.

58. E.g., Sohn, "The New International Law: Protection of the Rights of Individuals Rather Than States" *American University Law Review* 32 (1982): 1. The Universal Declaration of Human Rights, "as an authoritative listing of human rights, has become a basic component of international customary law, binding on all states, not only on members of the United Nations" (ibid., 17).

59. The Restatement lists the following rights as having attained the status of norms of customary international law:

(a) genocide;
(b) slavery or slave trade;
(c) the murder or causing the disappearance of individuals;
(d) torture or other cruel, inhuman, or degrading treatment or punishment;
(e) prolonged arbitrary detention;
(f) systematic racial discrimination, or
(g) a consistent pattern or gross violations of internationally recognized human rights (Restatement (Third) of the Foreign Relations Law of the United States 2, sec. 702 [1987]).

60. See Bruno Simma and Philip Alston, "The Sources of Human Rights Law: Custom, Jus Cogens, and General Principles," 12 Australian Yearbook of International Law 1992, 82.

61. Meron, *Human Rights and Humanitarian Norms*, 98.

62. See note 40 above.

63. International Labor Office, "Chart of Ratifications of International Labour Conventions," Jan. 1, 1991. The references are, respectively, to Conventions No. 1, No. 5, and No. 131. Geneva, ILO.

64. Meron, *Human Rights and Humanitarian Norms*, 81.

65. See Ghebali, *The International Labour Organisation: A Case Study on the Evolution of U.N. Specialized Agencies* (Deventer, Martinas Nijhoff, 1989).

66. *Human Rights Report No. 285*, 99th Cong., 1st sess. 6, reprinted in *1985 U.S. Code Congressional Administrative News*, 2577.

67. Lawyers Committee (1991), 6.

68. See the detailed reviews of agency practice contained in Lawyers Committee (1991) and Mandel, "In Pursuit of the Missing Link."

69. See *Country Reports on Human Rights 1990* at 1552.

70. See, for example, the lengthy discussion of this issue contained in Valticos, *Le Droit international du travail*, 243–71.

71. David Forsythe, "The United States, the United Nations, and Human Rights," in *The United States and Multilateral Institutions: Patterns of Changing Instrumentality and Influence*, ed. Karns and Mingst (Boston: Unwin and Hymen, 1990), 261, 283.

72. Richard Williamson, *The United Nations: A Place of Promise and of Mischief* (Lanham, MD: University Press of America, 1991), 118.

73. For a discussion that places the double standards issue in its proper per-

spective see Thomas M. Franck, *Nation Against Nation* (New York: Oxford University Press, 1985), ch. 12.

74. Mandel, "In Pursuit of the Missing Link." Mandel notes, however, that a small element of accountability is introduced by the requirement contained in some of the legislation to the effect that a determination, and the basis on which it was made, must be reported to Congress ("In Pursuit of the Missing Link," nn. 134 and 144.

75. *International Labor Rights Education and Research Fund v. Bush*, 752 F. Supp. 495 (D.D.C. 1990).

76. 19 U.S.C. sec. 2462 (b) (7).

77. 22 U.S.C. sec. 2191a(a) (1).

78. Lawyers Committee (1991), 9–11 (see especially n. 37, citing a case involving Malaysia), and Mandel, "In Pursuit of the Missing Link," 470–72 (see especially n. 151, citing a case involving South Korea).

79. Trade Act of 1974, sec. 301 (d) (3) (c) (i) (1), 19 U.S.C.A. sec. 2411 (d) (3) (c) (i) (1).

80. Mandel, "In Pursuit of the Missing Link," 463.

81. Ibid.

82. Lawyers Committee (1989), 25.

83. Office of the United States Trade Representative, "Kantor Announces Results of 1992 GSP Reviews—Emphasis on Worker Rights Is Underscored," June 25, 1993.

84. Lawyers Committee (1991).

85. Ibid., 19.

86. International Labor Conference, 76th sess., Geneva, 1989, *Provisional Record* 24:6.

87. See note 1 above.

88. See, e.g., Lawyers Committee (1991) and Mandel, "In Pursuit of the Missing Link."

89. See Philip Alston, "Revitalising United Nations Work on Human Rights and Development," *Melbourne University Law Review* 28 (1991): 216.

90. Constitution of the ILO, 3rd preamble.

91. Human Rights Report No. 1090, 98th Cong., 2d Sess. 11–12, reprinted in *1984 U.S. Code Congressional and Administrative News* 5101, 5111.

92. Charnowitz, "Fair Labor Standards and International Trade," 61–62.

93. Mandel, "In Pursuit of the Missing Link," 443.

94. On the important role of hypocrisy in this general context see Henkin, *The Age of Rights* (New York: Columbia University Press, 1990).

95. See Thomas L. Friedman, "U.S. Is to Maintain Trade Privileges for China's Goods," *New York Times*, May 27, 1994, A1.

96. *The United States and the International Labor Organization: Twenty-Sixth Report of the Commission to Study the Organization of Peace,* (New York: Commission to Study the Organization of the Peace, 1979) 22, n. 14.

97. *Report of the Committee on the Application of Standards*, International Labor Conference, 76th sess., Geneva, 1989, *Provisional Record* 26:4, para. 10 (statement by U.S. government member).

98. "Trade's Hidden Costs," 7.

99. Edward Potter, *Freedom of Association, the Right to Organize and Collective Bargaining: the Impact on U.S. Law and Practice of ILO Conventions No. 87 and No. 98* (Wash., D.C., Labor Policy Association, Inc., 1984), 92.

100. See, for example, the highly critical memorandum presented on behalf

of nine socialist countries at the 1983 International Labor Conference (International Labor Conference, *Record of Proceedings* 7.

101. Oscar Schachter, "International Law Implications of U.S. Human Rights Policies," *New York Law School Law Review* 24 (1978): 87.

102. Philip Alston, "International Trade as an Instrument of Positive Human Rights Policy," *Human Rights Quarterly* 4 (1982): 155.

103. "Prosperity for Welfare: Social Purpose in Economic Growth and Change —the ILO Contribution," *Report of the Director-General*, pt. 1, International Labor Conference, 58th sess., Geneva, 1973, 39.

104. "Human Rights: A Common Responsibility," *Report of the Director-General*, International Labor Conference, 75th sess., Geneva, 1988, 57–62.

105. Ibid., 58.

106. See Lawyers Committee (1991), 68–69.

Part II
Labor Rights and Trade

Chapter 5
In from the Margins
Morality, Economics, and International Labor Rights

Stephen Herzenberg

My introduction to the contemporary international labor standards debate consisted of hearing a talk in 1987 by the Carter administration Secretary of Labor, the current president of the International Labor Rights Fund, Ray Marshall. While he acknowledged that many details would need to be addressed, Marshall maintained that international labor standards would not be difficult to implement. The International Labor Office (ILO) had published conventions defining a wide range of labor standards, including such core rights as the freedom to organize and bargain collectively. In non-labor areas such as protection of intellectual property rights, Marshall added, the General Agreement on Trade and Tariffs (GATT) was willing to grapple with the complexities raised by variations in institutions, legal traditions, and history.

Despite my sympathy for adopting international labor standards, I had trouble accepting the view that international labor standards would be easy to implement. Upon reflection, I decided that Marshall's expression of this view stemmed in part from his role as their promoter. He projected confidence to instill confidence. Beyond this, however, there appeared to be two elements to Marshall's confidence.

First, Marshall understood international standards to play an economic as well as a normative role—to be a prerequisite for renewed national and global prosperity rather than, as many economists claim, a drag on development. Second, Marshall had lived through the post–World War II "Golden Age," when minimum labor standards, industrial unions, and industry-wide collective bargaining had helped sustain U.S. aggregate demand and the productivity growth that resulted from the spread of mass production. Marshall's experience with and knowledge of this period converted the abstract idea that basic labor standards could serve economic functions from a theoretical argument to a core conviction.

Moving international labor standards in from the margins of U.S. political debate requires its proponents to make more widely accessible the understandings that underlie Ray Marshall's conviction about the feasibility of standards. Moral arguments alone will not be enough. These cede, by default, the economic ground to conventional economists (aka "marginalists") who see international standards the same way they see labor market regulation and unions in the United States—as "distortions" of the free market that conflict with static efficiency. The perception that international standards conflict with economic goals intensifies opposition to them from the business community and developing countries. In addition, it gives opponents of standards a powerful argument in battles for broader public and political support.

To make the understandings that underlie Marshall's conviction broadly accessible requires making an analytical economic case for international labor standards and bringing this case to life in concrete proposals for how abstract rights and vaguely defined standards can be embedded in today's industrial, national, and global economic structures. The development of such a practical vision has the potential to give a progressive political coalition the confidence and broad support necessary to transform the character of development in the global economy.

The rest of this chapter begins by contrasting the moral or normative approach to advocating standards with a more integrated and economic approach and explores the particular role of labor standards in the post–World War II United States. It then describes the evolution of advocacy for international labor standards from an exclusively normative approach toward a partly economic one. The following section develops the economic case for standards into a sketch of the role labor protection would play in revitalizing the U.S. and global economies. The chapter closes with a brief conclusion.

Labor Standards and Business Strategy

My argument concerning the relationship between labor standards and business strategy draws on a distinction made by Michael Piore between what he calls lists and strategies.[1] Piore notes that we in the United States tend to think of minimum labor standards as a list of discrete items with which firms, for moral reasons, ought to comply. Despite the contemporary notion of a discrete set of standards, however, Piore says that the public pressure that led to the establishment of U.S. minimum labor standards was concerned with a holistic entity, the sweatshop. Properly understood, the fight for minimum labor standards in the United States revolved not simply around an effort to eliminate child labor, reduce working hours, enforce a minimum wage, and raise health and safety standards, but rather around eliminating the sweatshop way of doing business (or "business strategy"[2]).

Sweatshop business strategies reflect the low capital costs of garment production, which consist only of rent for the shop itself and for any sewing machines.[3] Low capital costs focus employers primarily on the labor cost of sewing garments—the per piece rate that they pay their workers. Given this preoccupation with labor cost, and the lack of attention to capital costs (and capital cost per piece), sweating employers do not focus on productivity. In fact, employers are not centrally involved in organizing production at all.[4]

The nature of this business strategy accounts for the type of labor violations that cluster in sweatshops: low wages, the employment of children whose low productivity does not matter to the employer, and the health and safety problems associated with lack of employer responsibility for shop layout and with crowding workers to minimize rent per worker.

The labor standard most critical to eliminating the sweatshop, Piore says, is

a minimum hourly rate high enough to create an employer concern with productivity. This rate alone will deter the use of low-productivity workers such as young children. . . . The reorganization required for an efficient work force itself remedies the most serious health and safety violations, . . . the major fire hazards, . . . and the excessively crowded work spaces which are a major source of health hazards. But a more basic result is that minimum hourly rates force the employer to extend his or her control over the work process and once he or she has done that, compliance with particular regulations becomes a marginal adjustment whereas before, compliance required the employer to extend his or her control into a realm of the business about which he or she was completely ignorant.[5]

The general lesson Piore draws from this is that the role of labor standards is to push business strategy toward productivity—and quality-enhancing types of competition—and away from reliance on low wages, high levels of physical effort, and worker vulnerability.

From Mass Production to Low-Social-Standard Export Processing

The period since the fight to establish minimum labor standards that would help eliminate sweatshops is now thought of as the age of mass production. Mass production is a business strategy based on using scientific management to subdivide production into small operations, and then developing machinery dedicated to performing the resulting, highly simplified tasks. Mass production is limited by the size of the market because specialized machinery cannot be readily redeployed to serve other markets. In markets for low-cost, low-quality goods, mass producers can be outcompeted at low volumes by sweatshops. In low-volume production of specialized, high-quality goods, mass production can be outcompeted by craft production (and, recently, by flexible production that combines broadly skilled workers with more flexible capital equipment).

Minimum labor standards contributed to the receptivity of labor-intensive employers to mass production by, as Piore suggests, making them focus on productivity. As it diffused, mass production, in turn, helped eliminate labor standards violations characteristic of sweatshops. Mass production did this because it involved employer control of production and because its capital intensity led employers to worry about minimizing capital costs and thus raising output per worker. The focus on productivity and capital costs contributed to a decline in child labor, to a lessening of individual employers' preoccupation with cutting wages, and to increased employer capacity to eliminate health and safety problems. Employer interest in extending the market for mass production goods also created a macroeconomic reason for employers to accept wage increases.

Of course, while mass production helped eliminate the low wages, child labor, and health and safety problems characteristic of sweatshops, it also had some undesirable consequences. As Piore notes, mass production created monotonous jobs and pressure to increase the work pace to reduce capital costs. Managerial fears of work stoppages that would paralyze expensive interconnected mass production lines also reinforced opposition to unions, at least until employers perceived unions as a means of increasing wages generally and thus the consumption of mass-produced goods.

Acknowledging its limits, mass production helped deliver a generation of material prosperity in the United States after the Depression and World War II. Labor standards and workers' exercise of basic labor rights played a central role in the institutional structure that generated this prosperity.[6] In the workplace, industrial unions negotiated work rules and grievance procedures that ameliorated the potential for speed-up while simultaneously assuring management that unionized mass producers would not face random work stoppages. In large mass production firms, unions negotiated cost-of-living adjustments and "annual improvement factor" wage increases that kept blue-collar real wages growing at roughly 3 percent per year. In smaller, less capital-intensive, and more commonly non-union firms the minimum wage ensured that sweatshop strategies could not reemerge to challenge mass production. Union political influence helped to establish unemployment compensation and social security systems that sustained consumer demand during economic downturns. Taken together, unions and the minimum labor standards and social insurance schemes that they helped construct prevented a reoccurrence of the kind of underconsumption crisis thought to have produced the Great Depression. Aggregate demand now kept up with potential output as mass production diffused and deepened.

Since the early 1970s, the prosperity of the postwar mass production Golden Age in the United States has passed. In retrospect, this seems inevitable given the way mass production designed production worker jobs to require minimal formal education and on-the-job training. Advances in telecommunications and reductions in transportation costs have made it possible for developing countries to approach advanced country productivity levels in mass-production operations. Multinationals have played a critical role in the transfer of the necessary maintenance skills and managerial knowledge. With production now spanning labor markets with vastly different wage levels, and in the absence of any regulatory structure to prevent it, wages and social standards generally have been forcefully reinserted into competition. In export-processing zones and in the United States itself, this global competition has also exacerbated the traditional labor standard problems of mass production, including high levels of work intensity and opposition to unions.

As a result, if the diffusion of mass production in advanced economies helped eliminate classic sweatshops, its diffusion throughout the global economy has given birth to a new phenomenon that is often called a sweatshop despite the fact that it is part of a global mass production system — the low-wage, low-social-standard export-processing plant. Some of these plants actually involve sweating in the sense that they perform highly labor-intensive operations spun off from mass production firms, but in which capital costs are irrelevant and managerial supervision of the production process is limited (e.g., sewing large volumes of shirt sleeves rather than whole shorts and some wire harness assembly) (Green, this volume). Increasingly, these plants practice mass production even within their internal operations, combining significant capital costs and managerial attention to productivity with efforts to lower labor and environmental costs.

What this analysis suggests is that the real enemy of labor and other social standards today is the new business strategy that gives rise to low-social-standard export-processing plants—that is, the effort to compete by combining low social standards with mass production.[7] If so, the real challenge facing the international labor rights movement is to eliminate this business strategy and give birth to an alternative one. In the context of this challenge, the notion of a Social Charter, a term imported from Europe during the recent debate about a North American Free Trade Agreement (or NAFTA), takes on a new meaning. Rather than a list, a set of important but separate social principles that are threatened by economic integration between high- and low-standard countries, a Social Charter can be seen as a tool for pushing employers toward an alternative to low-wage, low-social-standard mass production. The next section suggests that the NAFTA debate brought the international labor rights movement toward the understanding of labor standards and a Social Charter as tools for shaping employer business strategy.

From List to Strategy: The Evolution of the U.S. International Labor Rights Movement

Until recently, the notion of labor standards as a list of moral principles has been the dominant one put forward by the U.S. coalition for international labor rights.[8] The emphasis on norms goes back, in part, to the emergence of the U.S. coalition out of the human rights groups catalyzed by the Carter administration's emphasis on human rights in foreign policy.

After experiencing frustration trying to use human rights legislation to influence U.S. foreign policy, particularly in the first two years of President Reagan's first term, human rights activists conceived of the possibility of conditioning unilateral U.S. benefits to developing countries on the state of basic labor rights in these countries. This idea made it easier for human rights groups to gain support from the labor movement, which was worried about competition from low-labor-standard exporters. From a human rights perspective itself, labor rights conditionality put teeth in U.S. foreign policy designed to promote social progress in authoritarian developing countries.

The emphasis on labor standards as a list was evident in the language of the first U.S. trade-linked labor rights laws passed in 1983 and 1984. When U.S. human and labor rights activists drafted legislation to condition the tariff benefits granted to developing countries under the Caribbean Basin Initiative (CBI) and General System of Preferences (GSP), they listed five labor standards: the freedom to associate, the freedom to organize and bargain collectively, a prohibition on forced labor, a prohibition on child labor, and minimum standards for wages, hours, and health and safety.[9] This list has since been incorporated in several pieces of trade legislation and the laws governing the operation of the Overseas Private Investment Corporation (OPIC).[10]

In proposals for a North American Social Charter precipitated by the debate over labor and environmental standards in NAFTA, labor and other social concerns were again presented initially as a list of discrete social norms. In the labor area, this approach was a descendant of the same approach in earlier trade-linked labor rights legislation, with the list of five basic standards now augmented by an anti-discrimination provision. To these labor standards were added a separate list of environmental, consumer product, and agricultural standards. The idea of a list was even implicit in the title of a bill that incorporated these demands—the North American Environmental, Labor, and Agricultural Standards Act of 1992. This language contrasted with the more holistic perspective of NAFTA skeptics in Mexico, who called for a "Continental Trade and Development Plan."

That the social standards that non-governmental organizations (NGOs) wanted incorporated in trade agreements were perceived as a list of disconnected regulations was underscored by the *Wall Street Journal*'s labeling, in spring 1991, of one branch of the social standards coalition as a "motley crew."[11] To the *Wall Street Journal*, the environmentalists, unions, health and safety groups, child labor organizations, family farmer organizations, consumer safety groups, and religious organizations that fought the extension of fast track authority to negotiate a NAFTA and new GATT agreement (and many of which later fought NAFTA's passage) were a strange amalgam of special interest groups that shared only misplaced doubts about the benefits of trade liberalization.

There was, nonetheless, some movement in the NAFTA debate toward the alternative conception of social standards or a Social Charter as tools for shaping the dominant business strategy and overall pattern of development. A principle reason was that the debate around free trade with Mexico helped make concrete one vision of low-social-standard mass production, the *maquiladoras* (labor-intensive assembly and processing plants concentrated near Mexico's northern border).

Whatever the factual ambiguities regarding wages, health and safety standards, environmental conditions, and business strategy in and around maquiladoras, these plants were seen by many NAFTA opponents as an expression of what the wrong business strategy implies for the United States—a glimpse of the wages and living conditions that U.S. workers and communities might have to endure if the United States competes based on low labor, social, and environmental costs with countries that have much lower per capita GNPs. Understood in this way, maquilas were just the closest and most concentrated expression of a more general threat, the low-social-standard export-processing plant.

Fear of the maquiladorization of the United States began to consolidate the view among a broader cross-section of U.S. organizations that politics must change far more than this labor standard or that environmental standard. These diverse organizations groped instead toward the view that if the maquiladoras, as seen through their eyes, indicate what the future looks like, we have to define a different future.[12]

The potential of the loose, emergent U.S. international social standards coalition to transcend tactical cooperation does not deny the fragility of the links between its labor and environmental elements nor the weakness of the coalition's ties to major domestic constituencies such as minorities, women, and, to a lesser extent, community and regional development groups. It does suggest that what looked to the *Wall Street Journal* like a loose amalgam of activist organizations with unrelated social agendas looked from another perspective like an embryonic organic progressive coalition in American politics. And the notions of a Social Charter or alternative development strategy looked like instruments that might help the coalition to define a common vision of adaptation to globalization, in the process overcoming the boundaries between the particular concerns of its constituent elements and creating an enduring political force with the capacity to transcend the fragmented nature of progressive U.S. politics. This brings us to an attempt to sketch a vision that would make concrete an alternative to low-social-standard business strategies and give social forces opposed to and threatened by this a more organic unity.

The effort below to sketch an alternative to the low-social-standard mass production approach to economic integration does not imply a presumption that this will lead to its implementation. Such a sketch is seen as a means to unify the coalition in favor of stronger social standards and to increase support for standards more broadly. Outlining such a vision can help generate political support for new and higher standards; it is not a substitute for political power or the organizing necessary to achieve it.

An Alternative to Low-Social-Standard Mass Production

Global economic integration has undermined the national mass production pattern of development that generated prosperity for the United States during the post-World War II period. The national development strategies in individual European countries and highly protected developing countries such as Mexico have also broken down, probably irrevocably.

With these breakdowns, the United States and other countries have entered a period of economic uncertainty in which virtually all their major economic institutions—corporate structure, interfirm relations, labor-management relations, and government policies—are in flux. Amid this instability, particular interests have been searching for new approaches to protecting themselves and, less self-consciously, for a new institutional system that would restore the prosperity of the post-World War II period. In the United States, this search has led an increasing number of observers to see two possible futures: a high-wage, high-skill path that seeks to capitalize on the education and technology advantages that the United States has over developing countries and a low-social-standard path in which the United States tries to lower its labor, environmental, and other social standards enough to contain the movement of traditional mass production offshore.

Given the choice of pursuing a high-wage, high-skill or low-social-standard future, the central question becomes how to get to a high-wage path.[13] To think about this question, and to understand the importance of international labor standards, it helps to recognize that the essential difference between a high- and low-social-standard path concerns the way in which labor is used and the social relations at work.

In the low-wage path, lower-level workers will continue to have the highly delimited responsibilities emblematic of mass production. In large, core firms, these responsibilities might be integrated into a variant of the Japanese or *lean production* system. In lean production, job security, above-average wages, and investment in training (primarily acculturation to the norms of cooperation and teamwork, rather than deep, portable, general skills) might generate some worker commitment and give mass producers somewhat greater flexibility and higher quality. Especially in North America, nonetheless, lean production operates primarily as a more thorough imposition of scientific management and a way of extending machine-pacing and high levels of work intensity beyond the assembly line.[14] In more peripheral firms and in parts of large firms where management actions and the intensity of work destroy even the cooperation typical of lean production, a low-wage path would represent a return to the more primitive *autocratic management* reminiscent of the 1920s in the United States. Since managerially dominated lean production and autocratic management have both been mastered in low-wage countries such as Mexico, their predominance in the United States implies a continuation of downward labor standards harmonization.

By contrast, in a high-wage, high-skill path, work reorganization and teams would represent a fundamental expansion of the role of workers in production and toward less coerced cooperation. In developed countries, such *negotiated flexibility* would result in more complementary utilization of technology, flexible organizational structures, and workers' education, skills, and experience in ways that cannot be emulated in low-wage countries.[15] In developing countries, more negotiated and genuine workplace cooperation would generate more rapid human resource development and industrial upgrading than would lean production and autocratic management.[16]

One way of expressing the contrast between a high-wage, high-skill and a low-wage, low-skill future, then, is in terms of the predominance of each of the three variants of workplace relations described above — lean production, autocratic management, and negotiated flexibility. In the low-wage, low-skill future, negotiated flexibility would be confined primarily to professional workers and managers. These employees' skill and power as individuals or at the informal work group level would lead employers to recognize the counterproductive consequences of unilateral cuts in wages and benefits or other unilateral actions. In the high-wage, high-skill path, negotiated flexibility would also come to characterize social relations among non-professional workers, including not only the permanent employees of core firms, but contingent workers at core firms and workers in suppliers and small firms. Getting to a high-wage, high-skill path, then, means establishing conditions in which attempts to pursue low-social-standard business strategies do not lead lean production and autocratic shop floor relations to displace negotiated flexibility in all but a small part of the economy.

Three different types of labor standards are likely to be necessary to spread negotiated flexibility. Werner Sengenberger labels these three types promotive, preventive, and participative standards.[17] Promotive standards facilitate the development of human resources and technological knowledge necessary to pursue a high-wage strategy. Examples include laws requiring that firms spend money on training or join with unions to establish multi-employer apprenticeships or training consortia. Preventive standards make it more difficult to pursue low-wage strategies. The minimum wage and prevailing wage laws are classic U.S. examples. Participative standards, including basic labor rights, directly foster the workplace cooperation and labor-management consultation characteristic of high-wage strategies.

As Sengenberger notes, the three types of labor standards have synergistic effects. Promoting human resource-intensive strategies will have limited success if firms can easily pursue low-wage strategies. Companies will find ways around limits on low-wage strategies unless they have the tools necessary to follow human resource-intensive strategies. Worker representation and other participative standards facilitate the design and operation of effective promotive and protective rules and institutions. A corollary of the synergistic way the three types of standards operate is that the absence of any one type can render the others ineffective.[18] Without a sufficiently dense network of labor standards, low-social-standard strategies are likely to dominate major parts of the economy. This is not the same as saying that all labor standards are suitable and would promote productive development: standards must be adapted to the particular technological, economic, and social context in which they are introduced.[19]

Recently in the United States, there has been some agreement that promotive standards (e.g., more training) will increase investment in training and give employers the skills necessary to compete based on productivity and quality. Less consensus exists for restraints on low-wage strategies or the need for more widespread and powerful worker voice. However, given the historic attachment of U.S. firms to mass production and scientific management—as well as the opportunities they have to seek lower social standards at home or abroad—training alone will not generate a broad shift to high-wage, high-skill strategies.

To supplement promotive standards, domestic and international preventive standards are likely to be necessary. Relevant domestic preventive standards include a higher minimum wage and laws that foster industry-wide and occupation-specific wage patterns. Such patterns would help prevent low productivity, and would keep low-social-standard firms from undercutting more dynamic ones. To prevent the consolidation of a core-periphery economy in which human resource development and cooperation diffuse to only small parts of the economy, regulations may also be needed to protect temporary and part-time workers from being used as low-wage workers—for example, comparable worth legislation, laws mandating pro-rated benefits for part-time workers, and reforms of unemployment insurance to make it more accessible to contingent workers.

To complement stronger domestic constraints on low-wage strategies, analogous international constraints will be necessary. One critical standard will be an international minimum wage. Such a minimum could be defined by using the notion that workers as a whole should receive some minimum fraction (e.g., 40 percent) of manufacturing value-added to calculate an acceptable average wage for each country and then dividing this by about 2 based on the established notion that the minimum wage in individual countries should be roughly one-half the average manufacturing wage.[20] In many manufacturing and some service industries, of course, an international minimum alone would not constitute sufficient wage regulation any more than did the U.S. national minimum in the post–World War II period. Higher industry-specific international wage patterns are also necessary. In this regard, I have elsewhere proposed establishing a "Continental Improvement Factor" that raises Mexican auto industry wages toward U.S. and Canadian levels at a few percentage points per year.[21] As well as promoting more dynamic business strategies, industry-specific upward harmonization could, analogous to pattern bargaining in the postwar United States, help ensure that global consumption demand keeps pace with potential output.

Turning finally to participative standards, a variety of options have been proposed for the United States, which include legislatively mandated workplace committees with specified statutory rights.[22] Such committees would give worker representatives a consultative role even in non-union workplaces as well as specific rights in the implementation of health and safety standards, new training requirements, layoff notice laws, and so on. A second set of reforms of U.S. worker rights would deter U.S. employers from firing union supporters or intimidating worker attempts to form unions in other ways. While important reforms, neither workplace committees nor reaffirming the Wagner Act protections that gave birth to industrial unions are likely to spread negotiated flexibility beyond privileged employees in large core firms. The smaller enterprises and high degree of employment instability characteristic of most of the rest of the economy, especially the private service sector, make them inaccessible to unions or other forms of voice built, Wagner Act style, one workplace at a time.[23] More fundamental legal reforms and new forms of unions are necessary to transcend low-wage strategies in suppliers, small manufacturing firms, and the low-wage service sector.

In suppliers, facilitating the formation of unions that encompass both suppliers and core firms (and contingent and permanent workers) would limit the tendency to pursue low-wage strategies outside the core. In the low-wage service sector and manufacturing networks of small firms, geographically based occupational unionism could help raise productivity and transform dead end jobs into higher-wage, higher-skill jobs.[24] In some low-wage services, if productivity did not support wage increases negotiated by occupational unions, prices might rise and demand shrink.[25] Compensating expansions in demand for services with less polarized job structures could take place through decentralized delivery of public or state-subsidized social services—particularly child care, education (broadly defined to include all ages and levels as well as cultural activities), environmental clean-up and recycling, and infrastructure. In time, geographically based occupational unions could serve the full spectrum of U.S. occupations—from doctors to engineers to machinists to clerical workers to retail clerks—and become the predominant form of unionism in the United States.

As in the United States, enforcing labor rights in developing countries will be necessary to promote formation of unions adapted to the evolution of the economic structure and to promote the construction of preventive standards that limit domestic and international low-wage competition. The appropriate union forms may look similar to those in the United States. In Mexico, for example, more independent unions might push workplace reorganization toward negotiated forms of cooperation rather than autocratic management and lean production. Union forms appropriate for the service and small firm sectors in the United States may also have applicability in Mexico.[26]

Labor standards, of course, cannot carry the weight of transforming U.S. and global development alone. The necessary complementary policies—all the more likely to emerge in a context where labor has significant political power—include technological, industrial, and labor market policies that support the formation of geographically dense vertical and horizontal networks of dynamic manufacturing and service firms.[27]

Nationally and supranationally, regional development institutions disproportionately funded by prosperity in the most advanced regions would accelerate recovery in depressed areas and upward harmonization in developing countries. Macoeconomic policy coordination would help bring renewed global expansion. Shorter work time at the national and international level would help ensure full employment.

Successful institutionalization of an alternative to low-social-standard business strategies would yield enormous economic, social, and environmental benefits. Some of the economic benefits would result from giving more than a select few workers the skills and commitment to participate in efforts to improve productivity, quality, and service. The geographical proximity and social relations associated with manufacturing and service networks, in addition, would facilitate innovation, quality enhancement, and specialization based on modifying products and production processes at the level of the system or major subsystem as a whole. In contrast, mass production in which individual operations are dispersed across large geographical distances limits innovation beyond the level of the individual operation. Increasingly, as the potential for productivity growth within individual operations is exhausted, low-social-standard mass production risks being reduced to a search for lower-standard areas to place equally and sometimes less productive plants.[28] It would thus prolong the global productivity slowdown.

In the United States, low-social-standard mass production offers more relocation abroad by U.S. companies, more whipsawing of U.S. workers into accepting wage and benefit cuts, more recruitment through social networks of unskilled immigrants to take jobs that native workers (including the children of earlier immigrants) will not accept. The pools of jobless native workers will grow, wages will continue harmonizing downward, and the gap between professionals and less educated workers will yawn ever wider. Social division and violence in the United States will worsen. By contrast, embracing human resource development and networks of dynamic firms glued together, in part, by occupational unions offers to restore widespread opportunity in the U.S. labor market. The negotiated flexibility and occupational pride implied by a high-wage, high-skill strategy, moreover, would develop rather than corrode workers' dignity, personal capacities, and ties with members of other demographic and lifestyle groups on the job. In sum, social cohesion and a new sense of community could be undergirded by a shift in economic strategy.

Environmentally, the notion of a high-wage, high-skill strategy dispels the notion that there is, in the long run, a trade-off between jobs and the environment. A high-wage, high-skill future offers both greater economic promise and a cleaner environment. Moreover, intelligently applied environmental standards, as with labor standards, could yield dynamic economic benefits because they help rule out low-social-standard strategies. At worst, complying with tougher standards would require only marginal adjustment for flexible producers that see the capacity to adopt new technologies and adapt to new customer demands as basic to their survival. A high-wage, high-skill path also implies both a more efficient use of resources and an increasing appreciation of quality and specialized products rather than quantity. It represents a limited break with the assumption that more is better, a perspective reinforced since World War II by mainstream economics and the embrace of mass consumption. Shorter work time, particularly if accompanied by collective forms of non-work activity (including education and cultural activities) could further enhance a departure from material (and thus resource) consumption as an activity and source of identity. Finally, the social cohesion, at an international and national level, characteristic of a high-skill future would facilitate negotiation of any environmentally necessary limits on the use or production of particular resources, goods, or waste.

Restoring Labor's Place in the U.S. and Global Economies

The title of this volume echoes the normative thrust of much of the recent advocacy for international labor rights. Unfortunately, winning a taxonomic battle over whether labor rights should be classified as human rights will not, by itself, achieve improvements in labor standards.

Because of the fragile place of unions and labor rights in U.S. society, the limits of normative advocacy for international standards are particularly severe in the United States (and in the international forums in which we are the strongest power). Only for a brief period in the aftermath of the Great Depression have unions in the individualistic United States been seen as an essential institution. Unions, contractual wage rules, and industry-wide pattern bargaining were seen as critical to preventing a reoccurrence of the mass unemployment of the Depression. They checked managerial power in the workplace and corporate power outside it. In politics, unions fought for a social agenda widely seen as benefiting society as a whole, not only their own members.

Globalization has revealed just how contingent was the postwar place of labor in U.S. society. The core labor standards of the past, union wages and work rules, are now seen as contributing to the decline of U.S. industry. The buffeting of U.S. giants such as General Motors and IBM by foreign competition reduces the perceived need for countervailing corporate power. In politics, much of the public sees unions as a high-wage special interest fighting to protect its own membership, often at the expense of lower-wage workers.

U.S. proponents of international labor rights cannot wish away the ambivalence of U.S. society toward unions and thus toward labor rights. As long as unions and labor standards are seen as contributing to our economic problems, not to their solution, many in the United States will remain unconvinced that stronger international labor rights are really a good idea.

To bring the argument for international labor standards to the center of U.S. political debate requires directly addressing the view that labor standards and strong unions compete with economic goals. This chapter argues that the way to do this is to recognize that two fundamentally different business strategies now compete with each other in the U.S. and global economies. One, low-social-standard mass production, threatens to promote continuing economic decline, particularly for less skilled workers in the United States. An alternative, human resource–intensive business strategy promises a brighter economic future and superior social standards. Of critical importance to the case for labor rights, empirical study indicates that wide adoption of high-wage, high-skill strategies will not take place without significant strengthening of both U.S. and international labor standards. Designed to promote a change in business strategies rather than simply to prevent violation of a list

of moral norms, labor standards would help consolidate the cooperation within and among firms characteristic of an economically dynamic,
socially sustainable development path.

In sum, environmental, agricultural, consumer product, and labor
groups face a common enemy—that low-social-standard mass production business strategies will become increasingly dominant within an
unregulated regional and global economy. The same possibility threatens less skilled workers in the United States and the organizations of
workers, minorities, and women that represent them. Recognition of
this common enemy increased during the U.S.-Mexico free trade debate
due to the fear that NAFTA might generalize the low wages, environmental standards, and living conditions perceived in the *maquiladoras*.
By going beyond their common fear of the low-social-standard mass production that maquilas represent, and by trying to define a shared vision
of an alternative, the disparate groups that make up the social standards
coalition might coalesce into a more enduring and powerful strategic as
opposed to tactical alliance. Only in this way will these groups, and the
broader population to which they appeal, come to recognize the central place of labor and labor standards in economic prosperity as well
as social justice. Only in this way will they come to share Ray Marshall's
conviction that international labor standards that preserve labor's place
must, and can, be implemented.

Notes

1. This chapter aims to develop, in ways useful to proponents of international
labor rights, the ideas of Michael Piore. See Michael J. Piore, "Labor Standards
and Business Strategies," in *Labor Standards and Development in the Global Economy*,
ed. Stephen A. Herzenberg and Jorge F. Pérez-López (Washington, D.C.: U.S.
Department of Labor, Bureau of International Labor Affairs, 1990). This author
greatly appreciates the helpful conversations and comments on an earlier draft
provided by Howard Wial.

2. Piore's notion of business strategy includes the decisions firms make about
which markets to compete in and how to organize production to succeed in
these markets (Ibid., p. 35).

3. In homework, the clearest expression of sweating as a business strategy,
even these minimal capital costs are eliminated as the worker pays the rent for
the sewing machine and for the place in which work is performed.

4. Readers may find it implausible that sweatshop employers do not try to
improve productivity because it seems such an obvious way of reducing labor
costs per piece. It seems this way only because of the predominance today of
mass production, in which (see text below) employers do have a central role in
improving productivity. Most low-quality apparel producers in the global economy today are low-wage mass producers that produce standardized garments.
For evidence, see U.S. Congress, Office of Technology Assessment (OTA), *U.S.-*

Mexico Trade: Pulling Together or Pulling Apart (Washington, D.C.: U.S. Government Printing Office, Oct. 92), chap. 9. Except at very low volumes, mass producers outcompete pure sweatshops in which employers do not reorganize production (based on scientific management). Corroborating this claim, child labor in the United States, and in export-processing zones, consists primarily of increasing employment among young teenagers rather than even younger, and less productive, employees. In manufacturing today, sweatshops—and the employment of young children—exist primarily in the protected industries of developing countries or in specialized traditional production for export (e.g., rugs and carpets) that faces no mass production competition. For evidence, see Bureau of International Labor Affairs, *International Workers' Rights, Part I: International Child Labor Problems* (Washington, D.C.: U.S. Department of Labor, 1992).

5. Ibid., p. 38.

6. Two books that elaborate the role of unions and labor standards in postwar prosperity are Michael J. Piore and Charles F. Sabel, *The Second Industrial Divide* (New York: Basic Books, 1984) and Ray Marshall, *Unheard Voices: Labor and Economic Policy in a Competitive World* (New York: Basic Books, 1987).

7. It is tempting to give low-social-standard mass production the acronym LOSSMAP, which suggests that moving down this path represents having "lost our way."

8. As well as observation of the Washington debate about international labor rights over a period of five years, this section draws on interviews conducted in early 1991 with Pharis Harvey, director of the International Labor Rights Fund, and John Cavanagh of the Institute for Policy Studies.

9. The legislation originally included a sixth standard—against discrimination—but this was dropped as a political compromise. Karen F. Travis, "Women in Global Production and Worker Rights Provisions in U.S. Trade Laws," *Yale Journal of International Law* 17, no. 1 (Winter 1992).

10. An example indicates of the normative emphasis of the international labor rights community. When I asked one of its leading members if he could suggest a development economist sympathetic to the labor and human rights perspective who might participate in a 1988 conference, he half-jokingly responded, "You can't get here from there." Implicitly, he understood economics and labor rights as separate if not competing concerns.

11. Part of the coalition took this tag as its name for the next two years (the Mobilization on Development, Trade, Labor, and the Environment, or MODTLE).

12. For brief discussions of the anti-NAFTA coalition and its origins, see Jeremy Brecher and Tim Costello, *Global Village vs. Global Pillage: A One-World Strategy for Labor* (Washington, D.C.: International Labor Rights Education and Research Fund, 1991), pp. 32–34. See also Bob Davis, "Fighting 'NAFTA': Free-Trade Pact Spurs a Diverse Coalition of Grass-Roots Foes," *Wall Street Journal*, Dec. 23, 1992, pp. A-1, A-6.

13. The rest of this section draws substantially from OTA, *U.S.-Mexico Trade*, which I helped write. See also Stephen Herzenberg, "Towards a Cooperative Commonwealth? Labor and Restructuring in the U.S. and Canadian Auto Industries," unpub. Ph.D. diss., Massachusetts Institute of Technology, 1991, esp. chaps. 12 and 1.

14. For some evidence from the auto industry, see Stephen Herzenberg, "Whither Social Unionism? Labor and Restructuring in the U.S. Auto Indus-

try," in *Canadian and American Labour Respond: Economic Restructuring and Union Strategies*, ed. Jane Jenson and Rhiann Mahon (Philadelphia: Temple University Press, 1993).

15. The identification of lean production, autocratic management, and negotiated flexibility as alternative patterns of flexible workplace social relations is based in part on detailed studies of individual workplaces. For evidence and a more extended analytical discussion, see ibid. chaps. 3 and 8–11, especially chap. 11C. For an abbreviated version of the same analysis, see Stephen Herzenberg, "Whither Social Unionism?" in *Canadian and American Labour Respond*, ed. Jenson and Mahon.

16. For a brief discussion of workplace relations in Mexico, including examples of lean production, autocratic management, and negotiated flexibility, see OTA, *U.S.-Mexico Trade*, esp. pp. 81–86.

17. See Werner Sengenberger, *The Role of Labour Standards in Industrial Restructuring: Participation, Protection, and Promotion* (Discussion Paper 19; Geneva: International Institute for Labor Studies, 1990).

18. One of the reasons much of the U.S. economy is now pursuing low-wage strategies is because training and technology institutions that promote high-wage strategies were not highly developed in the mass production era. As a result, the protective (e.g., pattern bargaining) and participative (e.g., industry-wide unions) institutions that did exist after World War II have been undermined since the 1970s by companies that saw no alternative to low-social-standard mass production (a strategy they pursued first in the southern United States and now in developing countries).

19. Some of the critical labor standards of the post-World War II decades, such as narrow job classifications, could therefore impede the pursuit of high-wage national development. Union tactics regarding when to concede work rules—when enough new labor standards are being gained in exchange that are appropriate to a high-wage future—are enormously complex.

20. For some discussion of ways of implementing an international minimum wage, see Richard Rothstein, "Setting the Standard: International Labor Rights and U.S. Trade Policy," *Briefing Papers* (Economic Policy Institute, Washington, DC, March 1993).

21. See Stephen Herzenberg, "Continental Integration and the Future of the North American Auto Sector," in *Driving Continentally*, ed. Maureen Appel Molot (Ottawa: Carleton University Press, 1993).

22. For a summary and additional references, see OTA, *U.S.-Mexico Trade*, chap. 2.

23. This is a central reason that in Canada, which makes union organization easier within a Wagner Act workplace-based model, unionization is low in small firms and the private service sector, and income inequality has begun to grow.

24. For an extended discussion of the potential of occupational unionism in the low-wage service sector, and of specific legal proposals that would promote such unions, see Howard Wial, "The Emerging Organizational Structure of Unionism in Low-Wage Services," *Rutgers Law Review* 45, no. 4 (Summer 1993).

25. I owe this point to Eileen Appelbaum.

26. The Mexican Accord on Productivity and Quality, signed by labor, business, peasant, and government representatives on May 25, 1992, explicitly recognizes (in principle) the importance of unions and productivity-based wages to transcending footloose, low-social-standard mass production and to nourishing labor-management, assembler-supplier, and interfirm cooperation in geographi-

cally integrated small firm industrial networks. A progressive implementation of this vision is unimaginable without a preceding increase in the independence of the trade union movement from the government.

27. Deepening the economic and social ties among geographically linked enterprises also implies an increasing importance of regional government— groups of states and, in border areas in North America, of U.S. and Mexican states or U.S. states and Canadian provinces. Expanding the authority of relatively accessible regional governments could help rejuvenate democracy and the notion of "local control" and provide the confidence necessary to delegate responsibility for essential global rules to more distant, multilateral institutions.

28. Plants relocated to lower-standard areas may be less productive and flexible if they adapt more autocratic management as opposed to lean production. In addition, as suggested in the text, greater dispersal of production implies a loss in dynamic agglomeration economies.

Chapter 6
At the Junction of the Global and the Local
Transnational Industry and Women Workers in the Caribbean

Cecilia Green

The World Market Factory and Transnational Production

The world market factory is the site of the rendezvous between the global and the local. "World market factory" refers to globally dispersed production units home to "outsourcing" of manufacturing production for export to developed country markets. These enterprises are usually foreign subsidiaries or local contracting firms engaged exclusively in the assembly, subassembly, or finishing of manufactured products for a predetermined export market. They usually take advantage of special offshore assembly tax and tariff provisions put into place by many third world "host" governments on the one hand and advanced capitalist "home" governments on the other.

The typical arrangement observed in the Caribbean allows a foreign company—usually American, sometimes German or Japanese, but also increasingly Hong Kong Chinese, South Korean, or Taiwanese—to set up an offshore facility for the assembly or subassembly of goods. These operations use low-cost, labor-intensive methods and precut or prefabricated components supplied by the parent body. The finished or semi-finished products are then exported back to the home country (or perhaps first transfered to another third world subsidiary for finishing), where duty is paid only on the value added by the foreign operations. In the host country, companies can take advantage of cheap and compliant labor, as well as special fiscal concessions, subsidized facilities and infrastructure, and — they hope — a "stable" political climate.

In relation to capital investment, technology, raw materials, management decisions, markets, and profits, these outsourcing enterprises are completely sealed off from the local host economy. Their only links with the latter are through the labor market and central government. Their insulation from particular host economies and their homogeneous global character are underscored by their frequent location in special "export processing zones" (EPZs) that provide direct international access and bypass national customs barriers.

The typical unit is a labor-intensive light manufacturing operation employing mainly female assembly line workers at low levels of skill and pay. The most common examples are garment and semiconductor electronics assembly enterprises. The requirements and characteristics of garment and electronics assembly are highly compatible with the conditions offered by offshore facilities, requiring relatively light capital investment, high labor/low-skill intensity, and easy product transportability. The International Confederation of Free Trade Unions reports that "electronics components are well suited to 'offshore' assembly operations because they have a high value in relation to volume and weight so that transport costs are low."[1]

Technological advances in telecommunications and transportation have greatly reduced the cost and time required for world-wide commerce. In addition, garments and electronics constitute mass consumer goods with unlimited demand schedules, and the pressures to keep cheapening them are enormous. This has a particular significance for the United States, whose main rivals in the field often enjoy much lower labor costs.

Electronics and garments will provide the industry focus for this paper. Other products typically produced in export-processing zones are "footwear, leather products, plastics, toys, optical goods, sporting goods, furniture, car parts, housewares, artificial flowers, and minor transport equipment."[2] For most Third World countries, these are known as "non-traditional exports" to distinguish them from the raw materials exports of the colonial era. However, among them, clothing, textiles and footwear constitute a relatively more traditional and long-established category of merchandise exports — especially in those countries which have developed a national industrial base.

From the point of view of the parent company the main rationale for an offshore facility is the transfer of the labor-intensive portion of manufacturing operations to labor-cheap areas in order to maintain product competitiveness on the home and international markets. From

the point of view of the host country, labor-intensive foreign manufacturing operations are considered an ideal development aid since they
are "instant" bearers of multiple jobs and foreign exchange, two factors
which are in critical short supply in small dependent nations like those
of the Caribbean.

Indeed, enclave enterprises or world market factories are a "logical" offshoot of the unfolding global economy. They concentrate a
number of trends: the cross-cutting of corporate economic systems
and dependent national economic systems; an international (and intra-
national) division of labor between capital- and technology-intensive,
high-skill, high-wage, high-consumption areas on one hand, and capital-
and technology-poor, low-skill, low-wage, low-consumption areas on the
other. They also reflect a sexual and racial division of labor whereby
women, especially third world and racial or ethnic minority and immigrant women, form a special reserve pool of unskilled labor from which
they can be pulled at any time to fulfill specific requirements of international capital.

Subcontracting is becoming a recognized form of neocolonial pene-
tration of third world countries. It is the lowest link in the worldwide
chain of supply that also includes a division of labor among "developing" countries and within "developed" countries: Hong Kong's apparel
industry has begun to subcontract to countries like Bangladesh and
China, which also implemented the reverse process.[3] The U.S. high-
fashion domestic industry is critically dependent on small, "flexible"
contract shops owned by immigrant entrepreneurs in urban centers like
New York, Los Angeles, and Miami.[4] Within developing countries, too,
large local operators subcontract out garment orders to small local firms
and individuals who themselves may fare little better than their workers.[5]

International subcontracting is sometimes used as a general term to
cover both production by directly owned subsidiaries and production
contracted between nominally independent parties.[6] This perhaps appropriately reflects the fact that "host" enterprises, no matter the nature
of their ownership, are usually limited to simple assembly operations
that do not involve the sharing of industry technology and decision-
making. They involve little more than the purveyance of labor for assem-
bling imported components according to predetermined specifications.

A specific pattern has emerged in home/host production relations
whereby local electronics enterprises, especially those making semi-
conductors and other computer components, tend to be subsidiaries of
transnational companies, while the garment industry is much more reliant on the subcontracting of independent local suppliers and on non-
manufacturing intermediaries (jobbers, buyers, trading companies, retail chains). Some observers see the tighter and more direct control by

transnational electronics firms over local operations rooted in the concern to safeguard the firm's technology. In contrast, the greater reliance on subcontracting in the garment industry reflects a need to maintain flexibility and diversity of supply in the face of rapidly changing fashion.[7]

Subcontracting arrangements may be long term, short term, or for a single batch. Most locally owned electronics operations in the third world survive, if at all, on long-term subcontracting agreements with foreign parties. Another notable type of transnational arrangement that stops short of outright ownership is the management-contract system, where local operations are directed by a transnational team of engineers and managers supplied by a foreign corporation or consortium.[8]

In the global garment industry, increasing subcontracting at the assembly level is being paralleled by increasing concentration, automation, and integration at the preassembly textile fabrication, design, and manufacturing level, and at the postassembly retail sales level. Moreover, certain sectors of the apparel industry like standardized basic garments produced by giant firms are on the threshold of virtually eliminating labor-intensive assembly operations.[9]

This kind of high-tech/low-tech bifurcation has been the operational basis of the semiconductor industry from its inception. It is increasingly being reinforced by subindustrial segmentation between a competitive mass consumer industry and highly specialized, capital-intensive production for fields like defense, medicine, genetic engineering, and communications. Here, too, subcontracting is deployed "as part of a strategy to diversify risks and lower production costs. [It] creates links between advanced sectors and producers of simple components."[10]

The Legacy of Enclave Production in the Caribbean

Let us move from the global level to the local space of the host countries of the Caribbean. The "modern" Caribbean began its history as the sugar plantation enclave of European imperial systems. Workers from across the seas in Africa were brought to work the land in a forced labor system to produce sugar for European consumers and profits for European settler planters and their commercial agents. Today's West Indian might perhaps best understand his or her economy in terms of the past, in the heyday of the absentee planter, when the owner did not live in the country, the plantation was not his or her sole investment or way of life, and decisions about the fate of the slaves emanated from distant shores.

Afro-Caribbean society developed both in spite of and in accommodation and resistance to slave plantation society. Relatively autonomous Afro-Caribbean social forms and domestic economies sprouted in the interstices of "enclave sectors" tied directly to metropolitan capital and markets. But these would-be domestic economies were never allowed to flourish. They either maintained an uneasy coexistence with the dominant colonial-capitalist enclaves, or they came into direct conflict with the interests of those enclaves. In the long run, all "domestic" modes of production were functionally subordinated to "colonial" or "neocolonial" modes of production.[11] Furthermore, the efforts of working-class and peasant women in particular to provide for domestic needs (for example, through subsistence cultivation and marketing) and ensure the reproduction of labor power—or the sheer survival of their families— have always been uncounted and un- or under-paid. These "informal" initiatives have been steadily marginalized in the neocolonial agenda, even as they provide refuge and sustenance for increasing numbers of people shut out of the "formal" economy, and even though they are indispensable for the reproduction of the formal economy itself.[12]

In some islands, the decline of the planter class gave rise in the twentieth century to the consolidation of several plantations into subsidiary units of giant corporations. When transnationals exploiting mineral resources like bauxite and oil developed alongside transnationals in sugar production, the economies in which this took place—Jamaica, Guyana, Trinidad—came to be characterized as "mixed plantation-mineral export economies" rather than just "plantation economies."[13] These sectors, which so dominated the life of these countries, constituted enclave industries in which capital, technology, and markets were externally based. Very few backward and forward linkages were formed with the rest of the economy. In this type of development, it was the land and labor of the Caribbean people that were being exploited for overseas use and profit. These industries were location- and capital-specific.

The creation of the banana industry in the Windward Islands (as in Jamaica) provided another variation on the theme of export enclave– type development. In this case the transnational corporation, while effectively controlling price, quality, shipping, harvesting-marketing time schedules, and all other conditions of "exchange," and relentlessly binding the farmers, mostly smallholders, to the cash-crop imperative (at the expense of food production for the domestic market as well as agricultural diversification), relied on local "marketing boards" to manage the extraction of surplus from the growers and ensure a steady supply of the fruit.

One analyst sees the marketing board in this situation as little more than "a state agency acting as an agent of a transnational corporation."[14] Meanwhile, the foreign corporation effectively controls production in this sector without getting its hands dirty or becoming embroiled in unpleasant labor relations.

In this so-called "traditional" sector, production is tied to the export market, diverting resources from the domestic economy for the profit of the company and generating very few backward and forward linkages or increments within the economy. The appearance of a sale is illusory. Not only is the price the farmer receives for his or her bananas a disguised form of a wage; it also pays the farmer *less than* the value of his or her labor power, which is subsidized through the extra hours spent grow-ing subsistence crops as well as through other types of "re/productive" labor[15] typically performed by women.[16]

Postwar import-substitution industry, on which postcolonial Carib-bean governments pinned their hopes for development, did not repre-sent a substantial divergence from this general pattern. In this strategy, transnational corporations that had previously exported their products to the Caribbean simply moved behind tariff walls erected to protect local (or, more accurately, on-site or domestic-market) industry. They established branch plants that assembled or put the finishing touches on manufactured components transfered from the appropriate company division. Here, the key asset for the company was not even so much cheap labor, but a captive market. This captive market was enhanced by the establishment of a subregional free trade zone, giving a particular advantage to those firms that had been first in line, since one branch plant could often satisfy the needs of the entire subregion.[17]

The more developed countries of the region, as favored sites for these industries due to their superior "economies of scale" potential, gained a head start that enabled them to penetrate less developed country mar-kets before the latter could develop an industrial capacity of their own. The fact that these firms did not even have to do market research, which would indicate some genuine ties with or commitment to the local econ-omy, reflected the "enclave" character. Even today, the import intensity of these companies' production structure has not been lessened by the conversion of some of them into joint ventures with 51 percent or more local ownership and continued licensing arrangements with the parent company. Import-substitution enterprises typically produce such things as metal appliances, processed foods, shoes, plastic goods, paint, and pharmaceuticals.

Today, the Caribbean is more import dependent than ever. It is faced with inputs into import-substitution industry (which never replaced the bulk of imports), and also with cheaper American imports spurred on by free trade inducements promoted by successive U.S. administrations. These imports are now displacing even the more locally rooted and longstanding import-substitution industries like apparel, and are further eroding the fragile basis of the Caribbean Community (CARICOM).[18]

Since the Caribbean produces what it does not consume and con-sumes what it does not produce, most local "entrepreneurial" activity

is centered around import-export trade, sales, real estate, construction, and commercial services such as insurance, cargo handling, and
travel. All of this service sector, "non-productive" activity—overwhelm-
ingly carried out, moreover, by "white" ethnic elites—is financially
underpinned by yet another enclave sector: commercial banking, mostly
foreign-owned. Foreign commercial banks in the third world are primarily interested in mediating export production and import consumption, and not in providing venture capital for would-be indigenous
resource-based entrepreneurs. One scholar reports on Barbados:

> In 1987 two sectors, personal and distribution, accounted for almost 40 percent
> of commercial credit in Barbados. . . . This lending preference is not atypical of
> the region. An earlier study of CARICOM . . . found a similar pattern in com-
> mercial bank lending, a pattern which still exists. Codrington . . . writes that
> "in 1986 almost a quarter of new consumer installment credit went toward the
> purchase of private motor cars [whereas] the amount of credit used for manu-
> facturing and agriculture grew very little."[19]

The most recent enclave-type industry to proliferate within Caribbean
shores—export-processing manufacturing enterprise—is therefore heir
to a long tradition of enclave development. Such enterprises formed
the basis of the "export promotion" thrust that succeeded the phase of
import substitution in a development pattern repeated throughout the
third world. The turn to export manufacturing was prompted on the one
hand by the disappointments of import substitution—its inefficiency,
high cost, low employment generation, high import dependence, and
depletion of foreign exchange reserves. On the other hand, it was driven
by the demand for cheap consumer goods in developed-country markets and by pressure from the World Bank and international investors
in the third world to cater to this demand to repay debts incurred by
import-substitution industrialization.

The Caribbean is one of a multitude of interchangeable locations
around the world that are being opportunistically exploited by American, German, Japanese, or Chinese (Hong Kong) companies. The type
of enclave enterprise resulting from this development represents the
classic Marxian attainment, on a global scale, of the degeneration of
human subjects, otherwise distinguished by race, culture, personality,
and so on, into labor-power clones.

Norman Girvan has summed up these different stages of Caribbean
"enclave" development thus:

> Basically the attraction in the first case was for utilizing the natural resources of
> the developing countries for the purpose of satisfying certain requirements in
> the metropolitan developed countries. The attraction in the second type of de-

velopment was to circumvent the tariff barriers in developing countries which had been set up to protect domestic industry . . . whereas in the third case within which the garment industry falls, the attraction is to use the cheap labor of the developing countries.[20]

Caribbean state economic policy has essentially created a jumble of unrelated, externally linked enclave sectors rather than undertake a painstaking policy of internal generation and integration. The task of building "national economies" (not in the autarkic or single-island sense) is therefore still ahead, and requires local and popularly based coordination among production, distribution, consumption, and social needs in the context of integration of the subregional economies.[21]

Women Workers, Global Capital, and National Development

Caribbean women workers joining the global assembly line are reduced to labor-power clones, interchangeable with their counterparts in other parts of the third world. From an investor's standpoint, different weights may be assigned to different factors. For example, marginally less labor docility might be weighed against geographic proximity and lower transport costs, or vice versa. But in every case the bottom line is the same: lowest possible cost of production to ensure the greatest possible profits.

From the point of view of women, no such reduction of human subjects takes place. When they enter the global assembly line and become functional objects of that international process, they do not leave themselves or their particular historical identities behind. The "local" is swept into the vortex of the "global," but through its own circuits it continues to have a certain (relatively autonomous) integrity. In fact, the world market factory experience becomes part of local Caribbean history. Caribbean women workers occupy positions in two histories at once: that of the "global assembly line," which presses to homogenize and standardize, and that of the particular Caribbean society or subregion with its unique cultural expression. While these histories merge at certain points, they are never identical. The local never "collapses" into the global. Any movement toward a real or symbolic identity between these two histories will be constantly disrupted by resistance, especially coming from those contesting their own absorption, as objects, into the global assembly line.

Neophyte Caribbean women workers do not necessarily, and certainly do not immediately, experience themselves as part of an international circuit or as located in a global space. That, for them, is still an abstraction. Above all, in terms of experience, they occupy a concrete local space. They are products of a particular Caribbean historical time; their consciousness is rooted in that time and space. This is not to say that a subtle reconstitution of their cultural values and modes is not taking place, but there is no doubt that if they were to be asked they would see this process of reinvention as located within the confines of a *Caribbean* identity.

The confrontation between Caribbean women workers and global capital within the world market factory is not a naked one. It is mediated through the national state, which, in its neocolonial agency, tends to line up behind the foreign subsidiary. This partisanship is not without its contradictions, and, in certain circumstances, the national state can be shamed into upholding the labor rights and sovereignty of its citizenry against the worst incursions and depredations of foreign capital. However, such support is invariably temporary or nominal and is easily betrayed or abandoned.

Trade unions, where they exist or are allowed to operate, also mediate the relationship. They are supposed to line up behind their women members, but they, too, play a contradictory and equivocal role. Traditionally, most unions in the Caribbean have been affiliated with political parties in a relationship whose origins are to be found in the two-pronged struggle against the colonial state, which consolidated the ascendancy of petty bourgeois nationalist leadership over the anti-colonial movement in the 1930s and 1940s. I have pointed out elsewhere:

Unfortunately for the workers, it has long been obvious that the trade union/political party link conservativizes the unions to a far greater extent than it radicalizes the politics of the party. In or out of power, the party may use its trade union affiliate to sabotage worker militancy, control access to jobs, and intimidate or influence potential voters. Women workers are the most frequent victims of these tactics, since, as persons excluded from the inner chambers of power, they are more likely to fall prey to either promises of a special alliance between members of an "old boys" network, or threats of a confrontation between male patrons.[22]

In the recent past, women have made up about 25 percent of union leadership and a much higher percentage of union support and behind-the-scenes organizational work. The "new" export-oriented strategy and obeisance to "structural adjustment"[23] demands from international lending institutions threaten to reduce even further the already low inclusion of women workers in unions. These programs entail pressure from local governments and foreign enterprises to halt or moderate union activity in the free trade zones. Governments in the subregion have called for twelve- to twenty-four-month moratoria on union activity within these zones, knowing full well that this gives foreign companies the time they need to develop anti-union strategies among their workforces.[24]

There are yet other parties involved. In this contest, Caribbean women workers are not just at the intersection of systems of oppression based on race, class, and gender. They are also at the intersection of various interventions on their behalf—some of which clash with each other. Major examples are contending labor organizations, local and international NGOs of elitist or "grassroots" bent (including those of the "women and development" model), and feminist or proto-feminist organizations. Unfortunately, some—though not all—replicate the same invidious distinctions as the institutions they are contesting.

If we focus for a moment on the poles of the counterpoised forces, we can better see the contradictory relation of women workers to the nation. At one extreme, there are the global circuits of capital or commodity production, converting everything in their paths, including labor power, into commodities. At the other extreme, there are the local circuits of human reproduction, involving families, communities, and informal economies, providing physical, emotional, and social nurturance to both "incorporated" and "unincorporated" sections of the population, and to which women have been central. The dependent national economy has literally blocked the internal channels of sustenance of these local circuits of human reproduction, diverting them more and more into the global marketplace.[25] In this latest stage of Anglophone Caribbean development, there is an unabashed shift toward incorporation into the U.S. periphery, alongside the Hispanic Caribbean (excluding Cuba), through various kinds of "free trade" arrangements, the most important of these coming under the rubric of the Caribbean Basin Initiative (CBI).[26]

Jamaica has gone furthest in devaluing its currency and structurally adjusting its economy into a new role as a cheap labor-supplying, export-processing adjunct of the United States economy. It has joined the Dominican Republic, Haiti, and Costa Rica as a major assembler of garments and other goods for the U.S. market. In 1988, Edward Seaga (Jamaica's prime minister at the time) reported in the *Wall Street Journal*: "Four years ago, we had four plants doing this kind of work with 2,000 or 3,000 people. Now there are more than 70 plants that employ 20,000."[27] It has been estimated that 10,000 local manufacturing jobs were lost under Seaga.[28] The situation is said to have worsened under the regime of Michael Manley, erstwhile protagonist of "democratic socialism," who is overseeing one of the largest privatization drives in the third world at the behest of the International Monetary Fund. During the 1980s, Jamaica received U.S. foreign aid behind only that of Israel and Egypt on a per capita basis. By 1992, the results of Jamaica's structural adjustment were typified in a report that Jamaican sugar workers were earning less per day than their counterparts in Haiti.[29]

Barbados, with a longer and less volatile tradition of export-processing dependency, presents a somewhat different profile. More vulnerable and dependent than Jamaica because of a narrower resource base and less diversified economy, Barbados nonetheless has relatively high labor costs. Many industries have already transfered from Barbados to the "less developed" islands. But it has no "Research and Development" infrastructure to speak of or national entrepreneurial base to handle a shift to higher-stage manufacturing. This is particularly significant since Singapore and Taiwan are the most widely admired models among Caribbean governments.[30]

While Jamaica's assembly production of garments for the U.S. market skyrocketed, substantially displacing and distressing the local garment industry, Barbados was experiencing a dramatic drop in both electronics and garment assembly exports to the United States, signaling the end of its pioneering export-processing "boom" based mostly on electronics assembly. A downward slide in the Barbadian economy was accelerated by the 1986 closing of Intel, a subsidiary of the giant American electronics company. The closing sent shockwaves through the economy when it threw more than one thousand persons out of work, most of them women. In fact, the closing of just two of the country's biggest exporters and employers, Intel and Playtex, reduced total exports to the United States from over $200 million in 1985 to $61 million in 1987.[31]

In 1991 the government of Barbados was forced to enter into negotiations with the IMF. While resisting a devaluation of the Barbadian dollar, the government devalued the country's social base and living standards, long considered high and stable by Caribbean standards.[32] It did this by laying off public sector employees, cutting wages 8 percent, and increasing consumption, payroll, and other taxes to address balance of payment difficulties.

The purported lack of competitiveness of Barbados' wage rates is reflected in a comparison of American Airlines data-processing subsidiaries located in Barbados and the Dominican Republic, where Dominican wages are 25 *percent* of the Barbadian rate. The disparity in wage rates between the two countries is partly a function of different labor traditions. Historically, the English-speaking Caribbean has had a strikingly higher level of unionization than has its Hispanic subregional counterpart.[33] This tradition, with all its limitations, is currently under attack. In recent years Caribbean labor leaders have witnessed—many, for the first time—the aggressive implementation of union-busting tactics, American style.

Caribbean Women and World Market Factories

Women have been affected by this new development strategy of import-ing food, importing end-of-the-line jobs, and "processing" exports for the U.S. market in three critical ways. First, as "traditional" managers of the home and feeders of the family (and also as the sole or main providers in many instances), they have to contend with imported food that is both expensive and low in nutritional value. Secondly, the im-portation of supermarket-packaged foods increasingly and permanently disrupts or displaces the longtime female roles of provision farmer and marketer of domestic food products. (About 70 percent of the market-ing of domestic food products is in the hands of independent female vendors.) Third, as a vast reserve of supposedly unskilled labor, women are the ones being pulled as low-wage workers into the new export-processing industries.

In the last ten years, a Non-Formal Youth Skills Training Program, sponsored by the Organization of American States and the U.S. Agency for International Development, has been put in place in the English-speaking islands to train young people for industrial jobs.[34] Among other things, the training program has a clear gender bias. Local ad-ministrators admit that pressure is put on them to churn out a certain quota of "trained" persons from crash courses within a certain time. The crash courses are all in a narrow range of occupations related to some form of assembly or service work. The overwhelming majority of "graduates" are women. Male training recipients, on the other hand, are encouraged to take advantage of a much wider range of craft skills training that offers genuine prospects for self-employment (sometimes complete with follow-up entrepreneurial counseling and support) or at least higher-paid, skilled occupations. Even within the garment facto-ries, the few positions on the shop floor classified as skilled are reserved for men.

The gender bias in training is particularly ironic for the women of the subregion, since their "formal schooling" profile has been consis-tently higher than that of men for some time. Even at the tertiary level, women are catching up with men, in terms of numbers, in a *few* "non-traditional" (for them) disciplines and significantly surpassing them in other, less influential fields. Secondary-level figures show a marked female preponderance. This has prompted exaggerated and unfounded claims of the "rise of matriarchy" and the "marginalization of the Black male" in the Caribbean, claims stemming from an inadequate analysis of the facts, as well as, no doubt, threatened-male hysteria.[35] I have ar-gued elsewhere that formal schooling equips women for a very narrow range of sex-typed jobs and decision-making responsibility, and, at any rate, is constrained by the limited structure of job opportunities in a dependent and gender-biased economy.[36]

Caribbean men do not have to rely as much on formal schooling to acquire higher-valued and better-remunerated craft skills or top managerial positions. Although, on a whole, they have less basic schooling than women and leave school earlier, they receive more vocational training and acquire more skills both on the job and institutionally. The briefest survey will show that they have a higher and far wider range of skills than Caribbean women, whose "white-collar" and "professional and technical" occupations—which, according to the census, constitute a clear majority of such occupations—are concentrated in nursing, teaching, data entry, secretarial, and other service sector occupations. Thus, "[while] female employment structure has more of a "white-collar" and therefore pseudo-status image, Caribbean men get paid more for what they do and, moreover, retain a near-monopoly on top administrative and management positions, even in sectors of employment dominated by women."[37]

In summary, women's craft skills tend to be seen as part of the low-valued or informal economy, while men's craft skills are seen as having an independent "trades" or entrepreneurial basis. Women are therefore more reliant on post-primary formal accreditation to gain social and economic valuation in their jobs. They still have a hard time transcending a kind of permanent "auxiliary" status, no matter where in the job hierarchy they find themselves.

In manufacturing, a former home-based seamstress may actually go through a de-skilling experience, both ideologically and materially, and make one-half to one-third the wage of a "tradesman" or maintenance man. In spite of the crippling unemployment and low wages that plague both sexes, working-class men enjoy a measure of stability compared to women based on the continuous reconstitution of the concepts of "skill" and "responsibility" in their favor. Unemployment among female heads of household, who tend to be older than the average woman worker or male heads of household, and who typically make up one-third to one-half of all household heads in the English-speaking Caribbean, is often twice that of their male counterparts.[38]

Not all "assembly line" trainees get factory jobs, and, for those who do not, emigration is seen as the inevitable solution. Unprecedented numbers of literate, well-educated Caribbean women migrate overseas in search of jobs, opportunities, and dignity. Indeed, for many of those who would like to but cannot migrate, the new factory work may promise a next-best escape from humiliating ties of dependence on boyfriends and various kinds of patronage for which Caribbean societies are well known, and which go against the grain of the other Caribbean tradition of female economic autonomy and provision for the family.[39]

For a few garment or electronics workers, this promise may be partially fulfilled. Here and there, a few determined, tough, enterprising, and hardworking women are able to take advantage of the incentive pay offered in these establishments (elusive to most workers), perhaps rise to the rank of supervisor, and save enough money to make the down payment on a housing unit or small business. However, for the vast majority of Caribbean women workers, factory work brings a fresh round of tribulations, and a new set of social relations. Often they prove to be deeply traumatic, raising the specter of a new, better-equipped, more efficient, at once more insidious and more detached form of colonialism.

Case Studies

I want to refer briefly to two examples from a 1987 survey of world market factories in the Eastern Caribbean island of St. Vincent.[40]

St. Vincent Children's Wear was owned by Bayliss Brothers of Cincinnati, Ohio, a former U.S. Industries company and now a subdivision of Hanson Trust, a giant conglomerate. Bayliss Brothers marketed an upscale line of children's apparel called "Polly Flinders," which was sold in big chain stores like Sears.

The factory in St. Vincent produced hand-smocked children's dresses, employing 230 in-factory workers and 1,500 home smockers. The company operated on a system of subcontracting, meeting orders from large retail companies like Sears. Thousands of stenciled, pre-cut fronts were smocked in rural Vincentian homes every week by "self-employed" smockers and then collected by eleven or twelve area supervisors for shipment back to the factory, where they were assembled into whole dresses by the workers.

The work of designing, styling, cutting, and distributing was all done at company headquarters in Cincinnati in an automated plant employing mostly women. When asked about the company's motive for locating in St. Vincent, the white, male American manager replied bluntly, "No American woman would sit at home and smock." Hand-smocking, which is far more durable and elastic than machine smocking, gives the product high quality and value, a fact reflected in the price.

Two things were striking about St. Vincent Children's Wear. One was that the company enjoyed special tariff privileges. When the finished goods reentered the U.S. market, duty was paid only on the valued added abroad. In fact, the immense amount of value added in Vincentian homes translated, for the smockers, all women, into extremely low piece-rate wages. A 1982 study found that the income of the St. Vincent smockers rarely exceeded $27 per month.[41] The authors designated smocking "the most exploitive kind of work found in St. Vincent."[42]

U.S. duties were paid based on the extremely low wages, not on the painstaking labor time expended. However, "value added" in St. Vincent was certainly put forward as a justification for the high price of the product. Secondly, although St. Vincent Children's Wear was one of the few enclave companies to boast of a unionized workforce and a lack of anti-union paranoia, only the 230 in-factory workers were unionized; the 1,500 home-based smockers conveniently spared the company "overhead expenses" or "labor troubles."

PICO (St. Vincent) Ltd, the other company studied, was a wholly owned subsidiary of PICO Products Inc. of Liverpool, New York, a manufacturer of cable T.V. products.[43] It employed 150 workers, nearly all women, to assemble electronic filters used in security systems for cable T.V. (These scramble and unscramble signals for the benefit of home subscribers.) PICO effectively "busted" a union with the government's complicity, dismissed pro-union workers, and set up a "Workers' Council"—in the words of a local newspaper, "a Humpty Dumpty euphemism for a company union, headed by a PICO supervisor."

Labor relations at PICO had been volatile from the beginning. Within a year of its establishment in 1981, the company was locked in a major struggle with the island's biggest and most powerful union over the question of recognition. The struggle prompted a report from the Labor commissioner that pointed to "a management apparently given to the frequent use of expletives" and found the company in contempt of a number of workers' rights. The union won certification, but labor relations never settled down. Three years later, another major labor dispute erupted, stemming from the dismissal of a shop steward, a central figure in the union. Again, the Labor commissioner ruled in favor of the employee, upholding her right to seek redress on the ground of unfair dismissal. When the employee sought reinstatement in her job, management refused to reinstate her and closed down the operations, locking out 136 employees. In the midst of many acrimonious exchanges, in which the bulk of the island's population appeared to take sides against the company, the government intervened on behalf of the company and negotiated conditions for the re-opening of the factory.

Upon reopening, the company ignored most of the government's conditions, selected 50 of 138 workers for rehire, kicked out the union, and set up a Workers' Council and new management structures around the key figure of a female Vincentian assistant manager. This woman was expected to mediate between the American manager and the Vincentian "girls." In an interview, she explained to me that she had worked in the United States so she understood the requirements of American businesses, and she was both Vincentian and female so she understood the needs of the "girls." She was central to the functioning of the workers' council and the training of supervisors—who were represented on the council—to resolve disputes through persuasion and conciliation. The Workers' Council essentially functioned as a regular weekly meeting between worker representatives and the assistant manager "to discuss and find solutions to problems." The council also "negotiated" wage increases, on the basis of an individual reward system.

The intent was clearly to keep unions out and to persuade workers that they were being given a unique opportunity for self-management. Workers were being imbued with a new philosophy of individual responsibility and individual reward. They were told that this was their own union, that they would be able to resolve problems by themselves. Some of the workers' aversion to the abrasive, confrontational style of the male union leaders, which seemed to come down to a "macho stand-off" or battle of the wills between men (especially between the union president and the company president), was subtly manipulated and played upon to induce a sense of empowerment among the women.

The earlier volatility of labor relations at PICO had been replaced by the incorporation of some workers into a new identity as "PICO ladies," the very term used by a few of the workers I talked to. These workers distinguished themselves with pride from the "ruffians" or "unruly" women at the neighboring St. Vincent Children's Wear, where shopfloor relations were seen as turbulent and steeped in "confusion." A Children's Wear employee told me that, in spite of the higher wages she enjoyed at that company, she would prefer to work at PICO because of the demure and respectable image offered to the workers there. Other workers from both companies, however, were perfectly able to see through the ideological manipulation at work in PICO management, and understood that workers' councils served primarily to promote conformity and loyalty to the company and to isolate workers from a collective and integrated working people's movement. Interestingly, all the workers I spoke to expressed preference for a "real" union (as opposed to a company union), even when they were critical of local unions and their style of engagement.

This was not surprising. A major complaint of the expatriate company managers I spoke to was that people in these islands were too "pro-union," and in their view this included Labor Department officials. Needless to say, this point of view was not shared by any of the union officials or women workers who expressed their thoughts to me. One point of view that did strike me, however, was the concern and deep-seated desire of women workers to speak for themselves, and to participate in and determine their own representation.

Conclusion: Theoretical Implications

There are three processes that are critical to our understanding of the agenda for liberation of Caribbean women workers. These are the dynamics of the rendezvous between the global and the local, the intersections of national, racial, class, and gender subordination, and the interpenetration of the first and third worlds. In reality and up close, the patchwork or tapestry of interwoven and contradictory "histories" that consciously or unconsciously compose the lives of Caribbean women workers is much more complex and detailed.

What are all the pieces of the puzzle? Below, I consider briefly the overlapping parts of the bigger picture in which Caribbean women workers are "locally embedded," which one would need to know in order to make sense of their situation. These serve as both a survey and an agenda for future research.

(1) The transnational production of garments and electronics. What are the specific social and technical international relations of production, distribution, and consumption in each industry?

(2) The world market factory and its location in special free trade zones—not to be confused with the industry as a whole. What are the social relations and politics of the export processing zone enterprises?

(3) The dependent or peripheral nation-state, transmission belt of neocolonial relations, but not without contradiction and countervailing tendencies. What are and have been the national development trajectory and strategies? What is the relation of various classes and class subdivisions to the nation and to the national development trajectory?

(4) The histories of working-class Caribbean women in families, communities, and the national economy. What clues can their lives and their heterogeneous and contradictory relations to their multifaceted world provide as to how to place human needs at the center of a liberating political project?

(5) The histories and dynamics of labor-based, gender-based, nationalist, and other grassroots or "alternative development" organizations. To what extent do these different groups vie for different aspects of women's consciousness, and to what extent do they see themselves and their projects as alternatives to each other?

To what extent do they and can they work together to achieve a multifaceted vision and strategy of Caribbean people's liberation?

(6) The contemporary unfolding of center-periphery relations in the U.S.-dominated American regional bloc, facilitated by the mechanisms of such initiatives as the Enterprise for the Americas Initiative (EAI), the Caribbean Basin Initiative (CBI), and the North American Free Trade Agreement (NAFTA). How to resist the renewed economic domination of these "free trade" impositions, and the tendency to pose the problems, even among the resisters, within a discourse that naturalizes "globalization" and downplays the continuing significance of underlying neocolonialist structures (sometimes under the guise of being anti-nationalist)? While third world countries and people are increasingly told that the nation-state—and therefore nationalism—is obsolete and self-defeating, we see the wielding of powerful national institutions on behalf of global-regional capital and powerful nations controlling supposedly international institutions. And do not powerful individual nation-states—the United States, Germany, Japan—occupy the center of the competing regional blocs?

(7) The "ethnicization" and "feminization" of the global labor force; the growing circuits of transnational communities of subordinated labor, in which women play a critical role. How do we deal with competing theories of the declining significance of race, the declining significance of class, and the declining significance of gender, coming from many of those who claim to be on the cutting edge of the representation of oppression and the oppressed? Who speaks for third world women "at home" and "abroad"? Who speaks, for example, for the tens of thousands of non-white, third world, immigrant women working in "sweatshop" enclaves that are resurging in New York, Miami, and Los Angeles and along the border with Mexico? Clearly, notions of the feminization of poverty that do not also address questions of "colonialism" at the core are profoundly inadequate.[44] The reverse is also true. And finally, as the interpenetration of the first and third worlds continues apace, what are the implications for transnational labor organizing and international solidarity?

For those of us who are the direct heirs of five hundred years of colonialism and racism—experiences that have encompassed all facets of our existence—many of the existing theories provide us with no tools for understanding what is happening "at the junction of the global and the local." As an anti-imperialist "third world" intellectual, I do not see my relationship to theory as academic and non-political. Theory, for me, becomes part of the *work* of transformation. It is not in the interest of working-class third world people that we remain rigidly faithful to a single, all-encompassing theoretical scheme, whether it is world systems theory, dependency theory, classical marxist theory, or exclusively nationalist or feminist theory, or that we engage in silly, narcissistic games of theoretical one-upmanship and vanguardism. We need to derive a multifaceted framework for understanding and intervening in the interweaving and contradictory "histories" discussed in this chapter, always placing at the center, as the subject, the most victimized participants.

This does not mean that what is required is an entirely new set of theories. We need to draw on all revolutionary or transformatory theories or perspectives that focus on one or more of the dimensions of class, nation, race, ethnicity, and gender, as these are structured by the global capitalist system. For me, marxism, nationalism (defined specifically by anti-imperialism and political and cultural self-determination), and feminism continue to provide the three major cornerstones of the theoretical apparatus that enables me to make sense of my world.[45] To those who see these as mutually exclusive or as canceling each other out, there are millions of people who might offer the reality of their lives as counterproof.

I see these three theoretical and political points of departure, rather, as mutually limiting and mutually conditioning, and as historically necessary and complementary tools of resistance against global capitalist and male hegemony. As a friend and I determined in an informal discussion, during which we were examining the practical implications the three had held for our political lives to that point, "they keep each other honest." Caribbean women workers might well agree.

Acknowledgments. I wish to acknowledge the role of the Caribbean People's Development Agency (CARIPEDA), Kingstown, St. Vincent, in enabling the research upon which this chapter is based. Extensive reference will be made in this article to two documents, authored by myself, resulting from a nine-month investigation in 1986–1987 of export-processing industries and their working conditions in the Eastern Caribbean. The first is a research report, "The New Enclave Industries and Women Workers in the Eastern Caribbean," Joint Project of Caribbean People's Development Agency (St. Vincent) and the Centre for Caribbean Dialogue (Toronto), 1988 (which includes a host of useful appendices); the second is an edited version of the report (minus the appendices), published as a book, *The World Market Factory: A Study of Enclave Industrialization in the Eastern Caribbean and Its Impact on Women Workers* (Kingstown, St. Vincent and the Grenadines: CARIPEDA, 1990).

Notes

1. International Confederation of Free Trade Unions, *New Technology and Women's Employment* (Brussels: ICFTU, 1983), 46.

2. Cornelia H. Aldana, *A Contract for Underdevelopment: Subcontracting for Multinationals in the Philippine Semiconductor and Garment Industries* (Manila: IBON Databank Phils., 1989), 17.

3. See Carol A. Parsons, "The Domestic Employment Consequences of Managed International Competition in Apparel," in *The Dynamics of Trade and Employment*, ed. L. D'Andrea Tyson, W. T. Dickens, and Jonathan Zysman (Cambridge, Mass.: Ballinger, 1988), 113–155, esp. 134.

4. See Richard Rothstein, *Keeping Jobs in Fashion: Alternatives to the Euthanasia of the U.S. Apparel Industry* (Washington, D.C.: Economic Policy Institute, 1989), esp. 13–22.

5. Aldana, *Contract for Underdevelopment*, 46–47, 96–101.

6. Ibid., 4.

7. Ibid., 6.

8. Ibid., 22.

9. Rothstein, *Keeping Jobs in Fashion*.

10. M. P. Fernandez Kelly and A. M. Garcia, "Invisible amidst the Glitter: Hispanic Women in the Southern California Electronics Industry," in *The Worth of Women's Work*, ed. A. Statham, E. M. Miller, H. O. Mauksh (Albany: State University of New York Press, 1988), 265–90, esp. 283.

11. See Cecilia Green, "Towards a Theory of 'Colonial' Modes of Production: A Marxist Approach," M.A. thesis, University of Toronto, 1980.

12. Faye V. Harrison, "Women in Jamaica's Urban Informal Economy: Insights from a Kingston Slum," *New West Indian Guide* 62, nos. 3–4 (1988): 103–28.

13. See Norman Girvan, *Foreign Capital and Economic Underdevelopment* (Kingston, Jamaica: Institute for Social and Economic Research, UWI, 1971).

14. Michel-Rolph Trouillot, *Peasants and Capital: Dominica in the World Economy* (Baltimore and London: Johns Hopkins University Press, 1988), 149.

15. Re/production is the term I have chosen to designate the combined activities of goods production and human reproduction. Goods production is a general reference to the production and servicing of consumer and producer goods. Human reproduction is a combined reference to biological reproduction (which strictly speaking, includes childbearing and breastfeeding) and non-biological reproduction (which includes childrearing, the day-to-day physical and emotional nurturance and "servicing" of human beings, typically within a family household, and household maintenance activities).

16. See Trouillot, *Peasants and Capital*, 141–63.

17. The Commonwealth Caribbean, as the former British West Indian colonies are sometimes referred to, established a Caribbean Free Trade Association (CARIFTA) among themselves in 1968. In 1973, wider cooperation and collaboration was institutionalized in the form of a common market, the Caribbean Community, or CARICOM. CARICOM countries include Antigua and Barbuda, the Bahamas, Barbados, Belize, Dominica, Grenada, Guyana, Jamaica, Montserrat, St. Kitts and Nevis, St. Lucia, St. Vincent and the Grenadines, and Trinidad and Tobago.

18. See note 18 above.

19. Winston H. Griffith, "CARICOM Countries and the Caribbean Basin Initiative," *Latin American Perspectives* 17, no. 1 (Winter 1990): 33–54, esp. 37.

20. Norman Girvan, "The International Division of Labour and Free Trade Zones," unpubl. paper, 1986, 2.

21. See Clive Y. Thomas, *Dependence and Transformation: The Economics of the Transition to Socialism* (New York and London: Monthly Review Press, 1974); also my own review of that work, Cecilia Green, "Thomas' Dependence and Transformation: A Review," *Two-Thirds: A Journal of Underdevelopment Studies* 1, no. 2 (Fall 1978): 71–74. A brief but useful summary of Thomas's blueprint for "another development" can be found in the last chapter of his latest book, *The Poor and the Powerless: Economic Policy and Change in the Caribbean* (London: Latin America Bureau, 1988), 351–370.

22. Cecilia Green, "Trade Unions and Women Workers in the Eastern Caribbean," *Voices of the African Diaspora* (CAAS Research Review) 7, no. 2 (Spring 1991): 30–34, esp. 31.

23. "Structural adjustment" refers to the standard prescriptive program imposed by the World Bank and the International Monetary Fund (IMF) on third world countries as a condition for granting loans. These two institutions see the economic problems of most third world loan applicants as arising from too much government spending, inflated wages and wage increases, and an overvalued currency, resulting in excessive demand, especially for imports, and low export receipts. In the IMF's global program of "restructuring," in which it acts as a bureaucratic surrogate for international—and especially U.S.—capital, the IMF is forcing a rapidly growing number of third world countries to devalue currencies, lower wages, outlaw or break unions, raise prices, slash government social welfare spending, privatize state-owned enterprises, eliminate protective tariffs, and cut back on the production of food for the domestic market and turn instead to export agribusiness and assembly manufacturing for the global/U.S. market. In IMF and U.S. State Department parlance, this is all in keeping with "free trade." See two recent books on the Caribbean that treat this problem in great detail: Kathy McAfee, *Storm Signals: Structural Adjustment and Development Alternatives in the Caribbean* (Boston: South End Press in assoc. with Oxfam America, 1991), and Carmen Diana Deere, coord., *In the Shadows of the Sun: Caribbean Development Alternatives and U.S. Policy* (Boulder, San Francisco, and Oxford: Westview Press, 1990).

24. See Green, "New Enclave Industries," 88–89, 184–254 (pt. 3), or *World Market Factory*, 71–72, 151–203 (pts. 4–5).

25. In characterizing the tension between "domestic" and "national" economies, I invert somewhat the use of these terms made by Lloyd Best, perhaps the major dependency theorist of the English-speaking Caribbean. According to Best and Levitt, one can talk of "domestic" economies in the Caribbean as the spaces within which (foreign-directed) economic operations and activities are domiciled, but one cannot talk of truly "national" (internally integrated) economies. Kari Levitt and Lloyd Best, "Character of Caribbean Economy," in *Caribbean Economy*, ed. George L. Becutord 38 (Kingston, Jamaica, Institute of Social and Economic Research, 1975). While I sympathize with the latter—although I prefer to characterize the national economy as disarticulated and dependent rather than as the absence or negation of an ideal type—I prefer to associate the term "domestic economy" with a subterranean reality that is at odds with or suppressed by the dependent national economy. Women play an important role in that sublimated or informal economy, so that, in at least one way, Best's and Levitt's categories may be said to be gender-blind (as they are somewhat class-neutral).

26. The Caribbean Basin Initiative (CBI) was first enacted through the Caribbean Basin Economic Recovery Act (CBERA) of 1983 and went into effect in January 1984. The CBI program provides duty-free access to the U.S. market for a broad range of eligible products from Caribbean region beneficiary countries. See Emilio Pantójas-García, "The U.S. Caribbean Basin Initiative and the Puerto Rican Experience: Some Parallels and Lessons," *Latin American Perspectives* 12, no. 4 (Fall 1985): 105–128, for the first of several articles by that author on the implications of the CBI for the subregion.

27. Cited in Griffith, "CARICOM Countries and the Caribbean Basin Initiative," 41.

28. Kathy McAfee, "Hurricane: IMF, World Bank, U.S. AID in the Caribbean," *NACLA* 23, no. 5 (Feb. 1990): 13–41, esp. 22. Proponents of economic liberalization claim that "free trade" increases exports and creates jobs for "host" countries. Critics counter that more exports and jobs are lost than won with economic restructuring.

29. Jack Heyman, "Jamaica's Manley Converts to 'Free Marketeer,'" *The Guardian* 44, no. 16 (Feb. 12, 1992): 12.

30. See a recent report on Taiwan by Andrew Leonard, "Taiwan Goes Its Own Way," *The Nation*, April 13, 1992, 482–484. Leonard reminds us that Taiwan executed an effective land reform program and achieved self-sufficiency in food production as well as a domestic manufacturing infrastructure before embarking on its famous "export-led" drive (a reminder to which Caribbean governments touting Taiwan as their developmental model should pay heed). See also Bernado Vega, "The CBI Faces Adversity: Lessons from the Asian Export Strategy," *Caribbean Review* 14, no. 2 (Spring 1985): 18–19, 43.

31. OAS Division of Development Studies, "The Experience of Caribbean Basin Countries in Promoting Investment and Trade," in *Promoting Investments and Exports in the Caribbean Basin*, ed. George P. Montalvan (Washington, D.C.: Organization of American States, 1989), pp. 3–102, esp. p. 33.

32. Barbados boasts (or used to), among other things, a climate of political stability deriving from a long tradition of constitutional and parliamentary democracy ("the second oldest parliament in the British Commonwealth"), a 98 percent literacy rate, a low birth rate, relatively high wage rates and level of labor organization, a good communications and transportation infrastructure, and the best (or least inadequate) welfare provisions in the English-speaking Caribbean. Although wage rates are approximately 50 to 70 percent lower than those in the United States, they are much higher than in Jamaica and the "less developed" neighboring islands.

33. Green, "Trade Unions and Women Workers in the Eastern Caribbean".

34. "New Enclave Industries," 116–122; *World Market Factory*, 101–105.

35. See Errol Miller, *The Marginalization of the Black Male* (Kingston, Jamaica: Institute of Social and Economic Research, UWI, 1986), and "The Rise of Matriarchy in the Caribbean," *Caribbean Quarterly* 34, nos. 3–4 (Sept.–Dec. 1988): 1–21.

36. Cecilia Green, "Caribbean Woman Notes: Historical and Recent Trends in Labour Force Activities and Fertility Rates," app. A, in "The New Enclave Industries," 1–32, esp. 27–29.

37. Ibid., 28.

38. Ibid., 18–19.

39. See Helen I. Safa, "Economic Autonomy and Sexual Equality in Caribbean Society," *Social and Economic Studies* 35, no. 3 (Sept. 1986): 1–21.

40. See "New Enclave Industries" and *World Market Factory.*

41. Burghard Claus et al., *Youth and Employment in the Lesser Antilles* (Berlin: German Development Institute [GDI] in cooperation with Christian Action for Development in the Caribbean [CADEC], 1982), 82.

42. Ibid., 100.

43. See Frank Deale's contribution to this volume.

44. See Evelyn Nakano Glenn, "Racial Ethnic Women's Labor: The Intersection of Race, Gender and Class Oppression," *Review of Radical Political Economics* 17, no. 3 (1985): 86–108.

45. See Cecilia Green, "Marxist-Feminism and Third World Liberation," *Fireworks: The Best of Fireweed,* ed. Makeda Silvera (Toronto: Women's Press, 1986), 210–24.

Chapter 7
Multinational Enterprises and International Labor Standards
Which Way for Development and Jobs?

R. Michael Gadbaw and Michael T. Medwig

Multinational enterprises (MNEs) occupy a position in the world economy that subjects them to many risks unique to transnational trade. While the commercial risks they face are no more onerous than those faced by domestic businesses, they must also cope with a growing variety of political risks found only on a global level. Unlike domestic enterprises, which tend to be subject to the laws of only a single home country, MNEs must comply with numerous national laws, international law, and a growing body of transnational custom.

Reconciling the competing social, legal, and economic goals of various national governments has become increasingly difficult because of the tendency of many governments to link trade with policy goals in non-commercial areas such as human rights, labor standards, and environmental protection. MNEs fear that the linkage of trade with non-commercial policies will spawn new and less manageable political risks, and many question how much political risk can be placed on the system before international commerce is undermined.

This chapter addresses only one aspect of a much larger trade linkage debate encompassing numerous non-commercial policy goals. MNEs view the linkage debate from a perspective somewhat different from that of the labor unions and other pro-labor policy advocates. While it is undeniable that an individual enterprise can gain a temporary advantage by resorting to abusive labor practices, most MNEs realize that the prevalence of such practices can lead only to the suboptimal performance of the individual firm and, by extension, to the suboptimal performance of the economy as a whole. MNEs, therefore, are just as eager as unions and other worker rights advocates to eliminate abusive labor practices.

MNEs are equally eager to avoid misconceived labor policies, however well intentioned. MNEs find themselves opposing many of these proposals, not because of any anti-labor posture, or out of a desire to be free to engage in unfair labor practices, but because some policies are likely to create the very same market distortions as those produced by the practices they seek to remedy.

MNEs and workers both benefit from free, efficiently functioning labor markets. Therefore, MNEs support standards that permit both business and labor to maximize their productivity and to increase their joint contribution to economic development. Although there is little disagreement over the objective of International Fair Labor Standards (IFLS)—fair treatment for workers, respect for trade union rights, balanced growth and development to benefit whole societies, and so on—there remain numerous unanswered questions on how best to pursue these goals.

The History of IFLS

In recent years, International Fair Labor Standards have reemerged as a prominent factor in the formulation of U.S. trade policy. The United States government attempted to place IFLS on the agenda of the Uruguay Round of multilateral trade negotiations. Worker rights provisions have been added to a number of U.S. trade laws including the Caribbean Basin Economic Recovery Act,[1] the Generalized System of Preferences (GSP),[2] the authorization of the Overseas Private Investment Corporation (OPIC),[3] section 301 of the 1974 Trade Act,[4] and the North American Agreement on Labor Cooperation.[5]

The link between International Fair Labor Standards and international trade is long established.[6] Congress banned the importation of convict-made goods with the Tariff Act of 1890.[7] An entire section on labor was included in the Treaty of Versailles at the Paris Peace Conference in 1919.[8] The Treaty obliged nations to "endeavor to secure and maintain fair and humane conditions of labor . . . in all countries in which their commercial and industrial relations extend."[9] The Treaty also established the International Labor Organization (ILO), which, since 1919, has adopted 173 conventions establishing labor standards governing every aspect of employment relations.

Participants in the 1948 International Conference on Trade and Employment drafted a document known as the Havana Charter of the International Trade Organization (ITO), which provided that "the Members recognize that unfair labor conditions, particularly for export, create difficulties in international trade, and accordingly each Member shall take whatever action may be appropriate and feasible to eliminate such conditions within its territory."[10] The ITO, however, never went into operation because of the failure of the U.S. Congress to approve U.S. membership.

Since it had been assumed that the ITO would supersede the GATT, the ITO labor chapter was not included in the GATT. The United States has been seeking, unsuccessfully, to remedy this omission ever since. In 1953 the United States proposed the insertion of a IFLS clause into the GATT. However, no action was taken because of the parties' inability to agree on a definition of "unfair standards."[11] In 1979, during the Tokyo Round, the United States again proposed the addition of a short minimum labor standards code, but received the support of only a few Scandinavian countries.[12] IFLS was also a contentious issue in the final stages of the GATT Uruguay Round process in 1994.

The United States has been a prominent advocate of International Fair Labor Standards for several reasons. First, the legislation granting the President negotiating authority for multilateral trade negotiations has mandated the pursuit of International Fair Labor Standards. Second, labor groups and human rights organizations have worked with Congress to incorporate worker rights provisions in several recent pieces of trade legislation. Third, the United States is bound to play a central role, either through action or inaction, simply by virtue of the size of its economy. In 1987, for example, the United States accounted for over 57 percent of developed country imports of manufactured goods from developing countries.

The State of the Debate

A highly politicized and emotionally charged debate on trade and labor policy rages on both the economic and the legal aspects of linkage. There is disagreement both on the ends of trade and labor policy and on the means of linking the two. Unfortunately, because of the acrimonious nature of the debate and the advocacy tone of much of the literature, the salient issues have been obfuscated more often than illuminated.

The Legal Debate

There is considerable disagreement on the existence of internationally recognized standards and also on the question of whether such standards can even be articulated. While ILO conventions are identified by some as evidence of such standards, many others are quick to point out that, even the most basic conventions have not been ratified by a majority of the developing countries, nor even by the United States. Moreover, many developing countries question the utility of Western

European standards, and even some Europeans are beginning to question the role of their own labor standards in perpetuating persistent high unemployment in many European countries.

Despite these differences, an international consensus is emerging on certain basic fair labor standards. Forced labor, for example, is nearly universally condemned, and seems to be practiced in only a dwindling number of states.[13] Other practices, although widely condemned, are still common in many developing countries, among them prohibitions on freedom of association, exposure of workers to hazardous working conditions without risk disclosure, and the employment of children for long work hours simply because they are cheaper to hire than adults.[14]

Under U.S. trade law, international fair labor standards include: (1) the right of association; (2) the right to organize and bargain collectively; (3) a prohibition on the use of any form of forced or compulsory labor; (4) minimum age for the employment of children; and (5) acceptable conditions of work with respect to minimum wages, hours, and occupational safety and health.[15] Although there is some agreement on the primacy of these rights, the real challenge is to design policies that will actually secure better conditions for workers.

The Economic Debate

The vast majority of workers do not enjoy the labor standards listed above, especially those listed under number (5).[16]

The reason is simple: the economies in which they live are too poor. For example, if the choice is between subsistence needs and "decent" work hours, the work days will be very long. Or if the choice is between child labor on the family farm or a smaller harvest, children will work long and hard in the fields.[17]

In other words, conditions that many labor advocates point to as "abuses" may really be less a function of policy failure than the unavoidably harsh conditions of life in a developing economy. Many argue that the best hope for these workers lies in the improved conditions brought about by economic growth. Others insist that employment conditions can only be improved by the government imposition of labor standards.

While nearly all analysts agree that the objective of labor policy in developing countries should be the advancement of worker welfare, few agree on which strategy best achieves this goal. Not surprisingly, governments have experimented with a number of approaches. Gary S. Fields categorizes the government labor policies that have been tried as follows: (1) high-wage policy, meaning that the government encourages or creates institutions pushing wages above market levels; (2) market-wage policy, in which the government allows wages to be determined by supply and demand; and (3) repressive wage policy, where the government deliberately attempts to hold wages down below market levels.[18]

Many labor advocates maintain that the high-wage policy best promotes worker welfare, thereby confounding labor relations standards with labor market outcomes. Former Labor Secretary Ray Marshall, for example, has argued that "labor standards, especially the right of workers to organize and bargain collectively, make it possible for third world incomes to be higher and more equitably distributed."[19] Others challenge the assumption that this outcome will be secured by such a policy. "Incomes might rise and be distributed more equally even in the absence of collective organization and bargaining."[20] Likewise, it is possible that the exercise of collective bargaining will "result unwittingly in lower employment in covered sectors, higher unemployment in the economy, or lower wages for workers crowded into uncovered sectors."[21]

Neo-Classical economists argue that neither form of government intervention in labor markets is likely to benefit workers:

As long as labor demand curves are downward sloping, . . . pushing wages above market levels will result in reduced employment, and probably reduced national output too.[22] Equally important, as long as labor supply curves are upward-sloping, wage repression will cause labor shortages and will thus also have the same adverse effects on employment and national output. Market wage determinations may result in the best labor market outcomes of all. Good intentions do not necessarily make good laws.[23]

According to many observers, the objective of U.S. policy toward developing countries should be the promotion of economic growth. If pushed too far the promotion of labor standards may "hamper employment, reduce competitiveness, and impede growth. The poor workers of the world cannot afford this."[24] The Neo-Classical policy prescription is to increase efficiency at home, not to reduce efficiency abroad.[25] They argue that the best way to prevent the decline of labor conditions at home is to anticipate where developing countries will be making their next breakthroughs and moving out of those industries and into others where comparative advantage remains.[26]

The standard critique of the Neo-Classical position often amounts to a repudiation of the theory of comparative advantage on which the international trading system is built. Many labor advocates argue that business "takes advantage of workers' lack of alternatives."[27] Furthermore, they complain that in the absence of internationally enforced labor standards employers will resort to a "sweatshop" business strategy in order to meet international competition.[28] Neo-Classicists respond by arguing that "in many countries the alternative to using cheap labor in production is not to produce at all. Can this really be better for the workers involved?"[29]

Some labor advocates have concluded that labor policy must push employers away from a "sweatshop" strategy toward a strategy based on technological innovation.[30] In reaching this conclusion, however, many of these scholars underestimate the relative scarcity and mobility of the factors of production. The relative stocks of resources, including both capital and labor, vary both in quantity and quality from country to country. Businesses are forced by the pressures of competition to employ the production methods best adapted to local conditions. Businesses in capital-scarce developing countries, therefore, cannot easily switch from relatively abundant labor (in which they have an advantage) to relatively scarce capital without incurring additional costs—costs that then render them uncompetitive in the international marketplace.

From a Neo-Classical perspective, the solution is to provide for the freer movement of capital (e.g., the movement of U.S. manufacturing facilities to developing countries that have an abundance of workers) or the freer movement of labor (e.g., the movement of workers from developing countries to the United States). By permitting the free flow of resources across borders, the rates of returns on both labor and capital would gradually tend to equalize across countries. This solution, however, is often resisted by labor advocates in the United States who oppose both increased immigration and "runaway" factories. This resistance leads Neo-Classicists to suspect that these advocates object to wage competition itself.

The *idée fixe* animating much of the criticism of free trade is the familiar "race to the bottom": Labor conditions are driven down as developing countries compete for foreign direct investment through relaxed labor standards.[31] While Neo-Classicists argue that this competition would continue only until the level at which the wage structure clears the labor market, their critics believe that the competition would continue until the absolute "bottom" of worker welfare is reached.[32]

As never before, the global economy provides a variety of laboratories in which these competing policies are being tested and refined. International trade has become both a conduit for the exchange of ideas and a test of a country's success in applying them. The issue then is whether trade should take on a more proactive role in promoting certain labor policies and ultimately whether countries' access to the channels of international commerce should be conditioned on their labor policies.

Three Approaches to Linkage

There are three approaches, one might say paradigms, for the linkage of labor policy to trade policy: (1) the conditionality approach; (2) the unfair trade practice approach; and (3) the international agreement approach. From the perspective of MNEs, the international agreement approach is the most desirable, as this method produces the least uncertainty. For MNEs, the unfair trade practice approach is the least desirable, since it carries with it the threat of retaliation and counter-retaliation. This method is also least desired by the governments of developing countries, who view it as a kind of imperialist mechanism for imposing standards that they have not recognized.

The Conditionality Paradigm

The conditionality approach is premised on the notion that it is perfectly appropriate to condition certain trade concessions on the beneficiary country's recognition of certain minimum international fair labor standards. Problems arise from this approach, however, when the standards contained in the conditions diverge from those that the beneficiary country has accepted or that actually command international recognition. If international law does not provide a satisfactory basis for formulating the conditions, then the United States is, "in reality, imposing its own conveniently . . . elastic standards upon other states. The latter are, in effect, being required to meet standards which are not formally binding on them by virtue of any treaty undertakings or customary international law."[33]

Caribbean Basin Initiative (CBI)

One of the first pieces of legislation to embody this approach was the 1983 Caribbean Basin Economic Recovery Act (CBERA).[34] This act gave the U.S. President authority to extend duty-free treatment to most imports from beneficiary countries in the Caribbean Basin. CBERA eligibility is conditioned on whether the beneficiary country has "taken or is taking steps to afford to workers in that country . . . internationally recognized rights."[35] In determining eligibility, the United States measures a nation's compliance in four areas: (1) freedom of association; (2) freedom to bargain collectively; (3) workplace conditions (freedom from forced labor, child labor abuses, minimum wage, and occupational safety and health standards); and (4) labor standards in export processing zones (EPZs).[36]

The United States found that five CBI countries (the Dominican Republic, El Salvador, Guatemala, Haiti, and Honduras) fell short in least one of the four areas. In order to qualify for CBI benefits the governments of these countries agreed to improve work conditions in a number of problem areas.

Generalized System of Preferences (GSP)

The U.S. Generalized System of Preferences authorizes the President to grant duty-free treatment of imports from developing countries designated as beneficiaries.[37] The program was extended by the Trade and Tariff Act of 1984, which added respect for "internationally recognized worker rights" to the factors affecting GSP eligibility. "Worker rights" were there defined to include: (1) the right of association; (2) the right to organize and bargain collectively; (3) the prohibition of forced or compulsory labor; (4) a minimum age for the employment of children; and (5) acceptable working conditions with respect to minimum wages, hours of work, and occupational safety and health.[38]

During the first review of GSP eligibility conducted by the Reagan Administration in 1985, human rights groups and labor unions filed petitions against Chile, Guatemala, Haiti, Korea, Nicaragua, Paraguay, the Philippines, Romania, Suriname, Taiwan, and Zaire. In January 1987, the President removed Romania and Nicaragua from the list of GSP-eligible developing countries and suspended Paraguay.[39] Chile was suspended in 1988.[40] Burma and the Central African Republic were suspended in 1989, and Liberia was removed in 1990.[41] Chile, Paraguay, and the Central African Republic were reinstated in 1991,[42] and Nicaragua was admitted to the CBI after the election of the Chamorro government. In 1993, Mauritania was suspended, and six countries—El Salvador, Guatemala, Indonesia, Thailand, Malawi, and Oman—were placed on a six-month continuing review status during which "if [these] countries fail to make substantial concrete progress in addressing worker rights concerns their GSP benefits will be in serious jeopardy."[43]

Overseas Private Investment Corporation (OPIC)

The Overseas Private Investment Corporation (OPIC) facilitates private investment projects in developing countries by insuring U.S. investors against political risks.[44] In 1985 the U.S. Congress added a worker rights provision to the corporation's authorizing legislation: "The Corporation may insure . . . a project only if the country in which the project is to be undertaken is taking steps to adopt and implement laws that extend internationally recognized worker rights . . . to workers in that country (including any designated zone in that country)."[45]

OPIC follows a two-track approach with regard to implementing the worker rights provision. First, for countries that are GSP beneficiaries, OPIC abides by the presidential determination of compliance with the GSP worker rights criteria.[46] Second, for other countries OPIC will make its own determination "with a greater degree of independence, although always in consultation with State and Labor, as mandated by [its] legislation."[47] Consistent with presidential GSP findings, OPIC has indefinitely suspended insurance programs in Nicaragua, Paraguay, Romania, Chile, and the Central African Republic.[48] OPIC also took the same action with respect to non-GSP beneficiary Ethiopia.

Criticism of the OPIC provisions reveals the difficulties of using this conditionality approach. According to one writer, the OPIC workers' rights provision has an overall negative effect on developing countries for a number of reasons.[49] First, most OPIC projects adhere to higher labor standards than do indigenous operations.[50] Second, U.S. overseas operations pay higher wages, provide safer work environments, and offer greater benefits than do local operations. Therefore, requiring OPIC "to abandon a project on the basis of a country's worker rights record is tantamount to depriving a country of a role model for labor standards."[51] The worker rights provisions also thwart OPIC's development goals by impairing a developing country's ability to earn foreign exchange, attract new employers, and obtain new technology.[52]

Furthermore, the loss of OPIC assistance harms U.S. investors. For example, "when OPIC decided to cease its programs in Chile as a result of that country's labor practices, almost five hundred million dollars of U.S. investments were abandoned by OPIC."[53] Many of these investment proposals were withdrawn, and many investment opportunities were taken over by international competitors "including many from Japan, Germany, and Italy."[54] One should also note that the loss of OPIC assistance is likely to have a negative impact on U.S. exports to the affected countries.[55]

One proposed solution to this problem would be to provide an exception to the worker rights provision for investors who voluntarily agree to fulfill the worker rights requirements of the statute:

If an investor is willing to provide its employees with recognized employment standards and is willing to work with national and international collective bargaining units, the project should not be condemned because of the host country's shortcomings. . . . U.S. investors would become instruments of change while at the same time enabling domestic industries to expand into the global market. Such steps do more to advance living standards than the enactment of local labor laws that, in practice, may never be implemented. An exception for investors who voluntarily meet the worker rights requirements is a critical necessity at a time when the viability of U.S. global competitiveness is in question.[56]

The Unfair Trade Practice Paradigm

The unfair trade practice approach is based on the notion that maintaining standards below certain prescribed minimums is a form of "social dumping." Dumping is an internationally recognized unfair trade practice for which there are prescribed remedies under national trade law. These remedies are generally accepted in the international trading system, although their application to redress differences in countries' regulatory regimes is hotly contested. Many MNEs question whether the denial of worker rights confers a competitive advantage, and many have concluded that there is no evidence to suggest that it does.

The unfair trade practice approach is considered more threatening than the conditionality approach. Withholding a concession from a country for what might appear to be an arbitrary and unfair reason is far less controversial than accusing that same country of engaging in an unfair trade practice based on the violation of a standard that very well may not enjoy international recognition. Furthermore, this approach may not be consistent with our trade agreement obligations, and any imposition of sanctions may be a violation of the GATT.

The recent GATT panel decision on the dispute between the United States and Mexico concerning the U.S. embargo on tuna imports from Mexico illustrates the dangers of the unfair practices approach. The U.S. Marine Mammal Protection Act (MMPA) sets dolphin protection standards and prohibits tuna imports from any country that does not meet those standards. When imports from Mexico were prohibited, Mexico asked for a GATT dispute settlement panel, arguing that the U.S. embargo was inconsistent with GATT provisions. The panel found

that the standard of Article III—namely, that imported products be accorded no less favorable treatment than domestic products—required a comparison between products of the exporting and importing countries, and not a comparison between production regulations . . . that had no effect on the product as such. Therefore, the United States could not embargo imports of tuna products from Mexico simply because Mexico's regulations affecting the production of tuna did not satisfy United States regulations.[57]

Although the panel, in this case, was dealing with environmental regulation, labor standards could just as easily fit the category of "production regulation" to which the panel referred. A future panel could, without difficulty, find a labor-linked embargo to be inconsistent with Article III on the same grounds.

Omnibus Trade and Competitiveness Act of 1988 (OTCA)

The most recent provision of U.S. trade law to address workers rights is a 1988 amendment to section 301 of the 1974 Trade Act.[58] This statute authorizes the U.S. trade representative (USTR) to take action against any act, policy, or practice that "burdens or restricts United States commerce."[59] The USTR has used this statute to impose sanctions on countries that deny U.S. access to their markets. As part of the OTCA, Congress added the denial of internationally recognized worker rights, using the GSP definitions, to the list of "unreasonable" trade practices actionable under section 301. The act provides, however, that a practice will not be treated as unreasonable if the USTR determines: (1) that the foreign country has taken, or is taking, actions that demonstrate a significant and tangible overall advancement in providing the rights described in the act or (2) that such practice is not inconsistent with the economic development of the country.[60] To date, no section 301 case has been initiated under the worker rights provision.

The International Agreement Paradigm

General Agreement on Tariffs and Trade (GATT)

The United States has tried to raise the issue of worker rights at the Uruguay Round of negotiations on several occasions. The OTCA established three U.S. negotiating objectives with respect to worker rights: (1) to promote respect for worker rights; (2) to secure a review of the relationships of worker rights to GATT articles; and (3) to adopt, as a principle of the GATT, that the denial of worker rights should not be a means for a country to gain competitive advantage in international trade.[61] During the preparatory work that preceded the September 1986 start of the Uruguay Round, the United States tried to include worker rights in the negotiating agenda. The U.S. delegate to the GATT Preparatory Committee indicated that "the U.S. did not intend to impose its wage standards on the rest of the world, or to deny the legitimate comparative advantage of developing countries. Rather, the United States sought to ensure that trade expansion was not an end in itself, and that it benefitted all workers in all countries and contributed to the basic objectives of GATT."[62] The developing countries refused to entertain any discussion of the workers' rights issue, even though the U.S. offered to narrow the scope of the investigation to discriminatory labor standards applied to exports, such as the prohibition on union organization and collective bargaining in Export Processing Zones (EPZs).

When U.S. efforts in this area were blocked, the United States called for the formation of a GATT Working Party to study the relationship of internationally recognized workers' rights to trade.[63] These proposals were also blocked, principally by the opposition of developing countries. Later, the United States lost both the fight to include labor rights in the Marrakech ministerial declaration and the fight to include a specific reference to labor rights in the Preparatory Committee decision, but it did win the inclusion of a vague statement in the Preparatory Committee Decision that could permit the future discussion of worker rights.

In April 1994, United States Trade Representative Mickey Kantor announced that the U.S. had persuaded its trading partners to accept language in the "Decision on the Establishment of the Preparatory Committee for the WTO" stating that the body should discuss "suggestions for the inclusion of additional items on the agenda for the WTO's work program." Developing countries, however, inserted language that limits discussion to issues that fall "within [the WTO's] scope and functions."[64] While the U.S. believes that this includes worker rights, the developing countries are adamant that it does not.

Developing countries argue that worker rights are best handled by the International Labor Organization. The same developing countries believe that trade policy linkage constitutes an unacceptable abridgement of their national sovereignty and an obstacle to their enjoyment of a comparative advantage based on low labor costs.

This recent conflict illustrates a fundamental disagreement between the United States and developing countries on the basis of international labor standards. While many U.S. policy advocates assume that the U.S. or Western European model should necessarily inform the discussion of international labor standards, many developing countries, observing the high unemployment and slow growth engendered in Europe by labor market rigidities, question this assumption.

When one considers the newly emerging consensus among developed countries on the need for greater flexibility and lower labor costs in order to promote economic and employment growth, developing countries cannot be blamed for regarding proposals that may operate to raise their own labor costs with the greatest suspicion. With this in mind, the G7 (Group of Seven—the advanced industrial countries) ministers recently agreed, at the Detroit Job Summit, that free trade and labor market flexibility were essential to tackle the problems of persistent unemployment.

The International Monetary Fund (IMF) also addressed this issue in its October 1993 World Economic Outlook and concluded that "Reforms are needed to increase the flexibility of workers and of markets—particularly of labor markets—so that the private sector is better able to adapt to the process of dynamic change by creating new jobs as others are lost." The new consensus reflected in these consistent calls for labor market flexibility by international organizations will undoubtedly have a profound effect on the discussion of international labor standards, and consequently many of the "rights" that have long been regarded as sacrosanct by the labor community deserve thoughtful reassessment.

Take the right to bargain collectively as just one example. While many unions regard this as an essential feature of any regime of fair labor standards, the role of such bargaining systems in economic development is currently under reconsideration. The IMF's own review led to the conclusion that "Wage bargaining systems need to be reformed . . . so that real wages in different sectors reflect productivity differences, which would allow expanding industries to attract labor rapidly." The European Commission, in a recent White Paper on Growth, Competitiveness and Employment," published at the end of 1993, also found that many existing wage-bargaining schemes have had a negative employment impact, protecting those in work at the expense of job-seekers. While no one denies that collective bargaining schemes benefit workers in unionized sectors, the IMF suggests that it is "not clear that . . . such gains represent an increase in welfare to the population as a whole" and warns that "the market power of the currently employed—the insiders—should not be so great as to result in real wage levels that are too high to allow the unemployed—the outsiders—to find work."

In light of the emphasis on the importance of labor market flexibility, the rights that eventually may earn the recognition of the developing world may bear little resemblance to the models put forth to date by the Europeans, the United States, or even the ILO. Policymakers will need to acknowledge the fact that "worker rights" that do not promote employment growth and economic development are not in the best long-term interests of workers. Efforts to reach truly international agreement on a system of labor standards, therefore, may result in the creation of a system different from the proposals put forth to date by policy advocates.

The North American Free Trade Agreement (NAFTA) and the North American Agreement on Labor Cooperation (NAALC)

With respect to labor standards, the NAFTA parties first concentrated on "mutual cooperation and exchange of information" under the framework of the U.S.-Mexico Binational Commission under a Memorandum of Understanding signed by the U.S. Department of Labor and the Mexican Secretariat of Labor and Social Welfare (STPS).[65] In September 1993, Mexico, Canada, and the United States reached agreement on a "Labor Side Agreement" containing a mix of cooperative ventures alongside dispute resolution procedures under which a party's failure to enforce its own labor laws in certain areas can lead to trade sanctions.[66]

To be actionable, a matter must relate to a "persistent pattern" of failure to effectively enforce "occupational safety and health, child labor, or other minimum wage technical standards." "Persistent pattern" means a sustained or recurring pattern or practice. In addition, a matter must be "trade related," and "covered by mutually recognized labor laws."

The NAALC is remarkable for two reasons. First, it evidences agreement between three countries, at least, that a country's failure to enforce *its own* labor laws could lead to an unfair competitive advantage for its firms. Secondly, it evidences the great difficulty involved in reaching any sort of consensus on what constitutes IFLS. The failure to reach agreement on common standards among even these three neighbors suggests that agreement among over a hundred World Trade Organization (WTO) members will be even more complicated.

Voluntary Codes of Conduct

Although voluntary codes of conduct are not binding international agreements, they are, at least, evidence of an emerging international consensus on fair labor standards. The ILO, for example, has produced a code entitled "ILO Tripartite Declaration of Principles Concerning Multinational Enterprises and Social Policy."[67] The Tripartite Declaration "sets out principles in the fields of employment, training, conditions of work and life and industrial relations which governments, employers' and workers' organizations and multinational enterprises are recommended to observe on a voluntary basis."[68]

The voluntary codes also represent a non-coercive method of achieving many of the objectives of a labor-linked trade policy. By adhering to these voluntary codes, MNEs can raise labor standards in the developing countries and serve as role models for the domestic enterprises in host countries. U.S. and Mexican businesses have been working on a code to govern post-NAFTA labor employment practices. An early draft of this code, entitled "U.S.-Mexico Business Principles on Employment and Working Conditions," incorporated many of the employment, work conditions, and industrial relations provisions of the Tripartite Declaration.[69] The objective of the draft was to "reflect [the] commitment by the United States and Mexican business to promote positive labor and employment relations and safe working environment under the North American Free Trade Agreement within the framework of law, regulations and prevailing labor relations and employment practices in the countries in which they operate."[70]

There is concern, however, that labor advocates might formulate codes with unrealistic standards that can never be met, and then push for government imposition of the codes. Many MNE's watched the "Sullivan Principles" for the conduct of U.S. business operations in the South grow from a set of "common principles" adopted by twelve U.S. corporations in 1977 into a U.S. law with substantial penalties for non-compliance in 1986,[71] and fear the repetition of that process. Legislative mandates such as these restrict the MNE's ability to adapt their employment policies to changing competitive conditions across the world, and stifle their ability to creatively and constructively raise worker standards in foreign countries. Equally important is the fear of the creation of government administrative bodies to regulate MNE compliance with the codes and the consequent replacement of market mechanisms with bureaucratic administration.

Development, International Trade, and Labor Standards

Considering that the chief obstacle to the establishment of an international regime of labor standards is the opposition of developing countries, several questions arise: Why do so many Less Developed Countries (LDCs) so adamantly resist the imposition of IFLS? Why do these countries view IFLS as both a threat to their export trade and as a potential brake on their economic development? And why does the debate between labor advocates and developing country governments so often end in mutual accusations of bad faith?

Economic Development

Some labor advocates argue that high-wage policies are necessary to block undesirable development strategies based on sweatshop production. According to Michael Piore, a sweatshop competitive strategy is a form of labor-intensive production with minimum capital investment.[72] He argues that the goal of trade and labor policy should be to "foreclose the use of these techniques" in foreign firms.[73] Underpinning this policy is the view that one can transform low-wage, low-productivity workers into high-wage, high-productivity workers by decree. Neo-Classicists respond to this view by noting that if an employer is forced to pay workers a higher wage (either explicitly or implicitly), he or she can only maintain his or her competitive position by making those workers more productive—that is, by substituting capital for labor, by producing the same output with fewer workers. In other words, in order for some workers to receive a higher wage others must be rendered redundant.[74] Developing countries see this as a prescription for unemployment.

Many linkage policies, in fact, are premised on a development strategy that is loosely modeled on the experiences of Japan, Korea, and the emerging countries of Asia. Many advocates move from the empirical observation that workers fare better in capital-intensive industries to the policy of forcing employers to switch to this production strategy. The critics of this planned industrial development argue that it has failed where it has been tried with singularly disastrous results in postcolonial sub-Saharan Africa.[75] The reason, they argue, is simple. The advocates of this strategy have confused cause with effect: Improving labor conditions are not a cause of economic growth; they *result from* economic growth.

Protectionism

We have reached the point in the debate on trade and labor policy where even the most modest trade-linked IFLS proposals are perceived as a form of protectionism by the developing world. The developing countries, for example, staunchly opposed the inclusion of a labor clause in the GATT, arguing that "the ostensible expression of social concern were simply a disguise for protectionism."[76]

Part of the problem is the labor advocates' tendency to see trade itself as the problem and not as part of the solution. Pharis J. Harvey, executive director of the International Labor Rights Fund, explained the need for a labor standards clause in NAFTA in the following manner: "From an economic perspective, free trade in the context of continued labor repression in Mexico would force American and Canadian workers to relinquish hard-won protection and wages in order to remain competitive. It would reinforce U.S. employers' well-documented tendency to rely on low wages rather than more productivity enhancing competitive strategies."[77] Likewise, an AFL-CIO spokesman framed his concerns in this way: "Mexico will be a magnet for U.S. and foreign corporations which desire a low-wage alternative to relocate their production in Mexico free of worker . . . protections."[78] Arguments like this, unfortunately, only fuel the suspicions of the developing country governments that linkage is aimed at limiting trade in order to protect U.S. union workers rather than advancing the cause of workers' rights in developing countries.

Compounding the problem is the failure of labor advocates in the United States to distinguish between labor relations standards and labor market outcomes. Many advocates present international wage differences as *prima facie* evidence of exploitative labor practices overseas. The fact that wages differ from one country to another, however, is no indication in itself of unfair or exploitative practices.[79] One might look first to differences in factor endowments. These relative variations in factor endowments are the foundation of many developing countries' comparative advantage. Fair labor standards, in fact, could lead to lower level wages in some sectors as labor market distortions are eliminated across the economy. While such an outcome would enhance the ability of firms in those sectors to compete with U.S. firms, there would be nothing inherently "unfair" or "exploitative" about this result.

Advocates of labor rights, therefore, must demonstrate a willingness to support the developing country access to the U.S. market provided that progress is made on labor standards. Developing countries, believing that the unions' true motive is protectionism, fear that, as soon as they make progress on workers' rights, the unions will push for a higher standard in order to continue to deny them market access. Even if the labor standards goals were formulated in good faith, developing countries fear that they could later be manipulated by protectionist labor advocates in the United States, leading to the same result.

Many argue that the solution to the problem of displaced workers in the United States is not to restrict imports but rather to provide retraining and other forms of support to the affected workers. They argue that the goal of adjustment policy should be to facilitate the movement of workers from declining industries into those where comparative advantage remains and where it is emerging. These adjustment policies, while easing the transition of displaced workers to new industries, permit the economy as a whole to capture and retain the gains from international trade. This approach, unlike trade restrictions, helps domestic workers adjust to the changing global economy without punishing home country consumers and foreign workers.

Conclusion

Labor advocates must recognize the conflict between the promotion of worker welfare in developing countries and the protection of jobs in uncompetitive industries in the industrialized countries. Since the two goals are rarely compatible, it is far better, in the long run, to build an international consensus on fair labor standards than to pursue the unilateral imposition of modern labor regulation on our trading partners. While many thoughtful opinion leaders feel that some form of linkage between trade and worker rights is appropriate, linkage involves numerous risks that must be weighed against the likely results.

First, it involves the danger of unilateralism. One should question the legitimacy of holding countries to labor standards that they have neither recognized nor accepted. Second, linkage is a blunt instrument. Once trade benefits are denied, the United States loses all leverage over the target country. Furthermore, the denial of benefits is usually followed by a loss of whatever commercial interests the United States had developed in the target country to our foreign competitors. Trade policy, by itself, does not appear to be the best context in which to address labor standards. The advance of IFLS is best pursued through international mechanisms expressly devoted to labor policy, such as the ILO.

MNEs play an important role in building an international consensus on fair labor standards and in improving the welfare of workers in developing countries. Simply by opening facilities in developing countries and by employing local workers, the MNEs bid up both wages and working conditions in local labor markets. Likewise, by adhering to fair labor standards, the MNEs present a model of advanced employment practices that can be imitated by local employers. Furthermore, by increasing the productive capacity of the local economy, the MNEs contribute to the economic growth of developing countries, which, in turn, leads to the improvement of the welfare of all workers. Instead of a race to the bottom, MNEs and developing countries are engaged in a race to the top. Developing countries compete to attract MNE investment, and MNEs compete to contribute to the economic growth of the host countries.

The increasing calls for trade retaliation as a means of advancing labor conditions in foreign countries are part of a preoccupation with imports that reinforces the neglect of U.S. policy toward exports, which are the critical source of jobs and wage growth in the United States. Note in particular that wages in the export industries are 17 percent higher than those in the economy as a whole. When trade is cut off, be it through the denial of GSP benefits or a section 301 action, we deny foreign exchange to countries that would otherwise use it to buy U.S. goods and services. Labor unions should place a higher priority on helping the United States to become a more export-oriented economy. Critical to the growth of the U.S. export sector is the ability of U.S. multinational enterprises to compete in an increasingly global economy.

Notes

1. Pub. L. 98-67, 97 Stat. 384, codified at 19 U.S.C. secs. 2701–2706 (1988 and 1990 Supp.).

2. Trade Act of 1974 sec. 502, Pub. L. 93-618, 88 Stat. 2066, codified at 19 U.S.C. secs. 2461–2466 (1988 and 1990 Supp.).

3. Overseas Private Investment Corporation Amendment Act of 1985, Pub. L. 99-204, sec. 5, 99 Stat. 1669, 1670–1671, codified at 22 U.S.C. sec. 2191a(a)(1).

4. Trade Ac of 1974, Pub. L. 93-618 (1975), amended by Omnibus Trade and Competitiveness Act of 1988, Pub. L. 100-418, 102 Stat. 1107, 1164, codified at 19 U.S.C. secs. 2411–2419 (1988).

5. North American Agreement on Labor Cooperation between the Government of the United States of America, the Government of Canada and the Government of the United Mexican States (hereinafter NAALC).

6. Steve Charnovitz, "Environmental and Labour Standards in Trade," *World Economy* 15 (1992): 335, 337, 339–341.

7. Ibid., 339.

8. Ibid.

9. 225 Consolidated Treaty Series 188, 204.

10. U.S. Department of State, Pub. No. 3206, Havana Charter for an International Trade Organization 32 (1948).

11. U.S. Commission on Foreign Economic Policy (1954) at 437–438.

12. See Jorge F. Pérez-López, "Conditioning Trade on Foreign Labor Law: The U.S. Approach," *Comparative Labor Law Journal* 9 (1988): 253, 259.

13. Gary S. Fields, "Labor Standards, Economic Development, and International Trade," in *Labor Standards and Development in the Global Economy*, ed. Stephen Herzenberg and Jorge F. Pérez-López (Washington, D.C.: U.S. Department of Labor Bureau of International Labor Affairs, 1990), 19, 20.

14. Ibid.

15. See, e.g., Trade and Tariff Act of 1984, Pub. L. 98-753, secs. 501–508, 98 Stat. 2984, 3018–3024, codified at 19 U.S.C. secs. 2461–2466 (1988).

16. Fields, "Labor Standards," 20.

17. Ibid.

18. Ibid., 22.

19. Ray F. Marshall, "Linking Worker's Rights and Trade," paper presented to the International Metalworkers Federation Central Committee Meeting, Madrid, June 1988, 2.

20. Fields, "Labor Standards," 20.

21. Ibid.

22. As Nobel Laureate F. A. Hayek notes,

workers can raise real wages above the level that would prevail on a free market only by limiting the supply, that is, by withholding part of labor. The interest of those who will get employment at the higher wage will therefore always be opposed to the interest of those who, in consequence, will find employment only in the less highly paid jobs or who will not be employed at all.

F. A. Hayek, *The Constitution of Liberty* (Chicago: University Chicago Press, 1960) at 270.

23. Fields, "Labor Standards," 23.

24. Ibid., 21.

25. Ibid., 32.

26. Ibid., 32.

27. Stephen A. Herzenberg, Jorge F. Pérez-López, and Stuart K. Tucker, "Labor Standards and Development in the Global Economy," in *Labor Standards and Developments in the Global Economy*, ed. Herzenberg and Pérez-López, 1, 5.

28. See, e.g., Michael J. Piore, "Labor Standards and Business Strategies," in *Labor Standards and Development in the Global Economy*, ed. Herzenberg and Pérez-López, 35.

29. Fields, "Labor Standards," 31.

30. See Piore, "Labor Standards," 39–47.

31. "Social competition" is used interchangeably with "race to the bottom" to describe this phenomenon. See, e.g., Hugh G. Mosley, "The Social Dimension of European Integration," *International Labour Review* 129 (1990): 147, 160.

32. The "race to the bottom" is reminiscent of an argument made by Karl Marx in his *Capital* in which he predicted that the result of wage competition would be the "a progressive diminution in the number of capitalist magnates" and "a corresponding increase in the mass of poverty, oppression, enslavement, degeneration and exploitation."

33. See Phillip Alston, this volume.

34. Pub. L. 98-67, 97 Stat. 384, codified at 19 U.S.C. secs. 2701–2706 (1988 and 1990 Supp.).

35. 19 U.S.C. sec. 2702(b) (7).

36. See Pérez-López, "Conditioning Trade," 262.

37. The GSP review process constitutes a significant source of leverage for the United States. In 1991, for example, the United States imported $13.7 billion of goods under the GSP program.

38. See *Trade and Tariff Act, supra* note 15.

39. Proclamation no. 5617, 52 FR 7265 (1987).

40. Proclamation no. 5758, 52 FR 49129 (1987).

41. Proclamation no. 5955, 54 FR 15357 (1989) (Burma and Central African Republic); Actions Concerning the Generalized System of Preferences, 55 FR 18073 (1990) (Liberia).

42. Proclamation no. 6244, 56 FR 4707 (1991) (Chile); Proclamation no. 6245, 56 FR 4921 (1991) (Paraguay and Central African Republic).

43. See Office of the United States Trade Representative, "Kantor Announces Results of 1992 GSP Reviews—Emphasis on Worker Rights Is Underscored," June 25, 1993.

44. OPIC was established in 1969, P.L. 91-175, pursuant to the Foreign Assistance Act of 1961, P.L. 87-195 sec. 101, 75 Stat. 424, codified at 22 U.S.C. secs. 2151–2443 (1990), and went into operation in 1971.

45. See OPIC Act, *supra*, note 3.

46. The OPIC reauthorization legislation contains the same five-point definition of internationally recognized worker rights already in the GSP.

47. Letter from OPIC President Craig A. Nalen to Congressman Don Pease, Oct. 7, 1986.

48. Jorge F. Pérez-López, "Worker Rights in the U.S. Omnibus Trade and Competitiveness Act," *Labor Law Journal* 41 (April 1990): 222, 226.

49. James M. Zimmerman, "The Overseas Private Investment Corporation and Workers Rights: The Loss of Role Models for Employment Standards in the Foreign Workplace," *Hastings International and Comparative Law Review* 14 (1991): 603, 614–618.

50. Ibid., 615; Reauthorization of the Overseas Private Investment Corporation: Hearings on H.R. 3166 before the Subcommittee on International Economic Policy and Trade of the Committee on Foreign Affairs, 99th Cong., 1st Sess. 619 (1985) (hereinafter Hearings), 254, 266.

51. Hearings, 254, 266.

52. Zimmerman, "Overseas Private Investment Corporation," 615. Hearings, 253–255.

53. Zimmerman, "Overseas Private Investment Corporation," 616; Reauthorization of the Overseas Private Investment Corporation: Hearings on H.R. 3797

before the Subcommittee on International Economic Policy and Trade of the House Committee on Foreign Affairs, 100th Cong., 2nd Sess. (1988) (statement of Craig A. Nalen, president and chief executive officer of OPIC) (hereinafter Nalen), 84.

54. Zimmerman, "Overseas Private Investment Corporation," 616. Nalen, 84.

55. Zimmerman, "Overseas Private Investment Corporation," 616; Hearings, 266.

56. Zimmerman, "Overseas Private Investment Corporation," 616–617. OPIC insurance contracts with U.S. investors are required to contain the following worker rights clause:

The Investor agrees not to take actions to prevent employees of the foreign enterprise from lawfully exercising their right of association and their right to organize and bargain collectively. The Investor further agrees to observe applicable laws relating to a minimum age for employment of children, acceptable conditions of work with respect to minimum wages, hours of work, and occupational health and safety, and not to use forced labor. The Investor is not responsible under this paragraph for the actions of the foreign government.

See 22 U.S.C. 2191a(a)(1).

57. Trade and the Environment, GATT press communique (GATT/1529, Feb. 3, 1992), 15 (Box 2).

58. See Trade Act of 1974, supra, note 4.

59. 19 U.S.C. sec. 2411(a).

60. 19 U.S.C. sec. 2411(d)(3)(C)(i).

61. OTCA sec. 1101(b)(14).

62. Preparatory Committee (GATT), Prep. Comm. (86) SR 14 (May 23, 1986), 81 (record of discussions, 17–20 March).

63. The United States proposed the following language for the Marrakech political declaration:

Ministers recognize that the more open multilateral trading system resulting from the Uruguay Round should benefit workers around the world through the impact of increased trade on employment and income. They also express the view that trade gains should not come at the expense of the realization of social objectives and, in this connection, they agree to undertake early consideration of the relationship between the trading system and internationally recognized labor standards.

Text of Letter from Mickey Kantor to Peter Sutherland, March 24, 1994.

64. Decision on the Establishment of the Preparatory Committee for the World Trade Organization, April 7, 1994. See *Inside U.S. Trade*, Special Report, April 8, 1994.

65. Memorandum of Understanding Regarding Cooperation between the Department of Labor of the United States of America and the Secretariat of Labor and Social Welfare of the United Mexican States (1991).

66. See American Society of International Law, Basic Documents on International Economic Law, *Canada-United States-Mexico: North American Agreement on Labor Cooperation*, 1994 BDIEL AD LEXIS 6, Agreement.

67. Tripartite Declaration of Principles Concerning Multinational Enterprises

and Social Policy (adopted by the Governing Body of the International Labor Office at its 204th session in Geneva, Nov. 1977), ILO, *Official Bulletin* (Geneva), 61, ser. A, no. 1 (1978): 49–56.

68. Ibid.

69. U.S.-Mexico Business Principles on Employment and Working Conditions, draft of Jan. 8, 1992.

70. Ibid.

71. See Comprehensive Anti-Apartheid Act of 1986, Pub. L. 99-440, Oct. 2, 1986, 100 Stat. 1086, codified at 22 U.S.C. 5001 et seq.

72. Piore, "Labor Standards," 36–37.

73. Ibid., 42.

74. See Hayek, *Constitution of Liberty*, 270. The extent to which labor "advocates" resist this simple economic observation speaks volumes on the paucity of theory supporting their claims.

75. See generally P. T. Bauer, *Dissent on Development* (Cambridge, MA: Harvard University Press, 1971) and P. T. Bauer, *Equality, the Third World, and Economic Delusion* (Cambridge, MA: Harvard University Press, 1981).

76. J. M. Servais, "The Social Clause in Trade Agreements: Wishful Thinking or an Instrument of Social Progress," *International Labour Review* 128 (1989): 423, 425.

77. Hearings before the Subcommittees on International Economic Policy and Trade and on Western Hemisphere Affairs of the Committee on Foreign Affairs House of Representatives, 102nd Cong., 1st sess. (1991).

78. Testimony of Robert M. McGlotten, director, Department of Legislation, American Federation of Labor and Congress of Industrial Organizations, before the Subcommittee on Labor-Management Relations, U.S. House of Representatives on the North American Free Trade Agreement, April 30, 1991.

79. David M. Dror, "Aspects of Labour Law and Relations in Selected Export Processing Zones," *International Labour Review* 123 (1984): 705, 715.

Chapter 8
From Intention to Action
An ILO-GATT/WTO Enforcement Regime for International Labor Rights

Daniel S. Ehrenberg

Lawmaking or prescription within the area of international human rights has proliferated rapidly since World War II, but the problem of applying or enforcing human rights norms has remained a major difficulty. Most scholars concern themselves with the rules and not with the actual process under which international rules, including human rights rules, operate.[1]

A number of human rights standards are also viewed as international labor rights standards. They include freedom of association, the right to organize and bargain collectively, abolition of forced or compulsory labor, establishment of a minimum age for child labor, non-discrimination in employment, and minimum acceptable conditions of work regarding wages, hours of work, and workplace health and safety.[2] Because labor is an input in the production process of goods that enter the international trading system, various scholars,[3] unions,[4] and national governments[5] have argued that violations of international labor standards should be enforced through trade sanctions. Unfortunately, most of these proposals are extremely vague and ill defined.

This chapter proposes the establishment of an enforcement system jointly administered by the International Labor Organization (ILO) and the World Trade Organization (WTO), the successor organization to the General Agreement on Tariffs and Trade (GATT), which enforces GATT rules and standards. This joint enforcement system would rely upon the expertise and cooperation of both organizations to prevent violations of international labor rights.

The ILO has emerged as the principal international body with expertise in the area of labor issues. Its well-developed, integrated, and intricate standard-setting and enforcement machinery has produced positive results in persuading states to adhere to their obligations with respect to international labor standards, including those involving human rights concerns. However, the tools that the ILO currently has available to attain member compliance are limited to moral persuasion, publicity, shame, diplomacy, dialogue, and technical assistance. While able to enforce some standards and obtain positive results from some states, gross and persistent violations of international labor standards, including those classified as human rights standards, continue in a number of countries.

The GATT/WTO has become the premier international institution for the regulation of international trade. Within the GATT, a large body of international trading rules and standards have developed. An effective and frequently utilized dispute resolution system has also evolved. The GATT/WTO has been largely successful in its objective of liberalizing international trade through reducing trade restrictions. Thus, the international trading system, largely as a result of the activities of the GATT/WTO, has flourished by increasing the volume of international trade through the enforcement of a set of mutually beneficial rules and standards of conduct.[6] In contrast to the ILO, the GATT/WTO uses procedures that permit trade sanctions for violations of its rules.

Whenever the idea of establishing and enforcing labor standards has been introduced in the GATT, it has always been rejected.[7] In fact, the establishment of a working party to even broach the issue has been repeatedly refused.[8] Beside contending that such an approach is a form of disguised protectionism, a number of members claim that the establishment and enforcement of labor standards properly resides in the ILO.[9] Alternatively, whenever the idea of linking the enforcement of international labor standards with international trade is mentioned in the ILO, it has been rejected as being beyond the expertise and mandate of the organization.[10] In addition, neither the GATT/WTO nor the ILO has the expertise in both the international labor and international trade areas. If one organization attempted to regulate conduct pertaining to both areas, it would encroach upon the other's area of expertise.

"Supervision of compliance should be entrusted to those organizations with the greatest technical competence in the field."[11] Since the ILO is the most competent organization in the field of international labor and since the GATT/WTO is the most competent organization in the field of international trade, combining these two organizations would create the most effective enforcement regime in terms of establishing adherence to international human rights and labor standards with respect to goods that enter the international trading system.[12] This synergistic linkage, relying on each international organization's expertise, could be used as a model to demonstrate how cooperation between multilateral organizations can be effectively utilized to effectuate international human rights and labor rights policies, and optimize world public order.

Joint ILO-GATT/WTO Enforcement Regime: Preliminary Remarks

A synergistic combination of ILO and GATT/WTO expertise, creating one enforcement mechanism, would provide the most effective means of preventing violations of fundamental labor rights in the production of goods that enter the international trading system. The ILO is the premier body to examine the implementation of labor standards. It has over seventy years of experience, through its reporting and contentious supervisory procedures, in determining whether basic international labor standards are being observed and the degree of that compliance.[13] It has an established technical cooperation component to complement its supervisory activities.[14] Thus, the ILO should contribute these resources, its supervisory and technical cooperation expertise, to this joint enforcement regime.[15]

The GATT/WTO is the principal body that regulates international trade. Its expertise is in determining the existence and extent of unfair trade practices, such as dumping or subsidies, that breach existing GATT/WTO obligations or nullify or impair the receipt of reciprocal trade benefits. It also supervises the cessation of those practices through the imposition of countermeasures and economic penalties. Therefore, the GATT/WTO should bring its expertise on trade practices and its well-developed dispute settlement system and enforcement procedures to this joint enforcement regime.

This enforcement regime would operate with a bifurcated procedure. The first phase of the procedure would be the determination phase. The object of this phase would be to determine whether gross and persistent violations of labor rights occur in the production of goods that enter the international trading system, and the extent of those practices if they are found to exist. The second phase of the procedure would be the remedial phase. It would determine what measures—technical cooperation programs, certification procedures, and possible penalties— need to be established to eliminate those practices, and under what timetable compliance can realistically and fairly be achieved.

Although the procedure itself would be bifurcated, the organizations should not bifurcate their activities under this enforcement regime.[16] In the first and second phases, both organizations' expertise would be required. During the first phase, the ILO has the competence to determine whether gross and persistent violations of basic labor rights occurred and the extent of those violations. The GATT/WTO, in this first phase, has the knowledge to interpret the existence and impact of those practices in terms of trade flows, just as it does in cases involving dumping or subsidies. During the second phase, coordination by the ILO and the GATT/WTO would be essential to eliminate such practices from the international trading system. The organizations need to work in tandem to execute this enforcement regime since neither organization by itself has the expertise to administer either phase of the enforcement regime. This cooperation would benefit both organizations by creating possible synergies and would result in a greater appreciation of the symbiotic relationship between trade and labor practices.

The standards used to determine if a violation had occurred would be whether gross and persistent practices that violate fundamental labor rights occurred in the production of goods that entered the international trading system. This standard is distinct from those situations where random and isolated violations of these practices occurred that did not involve complicity by the state in either a direct or negligent manner.[17]

Countermeasures and economic sanctions would be viewed as a last resort, only to be used against recalcitrant states that did not respond to less drastic means.[18] First, a technical cooperation program, administered by the ILO, would be put in place. A certification program might also need to be instituted to ensure that products made under conditions involving labor rights violations would not enter the international trading system. A timetable would need to be placed on the utilization of these programs before countermeasures and economic sanctions would be activated so that violating states could not delay implementation under the pretense of cooperation. Economic sanctions would be applied only in the most extreme cases and their application would need to intensify over time. These sanctions might range from banning the importation of the specific products produced under conditions that violate labor rights to a wider ban on other products. This entire process of remedial measures would be coordinated by the ILO and the GATT/WTO so that a fair and realistic timetable would be put in place.

Access to the enforcement regime would include states as well as employers' and workers' associations. Allowing only states to initiate complaints would be insufficient to prevent labor rights violations. This is because states are reluctant to criticize each other on matters that may be perceived as being merely human rights concerns.[19] This problem is somewhat ameliorated since these practices bear upon the international trade in goods that directly affect each nation's material interests.

Yet states may still remain hesitant to confront each other on the use of these practices for fear that such action would be seen as a hostile and potentially volatile. Therefore, carefully filtered and controlled access by certain employers' and workers' associations, such as is used in current ILO practice, would be used. Not only would greater use and, therefore, more consistent compliance result; but as the use of this procedure became more frequent, it would appear less politicized, so that the initiation of complaints would not appear to be hostile, biased, and based upon totally unfounded acts.[20]

Joint ILO-GATT/WTO Enforcement Regime: A Proposal to Produce Effective Compliance

Any state that is a member of the ILO or of the GATT/WTO, or a bona fide employers' or workers' association from a state party of either organization would be able to file a complaint, thereby initiating the enforcement regime process. The first stage of the process would be to screen the complaint for admissibility. An admissible complaint would trigger the determination phase and the establishment of a joint ILO-GATT/WTO Dispute Panel.

To be admissible, a complaint must meet the following criteria:

(1) the complaint must be in writing and addressed to the International Labour Office or the GATT/WTO Secretariat;
(2) it cannot be anonymous;
(3) it must be filed by either a state that is a member of the ILO or of the GATT/WTO or a bona fide employers' or workers' association from a state that is a member of either organization;
(4) it must concern activities in a state that is a member of the ILO or of the GATT/WTO;
(5) it must allege that a pattern of gross and persistent practices of labor rights violations exist in the implicated state that results in the production of goods that enter the international trading system;
(6) it must specify the manner in which the state has failed to secure effective observance within its jurisdiction of the prohibition against violations of fundamental labor rights, indicating whether the violation is caused by direct state action or by a failure of the state adequately to police infractions of the standard in accordance with appropriate domestic legislation;[21]
(7) it must allege in which industry or sector these violations are occurring and which products are implicated; and
(8) it must provide some documentary evidence that these violations

are actually occurring. Mere allegations without proof would be insufficient to trigger the determination phase of this process.

Admissibility would be determined by a permanent "Admissibility Committee." This committee would be composed of nine members appointed in equal numbers by the ILO and the GATT/WTO. Members of the committee would have expertise in either international labor matters or international trade matters. They would be appointed for staggered two-year terms and would serve in their individual capacities. After being appointed, the members would be required to declare that they would perform their duties honorably, faithfully, impartially, and conscientiously. The committee would specifically be appointed as follows: four members would be appointed by the chair of the ILO Governing Body (GB); four members would be chosen by the chair of the GATT Council (Council); and one member would be a joint appointment of the ILO and the GATT/WTO Directors-General.

The duties of the Admissibility Committee would be to decide if a complaint is admissible based on the eight aforementioned criteria. The Admissibility Committee, in their discretion, could communicate the complaint to the member state concerned so as to afford the government an opportunity to reply. Once a determination had been made, a notice to that effect would be sent to all parties concerned: the party that initiated the complaint, the party or parties implicated by the complaint, the GB, and the Council. The determination of the Admissibility Committee would be final. If declared inadmissible, all further deliberations regarding that complaint would cease.

Once a complaint had been declared admissible, the determination phase would be triggered and a joint ILO-GATT/WTO Dispute Panel would be established. The Dispute Panel would be quasi-judicial body composed of seven prominent and professional persons who would serve in their personal capacity. Members of the committee would be chosen on the basis of their expertise in either international labor matters, or international trade matters. They would have a judicial temperament, a reputation for fairness and objectivity, sufficient formal training or practical experience in the operation of international legal rules, and good character and excellent ability. After being appointed, the members would be required to take an oath in which they would swear to perform their duties honorably, faithfully, impartially, and conscientiously.

The ILO and the GATT/WTO would each appoint three members to this Dispute Panel, with the remaining member being a joint appointment of the ILO and the GATT/WTO Directors-General. The ILO panelists would be selected from the current members of the ILO Committee of Experts or from a specially created pool of potential panelists formulated by the ILO.[22] The GATT/WTO panelists would come from the current list of governmental and non-governmental panelists.[23]

In the case of an interstate complaint,[24] the states would be given the opportunity to agree on the ILO and the GATT/WTO panelists, using the respective pools of panelists that each organization would have made available. If the parties could not agree on the panelists within twenty days, either party could request the ILO or the GATT/WTO Director-General to appoint the remaining panel members within ten days from the date of the request.[25] The Directors-General, in selecting the remaining panelists, would be required to consult with both parties, but would make the final determination. In the case of a complaint initiated by an employers' or workers' association, the ILO Director-General would appoint the ILO panelists and the GATT/WTO Director-General would appoint the GATT/WTO panelists. The remaining panelist would still be a joint ILO-GATT/WTO appointment. This method of appointment would be used to ensure complete impartiality, independence, and objectivity.

The duties of the Dispute Panel would be to consider fully the complaint and make an objective assessment of the matter. It would prepare a report that would include its findings on all relevant questions concerning the issues implicated by the complaint. The report would indicate what the panel perceived to be a reasonable period of time for compliance, recommendations and programs to aid in the attainment of compliance (i.e., technical assistance programs and certification procedures), and possible countermeasures. The timeframe for compliance, the aid programs, and retaliatory measures could be made part of the adopted report.

The panel would fulfill these duties by engaging in a quasi-judicial inquiry into the matter, allowing sufficient flexibility for all parties to prepare their submissions while ensuring that the matter would be resolved in an expeditious manner. The panel, after consultation with the parties, would fix a timetable for presentation and deliberations within one week from its establishment. Normally, each side would submit written submissions to the panel with the complainant or complainants submitting first. The respondent party or parties would receive a copy of the complainant's submission and would have an additional twenty days to prepare its submission.

After receiving the submissions, the panel would hold oral hearings during which each side would present their arguments and answer questions with the other party present. After this first round of written submissions and oral arguments, another round of simultaneous written submissions followed by oral hearings would take place. The panel also would have the right during this investigatory stage to listen to and examine witnesses, who would appear at the request of the parties or at the request of the commission. The panel could seek information and technical advice from outside experts; utilize the reports of the Committee of Experts and other international bodies; and conduct on-the-spot investigations, field visits, and field hearings. Other states, not directly involved in the complaint, would be asked to place any relevant information that they possessed at the disposal of the Dispute Panel. Those member states either bordering on or having significant trade relations with the country or countries involved in the complaint would be called upon to furnish any relevant information.

In the case of complaints initiated by employers' or workers' associations, the submissions and oral hearings would be performed by a joint-complainant committee of GATT/WTO and ILO officials, with expertise in dispute resolution procedures, appointed by the Directors-General of the ILO and the GATT/WTO. These appointed officials could not have been involved in any matter that would prevent them from effectively representing the ILO and the GATT/WTO in these proceedings. The task of this joint-complainant committee would be to uphold the interests of both the ILO and the GATT/WTO in preventing violations of international labor rights in the production of goods that enter the international trading system. They would prepare the case in consultation with the original complainant party. Yet they would be responsible for representing their organizations' interests. The Dispute Panel could accept written submissions from the original complainants and could even allow them to appear before the panel as witnesses. Yet the original complainants would have no standing before the panel. In the case of interstate complaints, the complainant would be the state or states that filed the complaint.

Panel deliberations would culminate in the drafting of a panel report. The report would be drafted in three sections. The first section would describe the disputants' arguments and would include findings of fact. This section would be submitted to the disputants for their comments before the final report would be completed. The second section of the report would include a determination by the Dispute Panel as to whether gross and persistent violations of fundamental labor rights had occurred and, if so, the industry, sector, and products implicated by the violation. The third section of the report would indicate what the panel perceived to be a reasonable period of time for compliance, recommendations and programs to aid in the attainment of compliance (i.e., technical assistance programs and certification procedures), and possible countermeasures. The completed reports would usually be submitted to the disputants before submission to the GB and the Council.

The determination phase from establishment of a panel to completion of the final report would normally not exceed nine months and would never take longer than twelve months.

The Dispute Panel report would be circulated to all members of the GB and the Council. Any state that is a member of the ILO or the GATT/WTO could also receive a copy of the report. The "consensus" rule would be followed with respect to Dispute Panel reports. Under this rule, the first two sections of the Dispute Panel report, dealing with findings of fact and a determination as to whether a violation had occurred, would be automatically adopted unless a consensus of either the Council or the GB decided to withhold adoption or delay consideration. The Council, at the meeting following the report's presentation, could decide to withhold adoption or delay consideration. Likewise, at the next meeting of the GB, automatic adoption of the report could be delayed or denied.[26] The report would be adopted unless a consensus by members of either the GB or the Council decided to reject the report. If this rejection by either the GB or the Council occurred, the dispute process would be completed and no violation would have been found to exist. Thus, no subsequent actions would need to be taken by any state concerning this matter.

Any contracting party with an objection to the report would be required to detail their objection in writing and circulate the writing to all GB or Council members at least ten days before the meeting of either body at which the panel report would be considered. The disputants would have a right to participate in the GB or the Council deliberations concerning the report and their views would be recorded. The entire dispute settlement process from the filing of a complaint to the decision on the Dispute Panel report should not exceed eighteen months. If the report were to be adopted, the date of adoption would be the ending date of the meeting of either the Council or the GB, whichever occurred later, in which the report had not been rejected or had consideration delayed.

If the report was adopted, the state implicated by the report would have up to three months to appeal the decision of the joint ILO-GATT/WTO enforcement regime to the International Court of Justice (ICJ). The ICJ could either affirm, reverse, or vary any of the findings and conclusions contained in the adopted Dispute Panel report. The determination of the ICJ on this matter would be final.

During this three-month period, the implicated state would also have the opportunity to formulate and develop a technical cooperation program with the ILO. This technical cooperation program would be specifically geared to eradicating any violations of fundamental labor rights.

This program would be required to be approved by the ILO Director-General and the appropriate state official within six months from the period in which the Dispute Panel report had been adopted.

The technical cooperation program could involve a number of activities. These could include rewriting existing domestic legislation; imposing stiffer penalties against domestic violators; strengthening the labor inspectorate and state enforcement mechanisms; instituting public education and other campaigns targeted at employers, workers, religious institutions, schools, judges, law enforcement officials, and others; developing efficient production processes to produce the goods without violating labor rights; generating poverty eradication programs; and instituting compulsory education programs.

The technical cooperation program would incorporate a timeline for compliance. The timeline would include a number of interim phases in which the program's implementation could be evaluated.[27] While the technical cooperation program would allow for some flexibility in terms of achieving compliance with the adopted Dispute Panel report's rulings, a period of no longer than two years from the date of adoption of the panel report would be permitted before either full compliance would be achieved or an export ban on all products made in violation of basic labor rights would be instituted.

Besides the development of a technical cooperation program, the GB and Council with the assistance of officials from the International Labor Office and the GATT/WTO Secretariat would meet and jointly decide upon the actions the violating state would need to take to comply with the adopted report's ruling. These bodies would also oversee compliance monitoring of the violating state.

A joint ILO-GATT/WTO remediation committee would be established. It would consist of ten members: five from the GB and five from the Council. The members would be appointed by their respective chairs in consultation with their respective Directors-General. The committee would be established within ten days from the date at which the Dispute Panel report had been adopted.

This joint ILO-GATT/WTO remediation committee would decide upon a timetable for compliance, the actions that the government would be required to take to achieve compliance, and a timetable for countermeasures and economic sanctions. The committee would use section three of the Dispute Panel report as the initial starting point for developing this remediation plan and timetable. The committee could either accept or alter the Dispute Panel's recommendations. They would be required to complete the remediation plan and timetable within a period of two months from the date of their creation.

Once devised, the plan would be submitted to the GB and the Council. This remediation plan would be adopted automatically unless a consensus of either the Council or the GB refused to adopt the plan as formulated by the joint ILO-GATT/WTO remediation committee. If the remediation plan was rejected as written, it would be revised until an acceptable plan would not be rejected by consensus of either body.

In the event that the new plan of the joint ILO-GATT remediation committee was rejected a second time, the plan would be formulated by a special unit consisting of the two Directors-General and the chairs of the GB and the Council. They would seek input from all interested states, but would make the final determination as to the content of this remediation plan. They would complete the development of this plan within two months.

Compliance would normally occur within one year from the adoption of the Dispute Panel's report. It would, in no event, take longer than two years. If violations continued beyond the period of time designated in the remediation plan for full compliance, countermeasures and/or sanctions would be instituted. First, a countermeasure would be activated. This measure would ban any products made in the state where the violation had been found to exist if those products continued to be produced under conditions violative of fundamental labor rights. Only products implicated in the adopted Dispute Panel report that have been certified as having been produced without such violations would be permitted to enter the international trading system. In other words, only those products that satisfied a strict certification procedure could be exported.[28] If, after an additional period as specified in the remediation plan,[29] the violating state had still not stopped producing goods that enter the international trading system under conditions that violate labor rights, wider trade sanctions or bans would be instituted. These sanctions would intensify until the violations had ceased.

In addition to these measures, a certification procedure would also be developed. This procedure would be constructed so to certify that the products implicated in the adopted Dispute Panel report were not actually made under conditions that violate labor rights. If the mechanics of this certification procedure could not be arranged to the satisfaction of the joint ILO-GATT/WTO remediation committee and included in the remediation plan, a ban of all implicated products would occur as soon as the period for compliance in the remediation plan had expired.[30] To be operative, this certification plan would require mandatory inspections by a joint inspection team, composed of International Labor Office and GATT/WTO Secretariat employees. The inspection team could enter and inspect all facilities where the implicated products are being produced, including the facilities of subcontractors and other intermediate producers. These mandatory inspections would take place periodically and could occur without prior warning.[31] Only those products certified as having been produced without labor rights violations to the satisfaction of the procedures agreed to in the remediation plan as worked out by the violating state and the joint ILO-GATT/WTO remediation committee would be permitted to be exported.

The progress of the violating state would be periodically reviewed by the ILO and the GATT/WTO. The joint ILO-GATT/WTO remediation committee would have primary responsibility for monitoring progress with respect to the remediation plan. They would meet once every three months to discuss the progress of the violating state with regard to the adopted Dispute Panel report's rulings and the remediation plan. They would expect to receive a mandatory report from the violating state on the progress it had achieved with regard to compliance. If the violating state had entered into a technical cooperation program with the ILO, a report by the ILO would detail the progress achieved with regard to the technical cooperation program and the eradication of the offending practices. If a certification procedure had been implemented, then a report on the status of that procedure, including reports by the inspection team, would also be delivered to the remediation committee. The joint ILO-GATT/WTO remediation committee could also seek information and hear witnesses from any other pertinent sources in order to evaluate the compliance of the violating state. States that are members of the ILO or the GATT/WTO and bona fide employers' and workers' organizations could furnish information to the committee. On-the-spot visits could also take place either by the joint ILO-GATT/WTO remediation committee or by a joint surveillance team composed of International Labor Office and GATT/WTO Secretariat employees with the permission of the violating state. If such visits occurred, reports of the findings of those visits would be presented to the committee. Based on all the information received, the joint ILO-GATT/WTO remediation committee would draft a report to the GB and the Council.

The GB and the Council would consider compliance four months after the remediation plan had been approved or implemented. The GB and the Council would review the report of the joint ILO-GATT/WTO remediation committee every four months and oversee the remediation committee's activities. This review would continue until full compliance had been achieved. The chair of the joint ILO-GATT/WTO remediation committee would be present at each of these review sessions to present the committee's report and to answer questions. If monitoring efforts were deemed ineffective, the chair of the remediation committee would meet with the chairs of the GB and the Council and the Directors-General of the ILO and the GATT/WTO to formulate a revised monitoring strategy.

Again based upon all the information received, the joint ILO-GATT/WTO remediation committee could decide that the implicated state had fully complied with the rulings reflected in the adopted Dispute Panel report. Alternatively, the implicated state, at any time, could declare that it had achieved full compliance and could request that a joint ILO-GATT/WTO inspection team visit to verify compliance. If an inspection occurred, the report of the joint ILO-GATT/WTO inspection team would be submitted to the joint remediation committee. Full compliance would occur when the implicated state ceased from violating labor rights to produce goods that enter the international trading system.

Once the joint ILO-GATT/WTO remediation committee determined that full compliance had been achieved, it would file a report to the GB and the Council, certifying its finding. The GB and the Council would each discuss the matter and adopt the recommendation of the joint ILO-GATT/WTO remediation committee that full compliance had been achieved unless a consensus of either body determined otherwise. If either body refused to ratify the recommendation of the joint ILO-GATT/WTO remediation committee, then the monitoring procedure and the remediation plan would remain in place.

If the GB and the Council adopted the remediation committee's recommendation—namely, that full compliance has been achieved by the implicated state—then all economic sanctions and any bans on export goods would cease immediately. The certification procedure, however, would remain in place. The implicated state would continue to be monitored by the joint ILO-GATT/WTO remediation committee for a period of one additional year. The GB and the Council would continue to receive reports from the remediation committee and review their activities every four months for the additional one-year period. During this one-year period, periodic and unannounced on-the-spot visits of the country and inspections of all facilities that were suspected of violating labor rights in the production of goods that enter the international trading system would take place. If, during the additional year, no gross and persistent violations of labor rights were uncovered that produced goods that entered the international trading system, all countermeasures, bans on exportation, and certification procedures would be terminated.

Conclusion

The international trading system and the world economy would benefit by the enforcement of international labor rights standards. The international trading system would signal its seriousness and impartiality in regards to enforcing rules that promote fair competition and fair trade. The benefits of an open trading system would accrue to all, not only those who are exploiters. More human resources would be available to increase the efficiency of and expand the world economy. Indeed, a multilateral enforcement regime of international labor standards would increase the amount of world trade controlled by multilateral institutions and would decrease calls for protectionism. Perhaps most important, developing countries would be able, more effectively, to promote social and economic advancement within their countries without having to compete against other nations that do not respect these standards. Thus, a country would not have to fear being penalized in the international marketplace for respecting the labor rights, human rights, and dignity of its people.

Although many developing nations are currently opposed to the enforcement of violations of international labor standards, a number of developed countries are moving toward enforcement of these standards on a unilateral basis. The United States has already included worker rights provisions in its trade laws and has taken unilateral action against a number of countries.[32] Rather than dissipate, these demands will only increase in the future. Thus, a multilateral enforcement regime that replaces what has been called "aggressive unilateralism" would be in the best interests of developing nations. It would allow them to participate in the formulation and implementation of objective multilateral procedures, rather than be at the mercy of the procedures and actions devised by the developed nations.

By viewing violations of international labor rights not only as human rights violations but also as unfair trade practices, states could more readily recognize the implications of these practices on their material interests. Strong incentives would thus be created for states to protect their interests by sanctioning transgressor states and preventing future violations. In effect, the self-interest of each state would be harnessed to promote and enforce human rights for all.

Acknowledgments. An earlier version of this chapter appeared as Daniel S. Ehrenberg, "The Labor Link: Applying the International Trading System to Enforce Violations of Forced and Child Labor," *Yale Journal of International Law* 20, no. 2: 361ff. Reprinted by permission of the staff of the *Yale Journal of International Law.*

Notes

1. See Mark W. Janis, "Forward: International Courts and the Efficacy of International Law," *Connecticut Journal of International Law* 2 (1987): 261.

2. These consensus international labor rights are contained in every international and regional human rights instrument. They are also characterized as

fundamental rights by the International Labor Organization, as reflected in the ILO's basic human rights Conventions. See ILO, *Human Rights: A Common Responsibility*, Report of the Director-General (Geneva: ILO, 1988). U.S. law characterizes these human/international labor rights (with the exception of non-discrimination) as "internationally recognized worker rights." See The Omnibus Trade and Competitiveness Act of 1988, 19 U.S.C. sec. 2411 (d) (3) (B) (iii) (1988); Trade and Tariff (General System of Preferences Renewal) Act of 1984, 19 U.S.C. sec. 2462 (a) (4) (1988). See also Ray Marshall, "Trade-Linked Labor Standards," *Proceedings of the Academy of Political Science* 37 (1990): 67, 71; Gijsbert van Liemt, "Minimum Labour Standards and International Trade: Would a Social Clause Work?" *International Labor Review* 128 (1989): 433, 436–438.

3. See Marshall, "Trade-Linked Labor Standards"; International Labor Rights Education and Research Fund, *Trade's Hidden Costs: Worker Rights in a Changing World Economy* (Washington, DC: ILRREF, 1988) (hereinafter *ILRERF*); Gote Hansson, *Social Clauses and International Trade* (New York: St. Martin's Press, 1983); Philip Alston, "International Trade as an Instrument of Positive Human Rights Policy," *Human Rights Quarterly* 4 (1982): 155; Gus Edgren, "Fair Labour Standards and Trade Liberalization," *International Labor Review* 118 (1979): 523.

4. See International Confederation of Free Trade Unions, *Free Trade Unions for a Democratic World Order: The Role of the ICFTU* (Brussels: ICFTU, 1992) (hereinafter *Role of ICFTU*); International Metalworkers' Federation, *Trade and Workers' Rights: Time for a Link* (Geneva: IMF, 1988) (hereinafter *Time for a Link*); Bureau of International Labor Affairs, U.S. Department of Labor, *Labor Standards and Trade Distortions* (1978), 7, 16 (quoting resolutions by the AFL-CIO supporting a code of international labor standards).

5. Since 1979, the United States has made submissions to GATT proposing international labor standards. Canada, in 1979, supported the concept of developing a fair international labor standards system (Hansson, *Social Clauses*, 27–28). During Lome II negotiations in 1978, the European Economic Community proposed and later withdrew a provision that would have linked trade relations to respect for international labor standards (Philip Alston, "Linking Trade and Human Rights," *German Year Book of International Law* 23 (1980): 126, 137–38.

6. For background on GATT, see generally John H. Jackson, *The World Trading System* (Cambridge, MA: MIT Press, 1989). On April 15, 1994, after over seven years of negotiations, leaders from more than 117 countries signed the Final Act of the Uruguay Round negotiations of GATT at Marrakesh, Morocco. This historic agreement not only established the WTO, the successor institution to GATT, but also achieved numerous other trade agreements on goods, services, intellectual property rights, trade-related investments, and dispute settlement practices (U.S. General Accounting Office, *The General Agreement on Tariffs and Trade Uruguay Round Final Act Should Produce Overall U.S. Economic Gains*, vol. 2, July 1994, GAO/GGD-94-83b Uruguay Round Final Act, 6, 8).

The WTO "provide[s] the common institutional framework for the conduct of trade relations among its Members in matters related to the [Final Act] agreements and associated legal instruments included in the Annexes to this Agreement" (Final Act Embodying the Results of the Uruguay Round of Multilateral Trade Negotiations, Agreement Establishing World Trade Organization, art. II, para. 1, opened for signature April 15, 1994). It creates a single institutional framework to implement and operate all trade agreements associated with GATT and the Uruguay Round (*GATT Focus No. 107* May 1994, 11) (hereinafter *GATT Focus*); Amelia Porges, "Introductory Note, General Agreement on Tariffs and Trade—Multilateral Trade Negotiations (the Uruguay Round): Final Act Embodying the Results of the Uruguay Round of Trade Negotiations," *I.L.M.* 33 (1994): 1, 2. The Final Act was entered into force on January 1, 1995 after being ratified by those nations that signed it (*GATT Focus*, 11).

7. Jeffrey Laurenti, *Labor Standards and Social Trade in a Stronger Hand: Shaping an American Agenda for a More Effective United Nations* (New York: United Nations Association of U.S.A., 1988), 56, 60; "Meetings on Workers' Rights and Trade, Geneva, 4–5 September 1990," International Confederation of Free Trade Unions Internal Doc. no. 98EB/12(a), ESC 2, Annex I at paras. 2–3 (Dec. 3, 1990) (on file with the author) (hereinafter *ICFTU Memo*); Harlan Mandel, "In Pursuit of the Missing Link: International Worker Rights and International Trade," *Columbia Journal of Transnational Law* 27 (1989): 442, 449, n. 31; *Worker Rights and International Trade American Society of International Law Proceedings* (1987): 59, 61, 64–65 (remarks of Jorge F. Pérez-López) (hereinafter *Worker Rights Proceedings*); see also Steve Charnovitz, "The Influence of International Labour Standards on the World Trading Regime," *International Labor Review* 126 (1987): 565, 574–575 (hereinafter Charnovitz, *ILR*); Steve Charnovitz, "International Trade and Worker Rights," *SAIS Review* 7 (1987): 185, 197.

8. See *ICFTU Memo*, Annex I; Submission to the Negotiators Preparing the Final Agreement of the Uruguay Round of GATT Multilateral Trade Negotiations, 4–5 undated (received from the ICFTU in 1993; on file with the author); Liemt, "Minimum Labour Standards," 442; Mandel, "In Pursuit of the Missing Link," 447–448; *Worker Rights Proceedings*, 64–65.

9. *ICFTU Memo*, paras. 8–9, 11; Economic Policy Council of the United Nations Association of the USA, *The International Labor Organization and the Global Economy: New Opportunities for the United States in the 1990's* (New York: United Nations Association of the USA, 1991), 31; Charnovitz, *ILR*, 581.

10. *ICFTU Memo*, para. 11; International Labour Office, "Report of Discussion of Informal Working Group on Minimum International Labour Standards Held on 8 November, 1990," from files of Lee Swepston of ILO, Geneva (notes on file with author); International Labour Conference, "Provisional Record of Conference: 1988," from files of Lee Swepston of ILO, Geneva (notes on file with author); Alston, "International Trade," 175–81.

11. Theodore Meron, *Human Rights Law-Making in the United Nations: A Critique of Instruments and Process* (New York: Oxford University Press, 1986), 214.

12. The idea of an ILO-GATT/WTO linkage to protect violations of international labor standards by using the international trading system has been suggested by a number of commentators. See, e.g., International Confederation of Free Trade Unions," The Social Clause: A Technical Note from the ICFTU Secretariat on Its Rationale and on Its Operating Mechanisms," undated, 2–4 (received from the ICFTU in 1993; on file with the author) (hereinafter "ICFTU Technical Note"); Economic Policy Council, *International Labor Organization*, 36–37; Marshall, "Trade-Linked Labor Standards," 67, 73, 76–77; Mandel, "In Pursuit of the Missing Link," 448; *Time for a Link*, "International Trade and Worker Rights," 46–47; Charnovitz, 580–581; Charnovitz, "Fair Labor Standards and International Trade," World Trade *Journal of Law* 20 (1986): 76–77; Hansson, *Social Clauses*, 180–182.

13. See "ICFTU Technical Note," 3; Charnovitz, "Fair Labor Standards," 76; Edgren, "Fair Labour Standards," 530–531.

14. See, generally, *International Labour Standards and Technical Cooperation. Gov-*

erning Body, International Labour Office, 25 2d Sess., ILO Doc.GB.252/15/1 (March 2–6, 1992) (photocopy on file with the author).

15. See "ICFTU Technical Note," 3; Charnovitz, "Fair Labor Standards," 75–77. See also Edgren, "Fair Labour Standards," 530–531 (suggesting that the ILO in a labor standard–trade enforcement regime could function as the research agency in terms of studying compliance to labor standards); Economic Policy Council, *International Labor Organization*, 37 (stating that the ILO's role in a social clause should be "to provide the necessary training and support for countries and industries as they attempt to improve labor conditions").

16. More than one commentator has maintained that the ILO should be used only in a supplementary manner as a research agency or more actively as the body that makes a determination as to whether a violation has occurred, but should not involve itself in the remedial phase. See, e.g., Economic Policy Council, *International Labor Organization*, 36–37, 49–50; International Labor Office, "Minimum International Standards Resume of Meeting of 13 December, 1988: Minimum International Labour Standards Analysis of Responses," 3, from files of Lee Swepston of ILO, Geneva (notes on file with the author); Edgren, "Fair Labour Standards," 530–531.

17. A negligent situation would occur where the state does not attempt or merely engage in feeble attempts to enforce laws that prohibit labor rights violations.

18. "ICFTU Technical Note," 3; International Textile, Garment and Leather Workers Federation, "The Social Clause Explained," *ITGLWF Newsletter* (June 1992, 12 (on file with the author).

19. See Scott Leckie, "The Inter-State Complaint Procedure in International Human Rights Law: Hopeful Prospects or Wishful Thinking," *Human Rights Quarterly* 10 (1988): 249.

20. In addition, if complaints would be initiated by employers' and workers' organizations, the state really would have no control over the actions of these organizations. Thus, the initiation of such complaints under these circumstances would not be seen as interstate complaints, with all of the consequent ramifications. See Leckie, "Inter-State Complaint Procedure," 251–255.

21. The domestic legislation would be deemed appropriate in the sense that it meets the minimum requirements of the international legal standards pertaining to fundamental labor rights.

22. A specially created pool of potential panelists could also be appointed for renewable three-year terms by the GB on the proposal of the ILO director-general. The criteria for appointment would be similar to that used for members of the ILO Committee of Experts.

23. The GATT currently uses a roster of governmental and non-governmental panelists from which panelists are chosen (Eric Canal-Forgues and Rudolf Ostrihansky, "New Developments in the GATT Dispute Settlement Procedures," *World Trade Law* 24 [1990]: 67, 74). The WTO dispute resolution system will expand that practice and favor non-governmental panelists. Final Act Embodying the Results of the Uruguay Round of Multilateral Trade Negotiations, Annex 2: Understanding on Rules and Procedures Governing the Settlement of Disputes, art. 8, opened for signature April 15, 1994.

24. An interstate complaint is one in which a state or states file a complaint against another state or states. In other words, it only involves states as the implicated parties.

25. Of course, the ILO Director-General would appoint the remaining ILO panelists while the GATT/WTO Director-General would appoint the remaining GATT/WTO panelists.

26. If the GB decided to delay adoption, it would be required to hold a special meeting to consider adoption within thirty days from the ending of the GB session in which it had decided to delay adoption.

27. If, during one of the interim evaluations, it were to be discovered that the technical cooperation program was not achieving its objectives, the program would have to be reconfigured so that positive progress would be made. If, in attempting to revise the technical cooperation program, it were to be discovered that the violating state was only feigning cooperation in order to delay the implementation of countermeasures or sanctions, the program would be immediately terminated and a ban on all products implicated in the adopted Dispute Panel report would be immediately instituted.

28. For a discussion of the certification program, see notes 30–31 below and accompanying text.

29. Normally, this period would be an additional twelve months from the period in which the certification procedure had first been instituted.

30. The certification plan would be part of the entire remediation plan subject to the approval of the GB and the Council as per the procedures described earlier in this section.

31. It is preferable that all or almost all of the inspections would take place without any advance warning.

32. For a description and critique of worker rights provisions in U.S. trade laws, see, e.g., Lawyers Committee for Human Rights, *Worker Rights Under the U.S. Trade Laws* (New York: Lawyers Committee for Human Rights, 1989); *ILRERF*; Theresa A. Amato, "Labor Rights Conditionality: United States Trade Legislation and the International Trade Order," *New York University Law Review* (1990): 79, 96–104; Mandel, "In Pursuit of the Missing Link."

Chapter 9
Private Labor Rights Enforcement Through Corporate Codes of Conduct

Lance A. Compa and Tashia Hinchliffe Darricarrère

Codes of conduct for international business operations are proliferating as investors, companies, and governments confront worker demands to respect human and labor rights claims. For the most part, until recently, the link between increasing global economic activity and human rights was tenuous. Investors and executives tended to see human rights as a matter for government officials and diplomats to sort out, and resisted pressures to have their businesses used as tools for political reform. In a nutshell, as one critic of "corporate social responsibility" puts it, "the company that seeks to pursue profit and do 'good works' at the same time is likely to do neither very well."[1]

For their part, human rights activists tended to stress the most egregious violations of political and civil rights—arbitrary arrest and detention, torture, political killings, one-party dictatorships, and the like—without taking up issues of labor rights, working conditions, and the role of international business in a country where such abuses occurred. International labor rights were largely seen as a narrow, technical concern of the International Labor Organization, a Geneva-based United Nations specialized agency that issues—but has no power to enforce—"Conventions" approved by government, management, and labor delegates to its annual conferences.[2]

Globalization of the economy and globalization of human rights concerns were both important phenomena of the second half of the twentieth century, but they developed mostly on separate tracks. The international community did elaborate charters, covenants, and conventions that spoke to labor rights and labor conditions, but these mostly remained statements of high intention rather than guides to actual practice.[3]

A prominent exception to the general "de-linking" of human rights and international business with respect to labor conditions arose in the anti-apartheid movement of the 1970s and 1980s. The revulsion against a country making racial discrimination a principle of its legal system prompted a broad movement of economic pressure that involved U.S.-based multinational corporations active in South Africa. This pressure took shape with the "Sullivan Principles," a 1977 code of conduct for U.S. companies in South Africa that targeted discriminatory work practices, employee housing conditions, and promotional opportunities for Black and Coloured South Africans.[4]

In addition to their contents, the Sullivan Principles established an elaborate compliance audit mechanism administered by an independent accounting and consulting firm. However, the author of the Sullivan Principles later repudiated the program as ineffectual,[5] and they were superseded by congressional passage of comprehensive economic sanctions against South Africa.[6]

In the past ten years the general resistance to linking human rights and labor rights to international business practices has begun breaking down. Since 1984:

- U.S. trade statutes have been amended to include labor rights conditionality in trade preference programs;[7]
- a labor side accord was negotiated as part of the North American Free Trade Agreement;[8]
- litigation has emerged in U.S. courts over international labor rights disputes;[9]
- U.S. unions have moved aggressively to develop international solidarity programs with foreign workers and unions;[10]
- agreement was reached to include worker rights issues in the agenda of the new World Trade Organization resulting from the Uruguay Round of GATT negotiations;[11]
- more U.S.-based firms have developed codes of conduct on worker rights and working conditions for foreign subsidiaries and suppliers.

This chapter examines the last of these new developments: codes of conduct promulgated by corporations. Such an examination has taken on a new urgency in the wake of the Clinton administration's 1994 decision to maintain China's most-favored-nation (MFN) trade status, despite its record of widespread human rights and labor rights violations.[12] Responding to criticism, the administration has promoted a voluntary code of conduct for U.S. companies doing business in China.[13]

The Clinton administration's idea for a corporate code of conduct is not new. In response to growing pressure over labor issues, several U.S. companies involved in international business have begun elaborating corporate codes of conduct that address worker rights, among other concerns. As a spokesman for Reebok puts it, "Consumers today hold companies accountable for the way products are made, not just the quality of the product itself."[14]

Codes of conduct for labor rights are taking shape as part of a broader movement of corporate social responsibility. The premise of the corporate social responsibility movement is that "corporations, because they are the dominant institution of the planet, must squarely face and address the social and environmental problems that afflict humankind."[15] The most visionary exponents of this movement call for a redesign of the current system of commerce to one where "doing good is second nature, in which natural, everyday acts of work and life cumulate into a better world as a matter of course, not a matter of altruism."[16]

Between altruism and "a matter of course" in some distant business paradigm lies a more immediate self-interest. As one observer puts it, "deteriorating social circumstances put at risk our ability to satisfy customers, provide a stable work environment, and meet our obligations to stockholders. . . . Business must actively continue to help ensure that the community has the economic policies to support business, the educational system to produce the workers of tomorrow, and the quality of life necessary to attract and retain employees."[17]

External Codes of Conduct

Before examining codes of conduct generated within the multinational enterprise, a look at externally generated codes suggests why companies are formulating their own internal norms of conduct. There are two main types of external codes: those created in multilateral government settings, and those shaped privately, but offered for company acceptance.

Multilateral Government-Initiated Codes

The United Nations Code

The United Nations has formulated, but never formally adopted, a Code of Conduct on Transnational Corporations. It was promoted in the early and mid-1970s at a time when the "Group of 77" developing countries was aggressively confronting the industrialized world. Evidence of malfeasance by multinational corporations (such as involvement in the

1973 overthrow of Chilean President Salvador Allende[18]) also spurred consideration of a corporate code of conduct.

The UN Code speaks generally to human rights and fair treatment of workers, requiring, for example, that "transnational corporations shall respect human rights and fundamental freedoms in the countries in which they operate. In their social and industrial relations, transnational corporations shall not discriminate on the basis of race, colour, sex, language, social, national and ethnic origin or political or other opinion."[19]

Since the time this code was elaborated, however, third world confrontation has largely given way to integration into a liberalized global economy. For most of the developing world, multinational companies are prized investors, not intruders. The UN Code stands as a worthy statement of principle, but, failing its adoption will remain just that, and nothing more.

The OECD Code

The Organization for Economic Cooperation and Development (OECD) established Guidelines for Multinational Enterprises in 1976, also in response to concerns about corporate interference in national political affairs. The code recognizes the right to organize and bargain collectively, and requires employers to provide facilities and information to union representatives so that they may engage in meaningful bargaining. The OECD code also requires companies to furnish financial and strategic information to unions so that they can "obtain a true and fair view" of operations. It further bans discrimination in employment, requires advance notice of layoffs and cooperation with unions to mitigate the effects of layoffs, and calls on management not to threaten plant closures or layoffs to influence contract negotiations or to interfere with the right to organize.[20]

Although the OECD avoids making specific findings of misconduct by individual companies under its code, it provides a complaint procedure that can result in "clarifications" of the guidelines as they apply to particular labor-management disputes. There is no coercive enforcement mechanism to ensure compliance with the guidelines, but workers and trade unions have occasionally achieved successful resolution of disputes through recourse to the OECD.[21]

The ILO Code

The International Labor Organization (ILO) has elaborated a Tripartite Declaration of Principles Concerning Multinational Enterprises and Social Policy. Since the ILO includes representatives of both employers and trade unions, this code is not strictly governmental in origin. The ILO code has a broader range than that of the OECD, extending to such issues as job creation, investment in the local economy, subcontracting, and so on. It also provides for a more detailed complaint procedure before a Standing Committee on Multinational Enterprises empowered to investigate and make specific findings of code violations by individual companies. Like the OECD code, though, the ILO Declaration has no sanctions to back up its rules. Enforcement is more a matter of private consultation or public embarrassment.[22]

Privately Drawn "Sign-On" Codes of Conduct

The MacBride Code

The Sullivan Principles remain the most prominent example of a corporate code of conduct drawn up by an outside private party, designed for companies to "take the pledge" to comply with its terms. This approach was replicated in the "MacBride Principles," a code of conduct issued in 1984 by the noted Irish statesman Sean MacBride to influence the activities of U.S. companies doing business in Northern Ireland. This code focuses on non-discrimination and affirmative action programs to overcome the deep antipathy between the Protestant majority and the Roman Catholic minority in that British-ruled territory.[23]

The Slepak and Miller Codes

The "Slepak Principles" and "Miller Principles"—the former named for a prominent Soviet dissident, the latter for the U.S. congressman who formulated them—sought to create codes of conduct for multinational companies doing business in the Soviet Union and in China, respectively. The Slepak code was issued in 1988 by a private foundation. The Miller Principles were contained in a 1991 bill introduced by Representative John Miller of Washington state. Both spoke principally to forced labor issues and military-related industrial projects. In the wake of the Soviet Union's dissolution, however, and continuing U.S. corporate interest in investment opportunities in China, neither has attracted support.[24]

The Maquiladora Code

Concerns about pollution, unsafe working conditions, and poverty-level wages have led to the issuance of a code of conduct for U.S. companies with operations in the *maquiladora* factory zone along the U.S.-

Mexican border. Promoted by the AFL-CIO and a coalition of religious and environmental groups, the "Maquiladora Standards of Conduct" code appeals to U.S. corporations to promote a safe environment, safe workplaces, and an adequate standard of living for workers.

The maquiladora code addresses hazardous waste disposal, chemical leaks, and transportation of toxic materials. It further requires disclosure to workers and communities on the use and risks of chemicals and other hazardous materials, and calls for workplace health and safety committees. The code would protect the right to organize and bargain, ban discrimination (including sexual harassment), and require a higher minimum wage and limits on working hours. Finally, this code would abolish barracks-style living quarters for workers and establish a trust fund to improve housing, health care, sanitary services, and other infrastructure.[25] In practice, however, at least through mid-1994, only one corporation reportedly committed itself to abide by the Maquiladora Standards of Conduct.[26]

Internal Corporate Codes of Conduct

Broad codes of conduct sponsored by groups seeking a declaration of acceptance and compliance by multinational corporations have not fared well in obtaining company adherents. Of the examples just noted, only the Sullivan Principles attracted support from U.S. companies, and they were concerned mostly with potential adverse reaction in their domestic consumer market. Even then, they came under fire from critics who contended that signatories to the Sullivan Principles were using them "as camouflage—as a justification for operating in (and profiting from) a fundamentally corrupt and odious system."[27]

Understandably, international business managers resist a "one size fits all" approach that includes a review of compliance by interests outside the corporation. But multinational companies still feel the pressure for human and labor rights in their international operations. As noted earlier, they face initiatives for unilateral labor rights legislation, the emergence of worker rights in the new GATT/WTO regime, innovative litigation by foreign employees claiming worker rights violations and other developments, many of them outlined in this volume, that can affect relations with employees and governments in countries where they do business.

The occasional media exposé of child labor or prison labor conditions, or environmental disasters, can also affect attitudes in multinational companies' target markets. Companies are most vulnerable in sectors of consumer goods heavily dependent on brand image and company good will. As one analyst points out, "In a global marketplace with almost instant communications, there are no hiding places for companies. International media will expose inconsistency and irresponsibility in corporate behavior, and vigilant consumers will respond." [28]

Multinational companies are also feeling pressure in board rooms and shareholder meetings and from sources of capital. Resolutions on human and labor rights are commonly proposed to boards of directors and offered at annual meetings.[29] This has traditionally been done by religious orders that hold company stock, and was viewed by executives as a predictable and manageable exercise. Now, however, larger institutional investors and a new breed of "socially conscious" mutual funds are raising questions and making demands about human and labor rights.[30]

Many companies have chosen a proactive route to outpace the curve of human rights criticism and have begun to issue their own self-initiated and self-supervised codes of conduct for human and labor rights in their international subsidiaries and suppliers. Two prominent U.S.-based firms are in the forefront of this movement: Levi Strauss & Company, and Reebok Corporation.

Levi Strauss & Company Terms of Engagement and Guidelines

In 1985 the family descendant of the company's founder undertook a $1.6 billion leveraged buyout of Levi Strauss & Company. As a privately held company with no shareholders to convince, it can go farther and faster with corporate social responsibility initiatives than many others. Levi Strauss's international code of conduct is just part of a broad-based program for a socially conscious approach to business.

The Levi Strauss Mission Statement declares that "we will conduct our business ethically and demonstrate leadership in satisfying our responsibilities to our communities and to society. Our work environment will be safe and productive and characterized by fair treatment, teamwork, open communications, personal accountability and opportunities for growth and development." [31]

The adoption of sourcing standards for overseas suppliers is an extension of Levi Strauss company values. "As we expand our production to more diverse cultures and countries, it makes sense to select partners whose practices are compatible with our aspirational and ethical values," says a company official. At the same time, such policies also serve to protect the company's valuable brand image. The official goes on to say, "Otherwise we may end up with contractors who don't abide by responsible business policies, and our association with them could damage the image of our brands and our company." [32] A Levi Strauss vice president responsible for offshore sourcing points out, "We'll pay more to deal with reputable people who take care of their employees and maintain our brand image."[33] "Sourcing decisions which emphasize cost to the exclusion of all other factors will not best serve our long-term business interests," concludes an internal company analysis.[34]

In September of 1991, Levi Strauss senior officials appointed a management task force, Sourcing Guidelines Working Group (SGWG), to develop its Global Sourcing Guidelines. The fourteen-member group was drawn from eight divisions within the company to reflect its broad internal interests. They were charged with also taking into account the concerns of company "stakeholders," including its employees, its customers, and the communities in which the company operates.

The Working Group reviewed the UN's Universal Declaration of Human Rights and other international human rights instruments in formulating its recommended country and supplier guidelines. In February 1992 the SGWG presented its guidelines to the Executive Management Committee for approval. The guidelines were approved in March 1992 with a certain eagerness, since their adoption followed hard on an embarrassing media exposé of abusive labor conditions in Saipan, a U.S. protectorate, in factories that supplied Levi Strauss, Sears, and other U.S. retailers.

Titled "Business Partner Terms of Engagement and Guidelines for Country Selection," the Levi Strauss code of conduct is a two-part instrument. The "terms of engagement" cover environmental requirements, ethical standards, health and safety, legal requirements, and employment practices to the extent that they are "issues that are substantially controllable by our individual business partners." The "guidelines for country selection" speak to "issues which we believe are beyond the ability of the individual business partner to control." They address issues of brand image, health and safety, human rights, legal requirements, and political or social stability, to the extent that each of them turns on policies of the government in countries where Levi Strauss maintains operations or contracts with suppliers, rather than corporate policies.[35]

The "employment practices" section of the terms of engagement is the only one of the terms or guidelines broken down in greater detail, addressing six specific types of employment conditions: wages and benefits, working hours, child labor, prison labor/forced labor, and discrimination and disciplinary practices (namely, "corporal punishment or other forms of mental or physical coercion"). Interestingly, from a labor rights perspective, the Levi Strauss code of conduct is relatively silent on the right to form and join trade unions and the right to bargain collectively, norms otherwise contained in every international human rights instrument. There is only a passing reference to freedom of association in an introductory passage of its code.

Levi Strauss has gone beyond a simply hortatory use of its code of conduct on human and labor rights. The company has created an elaborate internal monitoring and enforcement system that begins with a detailed questionnaire on employment practices in foreign supplier plants. The questionnaire covers every element of the terms of engagement. Results are fed to a unique, centralized global database on labor rights and conditions in company facilities worldwide.

The company's enforcement mechanism also provides for audits that can include surprise site visits, intense review by company personnel charged with enforcing the code of conduct, and a cutoff of contracts for violators. The company applies the mechanism in a flexible fashion, however, taking a three-tiered approach to its contractors. The first level of assessment applies to those whose practices are unworkable, and where the "business partners" appear indifferent and unwilling to improve the situation. These relationships are terminated. The second level looks at operations where there is some concern over conditions but there appears to be the possibility for improvement. Levi Strauss sets out a plan and a time-frame for resolving problems. If goals are met, the company will maintain a relationship with that contractor. If not, the relationship is ended. The third level applies to those contractors who appear to fulfill the Terms of Engagement but could do better. A severance of relations is not threatened, but Levi Strauss continues to work with the supplier in an effort to make it a model partner.

One of the first applications of the Levi Strauss code of conduct followed a burst of publicity in 1992 about working conditions in supplier factories in Saipan. NBC Nightly News, for example, aired a report about a factory owner who forced virtual slave conditions on his employees. Many of the workers were immigrant Filipinos housed in padlocked barracks with their passports confiscated during their contract period. They were working as much as eleven hours a day, seven days a week for as little as $1.65 an hour with no overtime pay (minimum wage in Saipain is $2.15 an hour).[36] The stories were even more embarrassing since Saipan is a U.S. protectorate governed by American labor law as part of the Commonwealth of the Northern Mariana Islands. All goods produced there can be labeled "Made in the USA" and shipped without quota limits or duty.

Levi Strauss code of conduct auditors inspected the Saipan factories using their Terms of Engagement questionnaire. The company quickly canceled its contract with those suppliers. In addition, contracts with suppliers in the Philippines, Honduras, and Uruguay were terminated when the auditors found that they failed to "conduct their business consistent with a set of ethical values not inconsistent with those of Levi

Strauss & Co."[37] In all, Levi Strauss terminated contracts with thirty suppliers worldwide, and forced reforms in employment practices in over one hundred others.[38]

In Bangladesh, Levi Strauss undertook an innovative program to address child labor conditions in two supplier plants where the company discovered that children under fourteen years old were working. After a dialogue with local officials, agreement was reached for the children to return to school but continue drawing pay from the contractor, while Levi Strauss paid for school tuition, books, and uniforms. The children will be offered jobs when they turn fourteen or finish school.[39]

Applying its guidelines for country selection, Levi Strauss code of conduct auditors cross-checked its suppliers with a list of facilities in China reported to utilize prison labor. They also conducted surprise inspections of Chinese supplier plants, and visited each supplier to inquire about their use of prison labor.[40] Similar moves were undertaken in Burma, where a repressive military regime crushed a human rights movement. As a result, the company announced that it would entirely withdraw from both countries.

Adoption of codes of conduct such as Levi Strauss & Company's Terms of Engagement provide a framework for acceptable business partner behavior. One Levi Strauss official points out that the code benefits its business partners as well. "Contractors value listing us as a client for sourcing. If they can meet our requirements, it means they can work for anybody in the industry."[41]

Reebok's Human Rights Production Standards

Reebok Corporation has developed an innovative international human rights support program that includes rock concert sponsorship, Reebok Foundation grants, annual Human Rights Awards, and a code of conduct for international labor rights called Reebok Human Rights Production Standards.

Amnesty International approached Reebok in 1988 about sponsorship of the Human Rights Now! tour by rock music groups, designed to raise consciousness about human rights. The tour also aimed to secure millions of signatures on petitions calling on governments to observe the Universal Declaration of Human Rights and protect human rights activists. Reebok executives worked with their then-chief advertising agency, Chiat Day, to underwrite the "Human Rights Now!" tour on a budget of $12 million, including advertising produced by Chiat Day.

The company tied the Reebok name to the tour for marketing purposes, but in an understated fashion. (in fact, several trade retailers actually requested less subtlety to help sell more shoes.) As one executive explained, "The fact that Reebok is making this possible is important to get across. We are a business entity, and for that I don't apologize. But we also care about issues like human rights. So, this is not an occasion to blast the name Reebok all over the place."[42]

T-shirts, sweatshirts, and jackets with the tour symbol and the Reebok logo and the note "Made possible by Reebok" were sold to concert-goers. Proceeds from the sale of these items went to Amnesty International. Reebok continues to support Amnesty International's efforts with its own AI chapter at the company and the offer for employees to use company time to write letters on behalf of political prisoners. It also continues to encourage retailers to carry membership applications to Amnesty International in their stores.

The Reebok Foundation provides video cameras, computers, and fax machines, as well as training for human rights advocates, in developing countries under the "Witness Program." This support is designed to amplify documentation of human rights conditions and presentation of the footage to the global media, in hopes of providing activists with a powerful weapon and deterrent against abuses.

The Reebok Foundation supports other organizations whose mission is to promote human rights. For example, it has funded El Rescate, a group that provides legal services for Central American refugees. Reebok has been a major donor to TransAfrica, a non-profit organization dedicated to ending apartheid, and helped support Nelson Mandela's tour of the United States after his release from prison.

Since 1988, Reebok has given annual human rights awards of $25,000 to young activists. As the company explains, "The Reebok Human Rights Award seeks to honor individuals from the United States and around the world who have made significant contributions to the cause of human rights, often against great odds. The purpose of the Award is to shine a positive, international light on the awardees and to support their work in human rights. . . . Award candidates mus be 30 years old or younger and working on an issue that directly relates to the United Nations Universal Declaration of Human Rights."[43]

The formulation of the Reebok Human Rights Production Standards begins with a statement of the company's commitment to human rights: "Reebok's devotion to human rights worldwide is a hallmark of our corporate culture. As a corporation in an ever more global economy we will not be indifferent to the standards of our business partners around the world."[44]

The Reebok code addresses seven defined areas of labor rights: non-discrimination, working hours/overtime, forced or compulsory labor, fair wages, child labor, freedom of association, and safe and healthy work environment. In contrast to the Levi Strauss code, which glides over the question of trade union rights, Reebok's worker rights code declares forthrightly that it "will seek business partners that share its commitment to the right of employees to establish and join organizations of their own choosing. . . . Reebok recognizes and respects the right of all employees to organize and bargain collectively."

Another contrast to the Levi Strauss approach is Reebok's application of its labor rights code only to business partners, not to governments in the countries where it does business. Levi Strauss has "terms of engagement" for suppliers and "guidelines" for country selection, and has applied those guidelines to withdraw from China and Burma. Reebok has chosen, in the case of China, to ensure that it was not sourcing from contractors employing prison labor, but not to leave China.

Reebok uses joint-venture factories rather than contract with a government or third-party investor-owned facility. This way, it could both manage the workplace environment and assure quality of the shoes, factors which company executives believe are positively correlated. "We believe that the incorporation of internationally recognized human rights standards into our business practices improves worker morale and results in higher quality working environment, which in turn helps us produce higher quality products."[45]

A further distinguishing feature of the Reebok code, compared to that of Levi Strauss, is an apparently less defined mechanism for auditing, evaluating, and enforcing the terms of its code. There is not the evidence of canceled contracts or country pullouts that Levis Straus has demonstrated. In effect, Reebok is faced internally with the same dilemma of "trade sanctions" that confronts the U.S. government in its own labor rights enforcement regime: applying sanctions by canceling contracts can harm the very workers the policy is supposed to protect. Over the longer term, maintaining the relationship with a supplier, and the influence that accompanies it, might bring improved labor rights and labor conditions. On the other hand, the fate of the Sullivan Principles showed that there is no guarantee of improvement without strong sanctions and a willingness to use them.

Conclusion: Corporate Vulnerability, Risk, and Reward

A further dilemma faced by a company that charts a proactive course on human rights and labor rights is that it can never fully satisfy its ideals. Most companies have not issued human and labor rights codes of conduct, or codes of conduct relating to any subject, preferring to maintain tersely that they obey the laws of countries where they do business. Companies like Levi Strauss and Reebok that claim to set a higher standard get the perverse result of making themselves easier targets of criticism.

Shortly after Levi Strauss received an award from the Council on Economic Priorities for its "unprecedented commitment to non-exploitative work practices in developing countries," reports surfaced alleging use of child labor, unsafe conditions, and unpaid wages at a Levi Strauss supplier plant in Juarez, Mexico.[46] Similarly, Reebok has been sharply criticized for its reliance on supplier facilities in Indonesia, where wage levels, though higher than the minimum, are lower than estimates of what is needed for basic necessities of life, and where the military-dominated government suppresses independent trade union organizing.[47]

Levi Strauss and Reebok are not alone in moving toward codes of conduct on human and labor rights in their international operations. Sears, JCPenney, Wal-Mart, Home Depot, Philips Van-Heusen, and others have all adopted similar measures for their overseas subsidiaries and suppliers.[48] Many companies have adopted codes of conduct on global environmental practices.[49] The code of conduct phenomenon is also prevalent domestically, where many U.S. companies have formulated codes for American employment relations, labor, environmental, and other social concerns.[50]

As we have seen, several factors are promoting the emergence of corporate codes of conduct that speak to human and labor rights as an important feature of modern multinational enterprise. There is a genuine humanitarian impulse at work in many cases, whether it starts with individual corporate leaders shaped by personal experiences or as a consensus arrived at by a more collective company leadership. Often the altruistic motive coincides with "bottom line" considerations related to brand name, company image, and other intangibles that make for core value to the firm.

From outside the enterprise, a more traditional pressure common in the modern regulatory state has an effect. Governments seeking to mandate behavior by companies are devising laws and regulations on labor rights in international trade, as in the Generalized System of Preferences and other U.S. trade statutes. International regulation is also beginning to appear, as in the NAFTA labor side accord, the "social chapter" of the European Union's Maastricht Treaty, and perhaps next in the new World Trade Organization.

A traditional response by corporations to such "mandates," as they are known in U.S. regulatory discourse, is an assertion of self-regulation that will allow for individual differences and needs while still achieving the overall social goal. From a historical perspective since the early twentieth century, this preemptive thrust toward self-governance on social matters has been more of an orderly retreat than a counteroffensive. But in the new global economy, where the regulatory state is coming under greater criticism, self-regulation by means of codes of conduct on human and labor rights may enjoy a greater chance to prove its effectiveness.

To become a permanent and positive feature of the global economy, private codes of conduct devised by firms to generate respect for worker rights in their international operations must be more than eccentricities. Drafting the content of such codes is relatively easy. Good models exist in United Nations human rights instruments, in International Labor Organization conventions, in codes drafted by multilateral governmental or economic coordinating bodies, and other sources. Effective implementation is the real test of such codes. Companies sincerely interested in making them work will have to create credible enforcement regimes to back them up, characterized by such elements as:

- ongoing auditing of company operations, either by independent examiners or, if by company officials, with results subject to independent verification;
- creating avenues of recourse for workers to invoke the code of conduct, with guarantees of non-reprisal;
- no-nonsense enforcement of the code, including cancelation of contracts, termination of responsible managers, withdrawal from offending countries, and similar sanctions;
- a willingness to accept trade union representation and collective bargaining where workers desire them, even if the firm's preference is to remain non-union;
- adding an independent human rights and labor (or environmental, in the case of an environmental code) advocate to the corporation's board of directors, or otherwise opening the board to independent advocacy; and
- regular public reporting on labor rights progress, and continuing dialogue with labor rights and human rights advocacy groups.

In the same way that a "first generation" of civil and political rights emerged in the human rights field, to be followed by "second"- and "third"-generation rights that expanded the scope of human rights appeals, the corporate codes of conduct that took shape recently are a first-generation effort. Making such codes the rule rather than the exception, and finding creative methods for making them effective, not just hortatory, are the next challenge for human and labor rights advocates within and without the international corporate community. Perhaps after that, a third generation of corporate social responsibility will find respect for human rights the "matter of course, not altruism" that its pioneers envision.[51]

Acknowledgments. An earlier version of this chapter appeared as Lance A. Compa and Tashia Hinchliffe, "Private Labor Rights Enforcement Through Corporate Codes of Conduct," *Columbia Journal of Transnational Law* 33, 3 (1995): 663ff. Reprinted by permission of *Columbia Journal of Transnational Law.*

Notes

1. See B. J. McCabe, "Are Corporations Socially Responsible? Is Corporate Social Responsibility Desirable?" *Bond Law Review* 4 (June 1992): 2, 18.

2. To date, the ILO has adopted 177 conventions. Most deal with working conditions in specific industries or employment sectors. A half-dozen are considered to constitute a "human rights core" of ILO conventions covering freedom of association, the right to organize and bargain collectively, forced labor, child labor, discrimination, and minimum acceptable conditions as to wages, hours, and workplace health and safety. See ILO, *Human Rights: A Common Responsibility*, Report of the Director General (Geneva: ILO, 1988).

3. The principal international instruments addressing labor rights concerns are the United Nations Universal Declaration of Human Rights and the two international covenants that flow from the declaration: the International Covenant on Civil and Political Rights and the International Covenant on Economic, Social and Cultural Rights; and what the International Labor Organization (ILO) calls its core human rights conventions. Regional groupings like the Organization of American States and the European Union have analogous provisions in their basic charters. See Universal Declaration of Human Rights, G.A. Res. 217A(III), U.N. GAOR, 3rd sess., pt. 1, 71, U.N. Doc. A/810 (1948); International Covenant on Civil and Political Rights, G.A. Res. 2200 (XXI), U.N. GAOR 21st sess., Supp. No. 16, 52, U.N. Doc. A/6316 (1966); International Covenant on Economic, Social and Cultural Rights, G.A. Res. 2200 (XXI), U.N. GAOR, 21st sess., Supp. No. 16, at 49, U.N. Doc. A/6316 (1966); ILO Convention No. 87 Concerning Freedom of Association and Protection of the Right to Organize (entered into force July 4, 1950); Convention No. 98 Concerning the Application of the Principles of the Right to Organize and Bargain Collectively (entered into force July 18, 1951); Convention No. 105 Concerning the Abolition of Forced Labor (entered into force Jan. 17, 1959); Convention No. 111 Concerning Discrimination in Respect of Employment and Occupation (entered into force June 15, 1960); Convention No. 138 Concerning the Minimum Age for Admission to Employment (entered into force June 19, 1976), in International Labor Organization, *ILO Conventions and Recommendations, 1919–1991* (Geneva: ILO, 1992); American Convention on Human Rights, OAS Official Records, OEA/Ser.A/16(English), T.S. No. 36 (Nov. 7–22, 1969); Convention for the Protection of Human Rights and Fundamental Freedoms, Nov. 4, 1950, Europ. T.S. No.5; European Social Charter, Oct. 18, 1961, 529 U.N.T.S. 89.

4. The Rev. Leon Sullivan, a prominent Philadelphia clergyman, was a member of the board of directors of the General Motors Corporation. His Principles

were a voluntary code of conduct to which U.S. companies would pledge compliance and report on their steps to effectuate the principles. Companies that refused to "take the pledge" or failed to live up to the Principles' requirements faced adverse publicity that might create uncertainties for their market shares or other economic interest. For a recent discussion of the Sullivan Principles in the context of voluntary corporate codes of conduct, see Daniel Pink, "The Valdez Principles: Is What's Good for America Good for General Motors?" *Yale Law and Policy Review* 8 (1990): 180, 181–185.

5. See Karen Paul, "The Inadequacy of Sullivan Reporting," *Business and Society Review,* Spring 1986, 62; Leon Sullivan, "The Sullivan Principles and Change in South Africa," in *Business in the Contemporary World,* ed. Herbert L. Sawyer (Lanham, MD: University Press of America, 1988), 175.

6. Comprehensive Anti-Apartheid Act of 1986, 22 U.S.C. sec. 5001 (1988).

7. See Jorge Pérez-López, "Conditioning Trade on Foreign Labor Law: The U.S. Approach," *Comparative Labor Law Journal* 9 (1988): 253. For a criticism of the U.S. approach to international labor rights as reflected in these statutes, see Philip Alston, "Labor Rights Provisions in U.S. Trade Law: 'Aggressive Unilateralism'?" *Human Rights Quarterly* 15 (1993); 1; Theresa Amato, "Labor Rights Conditionality: United States Trade Legislation and the International Trade Order," *NYU Law Review* 65 (1990): 79; Harlan Mandel, "In Pursuit of the Missing Link: International Worker Rights and International Trade?" *Columbia Journal of Transnational Law* 27 (1989): 443. For a defense of such clauses, see John Cavanagh et al., *Trade's Hidden Costs: Worker Rights in a Changing World Economy* (Washington, D.C.: International Labor Rights Fund, 1988); Terry Collingsworth, "American Labor Policy and the International Economy: Clarifying Policies and Interests," *Boston College Law Review* 21 (1989): 1.

8. For a discussion, see Lance Compa, "The First NAFTA Labor Cases: A New International Labor Rights Regime Takes Shape," *U.S.-Mexico Law Journal* 3 (Spring 1995): pp. 159–181.

9. See, for example, *Labor Union of Pico Korea v. Pico Products, Inc.,* 968 F.2d 191 (1992); *Dow Chemical Co. v. Castro-Alfaro,* 786 S.W.2d 674 (1990); *Van Blaricom v. Burlington Northern,* U.S. Court of Appeals for the Ninth Circuit, CV-90-1530-WD (1994); *ILA and Coastal Stevedoring,* 313 NLRB No. 53 (1993); *Osorio v. INS,* U.S. Court of Appeals for the Second Circuit, No. 93-4115 (March 1994).

10. See, for example, the "UE-F.A.T. Strategic Organizing Alliance: Statement on Joint Work" (Feb. 1992), a program devised by the United Electrical, Radio and Machine Workers of America (UE), a U.S. union, and the Frente Autentico de Trabajadores, a Mexican labor federation, for coordinated union organizing campaigns in the *maquiladora* sector.

11. See Alan Riding, "U.S. Envoys Gain a Forum for Labor Issues in Trade," *New York Times,* April 8, 1994, D1.

12. See, for example, Keith Bradsher, "Prison Labor Seen in China Imports," *New York Times,* Sept. 24, 1991, A9; Daniel Southerland, "China Said to Still Use Forced Labor: Report Contends Exports Violate Pact, Threaten Favored Nation Status," *Washington Post,* May 19, 1993, F3.

13. See Edward A. Gargan, "Business Objects to a Code in China," *New York Times,* May 24, 1994, D2; Steven Mufson, "For U.S. Firms, a Struggle over Rights and Roles," *Washington Post,* Aug. 25, 1994, B10. For an extensive treatment of this issue, see Diane F. Orentlicher and Timothy A. Gelatt, "Public Law, Private Actors: The Impact of Human Rights on Business Investors in China," *Northwestern Journal of International Law and Business* 14 (1993): 66.

14. See "Human Rights Production Standards Set in Worldwide Reebok Initiative," in *Reebok: Making a Difference* (company newsletter), June 1993 (on file with the author).

15. Paul Hawken and William McDonough, "Seven Steps to Doing Good Business," *Inc.*, Nov. 1993, 80.

16. Ibid.

17. George B. Harvey, "The Education of American Business," *Business and Society Review* 83 (Fall 1992): 62–63.

18. See "Multinational Corporations and United States Foreign Policy: Hearings before the Subcommittee on Multinational Corporations, Senate Committee on Foreign Relations," 94th Cong., 1st sess., 381–386 (1975).

19. United Nations Economic and Social Council, 2nd reg. sess. 1990, item 7 (d) of the provisional agenda, UN doc. E/1990/94, 7 (1990), cited in "Corporate Responsibility and Human Rights," *ABA Annual Meeting Document* (Minneapolis: Minnesota Advocates for Human Rights, Aug. 8, 1993).

20. See "Employment and Industrial Relations" clause, OECD, Guidelines for Multinational Enterprises (1976).

21. See Duncan C. Campbell and Richard L. Rowan, *Multinational Enterprises and the OECD Industrial Relations Guidelines* (Philadelphia: The Wharton School, University of Pennsylvania, 1983); John Robinson, *Multinationals and Political Control* (New York: St. Martin's Press, 1983).

22. For a discussion of cases arising under the ILO Declaration, see B. Glade and E. Potter, "Targeting the Labor Practices of Multinational Companies," in U.S. Council for International Business, *Focus on Issues* (New York: U.S. Council for International Business, 1989).

23. See Helen E. Booth and Kenneth A. Bertsch, "The MacBride Principles and U.S. Companies in Northern Ireland" (pamphlet; Washington, DC: Investor Responsibility Research Center, 1989).

24. See Jorge Pérez-López, "Promoting International Respect for Worker Rights through Business Codes of Conduct," *Fordham International Law Journal* 17, no. 1 (1993): 1, 12–19, 32–35.

25. See Lance Compa, "International Labor Rights and the Sovereignty Question: NAFTA and Guatemala, Two Case Studies," *American University Journal of International Law and Politics* 9, no. 1 (Fall 1993).

26. See "Activists Reached a Variety of Agreements in Withdrawing All 10 Maquiladora Resolutions," in Investor Responsibility Research Center, *News for Investors*, May 1992, 15.

27. See Pink, "Valdez Principles," 189.

28. See Martha Nichols, "Third-World Families at Work: Child Labor or Child Care?" *Harvard Business Review* 71, no. 1 (Jan.–Feb. 1993): 22.

29. Timothy H. Smith, "Pressure from Above," *Business and Society Review* 81 (Spring 1992): 36–37.

30. See, for example, Carole Gould, "A Social Responsibility Shake-Up," *New York Times*, June 12, 1994, F14.

31. Levi Strauss and Co., Mission Statement, *Levi Strauss & Co. Human Resource Policies*, June 1, 1992.

32. See "Sourcing Guidelines Working Group Report to Executive Management Committee, Levi Strauss & Co.," 1993 (on file with the author).

33. Ibid., p. 14.

34. Ibid., p. 26.

35. Levi Strauss & Co. company communications document, 14.

36. See "A Stitch in Time," *The Economist*, World Politics and Current Affairs section, June 6, 1992, 27.

37. Ibid.

38. See John McCormick and Marc Levinson, "The Supply Police," *Newsweek*, Feb. 15, 1993, 48–49.

39. See Nichols, "Third-World Families," 16.

40. Amy Borrus and Joyce Barnatham, "Staunching the Flow of China's Gulag Exports," *Business Week*, April 13, 1992, 51–52.

41. Richard Rapaport, "Import Jeans, Export Values: What Happens If a Company's Global Reach Exceeds Its Ethical Grasp?" *Fast Company* (1993).

42. Bruce Horovitz, "Reebok Walks Marketing Tightrope with Human Rights Concert Tour." *LA Times*, July 26, 1988, p. 6.

43. Reebok Human Rights Award application form, 1993.

44. "Reebok Human Rights Production Standards," 1993 (on file with author, available from Reebok corporate offices).

45. See "Human Rights Production Standards Set in Worldwide Reebok Initiative," in *Reebok: Making a Difference* (company newsletter), June 1993.

46. See Laurie Udesky, "Sweatshops behind the Labels: The 'Social Responsibility' Gap," *The Nation*, May 16, 1994, 665–667.

47. See "Labor Rights Group Asserts Reebok Human Rights Award Marred by Company's Exploitative Production Practices," press release from International Labor Rights Education and Research Fund, Dec. 10, 1991 (on file with the author). On wage levels, see Jeffrey Ballinger, "The New Free Trade Hell," *Harper's Magazine*, Aug. 1992, 46–47 (discussing salary at a Nike contractor). On trade union suppression, see Thomas L. Friedman, "U.S. Prods Indonesia on Rights," *New York Times*, Jan. 18, 1994, D1.

48. See McCormick and Levinson, "Supply Police."

49. See Stan Hinden, "Joan Bavaria's Crusade for the Environment: Social Activist Is Driving Force Behind the Valdez Principles, a Corporate Code of Conduct," *Washington Post*, Dec. 23, 1990, H1.

50. For a broad survey of company initiatives, see Joel Makower, *Beyond the Bottom Line* New York, Simon & Schuster (1994); see also Leslie Crutchfield and Luba Vangelova, "Can Companies Care?" *WHOCARES*, Summer 1994, 28–32.

51. See above, note 15.

Chapter 10
Labor Rights in the Global Economy
A Case Study of the North American Free Trade Agreement

Stephen F. Diamond

Congressional approval of the North American Free Trade Agreement (NAFTA) at the end of 1993 inflicted upon the American trade union movement its most visible and demoralizing defeat in recent years. Hoping against hope that a Democratic president would signal a turnaround in the fate of organized labor, trade unionists were stunned to find themselves on opposite sides of the barricades from an administration that had won the election on a nominally pro-worker ("It's the economy, stupid!") platform. But the President did pledge that NAFTA would only be put through after "side agreements" on labor and the environment were hammered out in new negotiations with Mexico and Canada. The labor side agreement, formally known as the North American Agreement on Labor Cooperation (NAALC), was a second-best compromise worked out in the last few weeks of negotiations.

Given the open hostility expressed by American labor leaders upon NAFTA's passage, it seems unlikely that the relatively weak provisions of the NAALC will be taken at all seriously by the labor movement. I think that this would be a serious mistake on the part of organized labor. It is the purpose of this essay to explore the emerging field of regulating trade between nations through social provisions such as the NAALC. I want to suggest that such provisions, no matter how weak, are essential to effective organization of an increasingly transnational economy. Further, the full and active participation of interested parties is critical to realizing the sociopolitical potential in such regulatory provisions. This is especially true in the case of institutions like trade unions, which have long been considered central to our very concept of democratic pluralism.

In my view, the NAALC represents a potential contribution to this new form of legal institution. It is, as currently written, problematic, but it confronts one of the key tensions now facing the world: that between nationally organized democratic regulatory frameworks and the emerging transnational nature of economic life. A shared, but silent, presumption of constitutional theories, whether based on *Chadha*-like formalism, a Burtian dialogue, or Ackermanian constitutional moments, is the alleged existence of a nation-state-based congruity between political decision-making and economic structures. This made a certain kind of limited sense during much of the "American Century" (from the Civil War to the Vietnam War). One can trace, for example, a concern over "the rising tide of economic concentration" through American antitrust jurisprudence that comports with some sense that political decisions, judicially enforced, will have a direct consequence on national economic life. Hence, the Supreme Court bowed to what it saw as congressional concern for "the economic way of life" that Congress sought to preserve. But this approach no longer makes sense today, as the globalization of capital markets, technological changes in communications and transportation, and the growth of transnational economic institutions (public and private) all reduce or, at least, reshape the role the state plays in economic life.[1] Further, it makes even less sense to assume that such congruity is a reality for other nations of the world. Yet that is precisely what the core doctrines of both constitutional theory—in its various approaches to legal process—and international law—in its presumptions against extraterritoriality and in favor of international law—do assume. Instead, as will be described below, we must understand that the increasing transnational flow of economic decision-making stands apart from the nation-state. Yet I believe we can draw on the strengths of previous nation-state–based legal thinking to help establish a stable form for the emerging world economic order.

To bridge the gap that this tension exposes requires attention to what has been critical to *legitimizing* democratic life in a national framework. If we understand that need for legitimation, we can turn to the new institutions and suggest means by which they can help fulfill the same role in a world economy. This essay will explore the issues outlined here in the following steps: first, I will review the changing place of the labor union in modern economic life; second, I will place the emergence of NAFTA into a context of changing conditions for U.S. capital and Mexican political and economic life; third, I will explore the emerging efforts to regulate labor in the global economy; fourth, I will suggest that institutions like the NAALC can play a crucial role in the process of opening the door to the reestablishment of democratic political life on a transnational basis.

What I hope that I will have demonstrated is that traditional dualist approaches to international law and institutions are no longer adequate. Instead, I will suggest that it is in the process of encouraging institutions like the NAALC that we can ensure that the core concerns of the national legitimation process, which lie at the heart of respect for dualism, can be reconstructed on a transnational (or, at least in this case, a trinational) basis. I believe this process can take place without drifting into some kind of "one worldist" monism.

The International Crisis of Labor

Over the last two decades, the trade union movement in most of the advanced industrial economies has been facing a complete restructuring of the international division of labor.[2] I believe it is important to explore four areas of change: (1) the simultaneous crisis of global employment and trade union membership in the advanced capitalist democracies; (2) the growing rift between the trade unions of those countries and the political parties they have traditionally supported or, even, controlled; (3) the end of Fordism and the rise of a very particular kind of trade union activity in newly industrializing countries such as Mexico, South Korea, and Brazil; and (4) the dramatic end of the statist era signaled most loudly by the collapse of the Soviet bloc regimes and the lack of a coherent response by the labor movement to that change.

The Crisis of Membership and Employment

The membership crisis of trade unions is, by now, a familiar story. Despite claims that certain strikes, such as those by the coal miners at Pittston or the food workers at Hormel or, more recently, the Teamsters strike against longhaul freight companies, herald a new era for American trade unionism, there is no way to avoid the conclusion that U.S. labor is at a nadir—its lowest membership density in the economy since the 1920s. This is not simply the result of aggressive anti-unionism by employers—a fact of American industrial life from the beginning of modern trade unionism. Rather, the decline in membership must be seen as part of a general structural change in the economy.

Even as early as 1961, labor economist Lloyd Ulman noted the deepset slowing of union growth in unorganized plants or firms.[3] Another leading industrial relations scholar noted that same year that "unions have lost much of their vitality and forward motion; they are playing an essentially conservative role in the plant community; seeking to preserve what they have rather than make gains. Management, on the other hand, is on the offensive and has acquired a new sense of sureness in dealing with industrial relations."[4]

Steady growth in wages in the centrally organized sectors of the economy, fuelled in part by Vietnam era inflation, and new union membership in public employment and the service sector enabled the labor movement to defer discussion of the problem. But with the victory of Ronald Reagan in 1980 and his defeat of the Air Traffic Controllers Union, it finally hit home that the House of Labor was resting on a crumbling foundation.[5]

One study at Indiana University has found, for example, that "collective bargaining has yielded much smaller compensation packages in the last few years than previously: from 1974 to 1982 the average collective bargaining settlement advanced the total compensation received by covered workers by 9.76 percent; from 1982–1985 that figure averaged only 4 percent. In real terms, the hourly earnings of production and non-supervisory workers, including overtime pay, declined almost 5 percent in the decade from 1975 to 1985. Most startling, [however, is the finding] that in 1985 compensation gains for unionized labor averaged 2.6 percent compared to 4.6 percent for unorganized workers."[6]

Some attempt to argue blithely that this is a cyclical process with a return to the heyday of the CIO just around the next economic corner. But this ignores the technological shift underway in the now global workplace. Manufacturing jobs can and do "return" to the United States— but, in doing so, they have been fundamentally transformed. A 1991 Commerce Department study found that manufacturing now represents an increasing proportion of the GNP—the apparent reversal of a long-term decline—but only due to "a wrenching contraction in payrolls and plants," as the number of jobs in that sector dropped from 21 million to 19 million over the last decade.[7] Such a setting alters in a basic way the premise of continued expansion on which the modern collective bargaining system was built.[8]

This turns out to be a general trend in the advanced industrial economies. The Indiana University study found that "more than three-fourths of the eighteen largest, politically stable capitalist democracies experienced sustained declines or stagnation in union density in the late 1970s or early 1980s."[9] Only the sharpness of the conflict varied, in proportion to the relative strength of labor in the previous period. In Great Britain, for example, the almost mythical coal miners, not the highly unpopular air controllers, had to be defeated in a brutally long strike in order to establish the neoliberal order of Margaret Thatcher.

Parallel to this trend, and certainly feeding it, is the striking emergence of underemployment, long-term unemployment, and the ever more ephemeral nature of regular employment. These trends can be found in the advanced economies as well as in both the newer "export oriented industrializing" (EOI) regions and the older "import substitution industrialized" (ISI) settings.

A report issued for the United Nations by the International Labor Organization in 1994 states that more than 820 million people worldwide are either unemployed or working at a job that does not pay a subsistence wage; this amounts to 30 percent of the world's labor force. The global jobs crisis is not just the result of the recession that has plagued the world economy in recent years, Ali Taqi, chief of staff of the ILO, said; it's something more endemic and longer lasting than that and reflects the rapid pace of technological change and increasingly fierce global competition.[10]

Despite rapid industrialization over the last generation in many parts of the developing world, there are still only 30 million industrial jobs there out of a population of 3 billion. The ILO notes that while export-oriented industrialization has "been responsible for rapid increases in employment in labour-intensive industries . . . many of these industries have followed an essentially low-wage, casual labour strategy, with high turnover rates being common. A slackening of demand is thus easily transmitted into layoffs. . . . Labour is also poorly organized and there is only limited statutory protection against retrenchments. . . . A fall in demand will be immediately passed on in retrenchments or shorter working time and lower earnings."[11]

One marxist economist drew this general conclusion about the dynamic underway in the new global economy: "What expansion of capital does take place does not require, as in the past, the same number of additional workers, even if the rate of expansion should be the same. The great mass of the world population, which is no longer able to exist in traditional ways, is also not able to find a way into the labor market. The fact, then, that the mass of unemployed and underemployed is constantly growing on a worldwide scale, means that while the world is not polarized between capital and wage labor, it is certainly polarized between the beneficiaries of the capitalist system and an ever growing proletariat of which only a declining number find themselves counted within the working class."[12]

This view is echoed by mainstream commentators. Jonathan Zysman notes that "labor is [now] a continually diminishing element of production costs."[13] And Jacques de Larosière, former chair of the International Monetary Fund, noted that in the early 1980s "a clear pattern [emerged] of substantial and progressive long term decline in rates of return to capital. There may be many reasons for this," he continued. "But there is no doubt that an important contributing factor is to be found in the significant increase over the past 20 years or so in the share of income being absorbed by employees. . . . This points to the need for a gradual reduction in the rate of increase in real wages over the medium term if we are to restore adequate investment incentives."[14]

A New Political Era

Both a reflection and a cause of labor's structural weakness is the growing rift between trade unions and politics. In the United States, alone among the industrial economies, labor failed to move to political independence, relying instead on a seat at the table in the quadrennial smoke-filled rooms of the Democratic party. But by the late 1970s, that party began to ask, as Stalin once did of the Pope, "And how many divisions does he command?" Labor is no longer viewed as representing a broad view of social justice in American life, a movement that had fought for free public education, affordable health care, social security, the minimum wage, and the end of child labor, but is seen instead as just one among many "special interest" groups. In Canada, this development is echoed by the stunning losses that have rendered the labor-based New Democratic party almost irrelevant in federal-level political life.

A similar development has been underway in Europe, where tensions between trade unions and labor or socialist parties have heightened. Neil Kinnock and François Mitterand, for example, made their ability to control labor a cornerstone of their appeal to the general electorate. This development merges with the technocratic vision that has long had a home in mainstream social democracy. The labor movement, in falling back on the narrower terrain of disputes over wages, hours, and working conditions, has lost a forum for debate and argument about the wider social consequences of economic change.[15]

The importance of this shift cannot be underestimated. It means the loss of a major constituent element in modern political and legal culture. Unions establish a form of democracy in the workplace, acting as an opposition party does in general political life—a constant source of "checks and balances" against what could become the arbitrary authority of the employer. Unions generally establish a grievance procedure that imports a judicial process into industrial life. These developments stimulate workers' appreciation for the value of democratic political life more generally. Not only do they wish to enjoy democracy in all realms of life, but they realize that their industrial democracy can only survive in a democratic political context. In the words of Clark Kerr, unions "create a new power center which can, if it wishes, stand against the power centers of the state and the corporation. . . . A rough balance between private and public power centers is the essence of a pluralistic society, and a pluralistic society is the only firm foundation for democracy in an economy based on industrial production."[16] A reckoning with the potential loss of this power center has yet to occur in democratic institutions or theory. Its possible reestablishment may be one of the outcomes, however, of an active approach to the NAALC and similar institutions.

New Unionism and the End of Fordism

Some in the labor movement have expressed the hope that the emergence of unions in the newly industrializing countries could presage a return to trade union health on a world scale. Indeed, the flip side of the deindustrialization of the United States and Western Europe has been the emergence of a large industrial sector in places like South Korea, Brazil, and Mexico.[17] This has been accompanied by new organizing efforts and, in certain cases, explosive strike waves for better wages and working conditions. In some cases this new unionism has fed deeper movements for democratic political change. The Brazilian Workers' party is one example of this process. An eastern bloc version of the same phenomenon is found in the history of Polish Solidarity. But there is a tenuousness about this new development, which seems to reflect the increasing divide between capital investment and society. The result is an industrialization process underway in these countries that trade unionism has never really faced off against before. It is built upon relatively high capital intensity. It has proved to be highly mobile. But its commitment to the development of forward and backward linkages is weak. One might suggest that capital is *certainly* geographically mobile, but appears to be increasingly immobile *socially*.[18] This new industrialization, then, does not appear to be a development akin to that of earlier American industrialization. The long-term ties between Virginia's coal mines, Chicago's steel mills, and Detroit's automobile assembly lines, which fueled the American CIO and its version of Fordism, do not seem to be present in these cases.[19] The global roller coaster even contributes, on occasion, to the return of some manufacturing jobs to the United States. An overvalued cruzeiro and huge price increases in raw materials and energy pushed Ford recently to shift final assembly of truck kits back to Kentucky from Brazil because it is cheaper.[20] Hence, despite offering the "comparative advantage" of cheap labor, even developing countries can be the victims of deindustrialization.

Harley Shaiken's research on the Mexican manufacturing sector, for example, provoked the following comment of central relevance to a trade union response to such development patterns: "One critical question from the perspective of national development is whether successful high-tech manufacturing precipitates significant backward and forward linkages, or whether high-tech plants become 'islands of automation' surrounded by 'footloose' production that is likely to relocate quickly based on fluctuations in wages, exchange rates, and political stability."[21] Similarly, Joseph Grunwald has noted the failure of the maquiladora program in northern Mexico. The firms there, Grunwald has written, "have remained on the fringes of the Mexican economy and have contributed little or nothing to advancing industrialization, technological growth, or international competitiveness."[22]

The South Korean example is also telling. Despite historically low unemployment, union militancy has declined dramatically there. There were more than 3,700 labor disputes in 1987, but half that number in 1988. In the first five months of 1990, there were only one-fifth as many disputes as in the first five months of 1989. Why? Manufacturing employment slowed steadily as the 1980s came to an end, going into negative figures at the end of 1989. This reflected, according to the Bank of Korea, "the automation of production facilities." Overall wage and job gains there are attributable to the construction and service sectors. This pattern appears, in a hothouse fashion, to mimic the long-term structural changes underway in the economies of the United States and Western Europe.[23]

The End of the Statist Era

Finally, in this survey of the strategic context in which the trade union movement finds itself, mention must be made of the end of the era where state-centered accumulation seemed inevitable. In one way or another, important segments of the labor movement had staked themselves on the state-led efforts at development found either in the Soviet bloc, within the state-centered programs of Social Democracy, or within the post–World War II national liberation movements. This perspective was stronger in France and Italy than in Great Britain or the United States, but the sudden collapse of bureaucratic and collectivist politics in the East and the trend to privatization in the West has put the left in disarray, unprepared for the aggressive pro-market social movements that have now emerged. One example of this development came in Germany, where Social Democratic ties to the old East German regime and its official labor movement helped Helmut Kohl move to a strong victory in the postunification elections. Another example is found in the success of Lech Walesa in breaking from his roots in Solidarity to usher in the shock therapy of Harvard's Jeffrey Sachs. The failure of a new socially conscious and democratic paradigm to emerge in the wake of the collapse of the Eastern bloc has contributed to a certain level of demoralization in labor generally.

In Mexico, this process is evidenced by what one analyst has called the "deinstitutionalization" of state-labor relationships.[24] The Salinas government has made several dramatic moves aimed at breaking the older corporatist arrangements between the ruling Institutional Revolutionary Party (PRI) and the country's major labor federation, the Confederation of Mexican Workers (CTM). Three developments stand out in the emergence of this new period: first, the replacement of entrenched union leaders with more compliant figures or, in the case of independent unions, outright union-busting efforts (Salinas replaced, even violently, older *charrazos* in the oil workers' union and the teachers' union, and allowed violent union-busting efforts against independent and militant unions such as at Ford's Cuatitlan plant); second, the encouragement of allegedly more "modern" union groupings to organize independently of the CTM (Salinas has encouraged a pro-modernization labor leader of the telephone workers' union to establish a new independent union federation;[25] and, third, the reining in of unions' bargaining power through national tripartite wage negotiations (in 1987 the Pact for Stability and Economic Growth superseded the CTM's role in the National Minimum Wage Commission).

All three elements of this strategy can be found in only slightly different forms throughout much of the developing world and have their parallel in the former Stalinist bloc, as well. The three-pronged strategy amounts to an effort, as yet quite problematic and unstable, to consolidate a new paradigm for labor organization in the neo-liberal global economic era. The replacement of union leaders who have an independent power base, either in the bureaucracy or rank and file, allows an executive leadership greater flexibility in negotiating wage and salary concessions, while creating a more compliant working-class base willing to withstand the social impact of wage cuts and unemployment that accompany restructuring. The encouragement of "modern" union formations can become a framework for the establishment of new non-adversarial relations on the shopfloor. These are considered crucial to productivity increases within a capitalist framework. Finally, when tripartite negotiations replace or set the terms for traditional collective bargaining over wages, the state and private investors can place greater reliability on macroeconomic developments. These negotiations reinforce the effort to move to a non-adversarial industrial relations structure as labor is asked to "take responsibility" for national economic planning. Such a strategy would appear to be essential if states are to continue to play a role in bargaining for inward capital investment. If such efforts are successful, the state will have helped to establish the kind of "credible" stability necessary to attract that investment.[26]

The reverse side of this coin is also significant. The close links between official U.S. labor and U.S. government foreign policy was built around a common program of anti-communism. Now that target has dissolved, the door would appear to be open to new initiatives for an independent and democratic foreign policy for U.S. labor. Trade union visitors to Eastern Europe, for example, find a tremendous potential for new union organizing, but find only token support for such efforts by the American labor movement. The open debate that could chart a new independent foreign policy for American labor has yet to be scheduled.

In sum, organized labor had narrowed its horizon in the fifties and sixties, often sacrificing organizing, militancy, and internal democracy for a strong dues base in what appeared to be the commanding heights of the American, European, eastern bloc, and developing economies. But the era of the social contract, of Fordism, corporatism, and neo-Stalinism, has come to an end. The stability and predictability of an earlier era has left much of labor unable to comprehend the nature of change underway.

Mexico and the United States

It was perhaps unavoidable, but the somewhat hectic reaction in all three capitals of the United States, Canada, and Mexico to the Salinas and Bush announcements about a potential North American Free Trade Area left the general public with the impression that there was something new underway. In fact, NAFTA should be understood as one of the final building blocks of a decade-long process of reintegrating the Mexican economy into the world economy and, more specifically, into the U.S.-dominated regional economy. The process can be said to have begun in the early 1980s with the collapse of Mexico's ability to repay its external debt. Since then, Mexico has taken, or has had forced upon it, a series of steps resulting in greater financial and economic integration with the United States and international institutions.

The U.S. government's International Trade Commission opened its 1990 analysis of the potential of a NAFTA with a detailed description of the reforms Mexico has implemented in setting the stage for the current situation.[27] In their view, the starting point was, indeed, the 1982 debt crisis, when Mexico announced that it would not be able to meet scheduled payments on its $86 billion debt. In a surprise move, Mexico turned to the International Monetary Fund for assistance. Expansion returned but the dramatic drop in oil prices and the 1985 earthquake once again led to a "virtual halt in Mexican growth." In 1986, Mexico "obtained new agreements with the IMF, World Bank, and commercial bank creditors. In exchange, Mexico agreed to major reform of its economic policies, including reductions in tariffs and restrictions on trade, liberalization on foreign investment, reductions in public spending, tax reform, divestiture of state-owned enterprises, and reform of domestic price controls." In 1985, Mexico began negotiations to join the multilateral General Agreement on Tariffs and Trade (GATT), becoming in August 1986 the ninety-second contracting party to that agreement. Mexico became a signatory to five of the Tokyo Round Codes of the GATT covering licensing, customs valuation, anti-dumping, standards, and subsidies. These moves came just in time for Mexico to take part in the Uruguay Round, where Mexico is viewed by the United States as a "moderate" and has been touted by U.S. representatives "as an example of a country that has eased investment restrictions without hampering development."

In summarizing Mexico's "achievements" in this new era, the ITC noted that "based on the premise that excessive and obsolete regulations were largely responsible for inefficiency in the use of Mexican resources, Mexico has implemented a far-reaching program of deregulation." More than twenty-five sectors of the economy have been deregulated or are under review for future deregulation, including trucking, telecommunications, petrochemicals, the financial system, insurance, commodities such as sugar, cacao, and coffee, technology transfer, trade secrets, and agriculture. "The Government of Mexico is proceeding with a program of privatization with the clear objective of divesting public enterprises in favor of private, including foreign, investors," the ITC said. Of the 1,155 entities owned by the government at the end of 1982, 801 had been privatized or authorized for privatization by early 1990. In the area of trade, Mexico "has reduced its maximum import tariff from a level of 100 percent in 1986 to a current level of 20 percent," exceeding the requirements of a GATT signatory, which require only a reduction to 50 percent. Mexico's trade-weighted average tariff is only about 11 percent—considered low by the ITC among developing countries.

As for foreign investment, the ITC sees Mexico's recent moves as "sweeping reforms" that "broaden significantly" the range of economic sectors open to wholly foreign ownership. Foreign investment of up to 100 percent is allowed in unclassified activities, which account for 72.5 percent of the 754 economic activities that comprise the Mexican economy. Included are certain industries such as glass, cement, iron, and steel, where majority foreign participation had been previously restricted. In August 1989, Mexico announced a major reclassification of petrochemicals which provide greater opportunity for private investment. Fourteen basic petrochemicals were reclassified as secondary, cutting the list of basic petrochemicals from 34 to 20 products. And the number of products in the secondary category was "drastically reduced" from more than 600 to 66 as some 539 products moved into the unrestricted tertiary category.

Other reforms include the increase in the level of foreign participation in insurance and telecommunications companies to 49 percent and the indirect foreign ownership through non-voting shares of 34 percent of state banks. In the maquila sector, companies may now sell products locally up to 50 percent of their total exports in the previous period, the number of regulatory agencies that review a maquila application has been reduced from nine to one, and licenses, previously valid for only two years, are now open-ended, creating, in the ITC's view, "a more predictable environment for long-term investments."

Put simply, the process of neoliberalization, of reintegrating Mexico into the world market, has been underway for a number of years. The ITC concluded that "Mexico's reforms comprise a movement toward a market-oriented, open economy with a disciplined public sector. . . . These policies allow increasing optimism about Mexico's future." This is, of course, the optimistic view—motivated as much by the need to promote a viable investment climate as by a scientific investigation into the existence of such a climate. The collapse of the peso and a dramatic fall in the Mexican bolsa in early 1995 confirm that the underlying strength of the Mexican economy was greatly exaggerated.

The social impact of the reforms has been dramatic. Real wage rates have fallen precipitously, in step with the implementation of neo-liberal restructuring. The minimum wage, which is used in Mexico as a benchmark for other wage rates, fell throughout the 1980s, reaching, in 1992, an amount equal to only 65 percent of its value in 1960. In the early 1990s wages in the industrial sector averaged about 1.8 times the minimum wage and about 1.5 times the minimum in commercial agriculture. It is estimated that the cost of a basic market basket of consumption goods was 4.78 times the minimum wage in 1988. It would cost 2.72 times the minimum to be above what the Mexican government considers extreme poverty. Some 60 percent of Mexican households are below this standard.[28] Extreme malnutrition threatened 15 percent of the population at the end of the 1980s, while only 8 percent were so threatened in 1974. Beef and pork consumption fell 50 percent from 1980 to 1990. Per capita milk consumption dropped in the same decade from 125 liters to 74 liters.[29] While it would be overstating the matter to suggest that the 1980s neoliberalization process is alone responsible for longstanding Mexican poverty, it is clear that what was a serious problem is now out of control.

The primary concern for U.S. business is the growing pressure of worldwide competition from the European community and the Japanese-led East Asian bloc. These regions were built anew in the post-World War II era, without the fiscal drag of large military expenditures and with heavily deflated labor costs. They emerged in the 1970s and

1980s as home to the most productive economies in the world. They continued to combine a relatively cheaper labor force (shifting to new pools of cheap labor as home country wages rose) with the best technology available, establishing flexible and innovative human resource policies and supplier networks to dominate critical areas of growth. Their success is the ultimate example of the emphasis that Fernando Fajnzylber has so correctly placed on added intellectual value in a modern economy.[30] But this should be understood in the widest social sense — including the innovative relationships between the state and industry, the organization of supplier networks, and the just-in-time and continuous improvement systems of production.[31]

This is a structure that has presented formidable obstacles for the U.S. economy. Where American management once found the detailed job descriptions of individual workers in an assembly plant a critical basis of productivity, control, and stability, employers now battle with trade unions, which in turn find themselves, somewhat paradoxically, defending the old Taylorist regime.[32] The recent walkout at United Parcel Service over weight limits serves as an excellent example of this conflict. The opportunity to move production into virgin territory, where new relationships can be established on a much lower wage scale and in a less regulated environment is understandably tempting. Employers are anxious to tap into what the *Financial Times* calls "a rich vein of cheap labour in [the] newly industrialising economies," which is "exert[ing] a gravitational pull on wages in the developed world." Mexico, then, appears as a natural target for U.S. manufacturers. As the *Harvard Business Review* quipped, "Where to find tens of millions of consumers, low-cost workers and a free-market revolution? Right across the Rio Grande."[33]

In Response: A Labor Rights Approach

This stark picture of economic and political change means that, more than ever, the labor movement worldwide must face up to the loss of its place in general social affairs. For that segment of our polity concerned about the maintenance of social equity and a democratic political culture, I would like to suggest that this is a crisis not only for the labor movement but for society as a whole, whether defined nationally, regionally, or globally. A recent confidential report by the Executive Board of the International Confederation of Free Trade Unions (ICFTU), the leading international labor umbrella organization, underscores the gravity of the situation. They suggest that "the current threat to [trade union] rights stands out as an unprecedented attack upon" organized labor, "unprecedented in its extent, in the variety of forms in which it appears, and in the pervasive nature of its ideological underpinnings and legitimation." "Viewed globally," the Board argues, "the offensive is aimed at putting a definitive end to trade unionism."[34]

In response, they propose that a worldwide effort be made, through national and international institutional frameworks, to reestablish three critical rights central to the healthy existence of democratic labor organizations: the right to organize, the right to collective bargaining, and the right to strike. They suggest efforts to link trade to rights through the promotion of a social clause and worker rights clauses in national and regional legislation, linking aid and assistance to rights by interventions with appropriate international agencies, campaigning for universal ratification of key ILO conventions, continuing to make full use of and reinforcing ILO and UN mechanisms for the defense of trade union and other human rights, developing closer and more cooperative relationships with human rights non-governmental organizations (NGOs) that share the objectives and concerns of the ICFTU, and, finally, the formulation and presentation of convincing arguments to counter the ideological foundations of the offensive against trade union rights.

There are already efforts being made in this direction by labor organizations affiliated with the ICFTU. In February 1994, the Teamsters and the United Electrical Workers union (UE) announced that they were filing charges with the new United States National Administrative Office (NAO) of the NAALC. The charges stemmed from the dismissal of several Mexican union activists by Honeywell and General Electric at plants located along the U.S.-Mexican border. The firings followed in the wake of a joint effort by the UE, the Teamsters, and an independent Mexican union to organize the plants. The U.S. NAO announced in April that they would investigate the charges. But a report released by the NAO in October 1994 concluded that there was "no evidence that Mexico failed to enforce its labor laws."[35] A second set of charges was filed against the Sony Corporation following the violent suppression in April 1994 of a demonstration by workers affiliated with an independent union at a Sony plant in the Mexican *maquila* zone. But the NAO backed away from this charge, refusing to even grant a review as it had done in the Honeywell/GE situation.[36]

Another example of this kind of transnational effort is the sponsorship by the International Metalworkers Federation, an international trade union body headquartered in Geneva, of a May 1994 world conference in Peoria, Illinois to discuss issues of mutual concern among the workers of Caterpillar, Inc. The union umbrella group, to which the United Auto Workers (UAW), the union representing Caterpillar's American employees, is affiliated, is attempting to develop unified strategies in a campaign for fair treatment by the company. Caterpillar workers from Australia, Belgium, Brazil, France, and South Africa were invited to the meeting. The conference followed a five-month strike by the UAW against Caterpillar in 1992. South African and Belgian workers had staged sympathy strikes in support of the UAW walkout.

In a similar effort, officials of the United Paperworkers International Union representing workers at the Staley Manufacturing Co. in Decatur, Illinois traveled to London in February 1994 to meet with officials of Staley's parent corporation, Tate and Lyle, at its London headquarters. They were backed during their visit by the British union representing Tate employees in England and by the British Trades Union Congress. The Staley contract had expired in the fall of 1992, and the Paperworks began an in-plant "work to rule" strategy to press for a new contract. Staley responded with a lockout of the 760 workers represented by the union.

Through its international trade union secretariats, organized labor has been pushing, with limited success in the final days of the GATT talks, for the establishment of international labor standards in the recently concluded GATT negotiations. This particular debate showed up some of the complexities of the new situation. The European Community (EC) commissioner for external affairs condemned efforts to push for the GATT labor standards. This is somewhat ironic given the extent to which the EC's Social Charter attempts to replicate the old corporatist nation-state protections for labor on a regional basis. But this particular commissioner, Sir Leon Brittain, is British and the United Kingdom's major objection to full participation in the EC process has often centered on its concern that having defeated labor at home, it did not want to concede to a new all-European form of "socialism." In addition, Sir Leon is largely credited for having pushed France into concessions on agricultural subsidies, helping to bring the Uruguay Round to a close.

With such strong winds at his back, Sir Leon zeroed in on the NAFTA as an example of how member countries in a trade agreement should be allowed to "tailor their own labor practices to the agreement rather than having an agreement forced on them from the outside." When President Clinton raised the labor standards issue on his recent trip to Europe, Sir Leon responded by noting that the ILO process was adequate to protect labor rights and that the first step toward improving labor rights might lie in the United States' ratifying the 160 or so ILO conventions of which it has yet to approve. Of course, as labor advocates have long noted, the ILO process, while very valuable in providing basic information about labor rights and often helpful in propaganda campaigns for improvements in working conditions, lacks an effective enforcement mechanism. In the end, pressure from the United States and France did result in the nominal agreement that at the preparatory meetings of the new World Trade Organization the issue of workers' rights would be given some form of consideration.[37]

One potential route to adding a layer of protection for workers in the global economy could be the extraterritorial application of U.S. legislation. The courts have long had little trouble expanding antitrust and securities law extraterritorially, but have been much more reluctant with so-called non-market legislation, such as that applying to labor and the environment.[38] Congress in 1991 responded to a holding that year by the Supreme Court in *EEOC v. ARAMCO*, that Title VII did not apply extraterritorially by giving U.S. citizens working abroad for U.S. corporations the right to sue their employers for discriminatory treatment.[39]

An effort to do something similar in the field of labor rights has been made, to date unsuccessfully, in a joint effort by the Center for Constitutional Rights and a South Korean trade union representing workers at a South Korean-based wholly owned subsidiary of an American multinational firm. The plaintiffs claimed a right to sue under section 301 of the Labor Management Relations Act for severance pay provided for in the union contract negotiated by the company. The explicit language of section 301 gives workers the right to sue for breach of contract without regard to citizenship. The union lost in District Court and the Second Circuit affirmed on appeal, arguing that despite the clear language, Congress could not have meant what it said. So much for a conservative judiciary's strenuous efforts to reestablish literalism and congressional authority as against the efforts of an activist judiciary.[40]

The Potential Role of the NAALC

It is within the context of such a labor rights offensive that I believe the NAALC should be placed. My argument will comprise five steps: first, I will describe the structure of the NAALC, with particular attention to its inherent dualism; second, I will discuss the internal divide within the NAALC between technical labor standards and labor rights—a distinction crucial to understanding the current limitations of the NAALC; third, I will argue that American experience with labor relations points to the need in modern economic life to promote a form of "industrial self-government" based on respect for basic labor rights; fourth, I will suggest how trade unions should relate to the NAALC to achieve their democratic goals; fifth, I will consider some of the basic objections that my approach will provoke.

An Overview of the NAALC

The NAALC is not a constituent part of the NAFTA. The latter is an international agreement between the three parties, the United States, Canada, and Mexico, which required legislative approval in all three states for its implementation. The NAALC is an executive agreement negotiated in tandem with the NAFTA by representatives of the executive branches of each government. It did not have to be submitted for legislative approval. There was some form of limited consultation with outside groups during its negotiation.[41] It does make some attempt to base its existence upon provisions within the preamble of the NAFTA, which, for example, commit the three states to resolve to "*create* new employment opportunities and improve working conditions and living standards in their respective territories; . . . and *protect*, enhance and enforce basic workers' rights."[42]

Its putative goal is "to promote . . . high-skill, high-productivity economic development in North America." But this effort must be built "in accordance with their [the three states'] respective laws." The side agreement "affirm[s] [the three states'] continuing respect for each Party's constitution and laws."[43] While "recognizing the right of each Party to establish its own domestic labor standards, and to adopt or modify accordingly its labor laws and regulations, each Party shall ensure that its labor laws and regulations provide for high labor standards, consistent with high quality and productivity workplaces, and shall continue to strive to improve those standards in that light."[44]

This obligation to provide a certain level of protection amounts to the starting point for a charter of economic development based on the protection of labor. While acknowledging current national labor laws, it attempts to provide a direction in which reform of those laws must move. More importantly, it establishes an institutional mechanism through which that process of reform can be encouraged, monitored, inspected, reviewed, tested, and disciplined. Unfortunately, the level of obligation is extremely weak. The ultimate sanction level is very low. The time-frame is defined softly and openly. The process can be said to be an advance on the "campaign of shame" approach adopted by the ILO and independent human rights groups,[45] but it does not approach anything like a level of enforcement consistent with the significance of the social problem that must be addressed.

Article 3 obligates each government to comply with and enforce its own labor law through governmental action. An outline of possible action is provided—including inspectors, monitoring of and investigating compliance, record-keeping, mediation, and possible sanctions. Article 4 requires that each party provide a right of private action to its own courts. A form of due process protection is outlined in article 5. All these obligations, of course, are to be provided for only in national law.

Perhaps most significantly, a trinational Commission for Labor Cooperation is to be established, made up of a ministerial council and a secretariat. It is this transnational body, especially the Secretariat, which can be the driving force for the NAALC and a possible source of support for the strengthening of labor's role in shaping the NAFTA itself. The Council meets only once a year, although irregular sessions can be called. The Secretariat, however, is to be a permanent institution with a professional staff of fifteen, drawn from all three states. The Secretariat is, in effect, the implementing organization for the Council itself. The primary activity of the Commission is to

promote cooperative activities between the parties, as appropriate, regarding:

(a) occupational safety and health;
(b) child labor;
(c) migrant workers of the Parties;
(d) human resource development;
(e) labor statistics;
(f) work benefits;
(g) social programs for workers and their families;
(h) programs, methodologies, and experiences regarding productivity improvement;
(i) labor-management relations and collective bargaining procedures;
(j) employment standards and their implementation;
(k) compensation for work-related injury or illness;
(l) legislation relating to the formation of unions, collective bargaining and the resolution of labor disputes, and its implementation;
(m) the equality of women and men in the workplace;
(n) forms of cooperation among workers, management and the government;
(o) the provision of technical assistance, at the request of a Party, for the development of its labor standards; and
(p) such other matters as the Parties may agree.

This is a broad and open-ended mandate. An active Council and an aggressive Secretariat could use this mandate to shape critical aspects of the social impact of the NAFTA. Although the NAALC must work in conjunction with national legislation, it could conceivably serve as a check against the impact of national legislation.

Standards Versus Rights

Labor advocates argue, quite rightly of course, that without greater enforcement powers the NAALC could become a dead letter. During the negotiations, representatives from the "trade policy" (as opposed to

"labor policy") layer within each government and the business community lobbied heavily for weak enforcement mechanisms.[46] Beyond the
traditional dualism already mentioned, the side agreement makes a critical distinction between so-called *labor rights* and *technical labor standards*.
In parallel, the enforcement mechanism is divided in two parts. Both
labor rights and labor standards are subject to the provisions of Part 4
(Cooperative Consultations and Evaluations Provisions). But only three
of the eight technical labor standards ("the enforcement of a Party's
occupational safety and health, child labor or minimum wage technical
labor standards") are subject to the provisions of Part 5 (Resolution of
Disputes). It is only Part 5 that contains an arbitration step with the possibility of imposing a financial penalty.

Even this process is severely weakened by the lengthy, complicated,
and opaque steps outlined in the NAALC. In traditional labor dispute
resolution, one can expect three or four steps in the process, from initial review of a decision by labor and management representatives to
some form of final-step arbitration. The process can take up to a year,
but is often resolved more quickly. Only those cases that must be taken
to a state agency or the courts can be expected to drag on for longer
periods of time. The relative simplicity, flexibility, and openness of the
procedures used at each step makes grievance processing relatively accessible to any literate worker or union representative. But to get to
the final step in the NAALC over a dispute regarding a technical labor
standard can take as many as 1,320 days—nearly four years. In addition,
business is now lobbying for an interpretation of the NAALC that would
require that domestic administrative and judicial remedies be exhausted
before the dispute goes to the NAO for review. This could add several
years more to the process. Access to the process requires far more than
a single incident. A "persistent pattern of failure" in a party's enforcement of its technical standards is required.

A complaint must wend its way through consultations between national representatives (housed in the new National Administrative Offices within the NAALC) to ministerial consultations, through an evaluation by a committee of experts, to a draft and final evaluation report,
to party-to-party consultation, to an arbitration panel, through an initial and final report by the arbitration panel, to an implementation of
the final report, to the possible reconvening of the panel, to a second
possible reconvening of the panel, to the imposition of a "monetary enforcement assessment," to the possible reconvening of the arbitration
panel, to a final report to the parties in dispute.

The procedure established here contrasts sharply with other forms of
dispute resolution found within the main NAFTA itself. Investors, for
example, and defenders of intellectual property rights are granted di-

rect access to the courts of any of the parties. That right of access is explicitly ruled out of the NAALC. (See article 42.) In addition, the labor enforcement mechanism is controlled by the contracting parties; no private right to intervention by concerned parties exists. Clearly, labor and business organizations can play a supplementary role, but their direct control of the process is non-existent. Again, this contrasts with the rights of investors and property owners in disputes over their economic rights. (See, for example, article 1714: Enforcement of Intellectual Property Rights: General Provisions; or article 1715: Specific Procedural and Remedial Aspects of Civil and Administrative Procedures.)

The American Approach to Industrial Relations

The basic building blocks of an active and democratic labor movement are the right to organize, the right to bargain collectively, and the right to strike. These rights run parallel to basic political rights found in general social life—the right to assembly, the right to freedom of speech, and the right to petition the government for the redress of grievances. As such they form what Justice William O. Douglas has called a form of "industrial self-government," which lies at the heart of the American industrial relations system.[47] As suggested above, the existence of this system has long been considered a vital part of our understanding of democratic pluralism. The political branches, backed by the Supreme Court, recognize the right of the federal courts to shape a federal common law of economic life based on the common law of the shopfloor. "The collective agreement covers the whole employment relationship. It calls into being a new common law—the common law of a particular industry or of a particular plant."[48] This common law of the shop guarantees that there is some check against arbitrary power in economic life, just as the separation of powers operates in political life. Together, this form of economic and political *process* guarantees the health of our democratic culture.

To ignore this, and relegate basic labor rights to no more than paper status as the NAALC attempts to do, is a fundamental flaw in the accord. Never in the history of modern economic life has child labor, occupational health and safety, or the minimum wage been protected without a vigorous trade union movement. These very concepts owe their existence and motivation to the trade union movement. Hence, expert or technical concern about working conditions will fail to do anything to correct "persistent failures" in these areas unless there is simultaneous support for basic organizing rights.

To propose that a regional economy be built on this basis is to risk sacrificing the standards by which our elementary notions of democracy came into being. It is concern over the effective operation of pluralism that provides our polity with some concept of the legitimation of economic and political decision-making. We continue to advocate the doctrine of dualism, with its presumption against extraterritorality and presumption in favor of international law, precisely because we believe that legislation must be shaped and checked by a *process*. "The dualistic preference for municipal sources stems from a strong belief in legislative supremacy and thus naturally suits a Madisonian system that values deliberative and pluralistic decisionmaking."[49] To divide political rights from the standard of life that results from the exercise of those very rights borders on legal pathology.

A Trade Union Approach to the NAALC

Nonetheless, the very existence of the NAALC, especially the Secretariat, provides an opportunity to strengthen the participatory components of democratic politics and promote stable and equitable economic growth. By giving life to a stage in legal process it can also help undermine the traditional "municipalist" bias in our legal structure against international law.[50] The trade union movements in all three countries have an obligation, not just to society as a whole, but to their own organizational future, to take a full and active role in every possible way in the proceedings of the NAALC. The goal should be the same as that advocated by Justice Douglas—the establishment of a common law of trinational economic life. A long-range goal should be to remedy the types of limitations described here. The NAALC provides for a four-year evaluation period, after which the parties to the agreement are to make proposals for improvement. In addition, article 52 provides that "the Parties may agree on any modification of or addition to this Agreement."

But the variety of activities that the NAALC allows provides an *immediate* opportunity for labor activism on a trinational basis. Through the labor secretariat, the NAALC legitimates the exploration of domestic labor problems by a new international institution. If that body bears in mind the legitimation concerns that lie behind dualism, it will welcome the active support and participation of independent democratic organizations such as trade unions in support of its activity. I believe that labor unions should endeavor to establish their own parallel forms of trinational cooperation to make this exploration a reality. It is only by such activity that the opportunity for a genuine trinational democratic approach to economic development will be possible. This will mean the overcoming of very serious divisions within and between the labor organizations of each county. But only by making such a proposed trinational effort, can such divisions be confronted. As the ICFTU Confidential Report noted, the very future of trade unionism is at stake.

Possible Objections to the Argument

Let me conclude by recognizing some of the limitations to the approach I have outlined above. I do not want to answer these objections here in any detail. I raise them only to throw into perspective the challenges that lie ahead. First, the NAALC represents a kind of pooled sovereignty, similar, though on an obviously smaller scale, to the efforts made in Europe to put in place a social charter. A major problem in Europe, of course, was the success of Great Britain in opting out of full recognition of the Charter. There is a risk of a similar problem with the NAALC. In particular, Mexico, which is likely to become the initial significant target of labor rights efforts, may come to resent the apparent intrusion into its previously sovereign territory. Down the road, accession to NAFTA by other Latin American countries, such as Chile, may lead to problems with extending the NAALC.[51] Many Latin American countries have made economic advances in recent years by breaking preexisting obligations to labor movements.

Second, as noted briefly above, there are significant divisions within the trade union movement of each contracting party state, and between the movements of each country. This was evident during the campaign for NAFTA's passage. Little opposition was heard from Mexican labor to the NAFTA. The Salinas view that the agreement would bring jobs to Mexico was largely accepted as reality. American labor's opposition to NAFTA was motivated in large part by a narrow protectionist view, with an occasional racialist flourish added in reference to Mexican backwardness. Within American labor, efforts to bring Mexican and American trade unionists together to try to hammer out a joint strategy were largely ignored by top union leaders. Proposals for a social charter were often heard, but were largely pushed by labor officials as a kind of legislative "rider" aimed at defeating the NAFTA entirely. Proposals for a joint Continental Development Plan made by some on the Mexican left got very little consideration from American unionists.[52] American labor is divided as well along traditional occupational lines. Public sector unions were largely immune to requests for help from the industrial unions.[53]

Today, the impact of these pre-NAFTA fault lines in labor continue. At a recent trinational meeting to discuss a proposal for a social charter, Mexican representatives of the leftist opposition, the Democratic Revolutionary party, expressed anxiety about confronting the conservative CTM's hold on Mexican unions. Canadian representatives remained steadfastly opposed to any attempt to improve the NAFTA. They want nothing less than its full repeal. American unionists expressed interest, but at the same time felt that the momentum for a major political campaign on this issue does not exist.

A final concern, of course, remains the larger context in which this discussion takes place—the intensely competitive and global nature of economic life today. The major changes underway were described above. As mentioned by the ICFTU, these changes are accompanied by an ideological and theoretical assault on the very basis of the trade union in economic life. This points to the possibility of a very long period in which labor and the democratic left will be playing only a minor role in economic decision-making. This should alarm anyone committed to the democratic underpinnings of modern political and economic life. In my view, restoring the trade union and its traditional political representatives in labor and social democratic parties is critical to the future organization of the world community. Transnational institutions such as the NAALC will represent one of the critical arenas for this effort.

Acknowledgments: The author wishes to express his appreciation to the Program in International Peace and Security of the MacArthur Foundation and the Social Science Research Council for its financial support of the research that led to the development of this argument. In addition, the author expresses his thanks to both Allan Hunter, Director, A. E. Havens Center for the Study of Social Structure and Social Change, Department of Sociology, and Professor Robert Aubey, Center for International Business Studies, School of Business, University of Wisconsin, Madison, for their invitation to present this research to a seminar at the University of Wisconsin.

Notes

1. For an argument that the Court recognizes this in antitrust law, but not in labor law, see Jonathan Turley, "Legal Theory: "When in Rome": Multinational Misconduct and the Presumption Against Extraterritoriality," *Northwestern University Law Review* 84 (Winter 1990): 598–664.

2. Joyce Kolko, *Restructuring the World Economy* (New York: Pantheon, 1988); Robert J. S. Ross and Kent C. Trachte, *Global Capitalism* (Albany: State University of New York Press, 1990).

3. Lloyd Ulman, *American Trade Unionism: Past and Present* (reprinted from *American Economic History* by Institute of Industrial Relations, University of California at Berkeley, 1961; Reprint Series no. 157).

4. George Strauss, "Shifting Balance of Power in the Plant," *Industrial Relations* 1 no. 3 (May 1962).

5. Harvard Business School, *Air Traffic Controllers* (Case Study no. 9-483-054; Boston: HBS Case Services, 1984). See Kim Moody, *An Injury to All: The Decline*

of American Unionism (New York: Verso, 1988), for an argument that the Chrysler strike of 1980 was equally significant in signaling a new era of aggressive anti-unionism.

6. Larry Griffin, Holly J. McKammon, and Christopher Botsko, "The 'Unmaking' of a Movement? The Crisis of U.S. Trade Unions in Comparative Perspective," unpub. paper, n.d., pp. 1–2.

7. Sylvia Nasar, "American Revival in Manufacturing Seen in U.S. Report," *New York Times*, Feb. 5, 1991. For a dramatic description of this process see Richard Preston, "Annals of Enterprise: Hot Metal," *New Yorker*, Feb. 25 and March 4, 1991.

8. Thomas A. Kochan, Harry C. Katz, and Robert B. McKersie, *The Transformation of American Industrial Relations* (New York: Basic Books, 1986); Michael J. Piore and Charles F. Sabel, *The Second Industrial Divide: Possibilities for Prosperity* (New York: Basic Books, 1984); Michael J. Piore, "The Decline of Mass Production and the Challenge to Union Survival," paper presented to the International Working Party on Labour Market Segmentation, Santiago, Chile, 1985.

9. Griffin et al., " 'Unmaking' of a Movement."

10. Rich Miller, "World Economy Faces Jobs Crisis, UN Agency Says," *The Reuter European Business Report*, Feb. 2, 1994; Bureau of National Affairs (BNA), "Global Unemployment at Record High Level, ILO Says in New Study," *Daily Labor Report*, Feb. 4, 1994, D18.

11. International Labor Office, *Report of the Director-General: Growth and Adjustment in Asia—Issues of Employment, Productivity, Migration and Women Workers* (Geneva: International Labour Office, 1985).

12. Paul Mattick and Paul Mattick, Jr., eds., *Marxism: Last Refuge of the Bourgeoisie?* (Armonk, N.Y.: M. E. Sharpe, 1983).

13. Jonathan Zysman, "Technology and Power in a Multi-Power Global Economy," paper presented to seminar at the Graduate School of International Relations and Pacific Studies, 1990.

14. From an address to the Economic and Social Council of the United Nations in Geneva in 1984, cited in Howard Wachtel, *Money Mandarins: The Making of a New Supranational Economic Order* (New York: Pantheon, 1986), 137; David Ranney, "NAFTA and the New Transnational Corporate Agenda," paper presented to the International Conference on the North American Free Trade Agreement, Mexico City, March 17–19, 1993, 10.

15. On the significance of the relationship between labor and politics, see Andrew Martin, "Labor, Politics, and the Changing International Political Economy," paper presented to the 14th Congress of the International Political Science Association, 1988. On social vision see Piore, "Decline of Mass Production."

16. Clark Kerr, *Labor and Management in Industrial Society* (Garden City, N.Y.: Anchor Doubleday, 1964), 25–26.

17. Nigel Harris, *The End of the Third World: Newly Industrializing Countries and the Decline of an Ideology* (London: Penguin, 1987); Richard Peet, ed., *International Capitalism and Industrial Restructuring: A Critical Analysis* (Boston: Allen and Unwin, 1987).

18. Michael Kidron, *Western Capitalism Since the War* Middlesex: Penguin, 1970 [1968]).

19. On the end of the Fordist era, see Loren Goldner, "The American Working Class in the Current World Crisis: The Restructuring of Global Capital and the Recomposition of Class Terrain, unpub. paper, 1981 and "On the Non-

Formation of a Working-Class Political Party in the United States," unpub. paper, 1983.

20. Christina Lamb, "Imports Take on Brazil's Car Makers," *Financial Times,* Jan. 10, 1991.

21. Harley Shaiken, *Mexico in the Global Economy: High Technology and Work Organization in Export Industries* (San Diego: Center for U.S.-Mexican Studies, University of California, 1990), 122.

22. Joseph Grunwald, "Opportunity Missed: Mexico and Maquiladoras," *Brookings Review* (Winter 1990–1991): 44–48.

23. Bank of Korea, *Quarterly Economic Review,* June 1990. See also Ezra Vogel and David F. Lindauer, "Toward a Social Compact for South Korean Labor," Harvard Institute for International Development, Harvard University, Development Discussion Paper no. 317, November 1989; Jong-il You, "Capital-Labor Relations of the Newly Industrializing Regime in South Korea: Past, Present, and Future," unpub. paper, Harvard University, 1989; Alice H. Amsden, *South Korea's Labor Market in the Context of Early and Late Industrialization* (Cambridge, Mass.: Center for International Studies, MIT, Fall 1988).

24. Maria Lorena Cook, "Economic Restructuring and Political Change in Mexico: The Role of Labor," paper presented to the Latin American Studies Association, Los Angeles, 1992.

25. Steve Dubb, "Trozos de cristal: Privatization and Union Politics at Telefonos de Mexico," paper presented to the Latin American Studies Association, Los Angeles, 1992; Stephen Baker, "Salinas Goes after Another Monster: The Phone System," *Business Week,* March 6, 1989, 42.

26. Lawrence Krause, "Social Capability and Long Term Economic Growth," unpub. paper, Graduate School of International Relations and Pacific Studies, University of California at San Diego, La Jolla, Calif., Aug. 9, 1991; Lance Compa, "American Trade Unions and NAFTA," paper presented to Conference on International Trade Unionism, Saitama University, Saitama-Ken, Japan, 1994.

27. United States International Trade Commission, *Review of Trade and Investment Liberalization Measures by Mexico and Prospects for Future United States–Mexican Relations: Phase I and II* (Washington, D.C.: USITC, 1990).

28. David Barkin, "Salinastroika and Other Novel Ideas," unpub. paper, 1992.

29. Tom Barry, ed., *Mexico: A Country Guide* (Albuquerque, N.M.: Inter-Hemispheric Education Resource Center, 1992).

30. Fernando Fajnzylber, *Unavoidable Industrial Restructuring in Latin America* (Durham, N.C.: Duke University Press, 1990).

31. Zysman, *Technology and Power.*

32. Michael Piore, "Critical Notes on Dunlop's *Industrial Relations System,*" paper prepared for the colloquium "Les Systèmes de relations professionelles," Paris, March 1989.

33. "A Benign Scenario," *Financial Times,* June 3, 1989; Susan Walsh Sanderson and Robert H. Hayes, "Mexico—Opening Ahead of Eastern Europe," *Harvard Business Review,* Sept.–Oct. 1990.

34. International Confederation of Free Trade Unions, Executive Board, *Trade Union Rights Under Threat* (Brussels: ICFTU, Dec. 1–3, 1993).

35. Bureau of National Affairs, "NAO Decides to Review Union Charges against Honeywell, General Electric," *Daily Labor Report,* April 20, 1994, 14; BNA, "NAO Closes Book on Union NAFTA Charges Against Honeywell and General Electric," *Daily Labor Report,* Oct. 14, 1994, D3; BNA, "U.S. National Administra-

tive Office's Public Report of Review on Submissions No. 940001 and 940002," *Daily Labor Report,* Oct. 14, 1994, D23. For a detailed discussion, see Lance Compa, "The First NAFTA Labor Cases: A New International Labor Rights Regime Takes Shape," *U.S.-Mexico Law Journal* 3 (Spring 1995): 159–181.

36. BNA, "Four Groups Charge Sony, Mexican Government with Labor Law Violations under NAFTA Accord," *Daily Labor Report,* Aug. 17, 1994, D3; BNA, "NAO Refuses to Review Charges That Sony's Work Shifts Violate Mexican Labor Standards," *Daily Labor Report,* Oct. 20, 1994, D4.

37. BNA, "ILO Director Sees Difference over Coverage of Labor Rights," *Daily Labor Report,* April 28, 1994, D8.

38. Turley, "Legal Theory."

39. 499 U.S. 244 (1991).

40. *Labor Union of Pico Korea, Ltd. v. Pico Products, Inc.,* 968 F.2d 191 (2d Cir. 1992), cert. denied 113 S.Ct. 493 (1992).

41. Compa, "American Trade Unions and NAFTA."

42. American Society of International Law, Basic Documents on International Economic Law, *Canada-United States-Mexico: North American Free Trade Agreement,* 1993 BDIEL AD LEXIS 101, Agreement, emphasis in original.

43. American Society of International Law, Basic Documents on International Economic Law, *Canada-United States-Mexico: North American Agreement on Labor Co-operation,* 1994 BDIEL AD Lexis 6, Agreement, preamble.

44. North American Agreement on Labor Cooperation, pt. 2: Obligations, art. 2: Levels of Protection.

45. See chapter by Virginia Leary in this volume.

46. Compa, "American Trade Unions and NAFTA."

47. *United Steelworkers of America v. Warrior & Gulf Navigation,* 363 U.S. 574 (1960).

48. Ibid.

49. Turley, "Dualistic Values in the Age of International Legisprudence," *Hastings Law Journal* 44 (Jan. 1993): 186.

50. *Id.*

51. For a discussion of implications of extending NAFTA, see Lance Compa, "Going Multilateral: The Evolution of U.S. International Labor Rights Policy Under GSP and NAFTA," *Connecticut Journal of International Law* 10 (Spring 1995): 337ff.

52. See Stephen F. Diamond, "U.S. Labor and North American Economic Integration: Toward a Constructive Critique," *The Political Economy of North American Free Trade* (New York: St. Martin's Press, 1993).

53. Interview with Elaine Bernard, director, Harvard University Trade Union Program, 1993.

Part III
Litigating International Labor Rights

Chapter 11
International Worker Rights Enforcement
Proposals Following a Test Case

Terry Collingsworth

The emergence of the global economy in the last two decades has greatly affected conditions for workers around the world.[1] Employers are now free to search the world for cheap labor and pit workers in one country against another in a downward bidding spiral for rights and wages. Citing the dual goals of improving conditions for workers in developing countries and slowing the loss of manufacturing jobs in the United States,[2] Congress passed new laws designed to protect "internationally recognized worker rights" by conditioning some form of trade benefit on compliance with international standards of worker rights.[3]

The most significant of these laws is the Generalized System of Preferences Act (GSP),[4] which provides duty-free status for many products exported to the United States from developing countries. Under the labor rights clause, duty-free treatment could be denied unless the exporting country "has not taken or is not taking steps to afford internationally recognized worker rights to workers in the country."[5]

Unfortunately, successive U.S. administrations have been lukewarm at best, when not openly hostile, in enforcing the worker rights provisions of the law. They are careful not to offend the American multinational companies (MNCs) that benefit from ready access to cheap labor in developing countries and undertake large-scale transfers of production to developing countries. The real tragedy of the GSP program, as it has been implemented, is the failure to achieve one of the clear goals of the program: to supplant direct foreign aid to developing countries by giving their industries a competitive advantage, through tariff concessions, to allow them to grow and share the prosperity with workers, who could then be expected to increase global consumption.[6]

In 1990 the International Labor Rights Fund, joined by 22 other plaintiffs, including all the trade unions and human rights organizations that had ever filed a worker rights petition under GSP,[7] filed a lawsuit seeking judicial review of the Bush administration's record in undermining the statutory requirements of GSP. The case, *International Labor Rights Fund (ILRERF) et al. v. Bush et al.*, was ultimately dismissed by the Court of Appeals for the District of Columbia Circuit in a heavily divided opinion.[8] Decided on technical rather than substantive grounds, the Court's decision left undisturbed the executive branch's discretion in administering the GSP statute's worker rights provision. However, the decision did highlight the problems with the statute and clarified the course to ultimately enact an effective, enforceable statute.

The Clinton administration has taken a strong rhetorical stand in favor of worker rights. "Addressing the intersection of trade and internationally recognized labor standards is a high priority of the United States," said U.S. Trade Representative Michael Kantor in announcing that the United States won the right to raise labor rights issues in the new World Trade Organization.[9] But it remains to be seen whether President Clinton will depart from the practices of the preceding administrations and actively enforce the will of Congress with respect to international worker rights under the GSP program. His promoting a North American Free Trade Agreement without an enforceable worker rights provision, despite campaign pledges to the contrary, for example, or reneging on a firm commitment to remove China's most-favored-nation status unless significant progress was made on human rights, cast doubt on whether there will be effective GSP worker rights enforcement absent express amendments to the GSP statute.[10]

An opportunity for amendment during the GSP authorization renewal process should be utilized to ensure that future administrations cannot subvert the congressional policy to require compliance with internationally recognized worker rights as a condition of eligibility for substantial duty-free benefits under GSP. Now that the effort to include a "social clause" in the completed Uruguay Round negotiations on the General Agreement on Tariffs and Trade (GATT) has fallen short,[11] GSP reform is only viable option for concretely fashioning rules to protect workers to coincide with the protection of global investment by multinational corporations.

The purpose of this chapter is first to highlight the failure of U.S. administrations to enforce the GSP worker rights provision with a number of examples. Then, the legal issues in *ILRERF v. Bush* will be discussed to illustrate the minefield of administrative law issues that must be confronted in attempting to obtain enforcement of GSP or any of the other worker rights provisions in U.S. trade law. Finally, in the context of look-ing toward amendments to GSP, proposals will be made to cure the pro-cedural problems that precluded judicial enforcement and to clarify the substantive standards for "internationally recognized" worker rights.

The Bush Administration's Failure to Enforce GSP's Worker Rights Provision

There are several areas in which the Bush administration's GSP enforce-ment practices are in conflict with the statutory commands of GSP. The areas discussed are the major allegations that were made in the com-plaint in *ILRERF v. Bush*.[12]

The Role of the GSP Subcommittee in Enforcing the Worker Rights Provision

The GSP Subcommittee's regulations establish a petitioning process to enforce the worker rights provision requiring "interested parties" to submit documentation of worker rights violations.[13] The Subcommittee effectively requires the petitioners to bear the burden of proving the ineligibility of a beneficiary developing country (BDCs) for GSP bene-fits. In many cases, the U.S. government, through its embassy in a BDC or through the annual report on worker rights required by GSP, has independent knowledge of worker rights violations, yet the GSP Sub-committee has never taken action unless a petition has been filed by an outside party.[14]

This practice conflicts with the language of the statute, which places an affirmative burden on the president to remove a BDC from the pro-gram if it fails to comply with the requirements. Section 2462 (b) of GSP provides that "the President *shall not designate* any country a [BDC] . . . if such country has not taken or is not taking steps to afford internation-ally recognized worker rights to workers in the country."[15] Section 2464 (b) similarly provides that "the President *shall . . . withdraw or suspend* the designation of any country if . . . as a result of changed circumstances such country would be barred from designation as a [BDC]."[16]

The GSP process was intended to identify those BDCs that have failed to meet the statutory requirements, including compliance with the worker rights provision. Nothing in the statute or the legislative history supports the GSP Subcommittee's practice of acting only in response to petitions. In fact, the regulations expressly permit unilateral action, but at least with respect to enforcing the worker rights provision, this has never been done.[17]

The "New Information" Requirement in the Regulations as Inconsistent with the Statutory Language

Sections 2007.0(b) (5) and 2007.1(a) (4) of the GSP Subcommittee's regulations require that a petition include "substantial new information" before a previously reviewed country will be reviewed again, regardless of whether the country is in fact in violation of the statute.[18] In practice, the GSP Subcommittee has refused to review serious, undisputed violations of the statute simply based on the fact that similar allegations were made in a previous petition that was denied.

Although there are numerous examples of this practice, perhaps the clearest illustration of how far the Bush administration has gone to undermine the GSP worker rights provision using the "new information" requirement as a screening device is provided by the refusal to review Malaysia's worker rights practices. In 1988 the AFL-CIO filed a worker rights petition against Malaysia, alleging primarily that Malaysia failed to provide the rights to associate and collectively bargain, did not have a nationally applicable minimum wage law, and used force labor.[19] After accepting the petition for review, the GSP Subcommittee issued a decision in 1989 that recited the allegations and concluded without applying a discernable standard that Malaysia was "taking steps."[20]

Following the issuance of the decision, U.S. Trade Representative Carla Hills then wrote a letter to the Malaysian minister of trade and finance informing him that she recognized the finding that Malaysia was "taking steps," but she went on to say:

Our review finds that your government does not allow full freedom for workers to associate and form the labor organizations of their own choosing in certain export industries such as the electronics industry. We also find that certain aspects of your government's Pioneer Industries Program restrict some collective bargaining issues between workers and management at firms with foreign investment. Besides being inherently objectionable, these practices impede our efforts to obtain a consensus for open markets and liberal trade policies. I urge you to consult with your colleagues in government and the private sector and urge you to look toward the amendment or elimination of these measures. Taking action to modify these practices now can prevent these issues from becoming a focal point . . . in the future.[21]

Thus, the official government position expressly acknowledged that Malaysia, although cleared for that year, had serious problems that warranted further steps.[22]

In 1990, the ILRERF and AFL-CIO filed petitions documenting that Malaysia had not taken further steps with respect to the rights to associate and collectively bargain and that both rights continued to be restricted.[23] While the petitions also demonstrated that Malaysia likewise had not enacted a minimum wage law and still utilized forced labor, the primary focus was on the rights to associate and collectively bargain. These were the issues that USTR Hills had flagged as needing further steps, and they are the most essential of the specific rights enumerated in the GSP worker rights standard. Congress acknowledged this by saying that "The capacity to form unions and bargain collectively to achieve higher wages and better working conditions is essential for workers in developing countries to attain decent living standards and to overcome hunger and poverty."[24]

The GSP Subcommittee refused even to accept the petitions for review, issuing a summary rejection of the petitions, stating that the allegations made had been previously reviewed.[25] Thus, apparently Malaysia is effectively immunized from any future scrutiny as long as the terrible worker rights situation does not get worse. According to the GSP Subcommittee's interpretation of the statute, the failure to take further steps does not violate the statute under any circumstances because there is no "new information" if conditions remain the same.

The GSP Subcommittee's practice defeats the fundamental premise of the GSP statute that countries must continue to take steps until they are in complete compliance with the worker rights standard. Congress expressed its intent quite directly that "changed circumstances" could be a failure to improve, rather than new, affirmative violations. Congress envisioned a continuing review process[26] to determine whether a country "has taken or is taking steps" to comply with worker rights. It intended for the mandatory enforcement language to apply even if worker rights remained unchanged following the prior review, particularly if a country made economic progress and failed to spread the benefit of that progress to the workers. This is sufficient "changed circumstances," regardless of whether there is "new information," a requirement found nowhere in the statute.[27]

Failure of the GSP Subcommittee to Apply a Consistent, Identifiable Standard for "Internationally Recognized Worker Rights"

The most serious problem with enforcement of the worker rights provision to date has been the absolute failure of the GSP Subcommittee to apply any consistent standard of "internationally recognized worker rights" in making determinations under the worker rights provision.[28] The seemingly arbitrary application of the standard has drawn justified criticism. Philip Alston notes that "the form in which the standards are stated is so bald and inadequate as to have the effect of providing a *carte blanche* to the relevant U.S. government agencies, thereby enabling them to opt for whatever standards they choose to set in any given situation." [29] Unlike Alston, the Lawyers Committee for Human Rights focused its criticism on the enforcement record of the GSP Subcommittee, rather than the statutory language, and concluded following a comprehensive study of the GSP program that "Discretionary acceptance of petitions has sent signals to certain countries that the United States will ignore worker rights violations for foreign policy reasons and has reduced the credibility of the U.S. in promoting international worker rights." [30]

The core of the problem is simply that the GSP Subcommittee does not apply any of the recognized standards in determining whether a particular country is in violation of the worker rights standard. One of the most basic principles of administrative law is that agency determinations must include a clear standard and a reasoned analysis. [31] The GSP Subcommittee's record to date falls far short of this requirement.

The only written effort to provide an official interpretation of the worker rights standard is included as Appendix B in the State Department's annual *Country Report*. [32] That standard makes clear that the basic rights provided in the GSP statute are absolute: "No flexibility is permitted concerning the acceptance of the basic principles contained in human rights standards, i.e., freedom of association, the right to organize and bargain collectively, the prohibition of forced labor, and the absence of discrimination." [33] The standard goes on to note that the "taking steps" language of the statutory standard is meant to take account of differing levels of economic development with respect to the economically oriented factors: that is, minimum wage laws, child labor provisions, and health and safety laws. [34]

This standard has never been applied in any case reviewed by the GSP Subcommittee, which is in itself a violation of established administrative law principles, since an agency is bound to follow its own rules and regulations. [35] While the written record is clear that the GSP Subcommittee has never applied the Appendix B standard, there are numerous examples of cases that would necessarily have been decided differently if the standard had been applied. For the sake of brevity, the previously discussed example of Malaysia is illustrative. [36] Following the 1988 GSP review, even USTR Carla Hills acknowledged that Malaysia had serious problems and was not in compliance with the important rights to associate and bargain collectively. [37] According to the Appendix B standard, "no flexibility" is permitted with respect to those two important rights. Yet the GSP Subcommittee found that Malaysia had met the standard.

An additional failing is that the GSP Subcommittee consistently ignores internationally recognized standards that give substance to the five factors of the worker rights provision. [38] It is this issue that has generated the criticism that GSP violates international principles by "imposing its own conveniently flexible and even elastic standards upon other states. The latter are, in effect, being required to meet standards which are not formally binding upon them by virtue either of treaty undertakings or of customary international law."[39]

While the legislative history indicates that Congress intended to avoid such problems by utilizing universally recognized human rights standards,[40] and even Appendix B expressly notes that ILO standards should be used to define the scope of the protected rights,[41] there is little room to debate that the GSP Subcommittee has consistently ignored ILO conventions and specific findings of violations in making its determinations under GSP.

In many crucial areas the GSP Subcommittee has acted in conflict with well-established ILO conventions and rulings. For example, ILO Convention No. 87 on the Freedom of Association and Protection of the Right to Organize expressly prohibits violence or physical threats to workers, recognizing that such conduct is the most extreme and effective deterrent to unionization. The official position of the GSP Subcommittee has been that violence against trade unionists is beyond the scope of GSP since it involves violations of "human rights" not "worker rights."[42]

The GSP Lawsuit

Seeking to obtain judicial review of the GSP Subcommittee's disregard for the requirements of the GSP statute, the ILRERF formed a broad coalition of twenty-three labor and human rights groups including the AFL-CIO and its major affiliates, Human Rights Watch and the Lawyers Committee for Human Rights. However, the plaintiffs were never able to reach the merits, as the case became a struggle over questions of jurisdiction and administrative law.

First the government argued that the federal district court lacked jurisdiction and that the Court of International Trade (CIT) had exclusive jurisdiction under 28 U.S.C. sec. 1581. The District Court held that it had jurisdiction, as the matter turned on the interpretation of a federal statute, a traditional "federal question."[43]

The government then moved to dismiss on the grounds that the case was not justiciable and that the plaintiffs lacked standing to sue. The District Court dismissed the complaint on the justiciability issue, reasoning that the terms of the worker rights provision were so broad that there was "no law to apply" and therefore any determinations were committed to agency discretion. The court further stated that since the determinations under GSP involved foreign policy, the president was particularly shielded in his use of discretion.[44]

Plaintiffs appealed to the Court of Appeals for the District of Columbia Circuit, where the government seemingly abandoned most of its previous arguments and primarily asserted that the matter presented a non-justiciable political question.[45] The three-judge court, in a sharply divided opinion, affirmed the dismissal of the complaint. Judge Henderson ruled that the CIT had exclusive jurisdiction of all matters arising under the GSP.[46] She reversed the district court's ruling on the issue and ignored the government's express concession on appeal that jurisdiction was proper in the district court.[47] Both Judges Sentelle and Mikva disagreed with Judge Henderson on this point, creating a 2-1 majority in support of the District Court's jurisdictional ruling.[48] However, Judge Sentelle voted to dismiss on standing grounds, shifting the majority to a 2–1 affirmation of the dismissal.

Judge Sentelle focused exclusively on the standing issue, which the government had not raised on appeal. He reasoned that the human rights group plaintiffs suffered no legal "injury in fact" sufficient to meet the standing threshold. Then he held that while the labor union plaintiffs had suffered an injury in fact, that injury would not be redressed by proper enforcement of the GSP statute.[49]

Simply stated, the "redressibility" requirement is a development of the federal courts as a constitutional prerequisite to standing. The idea is that even if a party suffers an injury, judicial relief is not available if the requested remedy would not "redress" the injury.[50] In Judge Sentelle's view, even if he ordered the executive branch to enforce the GSP statute as plaintiffs requested, that would not necessarily result in restoration of lost jobs or a decline in the flow of jobs from the United States to developing countries.[51]

Judge Mikva, in dissent, strongly disagreed on this point. He found that the trade union plaintiffs have standing to sue, and noted that Congress had determined that the GSP statute would work and that common sense also indicates that improved worker rights in developing countries would make them less attractive to employers searching for cheap labor. He stated that "Congress's intentions about causation and redressibility must be deferred to unless they are plainly irrational. . . . [T]his Court has no business second-guessing Congress's judgment about the appropriate remedy for a perceived social ill."[52]

Judge Mikva agreed, however, that the human rights groups had not suffered a legally cognizable injury. He then went on to address the justiciability issue, the only judge to do so, and held that the standard was sufficiently clear and mandatory that it could be judicially reviewed.[53]

Lessons from the GSP Case: Proposals for Amendments

The problems with past GSP enforcement have been highlighted. The major problem has been the abuse of discretion, stemming from the lack of clear standards to implement the congressional policy. When the GSP program comes up for renewal, there is opportunity to ensure that its intent is realized. The GSP litigation provides important lessons that must be taken into account in designing a more effective law. In addition to clarifying the substantive standards, the GSP statute must take account of the pitfalls of jurisdiction and administrative law, and the likelihood that the conservative federal courts will be hostile toward advocates for worker rights.[54]

The proposals will be broken into two sections. First, problems that have prevented judicial review will be addressed. The assumption made is that judicial review is necessary to insure fair and responsive enforcement of GSP and to avoid the systematic abuses of discretion that have occurred when the GSP Subcommittee has operated on the assumption that its decisions would not be reviewable.[55] Then the discussion will shift to suggest changes to the substantive worker rights standard, both to add the necessary clarity to insure that questions as to its application will be justiciable and to bring it in conformity with true "internationally recognized" standards of worker rights.

Providing for Judicial Review

Subject Matter Jurisdiction

This is the one area in which there is the most agreement. Judges Sentelle and Mikva agreed that the lower court was correct in finding that the federal district had jurisdiction.[56] Absent the rather broad jurisdictional grant to the CIT of all actions arising out of laws "providing for . . . tariffs,"[57] there would be no debate that the district courts have jurisdiction over what would otherwise be a routine federal question, the interpretation of the GSP statute.[58]

There is no reason to leave this to chance. A simple clause stating that all questions relating to the conditions for eligibility for GSP must be brought in the U.S. District Court would put the matter to rest. Although the GSP statute lists seven conditions for eligibility,[59] including whether a given country is "Communist," or a member of OPEC, the only challenges to eligibility that have been brought related to compliance with the worker rights standard.

Standing

Standing has three components: (1) injury in fact; (2) the injury must be fairly traceable to the defendant's unlawful conduct; and (3) the injury is likely to be redressed by the requested relief.[60] The second and third factors are identical when the requested relief is ordering the government to cease a statutory violation.[61] There is a further requirement the courts have added, calling it "prudential," that requires that the plaintiff be within the zone of interests protected by the statute.[62]

The plaintiffs in *ILRERF v. Bush* had problems with both the "injury in fact" requirement and the combined second and third factors, demonstrating that the court's order to the government to comply with the GSP statute would redress the alleged injury. While there was no dispute that the labor unions suffered an injury in fact,[63] Judges Sentelle and Mikva agreed that the human rights groups had not suffered a legally cognizable injury.[64] As to redressibility, this is the point on which Sentelle and Mikva disagreed, Sentelle taking the position that even if the court ordered enforcement of the GSP it would not necessarily stop the flow of jobs to developing countries.[65]

The GSP statute could be structured to confer standing on both human rights groups and labor unions that seek to challenge determinations made under the worker rights provision.

The law in this area primarily stems from a 1972 Supreme Court case, *Sierra Club v. Morton*.[66] There the Supreme Court held that the Sierra Club could not sue to stop the development of a wilderness area solely because it had a societal interest in protecting the environment. In order for the Sierra Club to have standing, it needed a "direct stake in the outcome," something that could be achieved, for example, if its members would be deprived of the use of the particular wilderness area at issue. "Abstract societal interests" are not a sufficient injury to confer standing.[67]

While it seems inconceivable that human rights groups that devote their time and resources to improving the lot of workers in developing countries are not obviously injured when the government fails to apply the only law that these groups have to further their institutional aims, even Judge Mikva held that there was no legally cognizable injury. Rather than debate the merits of this position, it would be more constructive to discuss how the GSP law could be amended to create a legally cognizable injury that would confer standing on human rights groups.

First, the GSP law can expressly provide for a private right of action for human rights groups or any other groups. The Supreme Court and the District of Columbia Circuit have consistently held that "Congress may enact statutes creating legal rights, the invasion of which creates standing, even though no injury would exist without the statute." [68]

The proposed solution would provide the necessary "injury" to confer standing on human rights groups. However, a plurality of the Supreme Court very recently held in *Lujan v. Defenders of Wildlife*[69] that they would not automatically support such statutory grants of standing. To take extra precautions to avoid any problems with *Lujan,* an amended GSP statute should follow Justice Kennedy's moderate approach suggested in a concurring opinion joined by Justice Souter and make clear "the injury it seeks to vindicate and relate the injury to the class of persons entitled to bring suit." [70]

To confer standing on human rights groups, the articulated injury must be the exploitation of workers in developing countries. Either in the statute itself or the legislative history, Congress must make clear that one of the major goals of GSP is to improve the living and working conditions for workers in developing countries through the creation of an enforceable standard of worker rights.[71] Parties that have an interest in seeing that the poverty and deprivation of rights for workers in developing countries is eradicated can be designated as the class of persons entitled to file petitions and then file suit to have adverse decisions reviewed. Either on a theory that improvement of worker rights will allow these parties to focus their limited resources on other problems affecting workers in developing countries,[72] or perhaps on a theory that human rights groups are the best choice to serve as advocates for workers in developing countries who would otherwise be unable to protect their interests,[73] the groups entitled to bring suit would be substantially reduced from "all persons," a breadth that seemed to inflame the *Lujan* plurality, to groups that have a legitimate interest in seeing worker rights protected.

There are other ways in which Congress could ensure that human rights groups can allege a sufficient injury in fact. Most notably, Congress could create an informational right. The GSP statute currently requires the president to report annually on worker rights in developing countries.[74] This is currently accomplished by a special section on worker rights that is included in the State Department's annual *Country Reports.* Congress could make clear that accurate reporting, as well as thorough investigations and accurate written findings pursuant to the substantive provisions of the statute, are essential to the furtherance of the strong public policy in favor of worker rights. The failure to make accurate and complete determinations under the statute would result in the denial of information needed by human rights and labor groups to direct their efforts and limited resources toward the goal of worker rights enforcement.[75]

Despite the apparent ease with which the redressibility problem can be cured, it would still be quite useful for other reasons to directly confront Judge Sentelle's position, embraced by the *Lujan* plurality,[76] that the courts can disagree with Congress as to the appropriate method to remedy a problem.[77] And, in the event that human rights groups ultimately are held not to have statutory standing, labor unions would still have to show that the injury they have suffered, primarily the loss of jobs to offshore production, would be redressible through enforcement of GSP.

The solution for Congress is to develop a compelling case through extensive hearings on the need for and the probable success of an effective worker rights statute. The hearings could develop an extensive public record on the extent of capital flight from the United States by companies in search of cheap labor, the extent of domestic job loss to developing countries, wage and other benefit concessions that American workers have had to make to avoid a plant closing, the conditions for workers in developing countries, evidence that in the few cases in which the USTR has vigorously enforced the GSP mechanism it has worked, and examples of the USTR's failure to enforce the statute. Further, and perhaps most difficult, there must be some expert testimony as to the various alternatives that could be pursued, and that removal of trade benefits or other sanctions would be the most effective way of encouraging the improvement of worker rights. While Judge Sentelle chose to ignore the legislative history indicating that Congress had concluded that the GSP program would work to improve worker rights,[78] there would be little room for such an assertion if Congress acted following detailed hearings, which would provide the added benefit of gathering information essential to the worker rights movement.

Clarifying the Substantive Standard for "Internationally Recognized Worker Rights"

The current language of the worker rights provision is not the picture of clarity. The legal significance of this is that if the language is too vague, a court can conclude that there is "no law to apply," and the statute is not justiciable, leaving the executive branch with nearly complete discretion to formulate a standard.[79] In *ILRERF v. Bush*, the District Court did just that, ruling that the broad and vague terms of the worker rights standard, most notably that the president was to decide if a given country "has not or is not *taking steps* to afford internationally recognized worker rights," indicated congressional intent to leave the substantive determinations to the president's discretion and beyond the reach of judicial review.[80] Judge Mikva, the only appellate judge to address the issue, disagreed and held that the mandatory language preceding the "taking steps" language, which provides that the president "shall not designate" and "shall withdraw" countries that fail to comply with the standard, indicated Congress' intent to create a mandatory standard.[81]

Clarification of the worker rights standard is necessary to remove any question as to whether it is justiciable.[82] First, the "taking steps" language, which now is applied by the GSP Subcommittee to all five factors in the worker rights provision, must be removed. This language is primarily responsible for the vagueness in the statute and has allowed the GSP Subcommittee free rein to avoid ever defining the substantive rights. Rather than determine whether a country has complied with an objective definition, the GSP Subcommittee seems to focus on whether a country is moving in the direction of some abstract goal that need not be met.[83]

The concept behind the inclusion of the "taking steps" language comes from the legislative history. Congress stated that "it is not the expectation . . . that developing countries come up to the prevailing labor standards of the United States and other highly-industrialized countries."[84] Thus, there was a concern that developing countries might not be able to bear the economic costs associated with immediate and complete compliance with the worker rights standard. However, as the State Department's Appendix B recognizes in discussing the flexibility built into the standard by the "taking steps" language,

this flexibility applies only to internationally recognized standards concerning working conditions. *No flexibility is permitted concerning the acceptance of the basic principles contained in the human rights standards*, i.e., freedom of association, the right to organize and bargain collectively, the prohibition of forced labor, and the absence of discrimination.[85]

The GSP standard should expressly acknowledge this distinction and separate the five factors into two groups, human rights, including the rights to associate and collectively bargain and freedom from forced labor,[86] which must be completely satisfied, and working conditions, including laws regulating minimum wages and hours, child labor, and occupational safety and health, which would require compliance with a more flexible standard that takes account of the country's economic condition, but that contains some reasonable, absolute minimum.

As long as it is clear that all five factors of the standard must be complied with,[87] then there is little need to get bogged down in discovering some perfect formula to measure compliance with the flexible aspects of the standard. Many advocates for worker rights would agree that as long as the human rights are strictly enforced, then the economically determined factors will follow through collective bargaining and trade union political participation.

With respect to defining what is required for each of the five rights, the ILO conventions provide an excellent source. Appendix B acknowledges this and makes specific reference to the ILO. In many cases, the ILO has, in response to charges filed, specifically made findings that a particular country is not in compliance with one of its conventions.[88] The ILO has produced a great body of decisions and guidelines that could be used to add content to the specific rights. Eventually the GSP process itself will yield useful precedent once the GSP Subcommittee is required to apply an objective, uniform standard.[89]

The Benefits of a Revised GSP Statute

A more general criticism of the GSP program is that it violates international law because it is an attempt by the U.S. government to regulate the internal affairs of other sovereign nations. The credibility of the program is essential to its success, and international support for the program would facilitate that success.

A good deal of the international criticism has centered on the fact that the absence of "internationally recognized" standards in the GSP statute has subjected the countries in the program to an arbitrary process. The more fundamental violation of sovereignty argument stems from a basic principle of international law that all countries have some degree of sovereignty and that there are "powers that states claim for themselves in their mutual relations and to act without restraint on their freedom."[90] This fundamental principle of sovereignty is embodied in the documents and debates of the United Nations, which provide for the "non-interference in the domestic affairs of other countries, and therefore of the mutual respect for the forms of other peoples' governments."[91] The United Nations Declaration of Principles of International Law Concerning Friendly Relations among States declares that neither "political nor economic measures [may be taken that] coerce another state to subordinate its sovereign rights."[92]

Whether the removal or denial of GSP benefits constitutes a violation of sovereignty is determined by whether it has such a great impact as to constitute "interference" or "coercion." It has been argued that section 301 of the Trade Act of 1974, which gives the U.S. trade representative the authority to impose strict sanctions including a complete denial of access to U.S. markets, is of such a coercive nature that it interferes with state sovereignty.[93] However, GSP does not "condition *access* to the United States market on respect for labor rights but rather only condition[s] continuance of nonreciprocal trade benefits on respect for such rights."[94] Countries may continue to trade with the United States under the GSP law; they will merely be denied the benefit of duty-free trade. They may choose to comply with the labor standards set forth by the GSP or they may not.[95] If they are found to have not complied with the GSP labor standards, they will merely be denied a non-reciprocal benefit, not an absolute right.

The U.S. would be justified in taking action to protect its own interests that have been harmed by countries that refuse to comply with internationally recognized standards of worker rights, regardless of whether the action taken constitutes "interference" or "coercion."[96] The primary argument is that the United States could take steps to promote "fair trade" to protect its interests.[97] The United States has been damaged by the shift of investment from countries with more expensive labor and requirements of humane working conditions (such as the United States), to countries with cheap labor and poor working conditions. Based on figures compiled by the U.S. Department of Labor for the purpose of awarding Trade Adjustment Assistance to workers unemployed by "foreign competition," from 1975 to 1989 1,223,280 union and 542,795 non-union jobs have been lost.[98] Further, it is estimated that about 3 million jobs have been lost in the United States due to the trade deficit alone.[99]

Practices like the systematic suppression of worker rights are "driven by the desire to succeed in international trade. Certain developing and newly industrialized states suppress labor unions and depress labor conditions in order to support effective export sectors and/or to attract foreign investment."[100] Further, this type of international competition based on suppression of worker rights tends to harmonize downward labor conditions and wages; artificial depression in one state leads to declining labor conditions and wages throughout the world.[101] For a country like the United States, this translates directly into the loss of jobs and reduced living standards.

The fair trade justification would allow the United States to take steps to protect itself and seek to remedy the suppression of worker rights by foreign countries that has caused direct injury to U.S. workers and industry. Since gaining a competitive edge in the global marketplace promotes government suppression of worker rights, the most effective way to end these practices would be to eliminate their profitability through economic sanctions.

A variation on this theme is called the "undeserved benefit" justification. Based on this theory, GSP is a benefit that the United States grants to developing countries, to the detriment of competing U.S. workers and industries, to help their economic growth. One of the stated purposes of GSP is to allow workers in developing countries to improve their living and working conditions.[102] By extending benefits to oppressive regimes and by importing or even giving preferential treatment to goods produced by exploited workers, the United States is supporting the suppression of worker rights, something it is not required by international law to do.[103]

A distinct justification for the GSP program is that, to the extent that it furthers the enforcement of fundamental human rights, the United States can impose its standards, even at the expense of foreign sovereignty. All states have a duty to ensure that human rights are upheld. There is ample ground to assert that the current GSP program, with its arbitrary and unidentifiable standards applied in practice by the GSP Subcommittee, is not enforcing universally accepted principles of human rights.[104] However, while the debate rages as to which labor rights are human rights, both are being denied. The primary question perhaps is who gets to decide. Congress, in amending the GSP to include the worker rights provision, referenced the Universal Declaration of Human Rights and stated: "The Declaration specifically affirms for each person the right to a job, the right to form and join unions, and the right to an adequate standard of living."[105] Assuming that an amended GSP worker rights provision is tied to ILO conventions, the most important of which the ILO labels "basic human rights,"[106] it would be difficult to justify a sustained argument as to whether worker rights are "human rights" and whether the GSP program is enforcing universally recognized human rights.[107]

Conclusion

Fundamental changes are needed in the GSP review process to restore credibility to the idea that the United States is interested in promoting respect for international worker rights. Not only will this ensure that multinational corporations are no longer free to repudiate minimum and basic labor standards in their search for countries willing to sell their workers to the lowest bidder, but it holds the key to a new beginning in global development. Once workers in developing countries are able to realize their basic rights and gain a fair share of the economic pie, they can begin to purchase goods in the global market and contribute to global economic revitalization.[108]

Now that the GATT is completed without a social clause, the immediate opportunity for the optimum solution to the problem—global, multilateral enforcement of international labor rights—is gone for the moment.[109] Waiting any longer for the entire world to agree, and arguing over non-essential details, will simply prolong the opportunity for MNCs to take advantage of the situation. Congress has the opportunity in the GSP renewal process to take the lead and confront the twilight zone of the global economy where MNC's have extensive and effective laws to protect their property, but operate free of any regulations that would require them to honor the most basic and minimum standards for worker rights. An improved GSP program that enforces universally recognized worker rights will fill the gap in the short run and serve as a model for other countries to follow.

Notes

1. For a detailed discussion of the impact on worker rights due to the globalization of the economy, see Terry Collingsworth, "American Labor Policy and the International Economy: Clarifying Policies and Interests," *Boston College Law Review* 31 (1989): 31, 45–67.

2. The legislative history to the Generalized System of Preferences Act, 19 U.S.C. secs. 2461–2466 (1986) specifically mentions these two goals. See, e.g., *1984 U.S. Code Congressional and Administrative News* 4910, 5111–1112 (hereinafter Committee Report); 130 *Congressional Record* 977–979.

3. The Generalized System of Preferences Act (GSP), 19 U.S.C. secs. 2461–2465 (1986) (grants developing countries duty-free status on many exports to the U.S. conditioned on compliance with a five-factor worker rights standard); Caribbean Basin Economic Recovery Act (CBERA), 19 U.S.C. secs. 2701–2706 (1986) (operates nearly identical to GSP but applies only to countries in the Caribbean basin); Overseas Private Investment Corporation (OPIC), 22 U.S.C. sec. 2191 (1986) (provides financing and insurance to American companies investing in developing countries provided that the host country is in compliance with international worker rights); and section 301 of the Trade Act of 1974, 19 U.S.C. sec. 2411 (1988) (applies to all U.S. trading partners and makes failure to comply with international standards of worker rights an unfair trading practice and subjects the offender to a wide range of sanctions). For further discussion of the operation of these statutes see Collingsworth, "American Labor Policy," 67–86. Another law, the 1992 Amendment to the Foreign Assistance Act of 1961, 22 U.S.C. sec. 2151 et seq. (Supp. IV, 1992), was passed by Congress in November 1992 in response to widespread publicity of the use of United States Agency for International Development (USAID) money to encourage and subsidize offshore production by American firms. It restricts funding of programs that encourage offshore production or that contribute to the denial of internationally recognized worker rights. Most recently, in July 1994, Congress approved an amendment to the statutory authorization of U.S. participation in the World Bank, the International Monetary Fund, and other multilateral lending agencies, instructing U.S. representatives to the banks to assure respect for labor rights as a condition of receipt of bank loans and grants.

4. 19 U.S.C. secs. 2461–2466 (1986). GSP has been the most widely used of the available laws as a mechanism to attempt to improve worker rights in developing countries for a number of reasons. The most significant is that it has broader reach than the other two benefit-linked statutes, CBERA and OPIC. CBERA is very similar in operation to GSP, but applies only to countries in the Caribbean basin, 19 U.S.C. sec. 2702 (b), while GSP applies worldwide. OPIC has the same potential scope, but determinations of compliance with its worker rights provision are primarily tied to GSP determinations. See 22 U.S.C. sec. 2191a

(a). Section 301, while having the strongest remedy, expressly gives discretion to the United States trade representative to decline to take countervailing action against labor rights violations.

5. 19 U.S.C. sec. 2462 (b)(7). A five-factor substantive standard is provided in section 2462 (a) (4):

> (A) the right of association; (B) the right to organize and bargain collectively; (C) a prohibition on the use of any form of forced or compulsory labor; (D) a minimum age for the employment of children; and (E) acceptable conditions of work with respect to minimum wages, hours of work, and occupational safety and health.

6. See Statement of Purpose for GSP, 19 U.S.C. sec. 2461, note following text. Instead, the program has primarily served as an incentive for large MNCs to have the best of both worlds: cheap labor in developing countries and duty-free access to American markets. See, generally, Collingsworth, "American Labor Policy," 45–57, 67–82. For a discussion of global development through improved worker rights enforcement, see Collingsworth, Goold, and Harvey, "Time for a Global New Deal," *Foreign Affairs* 73, no. 1 (1994): 8.

7. GSP is enforced exclusively through a procedural framework that requires an "interested party" to file a petition with the GSP Subcommittee, an interdepartmental body set up by the GSP regulations to make decisions regarding eligibility under GSP. See 15 C.F.R. secs. 2007.0 and 2007.1. The petitioner is required to document a given country's failure to meet the worker rights standard (15 C.F.R. sec. 2007.1 [a]). The GSP Subcommittee then either summarily rejects the petition, or accepts it for review and makes a final determination as to whether the subject country is in compliance with the standard (sec. 2007.2).

8. 752 F. Supp. 495 (D. D.C. 1990), affirmed by a divided opinion, 954 F.2d 745 (D.C. Cir. 1992). For a discussion of the competing rationales, see below.

9. Statement by Ambassador Michael Kantor, press release, Office of the U.S. Trade Representative, April 8, 1994.

10. The Clinton administration halted a worker rights review of Indonesia in February 1994 despite evidence of severe labor rights violations. See "Review of Worker Rights in Indonesia Is Suspended," *Wall Street Journal,* Feb. 17, 1994, A4.

11. See, for example, Frances Williams, "Labour Standards Move Resisted," *Financial Times,* April 14, 1994, 5.

12. This discussion is limited to identifying the major failings of the Bush administration's record of non-enforcement of GSP. It does not raise all the technical statutory violations. For an exhaustive list of all the statutory issues, see the pleadings filed in *ILRERF v. Bush,* 752 F. Supp. 495 (D. D.C. 1990) (complaint paras. 53 a–k; Plaintiffs' Memorandum in Support of Motion for a Preliminary Injunction). All the pleadings are on file at the ILRF. In addition, this section does not exhaustively discuss legal arguments as to why the statutory violations should have been subject to judicial review. For a complete discussion of this issue, see the briefs filed on appeal in *ILRERF v. Bush,* 954 F.2d 745 (D.C. Cir. 1992). A general discussion of the issues of law that led to the dismissal of the plaintiffs' complaint can be found below.

13. 15 *C.F.R.* pt. 2007. For a discussion of the petitioning process, see note 7 above. The regulations define an "interested party" as "a party who has a significant economic interest in the subject matter of the request or any other party representing a significant economic interest that would be materially affected

by the action requested." Despite the emphasis on "economic" interests, the legislative history makes clear that Congress intended that "parties interested in the implementation and protection of internationally recognized worker rights" have the right to participate in the review process (Committee Report, 5125–5126). In practice, there has been no refusal by the GSP Subcommittee to accept petitions from human rights groups that arguably lack an economic interest.

14. My own inspection of the GSP Subcommittee's decisions since the worker rights provision was implemented confirmed that the GSP Subcommittee has never taken action against a country, regardless of the evidence available, unless a petition had been filed.

15. 19 U.S.C. sec. 2462 (b) (emphasis added).

16. Ibid., sec. 2464 (b) (emphasis added).

17. 15 C.F.R. sec. 2007.0 (f) provides that the Trade Policy Staff Committee, the body that reviews the GSP Subcommittee's actions (ibid., secs. 2007.3 [f] and [g]), "may at any time, on its own motion, initiate any of the actions described in [the paragraphs creating the petitioning process]."

18. 15 C.F.R. secs. 2007.0 (b) (5) and 2007.1 (a) (4).

19. The petition is on file with the ILRF and also is available at the office of the U.S. trade representative.

20. The decision is on file with the ILRF and is available at the U.S. trade representative's office. But for the unavailability of judicial review of the decision, discussed at length below, it would have been subject to challenge because of its failure to apply the standard in the statute and the lack of any meaningful analysis as to how the conclusion was reached. See, e.g., *Ashton v. Pierce*, 541 F. Supp. 635, 641 (D.D.C. 1982).

21. A copy of the letter is on file with the ILRF.

22. This cannot be reconciled with the State Department's Appendix B in the annual *Country Report*. See State Department, *Country Reports on Human Rights Practices for 1990*, submitted to the Committee on Foreign Relations, U.S. Senate, and Committee on foreign Affairs, U.S. House of Representatives, by the Department of State, 102d. Cong., 1st sess. (1991), at 1693. See below, notes 32–37, and the accompanying text.

23. The petitions are on file with the ILRF and also are available at the office of the U.S. trade representative.

24. Committee Report, 5111. Appendix B to the State Department's annual report on worker rights likewise states that "no flexibility is permitted" concerning these rights (*Country Report*, 1628).

25. Case No. 005-CP-90. The decision is on file with the ILRF and is available at the office of the U.S. trade representative.

26. Congress expected a periodic review of compliance:

[I]t is the Committee's intent that USTR establish a formal procedure through which parties interested in the implementation and protection of internationally recognized worker rights at least once a year can offer testimony or submit written comments during at least one public hearing on issues pertaining to countries' eligibility for designation as [BDCs]. (Committee Report, 5126)

27. Judge Mikva acknowledged that the GSP Subcommittee's regulation adding the "new information" requirement should be judicially reviewable to determine whether it conflicts with the statute (954 F. 2d 754, 758–759 [D.C. Cir. 1992] [Mikva, J. dissenting]).

28. In preparation for the litigation, the ILRERF conducted a comprehensive review of all the written GSP Subcommittee decisions either refusing to accept a petition for review or, in cases in which a petition was accepted for review, finding that a BDC was "taking steps." No discernible standard emerged from these decisions. Instead, the GSP Subcommittee mechanically recites the language of the statute, including at times the five factors of the worker rights standard, and reaches a conclusion without giving any indication of how it interpreted and applied the statutory standard. The decisions are on file with the ILRF and are available at the office of the U.S. trade representative.

29. Philip Alston, chapter in this volume. Alston's chapter reflects an unfamiliarity with the practical problems stemming from the GSP Subcommittee's enforcement practices, and he focuses on the statutory language asserting that it invites such arbitrary application (see pp. 74–78). He then notes that this uneven, elastic enforcement renders GSP an example of unilateral enforcement that violates international standards. While I strongly disagree that the language of the statute necessarily requires that conclusion, there is no doubt that the arbitrary enforcement record of the GSP Subcommittee has run afoul of international requirements. This issue is discussed further in the context of amending the statutory language to eliminate the potential for uneven enforcement. See below, notes 80–93, and the accompanying text.

30. Lawyers Committee for Human Rights, *Human Rights and U.S. Foreign Policy* Lawyers Committee for Human Rights, New York, New York 1992, 41–42.

31. See, e.g., *Motor Vehicles Manufacturers Association v. State Farm Mutual Automobile Insurance Co.*, 463 U.S. 29, 43 (1983); *Amalgamated Transit Union International v. Donovan*, 767 F. 2d 939 (D.C. Cir. 1985), cert. denied 475 U.S. 1046 (1986).

32. See *Country Report*, 1693–94.

33. Ibid., 1694.

34. Ibid.

35. See *Service v. Dulles*, 354 U.S. 363, 372 (1957); *Center for Auto Safety v. Dole*, 828 F.2d 799, 803 (D.C. Cir. 1987); *Padula v. Webster*, 822 F.2d 97, 100 (D.C. Cir. 1987).

36. See above, notes 19–25, and the accompanying text.

37. See Hill's letter, quoted in the text at note 21 above.

38. See note 5 above for the text of the five-factor worker rights standard.

39. Alston, chapter in this volume, p. 79.

40. See Committee Report, 5112.

41. See, e.g. 1990 *Country Report*, 1693–94.

42. While the GSP Subcommittee's position is well known, one written example is a letter from former U.S. Trade Representative Clayton Yeutter to Holly J. Burkhalter, Washington director of Americas Watch, explaining that Americas Watch's El Salvador petition was not accepted for review in part because of its emphasis on human rights issues. The petition documented numerous acts of violence against trade unionists. The letter is on file with the ILRF.

43. This was in a separate opinion devoted exclusively to the jurisdiction issue (752 F. Supp. 490 [D. D.C. 1990]). For further discussion of the issue of jurisdiction, see below, notes 56–59, and the accompanying text.

44. 752 F. Supp. 495, 498, 499 (D. D.C. 1990).

45. At oral argument, Judge Sentelle inquired of the government's counsel why the government had not briefed the standing issue. Judge Sentelle stated

that he had been forced to retrieve the briefs from the District Court. His ruling ultimately was that plaintiffs lacked standing (954 F. 2d at 752).

46. Ibid., 747–48.

47. In response to Judge Henderson's question at oral argument, government counsel expressly conceded that the District Court had jurisdiction. This was confirmed in a follow-up letter to the court. A copy of the letter is on file with the ILRERF.

48. 954 F. 2d at 748–49, 759.

49. 954 F. 2d at 750–52.

50. See, e.g., *Simon v. Eastern Kentucky Welfare Rights Organization*, 426 U.S. 26, 41–42 (1976).

51. 954 F. 2d at 751–752.

52. 954 F. 2d at 757. The question of how much deference is due congressional judgments regarding redressibility has been hotly contested on the D.C. Circuit. See, e.g., *Center for Auto Safety v. Thomas*, 847 F. 2d 843 (D.C. Cir. 1988) (en banc), vacated, 856 F. 2d 1557 (D.C. Cir. 1988) (en banc).

53. 954 F.2d at 757–758.

54. Judges Henderson and Sentelle did not approach the ILRERF case as disinterested jurists; they became advocates for the government by, as Judge Mikva described it, "resurrect[ing] jurisdictional objections that failed to persuade even the District Court and that had been conceded by the government" (954 F. 2d at 752). A similar trend is evident in conservative judicial opinions restricting access to courts for environmental and consumer activists. See, e.g., *Lujan v. Defenders of Wildlife*, 504 U.S. 555, 60 U.S.L.W. 4495 (No. 90-1424, June 12, 1992).

55. See above for a discussion of the GSP Subcommittee's record.

56. 954 F. 2d at 748–749, 759.

57. 28 U.S.C. sec. 1581 (i) (2).

58. 28 U.S.C. sec. 1331 is the general jurisdictional statute for "federal questions."

59. 19 U.S.C. sec. 2462 (b) (1)–(7).

60. See, e.g., *Allen v. Wright*, 468 U.S. 737, 751 (1984).

61. See, e.g., *Center for Auto Safety v. NHTSA*, 793 F. 2d 1322, 1334 (D.C. Cir. 1986).

62. See, e.g., *Consumer's Union v. FTC*, 691 F. 2d 575, 576 (D.C. Cir. 1982) (en banc) (per curiam), affirmed, 463 U.S. 1216 (1983).

63. 954 F. 2d 750–751.

64. Ibid., 750, 754.

65. Ibid., 751–752.

66. 405 U.S. 727 (1972).

67. *Spann v. Colonial Village, Inc.*, 889 F. 2d 24, 27 (D.C. Cir. 1990).

68. *Animal Welfare Institute v. Kreps*, 561 F. 2d 1002, 1005 (D.C. Cir. 1977), quoting *Linda R.S. v. Richard D.*, 410 U.S. 614, 617, n.3 (1973).

69. 112 S.Ct. 2130 (1992). There is a significant factual distinction between the situation in *Lujan* and the proposal to amend GSP to create a statutory right to petition. In *Lujan*, plaintiffs did not have a statutory right to participate in any review process. They were simply trying as outsiders to require the government to comply with statutory procedures, but they themselves were not participants in the statutory review process. Since, according to the plurality, plaintiffs had no interest in the outcome of those proceedings, they had no standing to challenge that outcome (*Lujan*, at 4497–4502). This is markedly different from the

situation if Congress gives interested parties the statutory right to initiate a GSP preceding. Following an adverse determination, it would then be a routine matter, consistent with basic due process, to have judicial review of that decision if such review is required by the statute. Presumably, the court would not overrule all its prior decisions indicating that in such cases judicial review would be available as a matter of course. See above, notes 67–68, and the accompanying text.

70. *Lujan*, at 4497–4502.

71. Congress did express this goal in the legislative history to the original GSP worker rights provision. See *Committee Report*, 5111–12.

72. See, e.g., *Community for Creative Non-violence (CCNV) v. Pierce*, 814 F. 2d 663, 668 (D.C. Cir. 1987) (CCNV's interest in helping the homeless was injured when the government underreported the extent of homelessness, creating the potential for a loss of donations and assistance).

73. Labor unions would also be a logical choice but are not discussed here as there was no dispute that labor unions were able to demonstrate their own injury from the non-enforcement of GSP due to job loss and forced concessions in collective bargaining. See above, note 63, and the accompanying text.

74. 19 U.S.C. sec. 2465 (c).

75. See, e.g., *Community for Creative Non-Violence v. Pierce*, 814 F. 2d 663, 668 (D.C. Cir. 1987).

76. The *Lujan* plurality likewise questioned whether the consultation required by the Endangered Species Act would in fact result in any increased chances that endangered species would be protected, thus accepting the view that it is appropriate for the courts to engage in this inquiry. Justices Stevens, Blackmun, and O'Connor vigorously disputed this second-guessing of congressional judgment.

77. 954 F. 2d at 751–752.

78. See 954 F.2d at 756–757.

79. *Citizens to Preserve Overton Park v. Volpe*, 401 U.S. 402, 413 (1971); *Getty v. Federal Savings and Loan Insurance Corp.*, 805 F. 2d 1050 (D.C. Cir. 1986).

80. 752 F. Supp. 495, 498–99 (D. D.C. 1990).

81. 954 F. 2d at 757–58.

82. If Congress creates an express right of judicial review, discussed above at notes 68–70 and the accompanying text, that would make it quite difficult to argue that Congress intended to leave the interpretation entirely to the discretion of the executive branch.

83. For a good example of this, see above notes 19–25, and the accompanying text for the discussion of the GSP Subcommittee's determination that Malaysia was "taking steps" even though there was no factual question that they had in fact not complied with the rights to associate and bargain collectively.

84. Committee Report, 5112.

85. *Country Report*, 1694 (emphasis added).

86. Appendix B, quoted in the text at note 86 above, also mentions "the absence of discrimination." GSP currently does not have an anti-discrimination provision. However, in the amended version being prepared by the ILRF, GSP will include such a provision. If this becomes part of the law, it would also be included in this "human rights" category.

87. The current worker rights standard uses "and" to connect the five factors, which would normally be taken to mean that all factors must be met. However, the GSP Subcommittee has allowed "taking steps" to consume the rest of the statute and has never removed a country for failure to comply with one or two

of the factors as long as it has taken some identifiable step, however small, in the other areas.

88. For example, regarding the controversy over Malaysia's failure to provide for the right to associate, discussed above at notes 19–27 and the accompanying text, the ILO has five times reviewed Malaysia's failure to comply with the Freedom of Association and Protection of the Right to Organize, Convention No. 87. See Case No. 1480 (1990) (on file with the ILRF).

89. To draw upon greater expertise, it would be preferable to have the GSP worker rights decisions made by a body that has experience with labor standards. See above, note 89.

90. R. P. Anand "Sovereignty of States in International Law," in Anand, *International Law and the Developing Countries: Confrontation or Cooperation?* (New Delhi: Banyan Publications, 1984), p. 77.

91. Francesco Capotorti, "Human Rights: The Hard Road Towards Universality," in R. St. J. Macdonald and M. Douglas Johnston, eds., *The Structure and Process of International Law: Essays in Legal Philosophy Doctrine and Theory* Dordrecht: Martinus Nijhoff (1983), 977.

92. Declaration on Principles of International Law Concerning Friendly Relations and Co-operation among States in Accordance with the Charter of the United Nations, adopted Oct. 24, 1970, G.A. Res. 2625, 25 U.N. GAOR, Supp. (No. 30), 9. See Schachter, "International Law, Implications of U.S. Human Rights Policies," *New York Law School Law Review* 24 (1978): 64.

93. Alston, chapter in this volume, pp. 79–80; Note, "Labor Rights Conditionality: United States Trade Legislation and the International Trade Order," *New York University Law Review* 65 (1990): 79, 82–83.

94. Ibid., 83.

95. Of course a particularly poor country could argue that the denial of GSP benefits puts it at such an economically competitive disadvantage that it has no choice but to comply with the U.S. statute. There are no economic studies that bear this out. While the argument has a strong surface appeal, it must be remembered that the developing countries have a distinct competitive advantage due to cheap labor. The choice they are put to is whether they are better off competitively by foregoing GSP benefits and continuing to have cheap labor or by accepting GSP and having their labor costs increase.

96. See, generally, Alston, chapter in this volume, pp. 79–80; Mandel, "In Pursuit of the Missing Link: International Worker Rights and International Trade?" *Columbia Journal of Transnational Law* 27 (1989): 452–55, 457.

97. Ibid., 452.

98. See para. 45 in Complaint filed in *ILRERF v. Bush.*

99. Culbertson, "A Realist View of International Trade and National Trade Policy," *New York University Journal of International Law and Politics* 18 (1986): 1119, 1125 n. 13.

100. Mandel, "In Pursuit of the Missing Link," 452.

101. See Steve Charnovitz, "Fair Labor Standards and International Trade," *Journal of World Trade Law* 20 (1986): 61, 73.

102. Committee Report, 5111.

103. See, e.g., Gus Edgren, "Fair Labour Standards and Trade Liberalization," *International Labor Review* 118 (1979): 523, 526; Lance Compa, "Eliminate Trade Benefits for Chile," *Oakland Tribune,* Dec. 15, 1986, A-9; Mandel, "In Pursuit of the Missing Link," 455.

104. See, e.g., Alston, chapter in this volume, pp. 78–80; Mandel, "In Pursuit of the Missing Link," 455–459.

105. Committee Report, 5112.

106. See ILO, *Human Rights: A Common Responsibility*, Report of the Director General (Geneva: ILO, 1988).

107. See Alston, chapter in this volume, p. 80.

108. See Collingsworth, Goold, and Harvey, "Time for a Global New Deal," 8.

109. GATT ministers agreed to permit the new World Trade Organization to discuss labor issues, but did not set any norms of behavior or enforcement of labor rights. See Alan Riding, "U.S. Envoys Gain a Forum for Labor Issues in Trade," *New York Times*, April 8, 1994, D1.

Chapter 12
The *Pico* Case
Testing International Labor Rights in U.S. Courts

Frank E. Deale

In February 1989, a United States-based multinational electronics corporation suddenly shut its subsidiary in South Korea. Nearly 300 workers, almost all women, lost their jobs. The closure was in violation of the terms of a collective bargaining agreement negotiated between the Labor Union of Pico Korea, which represented the Korean workers, and the Pico Korea Company, a subsidiary of New York-based Pico Products, Inc. The shutdown was also in violation of Korean laws requiring advance notification of the closing, severance pay, and back pay for work actually performed during the month of February.

After unsuccessful efforts in South Korea to track down company officials and bring them into compliance with their labor contract and with Korean law, the union members took the bold step of bringing their struggle to the doorstep of Pico Products in Liverpool, New York, a suburb of Syracuse. Beginning their campaign with a sale of pens on the streets of Seoul to earn air fare to the United States, four members arrived in the United States in April 1990 and started a historic political education campaign and legal battle against the company in the courts of the United States.

This chapter explores issues raised by the struggle of the Pico workers for recognition of their legal and contractual rights, and, just as important to them, their dignity. The case is the first of its kind, and presents new issues that go to the heart of the battle to establish internationally recognized and justiciable labor rights.

International investment and the widespread mobility of capital have two major and apparently contradictory effects on workers. As the engine of economic development for segments of the population in the initial stages of development, foreign direct investment helps some workers in developing countries advance their standard of living because it creates jobs that domestic capital could never generate on its own. Simultaneously, workers in the developed countries from which capital flows see their jobs move to other regions of the globe. As foreign employees of U.S. businesses abroad become familiar with the culture of the developed world, their desire grows for increased wages and benefits, often out of a belief that the company can afford to treat them better. However, the struggle of foreign workers to obtain such increases may force the investing companies to conclude that maintaining their profit margin requires relocating to yet another environment in the developing world where such worker organization and desire for greater employee benefits has yet to take place. As will be described in greater detail below, such was the fate of the Pico workers.

Cynical observers might take the view that workers in the developing world who are employed by U.S. companies have conflicting interests with workers in the United States. In this light, struggles such as that of the Pico workers are not deserving of international labor support because those workers earn the benefits of underselling the value of their labor power and must expect to pay the price of any attempt on their part to compete with workers elsewhere in the international market.

This view is misguided. Workers in the United States and abroad are seeking to obtain the best economic conditions that their bargaining power will allow them to obtain. Their employers are seeking to maintain maximum profits on their investments. Both groups of workers are seeking to better their position with respect to their employer and have the same interest in doing so. While they do not have conflicting interests with regard to each other, they are in competition with each other.

To eliminate this competition, international labor rights and human rights advocates have sought to establish standards of labor protection to be adhered to wherever an employer operates, and have succeeded in obtaining some protections that are carved out in international human rights instruments. For example, the Universal Declaration of Human Rights prohibits slavery and servitude, requires that workers have just and favorable conditions of work and the right to equal pay for equal work, and provides rights to join trade unions for the protection of their interests.[1] Some of these same rights are protected by the International Covenant on Economic, Social and Cultural Rights.[2]

Worker protections also can be found in guidelines promulgated by the Organization for Economic Cooperation and Development (OECD). These guidelines state that companies should respect the rights of employees to bargain collectively, engage in constructive negotiations with a view to reaching agreement on working conditions, refrain from coercive techniques such as threatening to remove subsidiaries or relocate employees to hinder the right to organize, provide reasonable notice of changes in company operations that would have major effects on the livelihood of employees such as closures and collective layoffs or dismissals, and provide employees and representatives with access to the multinational's real decision makers.[3]

While defining norms that all international labor rights advocates uphold and support, these instruments will not accomplish their goal without an effective means of enforcement, both of international standards and of labor terms that employers and employees agree are to govern the workplace. Moreover, such protections must include sanctions to prevent companies from walking away from such promises by relocating their plants. The Pico litigation sought to accomplish this goal.

The filing of a civil lawsuit in the courts of the United States is, at best, an indirect way of supporting the movement for international labor standards. The United States is only one of many countries from which multinational companies operate. Its subsidiaries operate throughout the world, but by no means exhaust the range of labor markets and employment circumstances that will be improved by heightened protection of international labor rights. Yet this litigation—which won for foreign worker employees of U.S. subsidiaries the right to sue their employer for violating the terms and conditions of a labor agreement in U.S. courts—will have important repercussions for all workers who are employed abroad by U.S. multinational companies. While the Pico workers were unsuccessful in their attempt to win their monetary claims in the courts of the United States, their litigation will serve as a model for subsequent cases designed to achieve similar goals.

Background

In 1984 the Korean government placed ads in a number of major Western publications offering significant incentives in return for investment from abroad. Pico Products took advantage of this opportunity and established a Korean subsidiary, Pico Korea, in 1984, under an investment plan that allowed the company to operate tax free for five years provided it stayed in business and complied with the labor laws of Korea. This was not the first instance of overseas investment by the company. Earlier operations had been established in the Caribbean, Taiwan, and the Philippines.

The company obtained factory space in Buchon City, a small town approximately forty-five minutes outside Seoul. After hiring a Korean manager, the company began to hire employees, almost all of whom were women. The wages paid to the employees hovered around five dollars a day for assembly line work soldering electronic parts, known as AB2 switches. The first year the company hired approximately forty employees. Thereafter, the number rose swiftly. In its second year of operation, the company was employing more than 250 workers.

Many of the workers were proud employees of Pico Korea. Yet conditions at the plant were less than desirable, causing the employees to organize for an improved work environment. Initial demands focused on improving basic working conditions, particularly occupational safety hazards and unsanitary dining conditions. After a number of unproductive meetings with company officials, the employees concluded that their strength could only be realized through collective action. They then organized a union.

This action by the Pico workers was not an isolated event. During this period, all of South Korea was paralyzed by waves of labor activity by workers. In 1987, the time that the Pico workers were starting their campaign for a union at Pico Korea, it was estimated that South Korea workers received no more than 11 percent of the average hourly pay of U.S. workers performing comparable work.[4] Moreover, in 1985, approximately 63.9 percent of women workers in South Korea received wages below the official minimum cost of living.[5] As a result of these disturbing figures, large numbers of South Korea workers began organizing simultaneously. Indeed, between 1987 and 1989, South Korea witnessed more than 7,000 labor disputes and the formation of 4,500 new unions.[6]

Negotiations toward a collective bargaining agreement at Pico Korea were difficult but successful, and, in November 1988, an agreement was signed by representatives of the labor union and the representatives of Pico Korea. It was a good agreement by any standard, providing for greatly improved working conditions, increased benefits, basic union autonomy, and protection against unjust discipline. The clauses essential to the litigation that the union was to bring against the company gave the union the right to prior notification and the right to object to any company closure, suspension of work, or reduction of personnel, and required that the company pay benefits to the affected personnel if any of these eventualities arose.

As is the case with any new labor agreement, there were disagreements between the union and the company about numerous provisions of the contract. These questions were compounded by the fact that none of the workers spoke English and none of the American managers spoke Korean. However, through the use of translators and a sincere attempt by the union and by Pico Korea to resolve their differences, work under the agreement proceeded.

At the same time, however, there was a major struggle brewing between the New York headquarters office of Pico Products, the California office of Pico Macom, an intermediary firm incorporated in that state and the immediate parent of the Korean subsidiary, and Pico Korea. The managers of Pico Macom and Pico Korea were aware that Pico Products was concerned about declining profits from the Korean subsidiary. They agreed that the best short-term method for dealing with this was to allow Pico Macom to provide a subsidy to Pico Korea to keep the plant open until the finances of Pico Korea, including profit margins, improved.

In New York, the management of Pico Products took an entirely different view and was escalating its plans to shut down Pico Korea. From every vantage point, the Pico Products managers were greatly disturbed that the Korean subsidiary had recognized and signed an agreement with a labor union. The New York managers were aware that the workers were organizing a union and were in touch with the management of Pico Korea during the union campaign. Yet their view was that success for the union would translate into more costs for the company and fewer profits. Indeed, Pico Products claimed that the onset of the union campaign directly caused halts in production that affected the company's financial viability. Looked at in conjunction with the approaching end of the five-year tax holiday, New York managers were more than ready to abandon Pico Korea.

Consequently, the board of Pico Products decided to dismantle the company. They concluded that this could best be accomplished by cutting off the lifeblood of the Korean subsidiary—the deficit financing that was being provided to the Korean subsidiary from Pico Macom. During the week of February 21, 1989, four months after the collective bargaining agreement was signed, Pico Products fired the head of Pico Korea, ordered that Pico Macom cease providing further deficit financing to Pico Korea, and effectively shut down the company. Although the collective bargaining agreement provided mechanisms for resolving issues concerning the productive capacity of the plant—means for laying off workers, reducing the size of the plant, relocating, and even shutting down production—Pico Products officials deliberately refused to follow these mechanisms. After firing the president of Pico Korea, the multinational abandoned the plant, leaving defective inventory and equipment and a mountain of debts. All these actions were accomplished over the objection of the terminated president of Pico Korea, and the president of Pico Macom, who resigned shortly after the events and informed the union that he supported their demands for justice.

At the center of the decision-making for Pico Products was its chief executive officer, who never went to Korea to observe the effects of company decisions. The CEO hired the president of Pico Korea and was informed by him of all developments at the Pico Korea subsidiary. In addition, the CEO was in constant communication with the Pico Korea president during the negotiations surrounding the collective bargaining agreement and was aware of the terms of the agreement. Ultimately, it was the CEO who called the board of directors of Pico Products together and arranged for passage of the resolution that was to result in the closing of Pico Korea.

In April 1990 five union officers arrived in the United States to confront the board at the New York headquarters of Pico Products and launch a campaign to educate U.S. communities about the case.[7] The workers began what was to be a three-month picket at Pico headquarters in Liverpool, New York, circulated petitions in support of the workers throughout the United States, and publicized the story of the workers campaign in the media.[8] The union members obtained supportive endorsements from human rights, labor, and religious groups throughout the United States.[9] The campaign accelerated to encompass midnight vigils at the home of the CEO and a week-long hunger strike. Before leaving the United States in July 1990, the union members secured counsel and filed a lawsuit against the company in the U.S. District Court for the Northern District of New York.

The primary cause of action asserted by the union was a breach of contract claim seeking to hold Pico Products, Inc. liable for breach of the collective bargaining agreement existing between the Labor Union of Pico Korea and Pico Korea. Plaintiffs alleged that the court had jurisdiction to adjudicate this claim under section 301 of the Labor-Management Relations Act of 1947. Section 301 states: "Suits for violations of contracts between an employer and a labor organization representing employees in an industry affecting commerce as defined in this Act, may be brought in any district court of the United States having jurisdiction of the parties, without respect to the amount in controversy or without regard to the citizenship of the parties."[10]

This theory of the case was complicated by the fact that Pico Products was not a signatory to the contract, which was executed between the Labor Union of Pico Korea and Pico Korea. Because of this fact, in order to prevail the union had to establish that Pico Products so dominated Pico Korea that Pico Korea did not have the ability to stay open against the wishes of Pico Products to close it. In legal parlance, the union members had to "pierce the corporate veil" insulating Pico Products from liability for the breach of contract of its subsidiary.

In a second theory of the case, also premised upon section 301, the union alleged that Pico Products' passage of a resolution preventing Pico Macom from providing subsidies to Pico Korea and dismissal by Pico Products of the head of Pico Korea caused the company to collapse. These acts of Pico Products constituted a "tortious interference" with the contract existing between the labor union and Pico Korea. In other words, the actions by Pico Products made it impossible for Pico Korea to live up to terms of the agreement that it existed between it and the union.

Finally, the union alleged that Pico Products, Inc. violated the federal Workers Adjustment Retraining and Notification Act[11] by closing Pico Korea without providing the union with sixty days' advance notice, as is required by that statute.

Shortly after the union filed its complaint, the company responded with a denial of the union's allegations. The union then exercised its right to gain access to the company's records and documents pertaining to the issues in the case.[12] Rather than responding to the plaintiffs' request, the company countered with a motion to dismiss the case on various procedural grounds, including jurisdiction, standing, and issues involving application of the *forum non conveniens* doctrine. The company sought to convince the court that the case should be tried by the Korean judiciary in an action against Pico Korea, not Pico Products, and that plaintiffs' federal action in the United States should be dismissed. Had the court ruled in favor of the defendants, the case would have been over without a trial. Having totally abandoned Korea, Pico Korea was a non-entity. The Korean courts had nothing over which they could exercise jurisdiction.

At the hearing on defendants' motion, the federal district judge hearing the case denied Pico Products' motion and refused to terminate the case at such an early stage. This unprecedented procedural victory for the union set the stage for the first trial in which a foreign union has taken a U.S. multinational to court for breach of a labor agreement.

While the judge's procedural ruling allowed the case to go forward to trial, he ruled in favor of the company on one crucial element of the case that haunted the plaintiffs throughout the course of the litigation. The judge concluded that plaintiffs' claims against the company could not be tried under *federal* law as the plaintiffs asserted, but would have to be tried under New York or under Korean law. According to Judge McAvoy, this was because section 301 of the Labor-Management Relations Act, upon which the plaintiffs based their breach of contract and tortious interference claims, did not reach "extra-territorially" to encompass a suit involving workers outside the United States. For the same reason, plaintiffs' claims under the Worker Adjustment Retraining and Notification Act could not be adjudicated in the case. For reasons to be explained below, the plaintiffs chose to litigate the case under New York State law governing contracts.

After extensive pretrial preparation, a six-day trial was held before the U.S. District Court for the Northern District of New York in October 1991. On the facts, the judge found that a breach of contract and interference with the contract occurred, with resulting damages to the plaintiffs. But unfortunately for the union, the judge concluded after trial that, under New York law, the union did not establish that Pico Products could be held responsible for the breach of contract. Moreover, under an obscure ruling on New York state corporate law known as the *"Felsen* privilege," Pico Products was permitted to interfere with the contract between the union and Pico Korea.[13] These rulings were affirmed on appeal by the U.S. Court of Appeals for the Second Circuit.[14] The U.S. Supreme Court refused to hear the case.[15]

Although the union members were unsuccessful in their legal proceedings against Pico Products, Inc., their suit accomplished a number of goals that would not have been achieved had the union members not brought their claims to the courts. First, the suit gave the union members a vehicle for further organizing around their cause. At the time the case was filed, the union's educational activity had not brought the company to the table to engage in serious settlement negotiations with the union members. Although the pickets outside of the company in Liverpool, New York, were continuing on a daily basis, the pressures on the union members in the United States leading the pickets were mounting. All the union members in the United States were spending significant time away from their families in Korea, and this was slowly draining them of their energy and dedication. Filing the lawsuit allowed the union members to return to Korea with the view that the struggle against Pico was continuing. Even though there were no longer pickets outside the company every day, the case was working its way through the court system. Furthermore, the suit forced the company to seek settlement of the case with the union. It gave the union an additional two years to educate and organize around the issues raised by their case—time profitably used by the union to pressure the company and to inform the public about the issues involved.

Moreover, the suit provides a guide to workers who, in the future, seek to hold accountable U.S. corporations operating abroad that violate collective bargaining agreements. The contacts made by the union members with individuals in the United States seeking to promote the cause of international worker solidarity will prove invaluable to other workers who find themselves in the same situation as the Pico workers.

The legal strategy followed in the case will assist lawyers who, in the future, will represent foreign workers seeking to rectify labor rights violations in the courts of the United States. Whether the litigation strategy parallels or diverges from that followed in *Pico*, it is the *Pico* case that will provide the guidepost of decision. Because the case was situated in the context of well-established law, the possibility remains that a strong factual case litigated before a more sympathetic judiciary[16] will bring about a result more favorable to the workers.

There are many issues that international labor rights supporters will need to examine if they are to bring *Pico* type cases in the future. The remainder of this chapter discusses these issues.

Political Strategies

The Pico Korea Labor Union could not have chosen a less auspicious time for coming to the United States to assert their claims against Pico Products. One problem was the long and continuing decline of the American labor movement.[17] Considering the drop in private sector unionism in the United States—less than 12 percent in 1993[18]—it is hard to imagine overall excitement about a union struggle rooted in a foreign country thousands of miles away, even though the target of the workers' struggle was a U.S.-based multinational corporation. Why is the strength of the U.S. labor movement relevant to the struggle of the Pico workers? Because the union members did not come to the United States solely to file a lawsuit against Pico Products. They also sought to utilize all means of public exposure of the company to force it to live up to its obligations, and the natural audience for this message consisted of American workers.

The second factor counting against the timing of the Pico campaign is the overall U.S. environment currently characterized by widespread concerns in the business community that private American companies are caught up in fierce competition with foreign companies, primarily those of Japan and Germany. U.S. employers point to what they perceive as governmental shackles limiting the manner of their operations, especially laws mandating environmental protection, workplace health and safety, and structural rights that enable workers to organize to improve their working conditions.[19] Moreover, attention must be given to the signing of the North American Free Trade Agreement (NAFTA) and the General Agreement on Tariffs and Trade (GATT). Both of these international instruments are designed to develop an atmosphere in which North American business (primarily United States corporations) can operate freely throughout the hemisphere unhampered by the regulations of sovereign countries, including those designed to provide and protect workers with health, safety, and environmental protections.[20]

By far, however, the most perilous factor facing the Pico workers in their quest for justice in U.S. courts was the altered condition of the federal judiciary. For a period of about twenty years, spanning roughly 1954–1973, the Supreme Court of the United States and the lower federal courts were sympathetic to litigation designed to achieve structural change.[21] Those days have long since passed.[22] In 1968, Richard Nixon campaigned explicitly for what he referred to as "strict construction-ist" judges who would not infuse judicial decision-making with personal biases. Although the terms of that debate have changed over the years,[23] the appointments of Ronald Reagan and George Bush have brought about a significant change in the composition of the federal judiciary that has made it increasingly difficult to extend many of the rights em-phasized by the Warren Court.[24]

The court's retrenchment over the years has not shut out all possi-bilities of obtaining social justice or structural change through the fed-eral judiciary. In 1973, some commentators noted that the then newly constituted "Burger Court" was primarily concerned with rolling back the rights of criminal suspects, the dispossessed, and disenfranchised in order to provide greater emphasis on middle-class property rights.[25] If this analysis is correct, the claims of the Pico union members would not necessarily be outside the purview of the Reagan-Bush judiciary since the union members were not seeking the creation or extension of rights disfavored by the now conservative federal judiciary. Instead, the union members were contesting the failure of their employer to pay them wages for work they performed and for refusing to adhere to agreed-upon contractual terms, claims firmly embedded in traditional common law claims of breach of contract and tort,[26] which they sought to exercise by piercing Pico Products' "corporate veil." Claims of the sort asserted by the union members would not alter structural institu-tions in the United States, or expand the powers of the judiciary at the expense of the legislative or executive branches of government. Breach of contract and tortious interference claims are causes of action with deep roots in the common law of the United States.

From another perspective, however, the case had profound implica-tions for the continued ability of U.S. corporations to move unencum-bered around the world in pursuit of cheap labor markets. If foreign union members use their economic power to force improvements at the workplace, and such improvements can be contained in a collective agreement that is legally enforceable in the corporation's home coun-try, workers will struggle to obtain such agreements. Whatever the com-pany's motivation for signing such an agreement,[27] the possibility that the agreement can be legally enforced in the corporation's home coun-try will add a new dimension to the future of the relationship between the company and the employees.

Legal Theories

The United States district judge tried the case not as an international labor rights impact case, but as an ordinary breach of contract and tort case against Pico Products to determine whether the company could be held responsible for the contractual obligations of its Korean subsidiary. His decision to treat the case as a common law contract and tort case, irrespective of the plaintiffs' Korean citizenship, was required by the established understanding that the federal courts are open to suits between citizens of foreign states and U.S. citizens. When federal courts are confronted with such suits, they are deemed to be sitting "in diversity," meaning that the constitutional basis underlying their power to hear the case is the diversity of citizenship provision of Article III of the Constitution.[28]

Under longstanding precedent in breach of contract cases before federal courts exercising diversity jurisdiction, the law that governs the controversy is state law.[29] Until 1947, this was true even though the contract at issue was a collective bargaining agreement signed by a union and an employer. In 1947, however, Congress passed the Labor Management Relations Act, which contained a provision opening the federal courts to suits between employers and labor unions in industries affecting interstate commerce, and required that such disputes be adjudicated according to federal law.[30] This provision, referred to as section 301 (a), was designed to help bring about labor peace by giving employers and unions the legal ability to enforce the collective agreement they had signed, and underscored the enormous federal interest in the peaceful resolution of such conflicts.

In addition to giving the federal courts jurisdiction to hear these cases, the Supreme Court, in *Textile Workers v. Lincoln Mills of Alabama*, held that section 301 "authorizes the federal courts to fashion a body of federal law for the enforcement of . . . collective bargaining agreements."[31] The "substantive law which the Courts are to apply would be federal law, which the Courts must fashion from the policy of our national labor laws."[32] Section 301 did not divest the state courts of jurisdiction over suits seeking to enforce collective agreements; it merely required that wherever such suits are brought, whether in federal court or state court, the law to be applied to dispute must be federal.[33]

As the *Pico* case moved through the federal judiciary, the question concerning the law governing the case became the dominant issue. This is because the rule that determines whether a U.S. corporation can be held responsible for the contractual obligations of its subsidiary in breach of contract cases is tied to the jurisdictional basis under which the court is operating. If the court is to treat the case as a routine breach of contract case, the law that will govern the veil-piercing rule will be that of the state either where the suit was brought or where the contract was executed. If, however, the court predicates jurisdiction under section 301, the law that governs is federal law.[34]

Why was this factor so important to the outcome of the *Pico* case? Primarily because federal precedents make it significantly easier to reach a parent corporation for the actions of its subsidiaries. Federal law moved in this direction in response to the mobility of capital. The investor seeks the cheapest labor markets, and the market, theoretically, responds to investor demands. This works at the domestic and international levels. In Korea, the government made it opportune for foreign investors to enter the economy by providing tax holidays and other benefits. Within the United States, the individual states operate similarly in creating investment breaks and laws protecting corporations that are chartered or simply doing business in the state. Because of the operation of market principles, each state has an incentive to protect corporations by maintaining high walls insulating corporations and their shareholders from the obligations of their subsidiaries. Most states and countries have responded to this incentive.

Federal law can modify these competing interests by setting bottom line standards for regulating corporate activities wherever they operate. The National Labor Relations Act, for example, was passed to provide the same standards for regulating management-labor relations throughout the United States, and testified to congressional recognition that the national economy would be served by uniform rules governing the treatment of worker organizations. Moreover, federal law has allowed suits seeking to surmount state barriers protecting corporations from liability to either their shareholders or subsidiaries to proceed in circumstances where, under state law, relief would have been barred.[35]

Does section 301 require that the suit of the Pico workers be adjudicated under federal law? The district judge in *Pico Products* did not think so. He concluded that section 301 did not apply to foreign workers, and his decision was affirmed by the U.S. Court of Appeals.[36] That court was of the view that Congress would have to amend section 301 to make it cover what the Court of Appeals viewed as a "collective bargaining agreement between foreign workers and foreign corporations doing work in foreign countries."[37]

Although the court recognized that a "rigid and literal reading of [section 301] might permit the instant action to lie,"[38] the court concluded that the contract between Pico Korea and the Labor Union of Pico Korea was not "the sort of labor contract . . . to be covered by 301."[39] And although the statute on its face applies to contracts where the commerce of the United States is affected, the court, relying on

Supreme Court precedent that has since been overruled by Congress,[40] deemed that this "boilerplate language" does not control.[41] The Court of Appeals was primarily concerned about the possibility that allowing section 301 and federal law to govern in this case "would inevitably lead to embarrassment in foreign affairs and be entirely infeasible in actual practice,"[42] and conflict with the principle that the "character of an act as lawful or unlawful must be determined wholly by the law of the country where the act is done."[43]

In reaching the above conclusions, the Appeals Court rejected the plaintiffs' claims that, in this case, the government of Korea was in full support of the litigation of the Pico Workers and that the act whose lawfulness was being challenged was the Pico Products' board ordering the cessation of funds to Pico Korea, a decision made in New York State. This was the act that triggered the tortious interference with the contract and resulted in the breach of contract.

The theory of the *Pico* case was that the unlawful act that provided the central focus for both causes of action, breach of contract and tortious interference, was the passage of a resolution and other acts undertaken by Pico Products in New York State that resulted in the inevitable closure of Pico Korea. The Appeals Court was totally uninterested in plaintiffs' arguments that the District Court judge had also misapplied New York State law, although his reading of New York law was briefed by both parties. In its opinion, the Court of Appeals did not discuss the District Court's state law conclusions, other than to agree with them.

In future litigation over international labor rights claims, plaintiffs will have to give careful consideration to the body of law under which they seek to litigate the case. As a strategic matter, the *Pico* plaintiffs sought to litigate the case under federal law for a number of reasons. Not only was there a conviction that federal interests greatly outweighed the interests of any state in resolving the dispute, a conclusion buttressed by the concerns of the U.S. Congressional Working Group on International Labor Rights, which urged Pico Products to settle the case, but, in addition, federal interests, once recognized, clearly outweigh the interests of states in protecting their host corporations from litigation challenging the illegal acts of their subsidiaries.[44]

Furthermore, a decision grounded in federal law would have initiated the development of a body of law to be applied evenly throughout the United States without regard to the state residence of the U.S. multinational and/or the site of the plant closure. If future cases turned on such factors, every plaintiff bringing such a suit would be precluded from building on previous litigation. In the *Pico* case, litigating under the law of Korea would have been extremely time-consuming and expensive. It would have prevented non-Korean-speaking attorneys and judges from engaging in first-hand research as opposed to learning the law from "experts" and would have resulted in a "battle of the experts" whenever the law was unclear and ambiguous, enhancing the complications of an already difficult case. Also, the law of Korea, as will be the case of the law of most developing nations seeking developed world investment, tends to protect foreign corporations because it seeks the financial investment and presence of such corporations. If, indeed, plaintiffs seek to litigate such a case under foreign law, it would make much more sense to litigate the case in the foreign jurisdiction, a possibility precluded in the *Pico* litigation because of the inability of any Korean court to obtain personal jurisdiction over any defendant.[45]

A Cautionary Conclusion

A number of words of caution must be advanced to anyone intending to become involved in litigation as a means of addressing international labor issues.

Resources

The *Pico* case was an expensive case to litigate, incurring huge costs for travel, depositions, filing fees and other court costs, and, of course, attorney time. Two trips to South Korea, a trip to the Philippines, and a trip to Taiwan were all necessary to conduct discovery from former Pico managerial employees who went to other parts of Asia after the plant closure. However, were this discovery not necessary, much of the travel could have been justified simply to understand the "culture" and "politics" from which the case emerged. Although the initial contact between lawyers and clients took place in the United States, most of the time that the lawyers spent with the Pico workers was in Korea. The understanding of the case and clients obtained during these periods provided the primary motivation and drive for seeking justice for the workers. Observing the plant where the workers were employed and the houses in which they lived, and participating in meetings at which they made their decisions, provided tremendous insight into the forces that moved the union to carry on its struggle against such overwhelming odds. Long distance discussions over the telephone and meetings with weary union members in the United States could not compare with the experience of seeing them in their home environment. It is only through such interaction that a relationship of trust, between lawyers and clients, Westerners and Easterners, Americans and Koreans, can develop. Had all of the discovery taken place in the United States, the lawyer-client relationship would have been greatly impeded.

Discovery abroad was not just valuable but necessary, because many of the managerial personnel of the company were in Asia and would not come to the United States to provide testimony. In addition to the expense of seeking them out to take their testimony, it was also necessary to bring to the United States union members whose testimony was sought by the defendants. The legal costs of taking testimony abroad to be used at trial is much greater than in the United States, because the testimony either has to be provided in English or translated into English. Primarily for this reason, the stenographers who transcribe such testimony abroad are much more expensive than they are in the United States. Indeed, in the *Pico* case, it was more economical to bring along a stenographer from the United States who would transcribe testimony either directly from an English-speaking witness or after it has been translated into English from a Korean-speaking witness.

In most cases of this type, the clients will not be able to afford the normal cost of lawyers and litigation.[46] If the case is being handled by a not-for-profit charitable and educational organization[47] established under section 501 (c) (3) of the Internal Revenue code, monies can be solicited from contributors, who can then deduct such contributions from their federal tax obligations. Defense or fund-raising committees can also be established and organized under section 501 (c) (3), which can solicit contributions from the public for the case. Although some statutes allow for the award of attorneys' fees to prevailing parties in litigation,[48] it will be a rare occasion when such an award can be justified in a *Pico*-type case. Attorneys should therefore expect to litigate such cases pro bono, unless the case is handled by a not-for-profit litigation group or a fund is established to solicit contributions.

Communication

Lawyers must be able to communicate with their clients, and any lawyer representing clients from a different language and culture, who knows neither the language nor culture of the clients, is starting off at a serious disadvantage. The *Pico* case could not have been litigated by the Center for Constitutional Rights without the invaluable assistance of a member of the legal team who shared the language and culture of the clients and the lawyers.[49] In addition to translating, this "facilitator" served as the proverbial bridge over troubled waters. In the *Pico* case, practically everything that the lawyers and clients understood about each other was mediated through the facilitator. The role of facilitator certainly includes that of translator but goes far beyond it. Every discussion about the case, whether in English or Korean, took place with the lawyer and the Korean facilitator. This was to enable the facilitator to know the case as well, if not better, than the lawyer.[50]

Because of the need for the lawyer to understand the personalities of the clients, the lawyer may have to interact with the clients in an extra-professional way. Where the lawyer and the client share the same culture and language, understanding the personality of the client can happen easily and quickly. The subtleties of communication in the same language can allow for such an understanding to take place directly and indirectly. When the language and the culture are a mystery, it takes much more interaction with the clients to understand the most basic things about them. Crucial strategic legal decisions, such as how to persuade the clients of a certain strategy, whom to call as witnesses, who should be deposed on behalf of the group, and whom to choose as a negotiating partner, cannot be made if the lawyer does not understand the characters and personalities of the people who are being represented.

In the *Pico* case, the visits to Korea helped to create such understanding. Ways were developed to increase the opportunities for interaction between lawyer and client that go beyond the bounds of a normal lawyer-client relationship. Eating and socializing together bring out aspects of client personalities that often will not be discovered in a regular professional relationship. Moreover, because lawyer and client are many miles apart, the interaction between lawyer and client is less frequent in occurrence, but more intense at each occurrence.

There is thus no substitute for effective communication and the presence of a facilitator. Without this, there can be devastating breakdowns. For example, during the trial of the case, the lawyers for the union members had to hire a translator for the court proceedings, a person who, of course, had to be unconnected to any of the parties. The mere use of a different translator resulted in failures of communication between lawyer and client at the very moment that clear communication was most important—when the witness was on the stand at trial during direct and redirect examinations.

Culture

Realistically, any lawyer must come to the realization that, at times, clients may harbor feelings that are not ascertainable by the lawyer. Notwithstanding the presence of an expert facilitator and numerous wonderful efforts and activities to understand Korea and Koreans, lawyer and clients in the *Pico* case were unable to agree on the most basic strategic decision of any case—when to continue fighting and when to settle.

Perhaps all plaintiffs, in litigation where the enormity of the injustice suffered by them has turned into an assault on their very dignity, wish to fight to the very bitter end. This is most certainly true for clients who are paying neither fees nor expenses for litigation. As almost all lawyers know, however, when decisions about settlement are looming, the lawyer-client relationship can be stretched to the breaking point.

The ultimate decision about settlement has to be made by the clients, but lawyers have various means by which they can respect that principle, yet simultaneously participate in the ultimate decision. In the *Pico* case, settlement offers began coming in as soon as it was clear that the case was not going to be dismissed on a pretrial motion. The strategy of the *Pico* lawyers was to refuse to recommend acceptance or rejection of a proposed settlement so long as the settlement was lower than what the lawyers felt was obtainable. This was because the lawyers did not want to discourage the union members from accepting a monetary settlement that, to Americans, might have seemed abysmally low but to workers in a third world country would seem exorbitant. It was also designed to empower the clients by avoiding a situation where the clients, already extremely dependent on the lawyer because of the distance, language, and lack of knowledge about American litigation, become even more dependent. The initial settlement offers by the company were, in the view of the lawyers, too low to justify recommending acceptance or rejection, and the workers, on their own, rejected them.

What happened in the *Pico* case typically happens in high-profile litigation: the closer the case got to trial, the larger and more appealing the settlement offers became. Eventually, the point was reached where the lawyers and the facilitator were of the view that what was on offer outweighed the risk of losing the trial and going home empty-handed. The legal team, however, failed to convince the union members that this point had been reached. On the Friday of the week before trial was to begin, the relationship between the workers and the legal team was fraught with tension amid heated arguments concerning the best course to pursue. The lawyers argued that accepting settlement would provide the union members with over 75 percent of what they could obtain had they prevailed at trial, in terms of the back wages and severance pay owed to the union. The company also offered to apologize to the union members throughout the American and Korean media. The union members, however, equated settlement with capitulation. The case was tried for six days, and four weeks later the district court judge issued a thirty-page opinion rejecting the claims of the workers.

Although the union members were deprived of any material symbols of their struggle, their victory in overcoming procedural and jurisdictional obstacles and forcing the company to negotiate opened the possibility that different factors operating together could yield a more favorable result. In the future, it will be important for labor rights advocates to study the *Pico* case and apply its lessons in the litigation sure to follow as corporate "restructuring" attains international dimensions.

Notes

1. Universal Declaration of Human Rights, arts. 4, 23.
2. International Covenant on Economic, Social and Cultural Rights, G.A. Res. 2200 A (XXI) of Dec. 16, 1966 at arts. 6 and 7.
3. Roger R. Blanpain, "Transnational Regulation of the Labor Relations of Multinational Enterprises," *Chicago-Kent Law Review* 58 (1982): 909, 940–947.
4. "South Korea's Economic Miracle," *Economist*, March-April 1989, 27.
5. Ramsay Liem and Jinsoo Kim, "The Pico Workers Struggle: Korean Americans, and the Lessons of Solidarity," *Amerasia Journal* 18, no. 1 (1992): 49, 55.
6. Walden Bello and Stephanie Rosenfeld, *Dragons in Distress: Asia's Miracle Economies in Crisis* (San Francisco: Institute for Food and Development Policy, 1990), 25.
7. This was not to be the first meeting the union members had with the company president. Some members met with him in New York over a year after the plant closing to see whether agreement could be reached. The hope was that an exchange could take place; inventory and equipment left by the company in Korea, which the union members protected from creditors and vandals, would be released to the company in return for the monies owed to the union members. However, what began as an attempt to obtain back wages and other benefits owed the union members degenerated into a shouting match when the company official accused the workers of criminal conduct.
8. See Liem and Kim, "Pico Workers Struggle," 58.
9. According to Liem and Kim, some of the groups supporting the Pico workers included the "United Auto Workers and the United Electrical, Radio, and Machine Workers of America; key state and congressional leaders, the U.S. Congressional Working Group on International Labor Rights; the Rainbow Coalition and Alliance of Philippine Concerns; the peace and justice community, including SANE/FREEZE and local chapters of the American Friends Service Committee; the international community, including the U.N. Observer Mission of the African National Congress; the religious community, such as Church Women United and the Columban Fathers; and individual groups in the Korean American community" ("Pico Workers Struggle," 58).
10. See Labor Management Relations (Taft-Hartley) Act, sec. 301(a), 29 U.S.C. sec. 185 (a) (1988).
11. See Worker Adjustment Retraining and Notification Act, 29 U.S.C. 2101 (1991).
12. This process is known as "discovery" and is governed by Rules 26–37 of the Federal Rules of Civil Procedure. The company, as defendant, had a corresponding right to view documents and take pretrial testimony from union members.
13. This privilege derives from a case called *Felsen v. Sol Cafe Mfg. Corp.*, 301 N.Y.S. 2d 610 (N.Y. 1969), and allows a corporation to interfere with the contract of its subsidiary to protect its economic interests.
14. See *Labor Union of Pico Korea, Ltd. v. Pico Products, Inc.*, 968 F. 2d 191 (2d Cir. 1992).
15. 113 S.Ct. 493 (1992).
16. For some time now, commentators and judges have argued that plaintiffs must consider greater utilization of the state judiciaries to avoid restrictive readings of the federal law by recently appointed conservative federal judges. See, e.g., William J. Brennan, Jr., "State Constitutions and the Protection of Individual Rights," *Harvard Law Review* 90 (1977): 489, 495–98; Project Report,

"Towards an Activist Role for State Bills of Rights," 8 *Harvard Civil Rights-Civil Liberties Law Review* 8 (1973): 271. As discussed below, the *Pico* court decisions require that future cases be litigated either in state courts or in federal courts construing state law. In some cases, plaintiffs may prevail. However, as argued below, state legislatures have an incentive to protect resident corporations from *Pico*-type suits and will enact laws that make it difficult, if not impossible, for plaintiffs to hold such corporations liable for the actions of their overseas subsidiaries.

17. Writing over ten years ago, Paul Weiler noted that "contemporary American labor law more and more resembles an elegant tombstone for a dying institution. While administrators, judges, lawyers, and scholars busy themselves with sophisticated jurisprudential refinements of the legal framework for collective bargaining, the fraction of the workforce actually engaged in collective bargaining is steadily declining" (Paul Weiler, "Promises to Keep: Securing Workers' Rights to Self-Organization under the NLRA," *Harvard Law Review* 96 (1983): 1769). In that article, Weiler produced figures demonstrating that the percentage of the non-agricultural private sector American workforce reached a high point in 1954 to near 35 percent, after which a steady decline set in, bringing it to a low of 20 percent in 1980. There have been further decreases since 1980, although public sector unionism has been increasing (Weiler, "Promises to Keep," 1773, n. 6). See also Paul Weiler, "Striking a New Balance: Freedom of Contract and the Prospects for Union Representation," *Harvard Law Review* 98 (1984): 351, citing Bureau of National Affairs (BNA), "Survey on Union Membership Statistics," *Labor Relations Report* 117 (BNA) (Oct. 1, 1984): 81; "Union Membership Falls to 16.8% in 1988," *Daily Labor Report* (BNA), no. 18, Jan. 30, 1989.

The decline in private sector union membership does not necessarily mean that Americans are against workers' rights, only that fewer and fewer American workers are choosing to join unions. Not only have many sectors of the economy traditionally dominated by unionized workers been eviscerated by overlapping recessions; in addition, National Labor Relations Board procedures and substantive rules have made it more difficult for unions to win elections. For some time now, the NLRB has been composed of judges who are less sympathetic to the claims of union members and who tend to side more often with management. See Lee Modjeska, "The Reagan NLRB, Phase I," Ohio *State Law Journal* 46 (1985): 95, 130–131; Morris and Turk, "A Labor Roundup and Forecast: The Balance Continues to Shift," *Employment Relations Law Journal* 11 (1985): 32, 54–55; Charles J. Morris, "NLRB Protection in the Union Workplace: A Glimpse at a General Theory of Section 7 Conduct," *University of Pennsylvania Law Review* 137 (1989): 1673, 1712–1713; Diane Avery, "Federal Labor Rights and Access to Private Property: The NLRB and the Right to Exclude," *Industrial Relations Law Journal* 11 (1989): 145, 153–154.

Although the National Labor Relations Board did not have jurisdiction over the Pico workers dispute, the highly restrictive view of workers' rights entertained by Reagan-appointed Board members is a further reflection of the difficulties facing the labor movement in the United States today. This situation may be changing with the appointment by the Clinton administration of William B. Gould IV to chair the Board. Gould was a participant at the conference at which this paper was presented and is considered sympathetic to the rights of labor and unions. See David Moberg, "Board Games," *In These Times*, Jan. 10–23, 1994, 25.

18. See U.S. Commission on the Future of Worker-Management Relations, *Fact Finding Report* (U.S. Department of Labor, U.S. Department of Commerce), May 1994, 24.

19. During the Bush administration, these concerns of the business community led to the establishment of a Council on Competitiveness, an extralegal body composed of members of the business community and chaired by the former vice president of the United States, Dan Quayle. The Council existed for the ostensible purpose of overseeing, and stopping if necessary, health, safety, and environmental regulations, among others, that in the view of the Council unduly interfered with corporate profits. Bill Clinton abolished the Council but proceeded to push for, and obtain, congressional ratification of the North American Free Trade Agreement (NAFTA) and the General Agreement on Tariffs and Trade (GATT), which many feel serve the same purpose but in an international context. See David Moberg, "The Morning NAFTA," *In These Times*, Dec. 13–26, 1993, 20. For an exchange on these issues, see Tom Wohlforth, "In Praise of NAFTA," *In These Times*, Jan. 24–Feb. 6, 1994, 28 and Jim McNeill, "Off the Marx," *In These Times*, March 7–20, 1994, 32.

20. For further discussion of NAFTA and GATT, see the materials cited in note 19.

21. See Abram Chayes, "Forward: Public Law Litigation and the Burger Court," *Harvard Law Review* 96 (1982): 4, 5–7.

22. A number of commentators have noted this change, including Chayes, "Forward." One of the most compelling presentations of this phenomenon is Erwin Chermerinsky, "Forward: The Vanishing Constitution," *Harvard Law Review* 103 (1989) 43, arguing that the Court has succumbed to the doctrine of majoritarianism by insistent deference to decisions made by elective branches of government.

23. Commentators have referred to a "constructionist" approach to the Constitution as one that places primary emphasis on the meaning intended by the framers and ratifiers of the Constitution to ascertain how it should be construed. This approach is often today referred to as an "interpretivist" approach, since one is seeking to "interpret" the meaning of the framers, or, even more commonly, a search of the "original intent." A "non-interpretivist" approach to the Constitution refers to the attempt to ascertain the meaning of constitutional language in light of contemporary times. See, generally, H. Jefferson Powell, "The Original Understanding of Original Intent," *Harvard Law Review* 98 (1985) 885; Richard H. Fallon, Jr., "A Constructivists Coherence Theory of Constitutional Interpretation," *Harvard Law Review* 100 (1987): 1189.

24. See Ronald Dworkin, "The Reagan Revolution and the Supreme Court," *New York Review of Books*, July 18, 1991, 23. Many of the decisions discussed by Dworkin are described in Archibald Cox, *The Warren Court: Constitutional Decision as an Instrument of Reform* (Cambridge, Mass.: Harvard University Press, 1968).

25. See William W. Van Alstyne, "The Recrudescence of Property Rights as the Foremost Principle of Civil Liberties: The First Decade of the Burger Court," 43 *Law and Contemporary Problems* (Summer 1980): 66; Chayes, "Forward," 57.

26. Writing as long ago as 1881, Oliver Wendell Holmes stated in a classic treatise that "the distinctions of the law are founded on experience, not logic. It therefore does not make the dealings of men dependent on a mathematical accuracy. Whatever is promised, a man has a right to be paid for, if it is not given." See Oliver Wendell Holmes, *The Common Law*, ed. Mark DeWolfe Howe (Boston: Little Brown, 1963 [1881]), 244.

27. Although many corporations will consider departing a country at the point when employees begin to seek some form of collective agreement, some

employers will sign such agreements either because they believe the corporation can live under the agreement until departure or because they are convinced that such an agreement will not inhibit continual production.

28. Article III provides the federal courts with jurisdiction over controversies "between a State or the Citizens thereof, and foreign States, Citizens or Subjects." See also 28 U.S.C. 1332, providing the district courts with original jurisdiction over civil actions where the matter in controversy exceeds $50,000 and is between "citizens of a State and citizens or subjects of a foreign state."

29. *Erie Railroad Co. v. Tompkins*, 304 U.S. 64 (1938).

30. See Labor Management Relations (Taft-Hartley) Act, sec. 301 (a), 29 U.S.C. sec. 185 (a) (1988).

31. 353 U.S. 448, 451 (1957).

32. Ibid., 456.

33. See *Local 174 v. Lucas Flour Co.*, 369 U.S. 195 (1962); *Charles Dowd Box Co. v. Courtney*, 368 U.S. 502 (1962).

34. *American Bell v. Federation of Telephone Workers*, 736 F. 2d 879, 886 (3rd Cir. 1984).

35. Stephen B. Presser, "Piercing the Corporate Veil § 3.01 (1991)," in James W. Moore et al., *Moore's Federal Practice* (2nd ed.; New York: Matthew Bender, 1985) 2, para. 4.25 [6] n. 33; Note, "Piercing the Corporate Veil: The Alter Ego Theory Under Federal Common Law," *Harvard Law Review* 95 (1982): 853, 870.

36. 968 F. 2d 191 (2d Cir. 1992).

37. Ibid., 195.

38. Ibid., 192.

39. Ibid., 193.

40. Citing *EEOC v. Arabian American Oil Co.*, 111 S. Ct. 1227, 1231 (1991) (superseded by Pub. L. 102-166 (1991).

41. 968 F. 2d at 195.

42. Citing *McCullouch v. Sociedad Nacional de Marineros de Honduras*, 372 U.S. 10, 19 (1963).

43. 968 F. 2d at 195, citing *New York Cent. R.R. v. Chisholm*, 268 U.S. 29, 31 (1925).

44. See sources cited in note 35 above.

45. In most cases, plaintiffs will be mandated to sue in the foreign country if the defendant corporation is still doing business in the country. After Pico Korea was closed, the workers sought to sue Pico Korea in Korea but could not find a defendant representative of the company. For this reason, Judge McAvoy refused to go along with the assertions of Pico Products that the absence of Pico Korea as a defendant mandated that the case be dismissed.

46. When employed, the Pico workers were paid somewhere between five and six dollars a day. The litigation began over a year after the plant was closed, and before those workers who obtained new jobs started them.

47. All the costs incurred in the *Pico* litigation were paid for by the Center for Constitutional Rights, a New York-based not-for-profit educational and charitable organization.

48. The Equal Access to Justice Act, Pub. L. 96-481, 94 Stat. 2325, only allows for the recovery of attorney fees when a party has "substantially prevailed" in a case involving the U.S. government or U.S. governmental agency. 42 U.S.C. 1988 allows for the recovery of fees in cases implicating specified civil rights statutes.

49. Jinsoo Kim was the administrative director during the *Pico* litigation, and later a member of the class of 1995 at Harvard Law School.

50. If all goes well, the facilitator will, in most cases, know the case better than the lawyer because the facilitator will have discussions and read documents in their original language.

Chapter 13
The *Castro Alfaro* Case
Convenience and Justice—Lessons for Lawyers in Transcultural Litigation

Emily Yozell

> The dissenters argue that it is *inconvenient* and *unfair* for farm-
> workers allegedly suffering permanent physical and mental injuries,
> including irreversible sterility, to seek redress by suing a multi-
> national corporation in a court three blocks away from its world
> headquarters. . . . The "doctrine" they advocate has nothing to do
> with fairness and convenience and everything to do with immuniz-
> ing multinational corporations from accountability for their alleged
> torts causing injury abroad.[1]

Proclamations of a "new world order"; the signing of the North American Free Trade Agreement (NAFTA) and the General Agreement on
Tariffs and Trade (GATT) Uruguay Round pact; controversy over the
Maastricht Treaty; recent international summit conferences on ecology
and development in Río de Janeiro, on population and development
in Cairo, on sustainable development in Stockholm, and most recently
on women in Beijing, are all indicators of a fundamental shift toward
a more systematic integration of the global economy. Before this shift,
global trade patterns developed with minimal planning or regulation
at the international level. Instead, national governments set tariffs and
otherwise managed their trade interests. There was virtually no supranational "lawmaking" or other form of regulation of multinational enterprise.

The "legalization" of this integration of capital at the international
level through various trade agreements is now provoking demands for
regulation of global economic activity from advocates for those interests

most affected by the new dynamic, and so far most voiceless—workers, trade unions, the environment, indigenous peoples, and women (who provide the majority of the workforce in many of the multinational, especially "maquila"-type assembly industries). The Social Chapter of the Maastricht treaty, environmental and labor "side agreements" to the NAFTA, and consideration of labor rights and environmental protection on the agenda of the new World Trade Organization are prominent indicators of the demands for increased responsibility on the part of the transnationals for the effects of their policies and products.

Requiring corporations to assume responsibility and pay the costs of their labor, health and safety, and environmental policies is a relatively new challenge for advocates working within the framework of existing United States law. Achieving such a goal when the corporation is U.S.-based and the affected persons, communities, and resources are in Costa Rica or India or Korea heightens the challenge. Lawyers who advocate in this area have to break new legal ground, learn new skills, and combine litigation with other forms of advocacy like effective use of the media, coordination with grassroots organizations, education, lobbying, and other tactics needed to change public perception and policy. They also need an understanding of cultures very different from that of North American (and European) lawyers, and perhaps more than anything, a humility of conduct to match boldness of concept.

This chapter discusses the *Castro Alfaro* case not so much for its controversial holding (defendants may not invoke *forum non conveniens* in Texas state courts to escape liability for personal injuries inflicted abroad to foreign nationals),[2] but as a prototype for worker rights cases brought against U.S.-based transnationals on behalf of men and women whose language, culture, and history differ radically from the one that created the system of law we use in attempting to vindicate their rights.

As one of a growing number of cases involving efforts by foreign plaintiffs to seek legal redress from the judiciary of the transnationals' home country, *Castro Alfaro* also contains vital lessons for *transcultural* litigation. It underscores the importance of recognizing that the legal system of the "North," where redress is sought by workers from the "South," is part of the wider system, encompassing both law and economics, that created those workers' jobs, then harmed them, all the while shaping our attitudes, work habits, and assumptions about human nature.

Lawyers and those who assist them in developing ways to make corporations responsible for these injuries face tremendous challenges as well as great rewards. The challenges are not all from the opponent; some are the fruits of our ignorance of other cultures and the arrogance that is part of the "developed world" culture. The rewards are not all monetary; they include not only the few precious legal victories, but also the opportunity to learn other values and world views that may, in the end, offer more hope for the future than the ones that produced the tragedy at Bophal or the pain, mental anguish, confusion, and loss, as well as physical damage, done to the protagonists in the case discussed here, the men, women, and children who have lived and worked on the banana plantations in Costa Rica.

The *Castro Alfaro* Case

Castro Alfaro concerns a group of farmworkers from Standard Fruit Company's Río Frío banana plantation located in Costa Rica's tropical Atlantic region.[3] These first plaintiffs were men and their spouses or partners who, born into a life of poverty, regarded the multinational plantations as an opportunity to improve their living standards, earn a minimum wage, have access to potable water, visit a medical clinic, and even learn to read and write at night school. Río Frío is an immense plantation composed of approximately fifteen large farms where row upon row of banana plants are grown within an infrastructure of railways and cabled passageways (for banana transport only) that go on as far as the eye can see, converging at the horizon.

Standard Fruit Company began breaking ground for the Río Frío plantation in the late 1960s. The initial labor force was comprised mostly of young men ages fourteen to twenty-five. By 1971, after a two-month strike, banana workers' unions were recognized and the first collective bargaining agreement was signed. The banana workers' unions became the strongest unions in Costa Rica, encompassing 70–80 percent of the workforce by the late seventies.[4] They achieved modest company-owned housing, transport to the fields, and greatly improved working conditions.

In the late 1970s, however, Standard Fruit began engaging in anti-union activities, including persecution and arbitrary firing and blacklisting of union activists. After the triumph of the Sandinista revolution in neighboring Nicaragua, the multinationals became much more aggressive, mounting a major campaign to eliminate the "communist" unions and introduce a new employer-worker relationship—"solidarismo."[5] In a successful effort to destroy the banana unions in Costa Rica, and as the final response to a long and violent strike in 1983, United Fruit Company closed down its extensive plantations and left the country crossing over the southern border in to Panamá. By the mid-1980s, the unions had lost most of their membership and union leaders were permanently banned from entering the farms. By the early 1990s, there were virtually no active banana worker unions functioning openly inside the farms. Workers have little bargaining power and very few recognized rights.[6]

During the 1960s and 1970s, thousands of Costa Rican banana workers were required to handle dibromochloropropane (DBCP), a highly toxic, but effective pesticide (nematicide) that kills nematodes that attack the roots of the plants. DBCP was manufactured in the United States by Dow Chemical, as Fumazone, by Shell Oil, as Nemagon, and by Occidental Chemical as Anvac and furnished to the banana companies for export. The application of DBCP to the banana plants contributed millions of dollars in increased profits for the defendant companies, increasing banana production by a phenomenal 35 percent. DBCP helped to eliminate crop losses caused by nematodes and ensure blemish-free bananas grown for export to the United States.[7]

DBCP also virtually ensures sterility in men who are exposed for as little as one hundred hours in sufficient doses. It also causes injury to testicles and birth defects in children fathered by DBCP-exposed men. Women also blame their sterility upon DBCP exposure. DBCP may cause cancer and is suspected of causing neurological damage. Sterility has provoked emotional and psychological effects, impotence, and a great social cost including the dissolution of families and social alienation of the victims.

The toxicity of the chemical was known to the manufacturers at least from the late 1950s on, when Shell and Dow researchers and independent scientists found that inhalation killed rats and, at much lower levels, produced liver damage and atrophied testicles.[8] The manufacturers successfully avoided a strong warning label that would have required the use of protective apparatus when handling the chemical. The information remained buried in technical journals and not provided as part of either Shell's or Dow's product data summary, much less to the workers who manufactured or applied it.

During the mid-1970s, plant workers at Occidental Chemical Company's agricultural products division in Lathrop, California became aware that they were sterile. In 1977, the Environmental Protection Agency (EPA) announced its intention to ban all food-related use of DBCP in the United States, shortly after the Occidental factory workers began to pursue their legal action, which eventually won an average of over $1 million per plaintiff for the DBCP-related sterility.

Standard Fruit and other banana growers redoubled their efforts to secure their DBCP supply. Dow and SHell, although reluctant after the Occidental scandal, continued to ship their products overseas for almost two years after the U.S. ban as Standard threatened breach of contract action. Workers were never told about the dangers of handling the chemicals, even after the problems at Occidental were known.

Thousands of the Costa Rican banana workers handled the DBCP with absolutely no protection, not even gloves. Workers responsible for preparing the diluted mixture to be applied to the plant handled full-strength DBCP by pouring the liquid from large barrels into smaller plastic jugs and adding water. The substance always spilled onto their bodies and clothing. Although spills stung the skin and fumes caused dizziness and nausea, the warehouse workers who performed these tasks were paid more and their chores were less physically demanding than was the field work. Besides, if they complained they were either demoted or fired. In the field, workers utilized a large syringe-like plunger to inject the DBCP mixture into the root of the banana plants. They, too, were constantly being splattered and directly exposed to the toxic substance.[9]

No news of the Occidental workers' injuries was transmitted to the banana workers in Costa Rica. The first complaints about sterility of the workers at the Río Frío and other plantations were publicized in 1978, but Standard Fruit continued using DBCP for another year and a half until receiving pressure from the Costa Rican authorities, and Dow and Shell stopped selling it to them in 1979.[10] By that time thousands of Costa Rican men had been exposed for a decade or more.

Costa Rican urologists and toxicologists presented the case to colleagues in the United States, who referred them to a Texas law firm specializing in large-scale personal injury lawsuits. Representatives of the firm visited Costa Rica and after meeting with workers and local health and legal professionals agreed to take the case on a contingency basis.

Domingo Castro Alfaro was one of the *afectados* (the term in Spanish commonly used to refer to the DBCP victims in Costa Rica, literally meaning "affected ones"). In 1984, the law firm filed a products liability suit against Dow and Shell in Texas on behalf of Castro Alfaro and forty-six other banana workers and their wives or partners from Standard's Río Frío plantation. Similar suits were also filed in state courts in Florida,[11] and California.[12]

The complaints were based on tort claims of product liability and negligence, and subsequent claims included Standard as a defendant as well as Dow and Shell. Defendants universally responded by removing the cases to federal courts, where they asserted a *forum non conveniens* procedural defense—that while there might be technical jurisdiction of the case in a U.S. court, the inconvenience of litigating here outweighed the technicality. "Let Costa Ricans sue in Costa Rica," they argued.

The problem with this position was that, at the time, the maximum recovery available to plaintiffs under Costa Rican law was less than $1,500.[13] As one of the judges who finally rejected that argument in the Texas Supreme Court wrote:

The plaintiffs, who earn approximately one dollar per hour working at the banana plantation, clearly cannot compete financially with Shell and Dow in carrying on the litigation. More importantly, the cost of just one trip to Houston to review the documents produced by Shell would exceed the estimated maximum recovery in Costa Rica.[14]

In other words, "If successful, Shell and Dow . . . would have secured a largely impenetrable shield against meaningful lawsuits for their alleged torts causing injury abroad."[15]

The Texas Supreme Court's decision to reject the assertion of *forum non conveniens* was not just a procedural nicety. It really determined the outcome of the case, since the evidence of negligence and injury was irrefutable. Faced with unassailable scientific evidence of the toxicity of DBCP, and their prior knowledge of this, accompanied by proof of their failure to warn or protect the workers, their only defense was to try to demonstrate that individual workers could not prove that they had been exposed to the toxin. Given such a weak defense, settlement discussions began within a year and a half of the Texas Supreme Court's decision, and an agreement was reached among U.S. attorneys for the plaintiffs and defendants in June 1992. This agreement was then offered to local counsel and plaintiffs.[16]

The concept of negotiating about one's rights, like the concept of plea bargaining, is utterly foreign to the Costa Rican legal system, and to the culture of the plaintiffs. Suffice to say that negotiating a settlement in a lawsuit—always exceedingly difficult, even for those of us inured to the process—is especially troublesome to those not used to it, particularly in a culture where corruption, bribes, and sell-outs are not uncommon. This is a stage of the litigation process at which sensitive communication, listening to the clients, and careful explanation of the real alternatives are critical.[17]

A Word About *Forum Non Conveniens*

Dow and Shell invoked the traditional discretion of courts not to hear controversies in cases "in which the Court may consider it more proper for the ends of justice that the parties should seek their remedy in another forum." Here defendants' interest in "the ends of justice" must be measured against their unwillingness to produce their personnel in Costa Rica, thereby defeating even the reduced recovery that may, theoretically, have been possible there. Like so many procedural devices cited by the powerful to resist the claims of the less powerful, application of the *forum non conveniens* doctrine is outcome determinative, because in this case there is no other adequate forum.

The Costa Rican workers sued in Texas not because it was convenient, but because they had no other hope of justice. Their case represents not just the advisability of using United States courts to make U.S.-based transnationals responsible for damages inflicted in the developing world. It also confirms the imperative to develop additional forums and alternative theories while the lessons of *Castro Alfaro* are analyzed and incorporated into practice.

The nine justices of the Texas Supreme Court permitted the suit to proceed to the merits, based upon a reading of the Texas statute. The legal issues were neither novel, complex, nor difficult, but the decision appears as a majority decision with two special concurrences and four separate dissents, with some of the most passionate (and at times insulting) dialogue found among jurists in their written opinions. And all this controversy was over a procedural motion about whether to provide a forum.

The U.S. law firm, local Costa Rican counsel, toxicologists and medical experts based in Dallas, Texas, and their Costa Rican counterparts, legal workers, law students, and liaison personnel who worked on *Castro Alfaro* and related cases put tremendous energy, effort, and resources into finding a forum in which the workers' injuries could be aired and, perhaps, partially redressed. Their victory puts transnational companies on notice of their responsibility and liability for the time-honored tradition of "us[ing] the Third World . . . as the industrial world's garbage can."[19] But the decision in *Castro Alfaro*, together with the efforts of plaintiffs and counsel in other ground-breaking cases like *Labor Union of Pico Korea v. Pico Products, Inc.* and *Labor Rights Fund et al. v. Bush*, discussed elsewhere in this volume, merely help us open the door to the courthouse. It will take several more years of experience and learning to begin to fashion these experiences into a way of making litigation an effective tool on behalf of victims of the transnationals' power and mobility.

This article does not purport to shed light on *forum non conveniens*, removal, pre-emption and other doctrines, or other defenses that those who litigate in United States courts on behalf of victims of U.S.-based transnationals will meet. Rather, it attempts to distill some practical lessons from the experience of working as part of the *Castro Alfaro* legal team, lessons to avoid practical, legal, and human problems that may prove as dangerous to successful litigation as the *forum non conveniens* doctrine. These transcultural lessons include the importance of developing the right combination of humility, empathy, and sensitivity necessary to serve as advocates within the United States legal system for those who have no other forum, but little understanding of how it works and how it will treat them. Finally, a measure of introspection and an openness to learning about other cultures may be the only ways to avoid exporting some of the same culture, habits, and attitude that permitted Dow and Shell to profit from DBCP use in Costa Rica and other developing nations.[20]

Plaintiffs and Defendants in a Global Economy

"I am not only mourning my personal loss of the son I could never have. . . . This injury is a loss to society of a whole generation of people." "I am good for nothing, a man who can not give his wife what he used to give sexually does not deserve to live anymore." "I would like to disappear, to escape, to walk forever, to be alone." "Nobody can understand how it feels to be only half a man, inferior to others, abnormal, castrated." "To be a real man you have to have children, I am afraid of the future and that of my wife. . . . Who will take care of us when we get older?" "Sometimes I think we should separate so that she could have a child, I wish I could kill those guilty at the companies, if only I knew who the people were."[21]

The theory of civil damage actions is that the remedy can compensate plaintiffs for loss and damage suffered as a result of defendants' negligent or wrongful action. When the loss is sterility, fear of cancer, inability to enjoy a sexual relationship, alcoholism, or thoughts of suicide, what compensation is able to make a man, a couple, or a community whole? When defendants can write off several million dollars in damages as a tax on the profits reaped by spreading toxic chemicals that will remain in the Costa Rican earth and water for the next fifty to one hundred years, what compensation is adequate? How do you measure justice in a different culture? Does it have a monetary price tag? Can the suffering of the Costa Rican workers and the damage to their communities be quantified? These are not merely abstract questions, but ones that a lawyer advocating settlement may be asked by plaintiffs, local counsel, or others concerned about the case. They are questions at the heart of this kind of litigation, which counsel must be prepared to answer in ways that are both realistic legally and humanly real. Again *Castro Alfaro* is merely an example. By looking at concrete issues and facts, we hope to make the challenge of multicultural litigation clear, and suggest some steps to avoid common errors.[22]

Consider the principle issue in the Costa Rican case. The measurable, irrefutable damage to plaintiffs was sterility. This is more than a physical loss. Domingo Castro Alfaro and his coplaintiffs are all Latin American men rooted in a rural culture in which virility and fertility are closely related to vitality, which is to say life—social, emotional, and economic life. In this world, the equation of virility with fertility and life is not abstract. Families of five to ten and more children are not uncommon; childless couples and those with one or two children are aberrant, objects of pity.

Men in the United States do not easily talk honestly about sterility and fears of sterility, about impotence, shrinking testicles, and sexual problems, even to their doctors. In the world of the Costa Rican banana workers, husbands and wives rarely exchange words about their sexual relationship, and men are not ready with words about the shame they feel when referred to as "the halfman" or "the gelding" for their failure to procreate. In a society in which the parish priest is the closest thing to a psychologist or psychiatrist these families will ever see, depression and emotional problems are rarely verbalized. Alcoholism, divorce, profound depression, and stigmatization are common reactions to such problems in a society that would find their airing undignified.

The Costa Rican suit was originally conceived as a version of the Occidental litigation, but absent claims of psychological damage: Workers sued for physical loss and their wives for loss of consortium. It was not until a U.S. lawyer who lived and worked in Costa Rica joined the team and began to prepare plaintiffs for depositions that the significance of the psychological damages became obvious and psychologists were called in to evaluate a sample. Intimidated by cultural differences and less common use of psychologists in the society, lawyers may hesitate to explore this dimension with clients when it is often the most significant.

Despite the difficulty of proving such damages, there is no hope of "making the victims whole" without understanding and looking for remedies to these injuries. This experience in *Castro Alfaro* underscores the importance of incorporating as a key member of the legal team from the outset a skilled interviewer who is both fluent in the plaintiff's language and culture *and* understands the concepts of damages and recovery, discovery and proof in the U.S. adversary system. Without such a person, civil actions that survive motions to dismiss will be subverted by weak and contradictory plaintiff's proof. It is impossible to overstate the critical nature of such a person, regardless of how skilled, respected, or close to the plaintiffs and their cause local counsel may be.

One of the problems in chasing the multinational tortfeasor to his domestic judiciary is that the injured must litigate by his rules, which in *Castro Alfaro*, as in most other transnational litigation, remained a mystery to those whose futures would be determined by them. One of the many jobs of the legal team in these already complex cases is to serve as, or provide for, a cultural intermediary and translator between the United States legal system and the culture, values, and legal system known to the plaintiffs, and from them to the U.S. legal system. Failure to do so can create legal, political, and personal disasters. Consider the following:

- Defendants sought to depose Domingo Castro Alfaro and another plaintiff in Houston. The plaintiffs were brought from the Río Frío plantation to Houston from San José on the first plane either had ever been in. They were welcomed and taken to the hotel, prepared for their interview, and left to rest. These two men had hardly even been in any city, let alone the English-speaking megalopolis of Houston. Lodged on the 35th floor of a high-rise hotel, neither had ever seen an elevator. Their region had recently survived a major earthquake that left it isolated from the rest of the country. Neither plaintiff had ever seen a building with 35 floors, but both knew it was a very dangerous place to be during an earthquake. Intimidated by the electric and electronic "gadgets" provided for their "comfort," the two could not sleep alone in their separate rooms; instead they huddled together in one for reassurance.
- A lawyer familiar with both U.S. and Costa Rican law was hired to prepare plaintiffs for deposition and trial. As part of her preparation, she reviewed each plaintiff's answers to the interrogatories. In the course of the interviews, she realized that they were fraught with factual errors. Dates were inaccurate or imprecise. One plaintiff would give different answers to questions about marital status at different times. This lawyer realized that in the culture of these workers, it was important to give the answer they believed the interviewer wanted to hear, and impolite to say, "I don't know," and that without a knowledge of local history, critical events could not be dated. The plaintiffs lived according to the rhythms of the natural world around them and did not need calendars or have date books.
- Several cases were dismissed because adequate arrangements were not made to maintain contact with plaintiffs who may live far from the nearest telephone and work at different sites from one part of the country to another. Dates for plaintiffs to provide information or sign documents came and went with no contact. When U.S.-based counsel advised local counsel that the cases had been dismissed for failure to meet a deadline, local counsel was incredulous.

Translating Justice: Practical Problems and Recommendations for Transnational, Transcultural Litigation

It is easier to write a formula for failure than a formula for success in these cases. The formula for failure is simple. Think first world or "North"; assume your values, experiences, culture, and legal system are (a) universal and (b) best. The consequences will be: frustration felt by all parties; lack of mutual understanding of critical issues; distrust among clients, local counsel, and U.S. counsel; and often procedural and factual errors that may prove fatal to the lawsuit and any hope of obtaining future compensation or curbing transnational corporate criminal and immoral actions.

There is no formula for success because success in these cases depends on learning diversity—learning about and valuing your client's perspective, culture, experiences, traditions, and values. If there is one ingredient without which this litigation cannot succeed, it is *humility*. So instead of a recipe, we offer suggestions and basic principles about transcultural litigation gleaned from *Castro Alfaro* and other cases involving litigation in United States courts on behalf of immigrants and others who use different words and different concepts to talk about justice.

Get to know your clients and help them to understand who you are and what your objective is in relation to them.

Go to your client's country. Go as soon as you possibly can and stay as long as you possibly can. Don't go at the last possible minute to take depositions or interview witnesses. Go in time to think about what you see and learn from it. Visit your clients' homes; get to know their families. If at all possible, learn the language. If you don't know it, find someone who knows both your client's language and your own well enough to answer your questions about problems in communication, which may be cultural as well as linguistic. Preferably utilize the same person so that he or she may get to know plaintiffs and the issues.

One of the most important issues in these cases is that Costa Rica (Colombia, the Dominican Republic, etc.) is *not* just like some warm part of the United States where Spanish is sometimes spoken. It is a vastly different culture with different roots, different traditions, different values, and a different legal system. You need to learn something about that before you can successfully communicate, even with local counsel, let alone your clients. Successful communication is not about good feelings, although it may help create some. It is about avoiding defaults, issue-preclusion, and the possibility of Rule 11 sanctions as well.

Before you go, read about the history and culture of the country, as well as its economy and political history. The purpose is not to make yourself a better person, but to help you to understand how to communicate with your clients, both substantively and mechanically.[23] It will also make you a more effective advocate in the United States, in relation to the opposing party, the judge, the jury, the public, and the news media. If you do not take the trouble to do this step, you will, in addition to reducing your effectiveness as an advocate, be reproducing many of the attitudes and practices that led your clients to identify all lawyers from the United States as agents of the corporations responsible for their suffering. Condition yourself to expect mistrust, understand the causes that may justify it, and work to counteract it by being open to learning and honest about your ignorance. Your clients don't need to be impressed about your wealth, your power, your command of the law. They are already impressed, but they are also intimidated by you.

Ask about formalities in the kinds of social situations you will be in. The humblest peasants in Latin America are more formal than most New York City socialites. Greetings and handshakes are exchanged on entering and leaving a room. The proper forms of address are used with strangers. Ask about the common forms of politeness and respect when greeting and leaving, the proper names and forms of address for persons you will be meeting. Be aware that the United States has a very informal culture compared to those of most of the rest of the world, and your informality may be confused with lack of respect. And "respect" is a key word in Latin cultures. To "disrespect" or "lack respect" for someone is to offend deeply.

Choose local counsel and other staff with care.

If lead counsel is in one U.S. state and local counsel is in another, the latter may do little but receive pleadings, file them according to the local rules, and forward responses. Local counsel in San José, Costa Rica will have to do much more. Local counsel will have to serve as chief intermediary and interpreter of both legal systems to the clients. Be sure that he or she is not only experienced with the legal system in your client's country but has some understanding of comparative law and the United States legal system as well, if at all possible. If not, you must provide a running seminar, not only in the theory and procedures that operate in your jurisdiction but also in the Anglo-American, common law system generally.

Usually you can find someone who understands the United States system, at least in theory. Things that are second nature to you—such as the process of cross-examination or the definitive nature of filing deadlines, issue-preclusion, and relevance rulings—are incomprehensible (not to mention counterintuitive) to most people not steeped in this system. Whenever in doubt, explain the purpose of a request or a procedure, and elaborate on any problems you anticipate as well as consequences of not complying with any orders entered or rules of procedure. If feasible, bring local counsel to the United States to observe court in session; their concepts are derived from old "Perry Mason" and "L.A. Law" television reruns.

Whenever possible, local counsel should also be bilingual and understand both cultures as well as both legal systems. He or she will need to help interpret the clients to you and vice versa. Prior to making any definitive decision about local counsel, do some research and some interviewing. Know prospective local counsel's reputation in the local bar, among law professors and constituency groups of your clients (e.g., labor unions); understand his or her place in local politics and society. Find out who past clients have been; your clients will undoubtedly know. Choose local counsel who will be able to interpret the local law for you, so that you will better understand the expectations and preconceptions of your clients, experts, witnesses, and so on.

Visit the offices of prospective local counsel and know what facilities are reliable: photocopier, computer, telephone, fax, modem, or mail? What methods of communication work best from abroad, and which can be relied on within the country? How will client contact be maintained? Whose responsibility will it be? Is local counsel's office in a place that is accessible to clients? Will local counsel travel to where the clients are? Are there any dangers to clients as a result of local political situations that local counsel is aware of? Does traveling to his or her office or meeting with him or her jeopardize them in any way, or increase their security? Finally, investigate the possibility of conflict of interest thoroughly. In many societies in the developing world, the concept is marginal, at best, and family loyalties and the traditional social structure virtually require that family, social, and political relationships be reinforced with whatever benefits are obtained from employment.

Once you have chosen local counsel, be as explicit as possible about the scope of the duties and the importance of each. Consider a memorandum of agreement that includes essential points you have discussed and provide copies for local counsel. Ideally, local counsel staff should include a bilingual attorney who understand both cultures and can help translate the demands of discovery and pretrial preparation into complete and accurate responses with regard to every factual situation. Staff must also include someone sufficiently familiar with local resources to identify expert witnesses and others who will be needed to develop the litigation in the plaintiff's homeland.

When considering "local counsel" consider the importance of an attorney who can serve as a bilingual, bicultural "facilitator" who can be responsible for much direct contact with clients (including locating them when necessary). This may be a sympathetic United States citizen living in the plaintiff's country, or one of plaintiff's nationality with extensive experience in the United States. The "facilitator" function is distinct from that of local counsel, although it may be combined. It is chiefly one of intense client contact, from interviewing and preparation to liaison with expert witnesses and local organizations and entities concerned about or involved in the case. The agreement with local counsel should include a chart of the responsibilities of all on the local and U.S.-based legal team, with clear descriptions of how information is expected to flow. It undoubtedly will not flow that way, but both sides will start with a map of expectations.

Optimally, part of the job of local counsel and/or staff should be the development of good working relations with sympathetic organizations, popular, political, governmental, religious, academic, and other institutions as well as the public information media. Litigation of this kind involves a great deal more than pleading and client contact. Strong support from significant sectors in the plaintiff's home country can often make the difference between winning and losing an argument, or a case, by generating probative documentary evidence. When local law supports a position or explains the nature of an injury, a term, or concept that becomes significant in the litigation, consider educating the court about it and, when appropriate, incorporating aspects of local law and history to help the court understand the litigation.[24]

In conducting client interviews, develop a transcultural vocabulary.

Interviewers, whether they are facilitators, local counsel, or paralegals, must understand the purpose of the interview and how the information obtained will be used. The importance of clarity, precision, and honesty over all other values must be made explicit, and communicated to the client. But no interviewer, no matter how well instructed, will succeed without establishing a rapport with the client. Interviewers must be chosen with both criteria in mind.[25]

Many concepts that seem basic to a North American attorney may be different to a client from another culture. It is not merely a question of language and nationality. Urban/rural, educated/unschooled, middle class/poor describe cultural dichotomies that also have a significant impact on vocabulary, style of expression, and ease of communication. The length of exposure to DBCP was a critical issue in the *Castro Alfaro* litigation, as was proof that DBCP was the exact pesticide to which workers were exposed. Questions about length of employment, duration of work at a particular farm, or assignment to specific tasks, such as injecting the chemical into the ground, all initially produced inaccurate, confusing, and misleading responses to interrogatories. It was not until a person familiar with the language and the day-to-day lives of the plaintiffs began to prepare them for depositions that the legal team began to understand the impact of different experiences and ways of measuring time on the litigation.

Most indigenous and rural people experience and describe time very differently from those of us accustomed to digital watches with alarms.

Question: How long did you work at farm number 13?

Answer: A long time.

Question: What is a long time? Two, five, or ten years?

Answer: About five years.

This exchange is hypothetical, but illustrates a situation in which the client understands that his answers are "not good enough" and tries to "guess" the "right answer" to please the interviewer. More objective responses can be obtained by asking the client to describe when he or she began a certain activity in relation to other events in his or her life, and to relate those events to major events in the larger world. For these clients and many who live in the developing world, time is not standardized and is intensely personal. Some relationship may be established between the two chronologies by resort to objective events — history, elections, strikes, floods, earthquakes and hurricanes, the birth of a child, the death of a community leader, and so on.

Social concepts are also relative. Attorneys in *Castro Alfaro* were surprised to learn that a single client would answer the question "were you married?" (e.g., while handling DBCP) differently at different times. The term and institution of "marriage" means different things to a North American lawyer and a Costa Rican peasant. Are you interested in civil marriage, religious marriage, common law marriage? Do you want to know if the couple was living together and raising children, whether they considered themselves and the community considered them a stable, established family unit, or whether they had formalized their relationship? Once such a couple/family is established, the woman is "my wife" and the man "my husband" regardless of their civil status — even if one or both is legally married to another. The expression "the father of my child/children" is commonly used to describe the biological father, regardless of whether either or both of the couples sought civil sanction for the relationship.

Clients are not going to find it easy to talk about many aspects of their injuries. Sterility was a major issue in the *Castro Alfaro* litigation. Initially the litigation focused on the physical aspects of the men that could be measured by science — zero sperm count, deformed sperm, poor motility, and so on, and also on the wives' loss of their husband's ability to procreate. As interviewers began to reinterview and know the plaintiffs better, other aspects became at least as important: fear of cancer, fear of deformed children in cases of less than complete sterility, fear of sexual rejection and impotence caused by it, shame and regret over not being able to contribute to the continuity of the family and the community.

These were both difficult subjects to talk about and extremely difficult matters to quantify. It was not until plaintiffs found people they could trust to "open up to" that the legal team could even seriously consider seeking damages for psychological injuries, which, in many cases, were the most severe. And it is not until such trust is established that the possibility of any real work toward "making [the client] whole" through counseling and therapy could even be considered. In addition, most of the marriages failed, and it became impractical to maintain contact with ex-partners.

Establish trust before embarking on settlement discussions with clients.

Trust can only be established when respect for the client, on his or her terms, can be conveyed. Whether it is established by person-to-person contact, or through intermediaries—bicultural legal workers and local counsel—litigation such as the *Castro Alfaro* case must be undertaken with a great deal of sensitivity toward the clients. They believe they are (and often are in fact) risking present and future employment, community ostracism, and often physical danger, not in the hope of recovering millions, but in order to vindicate their rights and see that "justice" is done.

The United States legal system tends to reduce "justice" in tort cases to a monetary award for damages. Victims of the torts and crimes of U.S.-based transnationals in other countries deserve to be "made whole" economically, as well as morally. But they rarely understand the economic compensation as the be-all and end-all of their struggles. This makes the issue of settlement a difficult one, indeed.

Nowhere in the litigation process is trust and accurate communication more important, and respect for the clients more essential. Damage awards can easily be negotiated without exchanging a word with clients, just as cases can be lost without their realizing it for failure to respond to interrogatories on time. The problem of "selling the settlement" can be relegated to local counsel or someone not involved in the tough job of litigating and negotiating. But attorneys involved in transcultural litigation must ask themselves whether this model of "justice" is very different from the model that resulted in the injuries in the first place. "First world knows best" is a hard attitude to shake, especially for those of us who have honed our skills in an adversary system, believing that using those on behalf of our clients was our best contribution to justice.

The trust essential to ethical long-distance negotiations cannot be created at the last moment, in order to settle the case. It must be built from the first client meeting, and must include counsel's willingness to understand that the feeling that "justice has been done" can be as important to clients as receiving a large damage award. Ethical and financial problems arise when, as in *Castro Alfaro*, U.S. counsel has spent very large sums of money to litigate on a contingency basis. Who decides when and if to settle? To avoid this dilemma, settlement as a possibility and U.S. legal processes in general must be discussed in depth with local counsel and plaintiffs to the extent possible.

Conclusion

Castro Alfaro brings to light a spectrum of issues concerning workers and human rights in today's global economy. The tenuousness of obtaining *any* forum for workers in developing countries in order to vindicate their rights against multinational corporations presents a great challenge for advocates, as do the logistical obstacles discussed above. Multinationals have become "globe-encircling enterprises" affecting people and the environment throughout the world. Advocates for such workers, for indigenous peoples, the environment, and others injured by transnationals must develop new theories of liability and jurisdiction, new forums of accountability, and new ways of using existing laws, both international and national, from both the forum country and the country where the injuries were suffered. As powerful as governments in many developing countries, the conduct of multinational corporations should be judged at least by the minimum international standards established by the Universal Declaration of Human Rights.[26] At least, they should bear the full human and environmental costs to maximize profits by producing the oversized, blemish-free perfect banana.

Notes

1. *Dow Chemical Co. et al. v. Castro Alfaro et al.*, 786 S.W.2d 674 (Tex. 1990) (hereinafter *Castro Alfaro*), concurring opinion of Doggett, J. This case is also commonly referred to as *Alfaro*. The name of the plaintiff was Domingo Castro Alfaro. In Spanish-speaking countries, two surnames are used—that of the father and that of the mother. If the name is shortened to only one name for convenience, it is of the first of the two last names, that of the father. Thus, the plaintiff could properly be referred to as "Mr. Castro," while "Mr. Alfaro" would probably be his maternal grandfather.

2. For comprehensive discussions of different perspectives on the controversial *Castro-Alfaro* holding regarding *forum non conveniens*, see F Woods, "Suits by Foreign Plaintiffs: Keeping the Doors of American Courts Open," *Arizona Journal of International and Comparative Law* 8 (1991); Manzi, "*Dow Chemical Company v. Castro-Alfaro*: The Demise of *Forum Non Conveniens* in Texas and One

Less Barrier to International Tort Litigation," *Fordham International Law Journal* 14, no. 3 (1990–1991); House, *"Dow Chemical Company and Shell Oil Company vs Domingo Castro-Alfaro, et al.:* The End of *Forum Non Conveniens?" Texas Bar Journal* (June 1991).

3. Standard Fruit Company is the local subsidiary of Dole Fresh Fruit Company, which at the time of the injuries was owned by Castle and Cook, Inc., now called Dole Food Company, Inc. *Castro Alfaro* was not a class action suit and subsequent cases were filed in groups of banana workers from other plantations and farms throughout Costa Rica; these were eventually joined to the *Castro Alfaro* group for settlement.

4. Other sectors peaked at 17 percent unionized by 1979.

5. *Solidarismo* (solidarity) is implemented through the creation of worker/ employer "associations" stressing "harmony" rather than "communist class struggle." Workers pay 5 percent of their wages to the Asociación, which in turn provides worker transport, cultural activities, and other benefits previously under the Company's domain. Today banana workers must purchase most of their own housing with the assistance from Asociación loans and financing. Overall, workers have become more dependent and no longer have the bargaining power to negotiate salaries and working conditions that they achieved during the height of their union activity fifteen years ago.

6. For further information about the history of banana development in Central America, see CSUCA, "Universo Banano en Centroamerica," *EDUCA,* 1977.

7. For a critical discussion of the social, economic, political, and cultural factors that led to reliance on toxic chemicals to increase agricultural production and a history of the DBCP controversy in the United States, see Cathy Trost, *Elements of Risk: The Chemical Industry and Its Threat to America* (New York, New York, Times Books, 1985). See also Weir and Matthiessen, "Will the Circle Be Unbroken?" *Mother Jones,* June 1989, for a more detailed rendition of the story of the injured banana workers in Río Frío and Castle and Cook's response.

8. Lori Ann Thrupp, "Sterilization of Workers from Pesticide Exposure: The Causes and Consequences of DBCP-Induced Damage in Costa Rica and Beyond," *International Journal of Health Services* 21, no. 4 (1991).

9. Excerpts from testimony of a Río Frío banana worker plaintiff demonstrating DBCP application at Senate hearings in Washington:

> Mr. Zumbado [interpreted from Spanish] . . . The other problem we ran into was that sometimes you would hit a stone at the bottom, and so the liquid which was supposed to come out of the little holes at the bottom would come up and spray your eyes and your face. And because of the constantly striking stones, this part of the plunger would become very loose, and we would constantly have to be touching this part of the whole apparatus and so you would get this liquid on your hands. . . .
>
> The other problem was that about every fifteen minutes or so you would be making applications and you would have to readjust the lower portion, the bottom part here. This had to be calibrated every fifteen minutes.
>
> The Chairman. How were you dressed during this?
>
> Mr. Zumbado [interpreted from Spanish]. Just normal clothes, a short sleeve shirt and pants, leather shoes. . . . No, sir, no gloves, no mask, and no rubber boots because nobody told us that this was harmful. . . . No safety lessons. The only lessons we received were how to make the application around the plant.

Circle of Poison: Impact of U.S. Pesticides on Third World Workers, Hearing before the Committee on Agriculture, Nutrition, and Forestry, U.S. Senate, 102nd Cong., June 5, 1991.

10. As the Costa Rican government was also being pressured to ban DBCP, Standard shipped much of their warehoused supply by land to Honduras, where they continued to use DBCP unchallenged. Banana workers in Honduras also suffered sterility and are presently attempting to obtain compensation from the banana companies. Some deposits of DBCP were left to rot out their metal barrels and drain into the grounds and creeks of the Costa Rican plantations and surroundings, causing large-scale fish and other wildlife killings and unknown environmental damages.

11. The first Costa Rican banana worker cases were filed in a Florida state court in May 1983— *Sibaja et al. v. Dow Chemical Co. et al.*—and dismissed by the federal circuit court based on *forum non conveniens* grounds, 757 F.2d 1215 (11th Cir. 1985), cert. denied, 106 S. Ct. 357 (1985).

12. A similar group of Costa Rican banana workers cases were filed in California as *Aguilar v. Dow Chemical Co.,* no. 86-4753 JGD (C.D. Cal. 1986), which was also removed to federal court, dismissed on *forum non conveniens* grounds, and dropped on appeal to the Ninth Circuit.

13. Compensation from the National Institute of Insurance (INS) for work-related injury available to worker employees of banana companies insured in Costa Rica.

14. *Dow Chemical Co. v. Castro Alfaro,* 728 S.W.2d 674 (Tex. 1990) at 683.

15. Ibid.

16. The settlement included 981 plaintiffs, all injured men who had filed suit by December 1991.

17. See below for more detailed suggestions for settlement procedure of trans-cultural litigation.

18. *Longworth v. Hope,* 3 Sess. Cas. (3d ser. 1049, 1053 [1865]), cited in *Castro Alfaro,* 786 S.W.2d at 676. Texas is one of a very few states that had statutorily abolished the *forum non conveniens* doctrine in death and personal injury cases. The statute was originally enacted in 1913, in language substantively the same as the statute in effect until 1993, Article 4678, recodified as Texas Civil Practice and Remedies Code sec. 71.031. What the legislature giveth, it can also take away. Defendants in *Castro Alfaro* took no time lobbying with tremendous support for the abolition of the abolition. The legislative attempt to restore the doctrine barely failed in 1991, and succeeded during the 1993 session. Meanwhile, those who litigate in other jurisdictions, including federal court, must remember that dismissal of such actions is *not required,* but rather merely permitted in the interest of fairness and convenience as long as there exists an adequate alternative forum. Unmasking the outcome determinative nature of such a dismissal and focusing on what is really in the interests of fairness is a critical stage of this litigation.

19. *Castro Alfaro* at 687, citing Comment, "U.S. Exports Banned for Domestic Use, but Exported to Third World Countries," *International Trial Law Journal* 6 (1980–1991): 95, 98.

20. For excellent case studies of the relationship between multinational profits and local effects, see e.g., Theodore Draper, *Abuse of Power* New York: Viking Press New Horizons, Press, 1990); Stephen Furber *Outrageous Misconduct* (New York: Arbor House/Morrow Pantheon, 1985); and Russell Mokhiber *Corporate Crime and Violence* (San Francisco: Sierra Club, 1988).

21. Quotes from plaintiffs during interviews, 1990–1992.

22. Multicultural or transcultural litigation must be distinguished from transnational business litigation in which parties belong to similar elite cultures and have more in common in today's global economy, notwithstanding other differences.

23. Not enough attention has been given to this issue in legal writing. One helpful article is Schirmer, "A Different Reality: The Central American Refugee and the Lawyer," *Immigration Newsletter* (National Immigration Project) 14, no. 5 (Sept.–Oct. 1985).

24. Obviously, this must be done with care, especially if *forum non conveniens* is at issue. Once that hurdle is passed, however, citation to local precedent can be incalculable in helping the court appreciate the significance of the case in the plaintiff's country as well as its significance to the defendants.

25. See, e.g., Diane Orentlicher, "Bearing Witness: The Art and Science of Human Rights Fact Finding," *Harvard Human Rights Journal* 3 (Spring 1990).

26. Ibid.

Bibliography

Philip Alston. "International Trade as an Instrument of Positive Human Rights Policy." 4 *Human Rights Quarterly* 155 (1982).

————. "Linking Trade and Human Rights." 23 *German Year Book of International Law* 126 (1980).

————. "Commodity Agreements: As Though People Don't Matter." 15 *Journal of World Trade Law* 455 (1981).

————. "Revitalizing United Nations Work on Human Rights and Development." 28 *Melbourne U. Law Review* 216.

Theresa A. Amato. "Labor Rights Conditionality: United States Trade Legislation and the International Trade Order." 65 *NYU Law Review* 79 (1990).

Alice H. Amsden. *South Korea's Labor Market in the Context of Early and Late Industrialization.* Cambridge, Mass.: Center for International Studies, MIT, 1988.

Ian C. Ballon. "The Implications of Making the Denial of Internationally Recognized Worker Rights Actionable Under Section 301 of the Trade Act of 1974." 28 *Virginia Journal of International Law* 73 (1987).

P. T. Bauer. *Dissent on Development: Studies and Debates on Development Economics.* Cambridge, Mass.: Harvard University Press, 1971.

————. *Equality, the Third World, and Economic Delusion.* Cambridge, Mass.: Harvard University Press, 1981.

Walden Bello and Stephanie Rosenfeld. *Dragons in Distress: Asia's Miracle Economies in Crisis.* San Francisco: Institute for Food and Development Policy, 1990.

Jagdish Bhagwati and Hugh T. Patrick, eds. *Aggressive Unilateralism: America's 301 Trade Policy and the World Trading System.* Ann Arbor: University of Michigan Press, 1990.

Roger R. Blanpain. "Transnational Regulation of the Labor Relations of Multinational Enterprises." 58 *Chicago Kent Law Review* 909 (1982).

Helen E. Booth and Kenneth A. Bertsch. *The MacBride Principles and U.S. Companies in Northern Ireland,* Washington, D.C.: Investor Responsibility Research Center, 1989.

Jeremy Brecher and Tim Costello. *Global Village vs. Global Pillage: A One-World Strategy for Labor.* Washington, D.C.: International Labor Rights Education Research Fund, 1991.

Bureau of International Labor Affairs. *International Workers' Rights, Part I: International Child Labor Problems.* Washington, D.C.: U.S. Department of Labor, 1992.

Duncan C. Campbell and Richard L. Rowan. *Multinational Enterprises and the*

OECD Industrial Relations Guidelines. Philadelphia: The Wharton School, University of Pennsylvania, 1983.

John Cavanagh et al. *Trade's Hidden Costs: Worker Rights in a Changing World Economy.* Washington, D.C.: International Labor Rights Education and Research Fund, 1989.

Steve Charnovitz. "Environmental and Labour Standards in Trade." 15 *The World Economy* 335 (1992).

———. "The Influence of International Labour Standards on the World Trading Regime." 126 *International Labor Review* 565 (1987).

———. "Fair Labor Standards and International Trade." 20 *Journal of World Trade Law* 61 (1986).

Richard Pierre Claude and Burns H. Weston, eds. *Human Rights in the World Community: Issues and Action.* 2nd edition. Philadelphia: University of Pennsylvania Press, 1992.

Terry Collingsworth. "American Labor Policy and the International Economy: Clarifying Policies and Interests." 31 *Boston College Law Review* 31 (1989).

Terry Collingsworth, William Goold, and Pharis Harvey. "Time for a Global New Deal." *Foreign Affairs* 73, no. 1 (1994).

Lance Compa. "Going Multilateral: The Evolution of U.S. International Labor Rights Policy Under GSP and NAFTA." 10 *Connecticut Journal of International Law* 337 (Spring 1995).

———. ". . . And the Twain Shall Meet? A North-South Controversy over Labor Rights and Trade." 23 *Labor Research Review* 51 (1995).

———. "The First NAFTA Labor Cases: A New International Labor Rights Regime Takes Shape." 3 *U.S.-Mexico Law Journal* 159 (1995).

———. "Enforcing Worker Rights Under the NAFTA Labor Side Accord." 88 *American Society for International Law* 535 (1994).

———. "Los Sindicatos Norteamericanos y el Tratado de Libre Comercio." *Revista de Trabajo* (julio–agosto 1994). Publication of the Ministry of Labor of Argentina.

———. "American Trade Unions and NAFTA." In Hideo Totsuka et al., eds., *International Trade Unionism at the Current Stage of Economic Globalization and Regionalization.* Proceedings of the International Conference held at Saitama University, Japan, April 6–9, 1994.

———. "Labor Rights and Labor Standards in International Trade." 25 Georgetown University Law Center *Journal of Law and Policy in International Business* no. 1 (Fall 1993).

———. "International Labor Rights and the Sovereignty Question: NAFTA and Guatemala, Two Case Studies." 9 *American University Journal of International Law and Policy* no. 1 (Fall 1993).

———. "The Global Economy and Working Women's Wages: The Utility of International Labor Rights Norms and Their Enforcement Regimes." Women's Bureau, U.S. Department of Labor, December, 1993.

———. "Migrant Worker Rights in the North American Free Trade Agreement." *International Union Rights* 1, no. 4, 1993).

———. *New Trade Union Strategies for Worker Rights in the Global Economy.* New York: City University of New York, Center for Labor-Management Policy Studies, 1992.

———. "International Labor Standards and Instruments of Recourse for Working Women." 17 *Yale Journal of International Law* (Winter 1992).

———. "Returning Rights to the Workforce." In Jonathan Greenberg and

William Kistler, eds., *Buying America Back.* Tulsa, Okla.: Council Oak Books.

———. *Labor Rights in Haiti.* Geneva: International Labor Rights Education and Research Fund, 1990.

———. "Unions in Chile: Laboring for Unity." *NACLA Report on the Americas* (March–April, 1988).

———. "Faces of Global Competition: Unions, Protectionism and Human Rights." *Commonweal* (September 12, 1986).

———. "The Case for Adversarial Unions" (with Barbara Reisman). *Harvard Business Review* (May–June, 1985).

———. "Fair Trade, Free Trade, Full Trade." *The Nation* (November 5, 1983).

Maria Lorena Cook. "Economic Restructuring and Political Change in Mexico: The Role of Labor." Paper presented to the Latin American Studies Association, Los Angeles, 1992.

Gary Cross. *A Quest for Time: The Reduction of Work in Britain and France, 1840-1940.* Berkeley: University of California Press, 1989.

Leslie Crutchfield and Luba Vangelova. "Can Companies Care?" *WHOCARES* (Summer 1994).

William S. Culbertson. "A Realist View of International Trade and National Trade Policy," 18 *NYU Journal of International Law and Politics* 1119 (1986).

H. T. Dao. "ILO Standards for the Protection of Children." 58 *Nordic Journal of International Law* 54 (1989).

Basil Davidson. *Special Operations Europe: Scenes from the Anti-Nazi War.* London: Grafton, 1987.

David Dembo. *Abuse of Power: Social Performance of Multinational Corporations: The Case of Union Carbide.* Westchester, N.Y.: New Horizons Press, 1990.

Stephen F. Diamond. "U.S. Labor and North American Economic Integration: Toward a Constructive Critique." In Ricardo Grinspun and Maxwell A. Cameron, eds., *The Political Economy of North American Free Trade.* St. Martin's Press, New York.

David M. Dror. "Aspects of Labour Law and Relations in Selected Export Processing Zones." 123 *International Labour Review* 705 (1984).

Gus Edgren. "Fair Labor Standards and Trade Liberalization." 118 *International Labour Review* 523 (1979).

Fajnzylber, Fernando. *Unavoidable Industrial Restructuring in Latin America* (Durham, N.C.: Duke University Press, 1990.

M. P. Fernandez-Kelly and A. M. Garcia. "Invisible Amidst the Glitter: Hispanic Women in the Southern California Electronics Industry." In Anne Statham, Eléanor M. Miller, and Trans O. Mauksch, eds., *The Worth of Women's Work.* Albany: State University of New York Press, 1988.

Anthony Ferner and Richard Hyman, eds. *Industrial Relations in the New Europe.* Oxford: Blackwell, 1992.

Gary S. Fields. "Labor Standards, Economic Development, and International Trade: The U.S. Approach." in Stephen Herzenberg and Jorge F. Pérez-López, eds., *Labor Standards and Development in the Global Economy.* Washington, D.C.: U.S. Department of Labor, Bureau of Labor Affairs, 1990.

David Forsythe. "The United States, the United Nations, and Human Rights." In Margaret P. Karns and Karen A. Mingst, eds., *The United States and Multilateral Institutions: Patterns of Changing Instrumentality and Influence.* 1990.

Thomas M. Franck. *Nation Against Nation: What Happened to the U.N. Dream.* New York: Oxford University Press, 1985.

Walter Galenson. *The International Labor Organization: An American View.* Madison: University of Wisconsin Press, 1981.

Mario T. García. *Mexican-Americans: Leadership, Ideology and Identity, 1930–1960.* New Haven, Conn.: Yale University Press, 1989.

Victor Y. Ghebali. *The International Labour Organisation: A Case Study on the Evolution of U.N. Specialized Agencies.* Boston: M. Nijhoff, 1989.

Norman Girvan. *Foreign Capital and Economic Underdevelopment.* Kingston, Jamaica: Institute for Social and Economic Research, UWI, 1971.

Evelyn Nakano Glenn. "Racial Ethnic Women's Labor: The Intersection of Race, Gender and Class Oppression." 17 *Review of Radical Political Economics* 3 (1985).

Cecilia Green. "Caribbean Woman Notes: Historical and Recent Trends in Labour Force Activities and Fertility Rates." Appendix A in Green, *The New Enclave Industries.*

———. "Marxist-Feminism and Third World Liberation," in Makeda Silvera, ed., *Fireworks: The Best of Fireweed.* Toronto: Women's Press, 1986.

———. *The New Enclave Industries and Women Workers in the Eastern Caribbean.* Caribbean People's Development Agency and Centre for Caribbean Dialogue, 1988.

———. "Thomas' Dependence and Transformation—A Review." *Two-Thirds: A Journal of Underdevelopment Studies* 1, no. 2 (Fall 1978).

———. *Towards a Theory of 'Colonial' Modes of Production: A Marxist Approach.* M.A. Thesis, University of Toronto, 1980.

———. "Trade Unions and Women Workers in the Eastern Caribbean." *Voices of the African Diaspora* (CAAS Research Review) 7, no. 2 (Spring 1991).

———. *The World Market Factory: A Study of Enclave Industrialization in the Eastern Caribbean and its Impact on Women Workers.* St. Vincent and the Grenadines: CARIPEDA Caribbean People's Development Agency, 1990.

Winston H. Griffith. "CARICOM Countries and the Caribbean Basin Initiative." 17 *Latin American Perspectives* 64, no. 1 (Winter 1990).

Joseph Grunwald. "Opportunity Missed: Mexico and Maquiladoras." *Brookings Review* (winter 1990–91).

Gote Hansson. *Social Clauses and International Trade.* Geneva: International Labor Organization, 1983.

Nigel Harris. *The End of the Third World: Newly Industrializing Countries and the Decline of an Ideology.* London: Penguin, 1987.

Faye V. Harrison. "Women in Jamaica's Urban Informal Economy: Insights from a Kingston Slum." 62 *New West Indian Guide* 3, 4 (1988).

George B. Harvey. "The Education of American Business." 83 *Business and Society Review* 62 (Fall 1991).

Paul Hawken and William McDonough. "Seven Steps to Doing Good Business." *Inc.* 80 (November 1993).

F.A. Hayak. *The Constitution of Liberty.* Chicago: University of Chicago Press, 1960.

Louis Henkin. *The Age of Rights.* New York: Columbia University Press, 1990.

Stephen Herzenberg. *Towards a Cooperative Commonwealth? Labor and Restructuring in the U.S. and Canadian Auto Industries.* Unpublished Ph.D. Dissertation, Massachusetts Institute of Technology, 1991.

———. "Whither Social Unionism? Labor and Restructuring in the U.S. Auto Industry." In Jane Jenson and Rhiann Mahon, eds., *Canadian and American Labour Respond: Economic Restructuring and Union Strategies.* Philadelphia: Temple University Press, 1993.

————. "Continental Integration and the Future of the North American Auto Sector." In Maureen Appel Molot, ed., *Driving Continentally*. Ottowa, Ontario: Carleton University Press.

Stephen A. Herzenberg, Jorge F. Pérez-López, and Stuart K. Tucker. "Labor Standards and Development in the Global Economy." In Stephen Herzenberg and Jorge F. Pérez-López, eds., *Labor Standards and Development in the Global Economy*. U.S. Department of Labor, 1990.

Human Rights—A Common Responsibility, Report of the Director-General. International Labour Conference, 75th Session. Geneva: International Labor Organization, 1988.

International Confederation of Free Trade Unions. *New Technology and Women's Employment*. Brussels: ICFTU, 1983.

————. *Peace Agreements and Violations of Human and Trade Union Rights in El Salvador*. Brussels: ICFTU, October 1992.

International Labor Organization. *International Labour Conventions and Recommendations 1919–1991*. Geneva: ILO, 1993.

John H. Jackson. *The World Trading System*. Cambridge, Mass.: MIT Press, 1989.

Mark W. Janis. "Forward: International Courts and the Efficacy of International Law." 2 *Connecticut Journal of International Law* 261 (1987).

C. Wilfred Jenks. "Human Rights, Social Justice and Peace: The Broader Significance of the ILO Experience." In Eide and Schou, eds., *International Protection of Human Rights* (1968).

Clark Kerr. *Labor and Management in Industrial Society*. Garden City, N.Y.: Anchor Doubleday, 1964.

Michael Kidron. *Western Capitalism Since the War*. Harmondsworth: Penguin, 1968.

Thomas Kochan, Harry C. Katz, and Robert B. McKersie. *The Transformation of American Industrial Relations*. New York: Basic, 1986.

Joyce Kolko. *Restructuring the World Economy*. New York: Pantheon Books, 1988.

Ernest Landy. *The Effectiveness of International Supervision: Thirty Years of ILO Experience*. Dobbs Ferry, N.Y.: Oceana Publications, 1991.

Lawyers Committee for Human Rights. *Human Rights and U.S. Foreign Policy* New York: Lawyers' Committee, 1992.

————. *Worker Rights Under the U.S. Trade Laws*. New York: Lawyers Committee, 1989.

Virginia A. Leary. "Learning from the Experience of the ILO." In Philip Alston, ed., *The United Nations and Human Rights*. Oxford: Clarendon Press, 1992.

————. *The Application of International Labour Conventions in National Law*. The Hague: Kluwer, 1982.

Scott Leckie. "The Inter-State Complaint Procedure in International Human Rights Law: Hopeful Prospects or Wishful Thinking." 10 *Human Rights Quarterly* 249 (1988).

Nelson Lichtenstein. "Great Expectations: The Promise of Collective Bargaining and Its Demise 1935–1965." In Howell Harris and Nelson Lichtenstein, eds., *Industrial Democracy, Past and Present*. New York: Columbia University Press, 1991.

Ramsey Liem and Jinsoo Kim. "The Pico Workers' Struggle: Korean Americans and the Lessons of Solidarity." 18:1 *Amerasia Journal* 49 (1992).

Gijsbert van Liemt. "Minimum Labor Standards and International Trade: Would a Social Clause Work?" 128 *International Labour Review* 433 (1989).

Staughton Lynd. *Labor Law for the Rank & Filer*. Rev. edition. San Pedro, Calif.: Singlejack Books, 1982.

Denis MacShane. "Is the Working Class Waking up in Asia." *Pacific Review* 1 (1992).

————. "The European Social Charter After Maastricht." *European Labour Forum* (1995).

————. "France: The Missing Link in European Labor." *New Politics*, 3, no. 2 (winter 1991).

Joel Makower. *Beyond the Bottom Line: Putting Social Responsibility to Work for Your Business and the World.* New York: Simon and Schuster, 1994.

Harlan Mandel. "In Pursuit of the Missing Link: International Worker Rights and International Trade?" 27 *Columbia Journal of Transnational Law* 443 (1989).

Ray Marshall. "Trade-Linked Labor Standards." 37 *Proceedings of the Academy of Political Science* 67 (1990).

Ray Marshall. *Unheard Voices: Labor and Economic Policy in a Competitive World.* New York: Basic, 1987.

Paul Mattick and Paul Mattik, Jr., eds. *Marxism: Last Refuge of the Bourgeoisie?* Armonk, N.Y.: M.E. Sharpe, 1983.

Kathy McAfee. "Hurricane: IMF, World Bank, U.S. AID in the Caribbean." 23 *NACLA Report on the Americas* 5 (Feb. 1990).

B.J. McCabe. "Are Corporations Socially Responsible? Is Corporate Responsibility Desirable?" 4 *Bond Law Review* 2 (June 1992).

Theodore Meron. *Human Rights and Humanitarian Norms as Customary Law.* Oxford: Clarendon Press, 1989.

————. *Human Rights Law-Making in the United Nations: A Critique of Instruments and Process.* New York: Oxford University Press, 1986.

Errol Miller. *The Marginalization of the Black Male.* Kingston, Jamaica: Institute of Social and Economic Research, UWI, 1986.

————. "The Rise of Matriarchy in the Caribbean." 34 *Caribbean Quarterly* 3, 4 (Sept./Dec. 1988).

Russell Mokhiber. *Corporate Crime and Violence.* San Francisco: Sierra Club Books, 1988.

Kim Moody. *An Injury to All: The Decline of American Unionism.* New York: Verso 1988.

Charles Morris. "NLRB Protection in the Union Workplace: A Glimpse at a General Theory of Section 7 Conduct." 137 *University of Pennsylvania Law Review* 1673 (1989).

Hugh G. Mosley. "The Social Dimensions of European Integration." 129 *International Labour Review* (1990).

National Advisory Council for Development Cooperation. *Recommendation on Minimum International Labour Standards.* Ministry of Foreign Affairs, Plein 23. The Hague, November 1984.

Frank Newman and David Weissbrodt. *International Human Rights: Law, Policy, and Process.* Boston: Little Brown, 1990.

Martha Nichols. "Third-World Families at Work: Child Labor or Child Care?" *Harvard Business Review* 22 (Jan.–Feb. 1993).

Diane F. Orentlicher. "Bearing Witness: The Art and Science of Human Rights Factfinding." *Harvard Human Rights Journal* (spring 1990).

Diane F. Orentlicher and Timothy A. Gelatt. "Public Law, Private Actors: The Impact of Human Rights on Business Investors in China." 14 *Northwestern Journal of International Law & Business* 66 (1993).

Emelio Pantojas-García. "The U.S. Caribbean Basin Initiative and the Puerto

Rican Experience: Some Parallels and Lessons." 12 *Latin American Perspectives* 47, no. 4 (fall 1985).

Carol A. Parsons. "The Domestic Employment Consequences of Managed International Competition in Apparel." In Laura D'Andrea Tyson, William T. Dickens, and John Zysman, eds., *The Dynamics of Trade and Employment.* Cambridge, Mass.: Ballinger, 1988. ｜

Karen Paul. "The Inadequacy of Sullivan Reporting." *Business and Society Review* 62 (Spring 1986).

Richard Peet, ed. *International Capitalism and Industrial Restructuring: A Critical Analysis.* Boston: Allen and Unwin, 1987.

Jorge Pérez-López. "Promoting International Respect for Worker Rights through Business Codes of Conduct." 17 *Fordham International Law Journal* 1 (1983).

———. "Conditioning Trade on Foreign Labor Law: The U.S. Approach." 9 *Comparative Labor Law Journal* 253 (1988).

———. "Worker Rights in the U.S. Omnibus Trade and Competitiveness Act." *Labor Law Journal* (April 1990).

Daniel Pink. "The Valdez Principles: Is What's Good for America Good for General Motors?" 8 *Yale Law & Policy Review* (1990).

Michael J. Piore. "Labor Standards and Business Strategies." In Stephen A. Herzenberg and Jorge F. Pérez-López, eds., *Labor Standards and Development in the Global Economy.* Washington D.C.: U.S. Department of Labor, Bureau of International Labor Affairs, 1990.

Michael Piore. "The Decline of Mass Production and the Challenge to Union Survival." Paper presented to the International Working Party on Labour Market Segmentation, Santiago, Chile, 1985.

———. "Critical Notes on Dunlop's Industrial Relations System." Paper prepared for the colloquium Les Systèmes de Relations Professionelles, Paris, March 1989.

Michael J. Piore and Charles F. Sabel. *The Second Industrial Divide: Possibilities for Prosperity.* New York: Basic, 1984.

Edward Potter. *Freedom of Association, the Right to Organize and Collective Bargaining: The Impact on U.S. Law and Practice of ILO Conventions No. 87 and No. 98.* Washington, D.C.: Labor Policy Association, 1984.

David Ranney. "NAFTA and the New Transnational Corporate Agenda." Paper Presented to the International Conference on the North American Free Trade Agreement, Mexico City, March 17–19, 1993.

John Robinson. *Multinationals and Political Control.* New York: St. Martin's Press, 1983.

Bruce Rockwood. "Human Rights and Wrongs: The United States and the I.L.O. —A Modern Morality Play." 10 *Case Western Reserve Journal of International Law* 358 (1978).

Robert J. S. Ross and Kent C. Trachte. *Global Capitalism: The New Leviathan* Albany: State University of New York Press, 1990.

Richard Rothstein. "Setting the Standard: International Labor Rights and U.S. Policy." Briefing Papers. Washington, D.C.: Economic Policy Institute, March 1993.

———. *Keeping Jobs in Fashion: Alternatives to the Euthanasia of the U.S. Apparel Industry.* Washington, D.C.: Economic Policy Institute, 1989.

Helen I. Safa. "Economic Autonomy and Sexual Equality in Caribbean Society." 35 *Social and Economic Studies* no. 3 (Sept 1986).

Oscar Schachter. "International Law in Theory and Practice." 178 *Recueil des Cours* 334 (1982-V).

———. "International Law Implications of U.S. Human Rights Policies." 24 *New York Law School Law Review* 63 (1978).

Stephen I. Schlossberg. "United States Participation in the ILO: Redefining the Role." 11 *Comparative Labor Law Journal* (1989).

Werner Sengenberger. "The Role of Labour Standards in Industrial Restructuring: Participation, Protection, and Promotion." Geneva: International Institute for Labor Studies, Discussion Paper 19, 1990.

J.M. Servais. "The Social Clause in Trade Agreements: Wishful Thinking or an Instrument of Social Progress." 12 *International Labour Review* 423 (1989).

Shaiken, Harley. *Mexico in the Global Economy: High Technology and Work Organization in Export Industries.* San Diego: Center for U.S.-Mexican Studies, University of California, 1990.

James T. Shotwell. *The History of the International Labor Organization.* 2 vols. New York, Columbia University Press, 1934.

Bruno Simma and Philip Alston. "The Sources of Human Rights Law: Custom, Jus Cogens, and General Principles." 12 *Australia T.B. International Law* 82.

Timothy H. Smith. "Pressure from Above." 81 *Business & Society Review* 36 (Spring 91).

Louis B. Sohn. "The New International Law: Protection of Rights of Individuals Rather Than States." 32 *American University Law Review* 1 (1982).

George Strauss. "Shifting Balance of Power in the Plant." 1 *Industrial Relations* 3 (May 1962).

Leon Sullivan. "The Sullivan Principles and Change in South Africa." In Herbert L. Sawyer, ed., *Business in the Contemporary World* (1988).

Clive Y. Thomas. *Dependence and Transformation: The Economics of the Transition to Socialism.* New York and London: Monthly Review Press, 1974.

Clive Y. Thomas. *The Poor and the Powerless: Economic Policy and Change in the Caribbean.* London: Latin America Bureau, 1988.

Hugh Thomas. *Armed Truce: The Beginning of the Cold War 1945–46.* London: Hamish Hamilton, 1986.

Towards an Action Program on Child Labour: Report to the Government of India of an ILO Technical Mission. Geneva: International Labour Office, 1984.

Lori Ann Thrupp. "Sterilization of Workers from Pesticides Exposure: The Causes and Consequences of DBCP-induced Damage in Costa Rica and Beyond." 21 *International Journal of Health Services* 4 (1991).

Karen F. Travis. "Women in Global Production and Worker Rights Provisions in U.S. Trade Laws." 17 *Yale Journal of International Law* 10 (Winter 1992).

Cathy Trost. *Elements of Risk: The Chemical Industry and Its Threat to America.* New York: Time Books, 1985.

Michael-Rolph Trouillet. *Peasants and Capital: Dominica in the World Economy.* Baltimore and London: Johns Hopkins University Press, 1988.

Jonathan Turley. "Legal Theory, 'When in Rome': Multinational Misconduct and the Presumption of Extraterritoriality." *Northwestern University Law Review* (Winter 1990).

———. "Dualistic Values in the Age of International Legisprudence." 44 *Hastings Law Journal* 186 (Jan. 1993).

Laurie Udesky. "Sweatshops Behind the Labels: The 'Social Responsibility' Gap." *The Nation* 665 (May 16, 1994).

Lloyd Ulman. *American Trade Unionism: Past and Present.* Reprinted from *American Economic History* by Institute of Industrial Relations, University of California at Berkeley, 1961.

U.S. Congress, Office of Technology Assessment. *U.S.-Mexico Trade: Pulling Together or Pulling Apart.* Washington, D.C.: U.S. Government Printing Office, October 1992.

U.S. Commission on the Future of Worker-Management Relations. *Fact Finding Report, U.S. Department of Labor, U.S. Department of Commerce.* May, 1994.

United States International Trade Commission. *Review of Trade and Investment Liberalization Measures by Mexico and Prospects for Future United States-Mexican Relations, Phase I and II.* Washington, D.C.: USITC 1990.

United States Senate Committee on Foreign Relations. *Report on the International Covenant on Civil and Political Rights.* Reproduced from U.S. Senate Executive Report 102-23, 102nd Cong., 2d Sess, Appendix B, 31 *I.L.M.* 645 (Jan 30, 1992).

Nicolas Valticos. *International Labour Law.* Geneva: International Labor Organization, 1979.

Bernardo Vega. "The CBI Faces Adversity: Lessons for the Asian Export Strategy." 14 *Caribbean Review* 2 (Spring 1985).

Ezra Vogel and David F. Lindauer. "Toward a Social Compact for South Korean Labor." Development Discussion Paper 317. Harvard Institute for International Development, Harvard University, November 1989.

Howard Wachtel. *Money Mandarins: The Making of a New Supranational Economic Order.* New York, Pantheon, 1986.

Sydney Webb and Beatrice Webb. *Industrial Democracy* London: Longman, 1987.

Paul Weiler. "Promises to Keep: Securing Worker's Rights to Self-Organization Under the NLRA." 96 *Harvard Law Review* 1769 (1983).

———. "Striking a New Balance: Freedom of Contract and the Prospects for Union Representation." 98 *Harvard Law Review* 351 (1984).

Howard Wial. "The Emerging Organizational Structure of Unionism in Low-Wage Services." 45 *Rutgers Law Review* 4 (Summer 1993).

Richard Williamson. *The United Nations: A Place of Promise and of Mischief.* Lanham, MD: University Press of America, 1991.

James A. Zimmerman. "The Overseas Private Investment Corporation and Workers' Rights: The Loss of Role Models for Employment Standards in the Foreign Workplace." 14 *Hastings International & Comparative Law Review* 603 (1991).

Index

Contributors

Philip Alston is Professor of Law and Director of the Centre for International and Public Law at the Australian National University. He is currently the Chairperson of the United Nations Committee on Economic, Social and Cultural Rights.

Terry Collingsworth is General Counsel of the International Labor Rights Fund. He has taught labor law at several U.S. law schools, and has published several articles on labor in the global economy, including "Time for a Global New Deal" in the January/February, 1994 issue of *Foreign Affairs*. He also served as Country Director of Bangladesh and Nepal for the Asian-American Free Labor Institute.

Lance Compa is Director for Labor Law and Economic Research of the Labor Secretariat of the North American Commission for Labor Cooperation. He was formerly a trade union attorney based in Washington, D.C., specializing in international labor law. He also held the post of Lecturer at the Yale Law School and the Yale School of Management, and served as the Director of International Labor Rights Advocates, a project of the International Labor Rights Fund. He has published numerous articles on international labor rights and trade union issues.

Frank E. Deale is an Associate Professor of Law at the City University of New York School of Law. He was formerly Legal Director of the Center for Constitutional Rights, where he served as chief counsel for the Labor Union of Pico Korea.

Stephen F. Diamond is an associate with a law firm in the San Francisco Bay Area, where he specializes in corporate finance. He is a graduate of Yale Law School and earned a doctorate in political science from the University of London. He is the recipient of a MacArthur Foundation Fellowship in International Peace and Security and has been a visiting scholar at Harvard University and the University of California at San Diego. He has also been a labor educator, union activist, and staff member of a large AFL-CIO local union.

Daniel S. Ehrenberg is an associate at the Washington, D.C. law firm of Wilmer, Cutler and Pickering. He received a J.D. from the Yale Law School and an M.P.P.M. from the Yale School of Management in 1993, and served a judicial clerkship on the Connecticut Supreme Court in 1993–94. His contribution to this book was made possible from a grant he received from the Ford Foundation Fellowship in Public and International Law.

R. Michael Gadbaw has been a General Electric Company Vice President and Senior Counsel for its International Law and Policy group since its creation in December, 1990. He came to that position from partnerships in Washington, D.C. law firms specializing in international trade law, and earlier served as a U.S. trade negotiator in the Treasury Department. His responsibilities at G.E. include international trade, investment and transaction financing, as well as the company's government relations strategy, corporate ethics and compliance policy.

Cecilia Green is a King/Chavez/Parks Visiting Professor in the Department of African Studies and the Women Studies Program at Wayne State University in Detroit, Michigan. She is the author of *The World Market Factory: A Study of Enclave Industrialization in the Eastern Caribbean and its Impact on Women Workers* (CARIPEDA, 1990). Her research interests include Caribbean women's and labor history; the role of the Caribbean Basin in the transnationalization of the U.S. garment industry; the Caribbean and global restructuring; the development of the African diaspora in the Americas.

Stephen Herzenberg is a Washington, D.C.-based labor economist and consultant. He was formerly Director of the Service Sector Employment project at the U.S. Office of Technology Assessment, and a senior researcher at the Bureau of International Labor Affairs of the U.S. Department of Labor. He received his doctorate in Economics from the Massachusetts Institute of Technology.

Tashia Hinchliffe Darricarrère is a Los Angeles-based international marketing and research consultant. She received an M.P.P.M. in 1994 from the Yale School of Management, where her studies focused on socially responsible business practices and alliances between the private for-profit and non-profit sectors. She has also worked in several European countries on issues of cross-cultural business dynamics.

Virginia A. Leary is a Professor at the School of Law of the State University of New York at Buffalo School, and a consultant to the United Nations Human Rights Commission in Geneva. She served at the International Labor Organization for several years, and is currently a member of the board of directors of the International Labor Rights Fund. She has written widely on labor and human rights issues.

Denis MacShane is a Labour Party Member of British House of Commons, elected in 1994 as the MP for Rotherham. He was formerly a Member of the European Parliament and Associate Director of the European Policy Institute. He also served as a policy advisor to the International Metalworkers Federation, an international trade union body. His 1992 book *International Labour and the Origins of the Cold War* was published by the Oxford University Press.

Michael T. Medwig is associate counsel of the International Law and Policy group of the General Electric Company, where he specializes in international trade and commercial law. He received his J.D. from the Georgetown University Law Center in Washington, D.C.

David Montgomery is Farnam Professor of History at Yale University. He is the author of *Citizen Worker: The Experience of Workers in the United States with Democracy and the Free Market During the Nineteenth Century* (Cambridge University Press, 1993).

Emily Yozell is the founder of *Justicia para la Naturaleza* (Justice for Nature), a non-profit legal research and advocacy center that works on environmental causes in Central and South America. She is a human rights lawyer based in San José, Costa Rica, where she also consults to several international organizations on human rights, labor rights and environmental protection. She acted as local counsel to farmworker plaintiffs in the *Castro Alfaro* case.

LaVergne, TN USA
08 June 2010
185348LV00006B/14/A